ECONOMICS HANDBOOK SERIES

SEYMOUR E. HARRIS, Editor

ECONOMIC DEVELOPMENT

ECONOMICS HANDBOOK SERIES

SEYMOUR E. HARRIS, Editor

Advisory Committee: Edward H. Chamberlain, Gottfried Haberler, Alvin H. Hansen, Edward S. Mason, and John H. Williams. *All of Harvard University.*

Burns · Social Security and Public Policy
Duesenberry · Business Cycles and Economic Growth
Hansen · The American Economy
Hansen · A Guide to Keynes
Hansen · Monetary Theory and Fiscal Policy
Harris · International and Interregional Economics
Hoover · The Location of Economic Activity
Kindleberger · Economic Development
Lerner · Economics of Employment
Mikesell · United States Economic Policy
   and International Relations
Schelling · National Income Behavior
Wright · Capitalism

ECONOMIC DEVELOPMENT

Charles P. Kindleberger

PROFESSOR OF ECONOMICS

MASSACHUSETTS INSTITUTE OF TECHNOLOGY

THE McGRAW-HILL BOOK COMPANY, INC.

New York   Toronto   London

1958

ECONOMIC DEVELOPMENT

Library of Congress Catalog Card Number: 57-10909

THE MAPLE PRESS COMPANY, YORK, PA.

To
E. R. K.

Editor's Introduction

For years many teachers of economics and other professional economists have felt the need of a series of books on economic subjects which is not filled by the usual textbook, nor by the highly technical treatise.

This present series, published under the general title *Economics Handbook Series,* was planned with these needs in mind. Designed first of all for students, the volumes are useful in the ever-growing field of adult education, and also are of interest to the informed general reader.

The volumes are not long—they give the essentials of the subject matter within the limits of a few hundred pages; they present a distillate of accepted theory and practice, without the detailed approach of the technical treatise. Each volume is a unit, standing on its own.

The authors are scholars, each writing on an economic subject on which he is an authority. In this series the author's first task was not to make important contributions to knowledge—although many of them do—but to present his subject matter so that his work as a scholar will carry its maximum influence outside as well as inside the classroom. The time has come to redress the balance between the energies spent on the creation of new ideas and on their dissemination. Economic ideas are unproductive if they do not spread beyond the world of scholars. Popularizers without technical competence, unqualified textbook writers, and sometimes even charlatans control too large a part of the market for economic ideas.

In the classroom the *Economics Handbook Series* will serve, it is hoped, as brief surveys in one-semester courses, as supplementary reading in introductory courses, and in other courses in which the subject is related.

Professor Kindleberger, in *Economic Development,* attempts to indicate the present understanding of the economic growth of underdeveloped countries. The book does not offer a thesis, unless it be its emphasis on the benefits to be gained from effectively working markets. It is rather eclectic in its approach, indicating along with its review of various theories which emphasize resources, capital formation, the economic capacities of the labor force, etc., how these ingredients of economic development can substitute one for the other; how a country can be rich and indolent if its resources are sufficient, or make the desert bloom if it has sufficient capacity for work and thrift.

Along with the ingredients of development, Professor Kindleberger discusses some general aspects of the developmental process: the change in technology employed, the increase in the scale of output, and the reallocation of resources from agriculture to services, including especially distribution, and to manufacturing. Following the treatment of ingredients and processes, Professor Kindleberger turns to a series of issues presently under debate in underdeveloped countries; on the internal front, planning versus the price system and the necessity for balance in investment decisions; and, on the international side, the merits and demerits of inflation and the roles of foreign trade, foreign borrowing, regional cooperation, etc.

The book emphasizes, more perhaps than some others in the field, the importance of social and political development along with economic growth.

With a rich experience in government from 1940 to 1948 and ten years on the faculty of Massachusetts Institute of Technology, where he is now a professor of economics, Professor Kindleberger is ideally suited to write on the problem of economic development. Early in the 1940s he studied, with Professor Hansen at the Federal Reserve Board, the postwar economic problems including development. He has also served with the Federal Reserve Bank of New York (1936–1939); the Bank for International Settlements (1939–1940); Office of Strategic Services (1942–1944); G-2 Section, 12th Army Group (1944–1945); as Chief, Division of German and Austrian Economic Affairs, Department of State (1945–1947); and as Adviser, European Recovery Program, Department of State (1947–1948).

In 1937, Professor Kindleberger wrote *International Short-term Capital Movements;* in 1950, *The Dollar Shortage;* in 1953, *International Economics;* and in 1956, *The Terms of Trade: A European Case Study.*

Seymour E. Harris

Preface

In the Research and Analysis Branch of the Office of Strategic Services, during the war, a running jurisdictional dispute was carried on between economists and historians over who was competent to speak as an expert on economic questions in foreign countries. The economists held that it was enough to understand economic problems. The historians were aghast that anyone would have the temerity to discuss, say, wheat production in the Ukraine who could not read Russian and who had not been there.

This book is written by one who has not been there. There is evidently something to the point of view expressed by the OSS historians, although I was unable to comprehend it at the time. It would be helpful in writing about economic development to have visited many countries and studied them thoroughly. I rationalize my innocence in this respect, as one might expect, in several ways. One who knows a little about a number of underdeveloped countries runs the danger of being superficial. One who knows a lot about one country is likely to mistake the particular for the general. As an example, certain economists who have visited only Latin America deny the existence of disguised unemployment.

While the book is based exclusively on armchair research, it represents the culmination of a long period of interest, dating back to early postwar planning days in Washington before Pearl Harbor.

My intellectual debts are high. I have appropriated facts and insights from a series of term papers prepared in a succession of classes at Massachusetts Institute of Technology, the Fletcher School of Law and Diplomacy, and the Harvard Summer School. When it comes to running down facts about the world, 100 heads are better than one. Everett E. Hagen, who originally undertook to prepare this book for the Economic Handbook Series, generously bequeathed me his outline when he found that he could not carry through the task, read my first draft, and made many valuable suggestions. Paul N. Rosenstein-Rodan, Max F. Millikan, Walt W. Rostow, and Francis M. Bator, of the Center for International Studies at Massachusetts Institute of

Technology, together with a series of distinguished speakers and participants at the Center's seminars, have been drawn on freely as sources of ideas and information. Harold J. Barnett has commented at length on Chapter 2, and Hiroshi Kitamura on Chapter 14. Seymour E. Harris, the expert editor of the Series, has given the manuscript a careful reading. It goes without saying, however, that these creditors are not responsible for the use to which I have put their intellectual property.

Miss Babette Solon and Miss Constance Hicks worked faithfully as graduate assistants, particularly in the collection of the statistical material. Once again Miss Beatrice A. Rogers polished the manuscript in giving it a final typing. Her devoted and efficient services are indispensable.

Charles P. Kindleberger

Contents

kets and National Income per Capita, 100; Markets and Money, 101; Impact of the Market on Entrepreneurs, Labor, Capital Formation, 103; Blocks to Development in Market Economies, 105; Distribution and Development, 107; Summary, 107.

CHAPTER 1

The Process of Growth

INTRODUCTORY

Anything that grows changes in growing.[1] This is obvious in animals and plants. In men, for example, a usual and convenient measure of growth is height, but along with increases in height come changes in weight, shape, intellectual and physical capacities, glandular activity, and a host of other aspects of body structure and functioning. Moreover, height by itself is frequently a misleading measure of growth, particularly when comparison is made between men of different cultures. Growth is broadly and generally measured by height, but no scientist would rely precisely or wholly on this single measure.

In economic growth the unidimensional measure is national income per capita. Economic growth implies an increase in this variable. But here the single measurement is much more subject to error and misinterpretation than height in the growth of men. This introductory chapter discusses first the drawbacks of using national-income statistics to measure growth—despite which drawbacks these data are used throughout the rest of the book—and then lists some of the structural and functional changes that are the inevitable and necessary accompaniment of economic growth. Subsequent chapters will develop these in detail.

NATIONAL INCOME PER CAPITA

The data on national income per capita are misleading for a variety of reasons. First is the question of determining what income is and what should be included in it. The costs of travel to work, and of

[1] F. Perroux, quoted in M. Moret, *L'Echange international: bilans de la connaissance économique*, Marcel Rivière, Paris, 1957.

1

wearing suitable clothes, are generally included in income, although they might appropriately be regarded as expenses or intermediate products and hence deducted from net income. Services previously produced in the household are diverted to outside agencies working for the market in a developed society—baking and even slicing bread, washing clothes, preparing meals. As this occurs, money income increases more than the real output of goods and services, and the money measure overstates growth. This underestimation is particularly acute in the agricultural sector.[2] Since economic growth involves the expansion of markets and the contraction of the subsistence or non-monetary sector, as we shall emphasize in Chapter 5, measures of money income in a growing economy tend to overstate the pace of development.

Another important source of error is exchange-rate conversion. International comparisons must be made in a single currency, but deviations of exchange rates from purchasing-power parities appear to be systematically biased. In many underdeveloped countries inflation has led to foreign-exchange control, or to a multiple-exchange-rate system, and confronts the estimator with the difficult problem of choosing the appropriate conversion rate. The official rate is generally overvalued; and the free rate, in a multiple system, is likely to be undervalued. But even where a single rate exists with something approaching foreign-exchange equilibrium, there is distortion. Gilbert and Kravis have demonstrated this in the case of Western Europe compared with the United States.[3] Putting aside exchange rates, they compared real income in the two areas by pricing goods and services actually bought by consumers, first at United States and then at European prices. With United States weights, money incomes understate the real products of Italy, the United Kingdom, Germany, and France by 88, 68, 64, and 53 per cent of the exchange-rate calculation, respectively. With European weights, the understatement is reduced to 35, 41, 29, and 21 per cent. M. F. Millikan has offered an estimate that the real income of Asian countries (excluding the Middle East), calculated through income estimates in local currencies, converted at the official rate of exchange, amounted to $58 per capita in 1950, but was probably nearer $195 when allowance is made for systematic bias in estimation. Comparable

[2] See S. Kuznets, *Economic Change*, William Heinemann, Ltd., London, 1954, especially the chapter on "National Income and Industrial Structure." See also V. K. R. V. Rao, "Some Reflections on the Comparability of Real Income of Industrialized and Underdeveloped Areas," in M. Gilbert (ed.), *Income and Wealth*, series III, International Association for Research in Income and Wealth, Bowes and Bowes, Cambridge, 1953, pp. 178–210.

[3] M. Gilbert and I. Kravis, *An International Comparison of National Products and the Purchasing Power of Currencies*, OEEC, Paris, 1954, p. 25.

figures for Africa are $48 and $177.[4] E. E. Hagen has observed that Burmese real income is understated by 300 per cent in the money measure, and has privately hazarded the hypothesis that the more underdeveloped a country is, the more its money income converted at an exchange rate understates real income. It would be rash to draw a straight line connecting these points to get a measure of the understatement of real income in other countries, as implied in Figure 1.1; but it is worth making the point that money incomes, carefully calculated, overstate differences in real incomes.

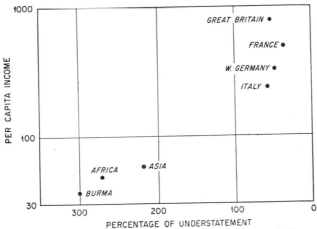

Figure 1.1. Degree to which money income converted into dollars understates real income, compared with income per capita, about 1949. SOURCE: Table 1.1, Average Income per Capita in Selected Countries, 1949 and 1953; for degree of understatement, see Chap. 1, pp. 2, 3.

While money measures exaggerate the differences between countries, there is evidence to suggest that they are not entirely useless. A study of consumption by M. K. Bennett indicates that income-per-capita figures give a fairly accurate picture of the ordinal ranking of countries with respect to real consumption, and that the differences in the latter are not a great deal narrower than in the former.[5]

Finally, a neglected point, there is a considerable counterweight to the understatement of real income through the use of money income in the way income is defined. In some ultimate sense, income should include leisure. If two people earn the same "income" but one works

[4] See statement of M. F. Millikan before Subcommittee on Foreign Economic Policy of the Joint Committee on the Economic Report, *Hearings, Foreign Economic Policy*, 84th Cong., 1st Sess., 1955, pp. 21, 28.

[5] M. K. Bennett, "Disparities in Consumption Levels," *American Economic Review*, September, 1951, pp. 632–649.

twice as hard as the other, there is substance in the view that the real incomes of the two are different. It is true that in some developed societies unemployment, either through layoffs or retirement, is painful per se and work may be counted as a good. But in the brutish conditions of work in many underdeveloped countries one can hardly

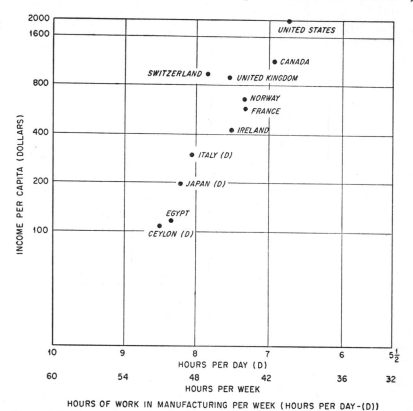

HOURS OF WORK IN MANUFACTURING PER WEEK (HOURS PER DAY-(D))

Figure 1.2. Hours of work in manufacturing, compared with income per capita, 1953. SOURCES: Hours of work, *Statistical Yearbook, 1955,* United Nations, New York, 1955, p. 76 (converted, where necessary, from hours per day on the basis of a six-day week); income per capita, see Table 1.1, Average Income per Capita in Selected Countries, 1949 and 1953.

put forward this position. The fact that the average workweek is forty hours in manufacturing in the United States and closer to sixty hours in Southeast Asia is a partial offset to the overstatement of real income differences implicit in the statement that United States real income per capita is twenty to twenty-five times that of the Southeast Asian inhabitant. Figure 1.2 sets out a relatively small amount of data on hours of work in manufacturing; if statistics of the average hours worked in manufacturing and agriculture together were available, the spread in hours would undoubtedly be wider. It is not that farmers in developed countries work shorter hours than those in underdeveloped: farmers are everywhere condemned to unremitting toil from sunup to sundown, and often longer, except in the off season. But there are more farmers in relation to the total labor force in underdeveloped than in developed countries, and many more hours worked in agriculture than in manufacturing and offices.

THE DATA

Table 1.1 presents a United Nations study of national income per capita in United States dollars for seventy countries in 1949,[6] along with a comparable set of estimates for 1953, prepared by the Center for International Studies of the Massachusetts Institute of Technology. Inflation of the United States price level in the period between the two selected years—the cost of living index rising 12 per cent, and the BLS wholesale price index 10.6 per cent—explains some of the differences between the two periods for given countries. Growth in real output per capita of 1 or 2 per cent, or in some unusual instances as high as 3 per cent per annum, will further help to account for them. But the table reflects an inevitable element of random error in the separate years and in year-to-year comparisons. It is evident, for example, that the United Nations estimate for Indonesia for 1949 is wrong. Indonesian income per capita was higher than Indian, not less than half its level. Similar statistical errors intrude throughout, partly through the crudity of the income estimates, partly through bias in the exchange conversion.

Nonetheless, it may be said that the general impression afforded by the table is substantially accurate. The figures in individual cases must be checked before they can be relied upon fully, and the statistical result achieved by the dollar calculation must be tempered by impressionistic evidence that weighs the real income of the country against those of neighboring regions. Throughout the book, as in Figures 1.1 and 1.2, these data will be used to serve as a base against which comparisons are made, and to indicate other economic measures positively correlated with income. The comparisons will be made exclusively in the form of semilogarithmic charts in which income is given in the vertical logarithmic axis and the other variable in arithmetic form along the horizontal. The other variable is oriented on the

[6] *National and per Capita Income in Seventy Countries*, United Nations, New York, 1949, p. 14.

Table 1.1. Average Income per Capita in Selected Countries, 1949 and 1953†

Country	Years 1949	Years 1953	Country	Years 1949	Years 1953
United States	1,453	1,908	Mexico	121	200
Canada	870	1,318	Yugoslavia	146	200
Switzerland	849	995	Japan	100	197
New Zealand	856	968	Costa Rica	125	180
United Kingdom	773	930	Greece	128	174
Australia	679	921	Jamaica	...	170
Sweden	780	910	S. Rhodesia	101	161
Denmark	689	740	Formosa	...	160
Norway	587	717	Domin. Republic	75	150
Belgium	582	717	El Salvador	92	150
Luxembourg	553	700	Honduras	83	140
France	482	600	Peru	100	140
Iceland	476	600	Nicaragua	89	135
Netherlands	502	600	Guatemala	77	125
Venezuela	322	530	Egypt	100	112
W. Germany	320	482	Syria	100	111
Finland	348	450	Paraguay	84	110
Israel	389	450	Ceylon	67	108
Soviet Union	308	440	Ecuador	40	100
Puerto Rico	.....	431	Hawaii	...	100
Uruguay	331	425	Saudi Arabia	40	100
Ireland	420	416	Indonesia	25	95
Czechoslovakia	371	370	Iraq	85	90
Hungary	269	370	Philippines	44	90
Poland	300	370	Thailand	36	76
Argentina	346	366	Haiti	40	70
Cuba	296	325	Iran	85	70
Italy	235	307	S. Korea	...	70
Panama	183	301	Nigeria	...	62
Austria	216	290	India	57	60
Union of S. Africa	264	283	Pakistan	51	60
Lebanon	125	265	Bolivia	55	55
Chile	188	250	Afghanistan	50	50
Colombia	132	250	China	27	50
Portugal	250	250	Ethiopia	38	50
Spain	.....	242	Liberia	38	50
Turkey	125	221	Burma	36	43
Brazil	112	215	Yemen	40	40

† In U. S. dollars of current purchasing power.

SOURCES: For 1949, *National and per Capita Income in Seventy Countries*, United Nations, New York, 1949, p. 14. For 1953, paper by M. L. Watkins, Center for International Studies, Massachusetts Institute of Technology, Cambridge, Mass.

horizontal axis in such a way, in each comparison, that positive correlation is represented by a scatter of cases sloping upward from left to right. In view of the uncertainty of the income data, to which is joined in many comparisons a degree of uncertainty in the measure of the other variable, no trends are fitted nor correlation coefficients calculated.

INCOME STATISTICS IN PLANNING FOR ECONOMIC DEVELOPMENT

Objections have been raised to overemphasis on the course of national income in the developmental process.[7] In the first place, net geographical product and net national product (or income) differ, owing to the fact that income produced by factors of production located in the country but owned abroad is part of the former but not of the latter.[8] Second, as discussed above, international comparisons are misleading. Third, it is argued that national income fails adequately to measure the change in output over time because of the index-number problem. Much of the increase in production comes in goods which are scarce and therefore high priced at the outset of development. To use a Laspeyres index, or base-year price weights, therefore, overstates the increase in output. On the other hand, the cheapening of these products in the course of development imparts a downward bias to the production record if end-year prices are used for weights in a Paasche index.

It may be admitted that national-income data contain many ambiguities requiring caution in their use, and that developing countries must not devote their statistical resources solely to the production of global income data, neglecting sector-output, population-census, census-of-manufacturing, and other important statistics. There is no other measure, however, so universally employed or so generally useful, provided it is not made to carry too much weight.

[7] See Dudley Seers, "The Role of National Income Estimates in the Statistical Policy of an Underdeveloped Area," *Review of Economic Studies*, 1952–1953, no. 53, pp. 159–168; also discussions in the same journal by A. R. Prest, 1953–1954, no. 56, pp. 223–228, and W. C. Hollinger and I. A. Stewart, 1955–1956, no. 59, pp. 220–225 and 226–227, respectively.

[8] It is of course important to distinguish the concepts of product and expenditure which are identical in a closed economy but tend to differ widely in commodity composition in an export economy, such as underdeveloped countries frequently are. Output includes exports, but not imports; expenditure includes imports, but not exports. If exports equal imports, output is equal to expenditure. Problems arising when the balance of payments on current account departs from zero and when terms of trade change will be indicated below.

INCOME DISTRIBUTION

Along with growth in total income, and in income per capita, there is generally a change in the distribution of income in favor of greater equality. The data to establish this as a universal proposition are lacking. Figure 1.3 contains fewer observations than any other in the

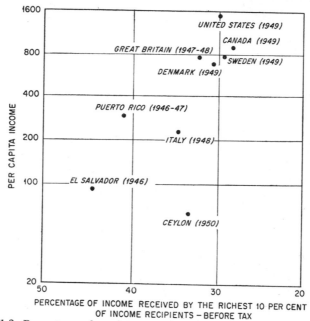

Figure 1.3. Percentage of total income received by richest 10 per cent of income recipients before tax, compared with income per capita, about 1949. SOURCES: Income distribution data, T. Morgan, "Income Distribution in Developed and Underdeveloped Countries—A Rejoinder," *Economic Journal*, March, 1956, p. 161; and *National Income and Its Distribution in Underdeveloped Countries* (Statistical Papers, series E, no. 3), United Nations, New York, 1951, p. 29; income per capita, Table 1.1, Average Income per Capita in Selected Countries, 1949 and 1953.

book. In fact, it must be stated at an early stage that there are few propositions about economic development to which there are not exceptions.[9] But the weight of the evidence indicates that, at least in the later stages and frequently in the earlier, economic development is accompanied by a more even distribution of income.[10] There may

[9] See K. E. Boulding, "In Defense of Statistics," *Quarterly Journal of Economics*, November, 1955, p. 488: "History seems to be a process system of almost infinite degree."

[10] See S. Kuznets, "Economic Growth and Income Inequality," *American Economic Review*, March, 1955, pp. 1–28; T. Morgan, "Distribution of Income in

be times in the early stages of development when income distribution becomes more unequal; in fact, this may be a vital part of the process of development, as entrepreneurs make large profits and reinvest them.[11] This source of savings will be discussed later. But an advanced stage of development requires both high average income per capita and a distribution of income which makes that average meaningful.

This proposition can be illustrated in reverse. Kuwait has a very high income per capita from the oil royalties paid to the Sheik by the Iraq Petroleum Company. With a small population and very large royalties, the average income earned per capita works out to something like $2,000, or well above the level for every country of the world. But Kuwait cannot be called a developed country. One aspect of development can be put in terms of a more equal distribution to income recipients; what is really involved is that all or most employed members of the population contribute to the high level of output and income.

PER CAPITA

One source of error in the calculation of income per capita is found in the estimates of population. Census data for a number of the underdeveloped countries are notoriously inaccurate, and the intercensal estimates, based on natural rates of increase derived from birth and death rates, are worse because of gross underreporting in both. But this source of error need not concern us deeply, since for any underdeveloped country the error is random, i.e., the population is just as likely to be overstated as understated.

A more fundamental question presents itself when income is adjusted for population. Should one divide by the total population or by the working force? We shall see in Chapter 12 below that these aggregates do not behave in the same fashion in the course of development, and that it makes a difference whether one divides national income by the one or the other. The answer is twofold. First, the fact: we have divided by total population. Second, the theory: income per capita is the concept appropriate for consumption, whereas income per employed head (or per head of the labor force, if one ignores unemployment) is the concept appropriate to income produced. In dis-

---

Ceylon, Puerto Rico, the United States and the United Kingdom," *Economic Journal*, December, 1953, pp. 821–834; W. Arthur Lewis, *The Theory of Economic Growth*, Richard D. Irwin, Inc., Homewood, Ill., 1955, p. 226.

[11] A. Sturmthal, "Economic Development, Income Distribution and Capital Formation in Mexico," *Journal of Political Economy*, June, 1955, pp. 183–201.

cussion of development, the emphasis should perhaps be more strongly focused on productivity than on the level of living, i.e., on income produced rather than on income consumed; but there is greater uncertainty as to the labor force than for the total population, and it is easier to divide by the population.

Population grows with an increase in income, as we note below throughout the discussion and in detail in Chapter 12. If there is to be economic growth in the sense of an increase in income per capita, this means, as is widely recognized, that total income must grow faster than population.

Professor Meade has suggested that total income is a more appropriate concept to measure welfare (or economic growth) than income per capita.[12] His argument, which has been roundly attacked,[13] rests on a demonstration like this: if there were two communities, A and B, whose incomes differed and were unconnected, income per capita would be increased by wiping out the community with the lower income, say B. But this could hardly be said to represent a gain in welfare. As Schelling points out, Meade's argument, which equates the death of existing people with the failure of unborn souls to get born, is more appropriate to a discussion of animals than of people. Meade himself departs from it when he deplores emigration under conditions in which the reduction in population in the country of emigration is rapidly made up by new births[14]—a judgment that implicitly rejects total income as a measure of welfare and uses income per capita. It is perhaps not necessary in this introduction to defend the use of income per capita, but it may be well to qualify the concept explicitly by outlawing any increase in income per head that comes from cutting off low-income heads.

THE INGREDIENTS OF DEVELOPMENT

What brings about the increase in income per head, as economic growth has just been defined? Here it is necessary to distinguish the ingredients from the process. The ingredients consist, evidently, of land, capital, and labor. The process includes changes in technology, in the scale of output, and in the allocation of resources. It is of course arbitrary to distinguish between the ingredients and the process, since the ingredients undergo change in the course of growth, and the

[12] J. E. Meade, *Trade and Welfare,* Oxford University Press, London, 1955, chap. VI.
[13] See the review by T. C. Schelling in *American Economic Review,* September, 1956, p. 717.
[14] *Op. cit.,* p. 463.

process could just as readily be described as the changes in the development of resources, capital, and people. But the present loose division is satisfactory for exposition. The six chapters which follow will discuss these ingredients and aspects of the process. By way of introduction, and to afford a summary view, it may be appropriate to offer a series of short paragraphs on them.

LAND, OR RESOURCES

Economic development requires some minimum of land as an input. The significant question is how much, and whether, if it is above the minimum, the variety and richness of resources condition the speed, the extent, or even the possibility of economic development. There are countries high in the list in Table 1.1 where the volume of resources appears to be limited, e.g., Switzerland. On the other hand, a country like Japan would seem to have undergone every step in the process of development that is to be described, but to be unable to rise very far in the scale of income per capita because of her low land/labor ratio.

The suggestion has been made that economic development should be measured against capacity for producing high incomes rather than against income itself. A baby elephant, it is said, may be larger but is not more fully developed than a mature rabbit.[15] If income is taken merely as an approximation of development, like height, there may be a necessity to observe that some countries only half developed in relation to existing technology, scale, and resource allocation have twice the income of others that are fully developed, and the difference in ultimate capacity for development is partly or largely found in differences in available resources.

On the other hand, capital and social capacity of the labor force for development are sometimes difficult to distinguish from land, and can be substituted for it under most circumstances. We are left with something of an unanswered question.

CAPITAL

Economic development brings with it an increase in the capital stock; and the process of economic growth involves a change in the rate of capital formation. In a static, stationary, or stagnant economy the production of capital goods is needed only to maintain the stock of capital as it gradually wears out through depreciation. In a devel-

[15] See B. M. Niculescu, "Underdeveloped, Backward or Low Income?", *Economic Journal*, September, 1955, p. 547.

oping economy, on the other hand, positive capital formation takes place as an essential part of the process, and growth entails increases in the ratios of capital to land, and of capital to labor.

Positive capital formation above the amount of depreciation may be needed in a stagnant economy to maintain the capital/population or capital/labor ratio, if the population and the labor force are growing. This is referred to as capital widening. More significant to economic development is capital deepening, in which the capital/labor ratio is increased. Production becomes more capital-intensive, more roundabout, and requires, in consequence, a change in technology and scale.

A central, but not necessarily the central, force in economic development is the increase in savings out of current income which makes possible this growth in capital stock.

LABOR, OR SOCIAL STRUCTURE

The changes in population numbers and in the size of the labor force have been referred to. More significant, and an important engine of economic change, is change in social structure, cultural patterns, and even personality traits. The need for such change is clear when one contrasts a traditional society that resists any departure from honored modes of behavior with a highly income-oriented culture that may even welcome change for its own sake. One part of growth is the simple acquisition of labor skills—knowledge of tools, machines, and techniques of their use. But more fundamental is the change in social behavior that makes economic growth a cumulative process rather than a once-for-all series of alterations in capital and skill imposed from without.

TECHNOLOGY

The historical process of development in countries now high in income per capita has depended significantly on a series of revolutions in techniques of production. New goods and new ways of making old goods have emerged from the Industrial Revolution, and from the lesser electrical, chemical, and mechanical revolutions that followed. In countries following the lead of the pioneers, the acquisition of techniques of production existing abroad has occupied a central role in the process of growth.

But invention, innovation, and imitation are not limited to the realm of production, as we shall see. They have important work in distribution, administration, and social relations and throughout economic, political, and social behavior.

The necessity for technological change raises the question whence it springs. In spontaneous economic development, the entrepreneur was its source. What, then, in the social matrix gives rise to entrepreneurs who lead change? In planned development, technological leadership devolves on the entrepreneurial class, if one exists, and on government.

SCALE

With growth comes an inevitable change in scale of operational units—in economic life, to be sure, but in political and social fields as well. Man's horizon expands from the household and the village to city, metropolitan regions, nation, and ultimately to the world. An essential part of the process is the linking of village markets into wider units, and of families and tribes into states and nations. Whether the change in the size of the operational unit follows or precedes the rise in income per capita is not altogether clear in every case, or even in most cases. But, as the village economy broadens into a regional and national one, it is vitally necessary to provide the communication and the appropriate monetary and market institutions if the process is not to be inhibited.

ALLOCATION OF RESOURCES

With more income per capita comes a change in the composition of output. At an early stage in the study of development it was noticed that the poorer countries have a large proportion of their resources engaged in primary production—mainly agriculture, but sometimes including mining—whereas the more developed countries concentrate their employment in manufacturing. An inevitable but erroneous conclusion was that the way to achieve higher income was by building manufacturing industry. It is now universally recognized that the transformation of the economy involved in the reallocation of resources is a more subtle process than appeared at first glance. In particular, more attention must be paid to tertiary industry, which consists in services such as transport, communications, trade, and government, as well as personal and domestic services; and secondary industry, or manufacturing, is neither a necessary nor a sufficient condition of growth. But it is a usual accompaniment of higher incomes, and may be their cause. And in any event, economic development requires transformation, or the reallocation of resources as growth in income entails change in the character of wants.

PLAN OF THE BOOK

This brief outline of the ingredients of growth and the major elements in the process constitutes the outline of the next six chapters. An attempt is made to assess the importance of each ingredient and element, largely with respect to historical cases of spontaneous growth. Exploration of the literature on economic development finds no difficulty in turning up writers who regard each of these ingredients and elements in turn as *the* central or crucial or strategic factor in the growth process. The position taken here is less courageous. Since the various ingredients can substitute for one another to a considerable extent, and since the process of development has at various times been led by one or another among these ingredients and elements, we refrain from ranking land, capital, labor and technology, scale and transformation as causes and effects, respectively, or in order of importance in the growth process. Everything has happened, and anything can happen. This is an unsatisfactory eclectic position in a world seeking answers to practical questions, and for students anxious to practice economic development. But it is the only answer that economics can afford in the state of our knowledge.

Following this general discussion of ingredients and elements, largely focused on the analysis of historical cases of spontaneous development, we turn to a series of more concrete issues currently under debate in underdeveloped countries. There is no uniquely logical form of organization of these issues. The subject can be started anywhere and worked over in any sequence. But in the present, necessarily arbitrary scheme, Chapters 8 to 13 deal with domestic questions, and Chapters 14 to 17 with international.

Chapter 8 addresses the extent to which a developing country should rely on the price system or turn to governmental as opposed to private market decision to make progress in development. Chapter 9 explores whether investment under governmental planning should provide "balance" among sectors, industries, regions, or on any other basis, as contrasted with priorities for one sector, industry, or region over others. Chapter 10 examines the choice between labor-intensive methods and borrowing the advanced technology of developed countries, which is usually capital-intensive and laborsaving. Chapter 11 investigates the extent to which inflation is inevitable in development and whether it can be used as a source of capital to speed the process.

Chapter 12 discusses the well-worn question of whether population growth will cut off economic development. Finally, among the domestic issues, Chapter 13 turns to social and political issues by asking whether economic development requires revolution as the "new men" insist on combining political domination with their economic leadership.

In the field of external relations, Chapter 14 is devoted to foreign-trade questions, and Chapter 15 to foreign borrowing. Chapter 16 examines the possibilities in regional cooperation among underdeveloped countries on which a certain amount of skepticism is expressed, whereas Chapter 17 looks into the relations between underdeveloped countries on the one hand, and developed on the other, and strikes a more optimistic note. A final chapter attempts to draw some of the conclusions of the book together into brief compass.

These sections of the book on domestic and international issues are somewhat arbitrarily cast into the form of choices to emphasize the point that economic policy has no universally valid answers to the policy questions raised by economic development, and that the questions give rise to controversy. Such controversy is sharper than that involved in many issues in developed countries, such as the use of fiscal policy in the United States to combat unemployment, or whether to nationalize or denationalize the coal and steel industries in the United Kingdom. To present these questions as still under debate, moreover, absolves the writer from the necessity of being too positive in providing answers, although he is not so timid as to refuse to express any opinion.

EMPHASIS ON EARLY STAGES

Given the nature of interest in economic development, it may not be necessary to state that the book, despite its title, focuses on the early stages of economic development and pays considerably less attention to middle and late. Problems of reviving developmental trends after a slowdown, or in gradual decline, such as are of concern to the United States and Western Europe, are not treated, despite their intense interest. Only when a developed country has been dormant so long that it can be regarded as young or underdeveloped again, as in the examples of Turkey, Egypt, India, or China, do its problems concern us. The writer is interested in senescence, advancing senility, and decline in countries—the gerontology rather than the pediatrics which are the focus of this book. Even though these problems may ultimately be more significant for the United States than the early stages of growth, which affect this country indirectly, there is little room for them in these pages.

POINT OF VIEW

It perhaps goes without saying, but should nonetheless be said, that the reader should be conscious of the writer's point of view, and should apply the appropriate discount. The latter is a native of the developed part of a developed country, and, although he attempts to keep a patronizing note out of his style, he may not succeed. There is, so far as he is aware, no regional bias in what follows. He has not been employed on development planning in any area of the world, has no conscious affinity for any special underdeveloped country, and is equally objective about (and ignorant of) Latin America, Africa, the Middle East, and Asia. He thinks economic development is a good thing and is disposed on moral and ethical grounds to think that the economic and political development in the rest of the world is of concern to his country. In addition, he is persuaded that events abroad have their repercussions on the United States—not all events, to be sure, but certainly cataclysmic ones.

If there is a bias, it is one of skepticism—surely the most appropriate attitude for a social scientist in the late 1950s. Anyone who claims to understand economic development *in toto,* or to have found the key to the secret of growth, is almost certainly wrong. "Everything is more complicated than most people think," as a nuclear physicist has told me.

And yet there is a positive element in what follows. The bias is in favor of the market. It is recognized that the market works badly at the earliest stages of development, and that the market alone cannot overcome all or even most deficiencies. Moreover, it is recognized, with Polanyi, that the market may sometimes work against desirable social goals, or require such heroic adjustments in the lives of people as to call for a veto of its dictates, or at least of the speed with which they would be put into operation. But development that ignores the market, or provides elaborate substitutes for it, is likely to fail in the grand manner. The market may not be very effective; but, in the present stage of economic wisdom, when allowance is made for its evident deficiencies, the result is better than any alternative. The reader who dissents vigorously from this position is warned.

CHAPTER 2 *Land*

INTRODUCTORY

How important to economic development are resources, or land in the familiar triad of factors of production—land, labor, and capital? A variety of conflicting opinion exists. Many people regard physical resources as a rather unimportant ingredient in development;[1] others, having in mind that most temperate countries are developed and most tropical are not, believe that resources—at least in the climatic aspect —are crucial.[2] A sharp debate has taken place over the historical evolution of economic growth in Europe, one school believing that the lag in French growth behind British and German was due to the French social structure, and particularly the family pattern;[3] others insisting that, if the French had had dominion over the Ruhr,[4] or if

[1] S. Kuznets, "Toward a Theory of Economic Growth," in R. Lekachman (ed.), *National and International Measures for Economic Welfare*, Doubleday & Company, Inc., New York, 1955, p. 36: "Every country has some natural resources. . . . The factors that induce formation of reproducible capital adequate as a basis for economic growth are unlikely to be inhibited by an absolute lack of natural resources." This remark is qualified to a degree in a footnote.

[2] See especially E. Huntington, *Civilization and Climate*, Yale University Press, New Haven, 1915.

[3] See D. S. Landes, "French Entrepreneurship and Industrial Growth in the Nineteenth Century," *Journal of Economic History*, May, 1949, pp. 45–61, and "French Business and the Businessmen in Social and Cultural Analysis," in E. M. Earle (ed.), *Modern France*, Princeton University Press, Princeton, N.J., 1951, pp. 334–353; J. E. Sawyer, "Strains in the Social System of Modern France," *op. cit.*, pp. 293–312, and "Social Structure and Economic Progress," *American Economic Review*, May, 1951, pp. 321–329; and D. S. Landes and J. E. Sawyer, "Social Attitudes, Entrepreneurship, and Economic Development: Comments (and Rejoinders)," *Explorations in Entrepreneurial History*, May, 1954, pp. 245–297.

[4] See A. Gerschenkron, "Social Attitudes, Entrepreneurship, and Economic Development," *Explorations in Entrepreneurial History*, October, 1953, p. 11.

17

steel technology had required charcoal instead of coal,[5] the course of economic history might have been very different.

Much of the disagreement and debate arises from differences in assumption and definitions. It is difficult to separate resources from capital, from the character of people, and from technology. Cleared land may be identical in agricultural productivity with acreage that once formed part of the virgin plain. The first incorporates capital; the second does not. The agricultural value of land is further intimately related to the system of inheritance. Primogeniture, which enables large tracts to be held intact from one generation to the next, will permit one type of production, such as wheat. Equal inheritance usually leads to small holdings and to another kind of output. Finally, a change in technology may alter the economic significance of land, as is clear from the new importance of uranium-bearing ores.[6]

The relation of land to economic development is a many-sided matter, since land itself has a variety of aspects, both physical and economic. In the rest of this chapter we shall discuss resources as an agricultural input, as an industrial input, and as a barrier to transport, and in relation to labor, including social structure, capital, and technology.

RESOURCES AS AN AGRICULTURAL INPUT

The productivity of land in agriculture varies greatly, whether it be measured in terms of crude output per acre, which may be called the land/output ratio, or in terms of the more refined net productivity of land, in which the comparison between two pieces of land runs in terms of output with other factor inputs identical, or with deduction for the contribution of other inputs. Soils differ widely in their productivity, due to physical and chemical properties, to temperature, rainfall, hours of light, and accessibility both to markets and to other inputs. Moreover, importance attaches in these aspects of land not only to averages but also to variability through time.[7]

[5] H. J. Habakkuk, "The Historical Experience on the Basic Conditions of Economic Progress," in L. H. Dupriez (ed.), *Economic Progress*, Institut de Recherches Économiques et Sociales, Louvain, 1955, pp. 157–158.

[6] Cf. the following quotation from B. Neumann, *Die Metalle*, Halle a. S., 1904, p. 408: "Metallic uranium has practically no uses. On this account, there are no production statistics" [author's translation].

[7] It has been asserted, with what accuracy I do not know, that one of the mistakes made in connection with the ill-fated groundnut scheme in Tanganyika was a miscalculation by a meteorologist about rainfall. The average rainfall over a five-year period was adequate for production. Unfortunately, almost all of it generally occurred in a single year. It seems more probable that the error, if there was one, concerned the distribution of rain within the year.

The land/output ratio will differ widely for land of roughly the same net productivity in the same commodity, due to different inputs of other factors. Thus Danish labor-intensive agriculture produces three times the average yield in wheat per acre of the United States.[8] But the variability extends further, both within the same latitudes, due to differences in rainfall, temperature, river flow, etc., and between latitudes where temperature differences are generally larger.

The nature of land has an impact on the character of the civilization. Major civilizations have not been built on the yam, cassava, breadfruit or—it may be added—the potato, since these commodities are not as easily transported or stored as cereals. In consequence, the density of population must be higher.[9]

This variability in the character of land makes it difficult to speak of the relationship between agricultural land and economic development. In addition, there is the possibility just mentioned of varying factor proportions. An extreme form of substitution is exporting other goods and services in exchange for food. Figure 2.1 shows very little correlation between arable land per capita, measured in hectares, and income per capita. The United States, Australia, Canada, and Argentina are high-income countries with high land/labor ratios; but much of this land is suitable only for grazing. For the rest, at every stage of development one can find countries of the same level of income, one having ten times the arable land per capita of the other—1 hectare per capita to 0.1 hectare: Australia and Switzerland; Argentina and the Netherlands; Syria and Japan; Liberia and Haiti.

Unfortunately, the data do not extend to some of the poorest countries in terms of arable land, such as Jordan and Libya, or to virtually uninhabitable areas of tundra, desert, badlands, and the like. Statistics of growth inevitably relate to places where people live.

There is a considerable difference between the two statements: (1) any existing country is likely to have enough resources to enable it to feed itself in the course of development, whether by agriculture, hydroponics, or trade; and (2) there are places in the world where it would be virtually impossible for a group of people large enough to constitute a country to establish what would ultimately be a viable,

[8] This was more than three times as much in the 1930s and less than three times as much after World War II. See, for example, L. D. Stamp, *Land for Tomorrow*, Indiana University Press, Bloomington, Ind., 1952, p. 94 (using data available in the FAO *Yearbook of Food and Agricultural Statistics*). The change was due to the increased application of fertilizer in the United States after the war.

[9] See M. Bates, *Where Winter Never Comes*, Charles Scribner's Sons, New York, 1952, p. 162. This work is an attack on the views of Huntington and Toynbee, with the thesis that the tropical blight on civilization is cultural rather than climatic.

self-sustaining economy. A minimum of resources may be needed;
but every existing country—Jordan? Libya?—is likely to have the
minimum.

More and better agricultural resources are better than less. This not
very profound observation is needed to correct the impression that

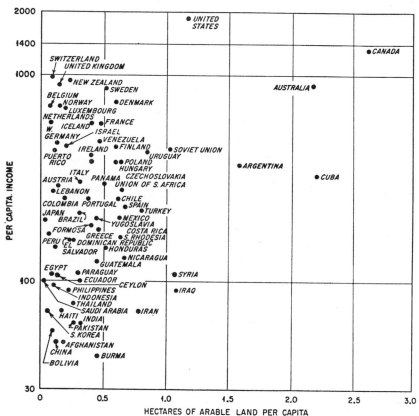

Figure 2.1. Arable land per capita (in hectares) compared with income per
capita, about 1953. sources: Arable land per capita (including fallow land and
orchards), *Yearbook of Agricultural Statistics—Production,* Food and Agriculture
Organization, Rome, 1956, pp. 3–7; income per capita, Table 1.1, Average Income
per Capita in Selected Countries, 1949 and 1953.

land may not be important. A rich country like the Netherlands can
do well with limited land—in fact, it has created land which is generally regarded as a fixed resource—but it could use more; and the
Netherlands land/labor ratio has been declining through time because
of increases in population after the country had already achieved a
considerable economic growth. A poor country with a high ratio of

people to land is under a severe handicap. Not only does it lack the social structure and capital that can be substituted for land, but it can confidently expect with development a further expansion of population and a further decline in the ratio of land to mouths. It is undoubtedly true that India has a considerable amount of unused land, and that it could, with capital projects, extend the productivity of land. Moreover, changes in social attitudes, such as the regard felt for cows, would change the effective availability of land for economic use. But India is crowded, and an Indian population of half the present numbers on the present land would have a better chance of economic development, other things more or less equal.

The abundance of resources may affect not so much the question whether economic development takes place as the levels of income per capita that a given rate of development starts from and ultimately reaches. Japan and the United States, for example, may each develop at the same pace, such as 3 per cent per annum compounded over long periods of time, with the rate unaffected by the different resource endowment; but the United States starts from and attains a level of living several times that of Japan. It is unlikely that the abundance or scarcity of resources has nothing to do with the rate of growth. But if it affects levels more than rates, it makes a great difference to the social and political outcome whether a country is more interested in the process of growth or in the income attained, as discussed in the preceding chapter.

LAND AS AN INDUSTRIAL INPUT

Land differs in its ability to provide industrial materials, as well as in its capacity to produce food. Certain types of industrial materials are ubiquitous, such as limestone; and some, like diamonds, are rare. Major importance attaches to the existence high-value materials, readily transported, or of lower-value products that are accessible. The economic value of an industrial resource in its natural state depends in an obvious way upon its grade (and the difficulty of refining or purifying it to normal market standards); its transportability; and its accessibility to means of transport, to other materials, and to markets. If iron ore is sufficiently abundant and high grade, a railroad will be built into the wilderness to bring it to the St. Lawrence River. But coal in the Antarctic is not an economic resource; nor are hydroelectric sites in the Andes, since the costs of their product and its transport outweigh the value at any possible market.

The significance of natural resources for industrial development is twofold. On the one hand, the country may produce and sell raw materials to other countries. Iran, Iraq, Saudi Arabia, and Kuwait produce and sell oil. Liberia, Labrador, Brazil, and Spain export iron ore. Chile, the Belgian Congo, and Rhodesia are the largest producers of copper outside of the United States. These obvious examples suggest that the possession of industrial resources is not a sufficient condition of economic development.

Or a country may produce materials for consumption in its own industry. But here we have a number of examples suggesting that the possession of a raw-materials base is not a necessary condition of development: New England with no domestic supplies of energy, no steel industry, no mines; Britain with no oil or nonferrous metals; Switzerland with only hydroelectric power; Japan with inadequate coal and few raw materials; New Zealand with no industrial raw materials to speak of.

It is nonetheless a fact that economic development implies big increases in the consumption of many industrial materials. Among the most important are steel and energy. Figures 2.2 and 2.3 show unambiguously that consumption per capita increases in these respects; and here the data suggest that the rate of consumption picks up as development gets beyond a certain point ($200).[10] Since iron ore, coal, and oil are bulky products and expensive to transport in relation to their value, is it possible for a country to develop with none of these materials in its industrial base and without hydroelectric sites? The issue is currently important for a number of countries, like Argentina, though its significance may shortly be eliminated by the more economical development of atomic energy.[11] The reduction in transport costs since 1870 and continuous changes in transport technology—represented, for example, by 100,000-ton tankers—have made possession of specialized resources less and less significant, provided a country is prepared to market the products in which it has a comparative advantage and to import the specialized products yielded by the

[10] Concerning the rate of increase, Harold J. Barnett has forecast that at least until 1965, United States requirements of energy per unit of national income will continue to decline at approximately 1 per cent per year as energy-saving innovations and high income-elasticity for non-energy-intensive goods and services continue to effect structural change. See *Energy Uses and Supplies, 1939, 1947, 1965,* U. S. Bureau of Mines Information Circular 7582, 1950, esp. pp. 25ff. But see *Resources for Freedom,* President's Materials Policy Commission, Washington, 1950, vol. I, p. 104, for a forecast of an increase in energy consumption in the United States from 8 tons per capita in 1950 to 13 tons per capita in 1975. This forecast implies a constant rate of energy consumption per unit of real national income.

[11] See E. S. Mason, *Energy Requirements and Economic Growth,* National Planning Association, Washington, 1955. Solar energy is another possibility.

missing resources. W. A. Lewis refers frequently to the necessity of having coal or iron ore in order to develop a broad basis for industry.[12] Is it possible, however, for a country to specialize entirely in the production of agricultural products, services, and products of light in-

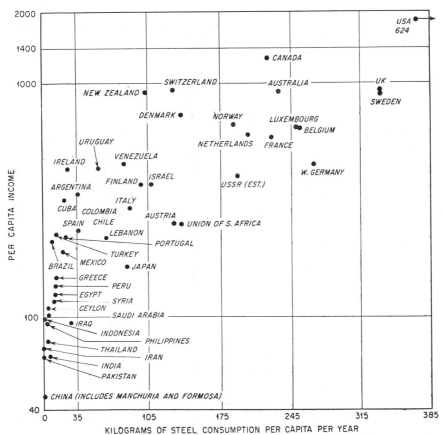

Figure 2.2. Steel consumption per capita compared with national income per capita, about 1953. sources: Steel consumption, *Statistical Yearbook, 1954,* United Nations, New York, 1954, pp. 282–283; income per capita, Table 1.1, Average Income per Capita in Selected Countries, 1949 and 1953.

dustry, exporting these in exchange for energy and metals, and to enjoy a high standard of living? If a country lacks almost all existing major forms of energy and metals, is its economic development foreclosed? Evidently not. Switzerland, Denmark, Iceland, and the Netherlands— to take four countries with incomes of over $600 per head in 1953—

[12] W. A. Lewis, *The Theory of Economic Growth,* Richard D. Irwin, Inc., Homewood, Ill., 1955, pp. 324, 329.

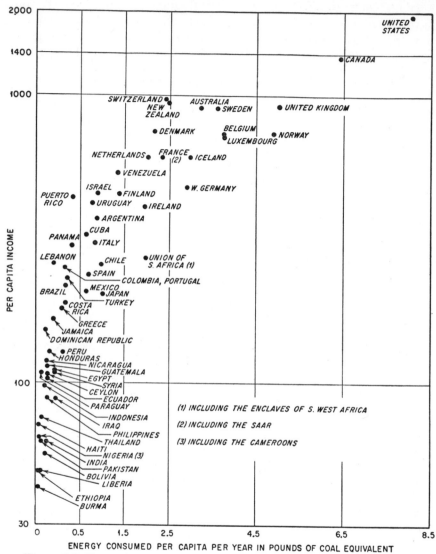

Figure 2.3. Energy consumption per capita compared with income per capita, about 1953. SOURCES: Energy consumption, *Statistical Yearbook, 1955,* United Nations, New York, 1955, pp. 302–304; income per capita, Table 1.1, Average Income per Capita in Selected Countries, 1949 and 1953.

24

testify in the contrary sense. Such countries must have a higher dependence on foreign trade than those which contain natural resources in greater abundance and variety within their borders, since the point goes beyond mere energy resources. The increased dependence on foreign trade, which skewed resources entail, will be discussed in a later chapter. But the absence of energy or any other particular resource need not fatally reduce a country's opportunity for development.

But it is not necessary to answer these questions in any ultimate sense, since a number of more immediate points can be made. First, most underdeveloped, and even a number of developed, countries have an inadequate idea of what their natural resources are. Technological innovations in the arts of geological prospecting, plus intensive exploration, have discovered new oil resources in Italy, France, and the Netherlands, for example, not to mention the Alberta oil fields in Canada and the Williston Basin in the United States.[13] In underdeveloped countries the possibilities are wide open. While it is true that the frontier is gone in the sense of vast territories in which civilized men have not set foot, many countries, especially in Asia, Africa, the Middle East, and Latin America, lack knowledge of existing resources.

Second, much development is possible on the basis of known resources and known technology, awaiting only the application of capital, labor, and entrepreneurship. Waste gases are being burned in the Middle East, Indonesia, and Venezuela for lack of complementary resources. Iron ores await development in Venezuela, Brazil, Chile. The copper belt of Northern Rhodesia and the Belgian Congo is capable of vast expansion. Venezuela has been holding back oil fields for later exploitation.

Finally, it is likely that after known resources have been developed, and new ones discovered and put to use, changes in technology will broaden the industrial base. The range of substitutability to overcome missing specialized resources is continuously widening. Capital and labor can substitute for land in producing a given good. Intermediate products traded domestically or internationally will replace a missing factor. Or substitution may take place in consumption. Wartime blockades showed how specific resource bottlenecks could be overcome and translated into general strain on total resources, especially manpower and capital. The German shortage of copper, it will be re-

---

[13] In the United States, it should be noted, exploration in oil since World War I has annually proved additional reserves equal to or greater than the reserves exhausted during the year. The limits of geological knowledge in petroleum, and perhaps to a lesser extent in other minerals, have been kept just about as far in the future, despite continuously expanding production.

called, finally produced the dismantling of high-power transmission lines and the replacement of copper with (abundant) aluminum wire, with some expense in aluminum and great cost in skilled labor. But the particular shortage was overcome.

All this does not dismiss resource problems as inconsequential. It is always better to have more resources rather than less. The countries that discover oil, like Iran and Venezuela, have a better prospect of economic development than if they had not, even though their prospects may not automatically be greater than those of countries that do not produce oil.[14] Moreover, in Venezuela, the conscious policy of reinvesting the profits from oil in capital assets—called "sowing the petroleum"—and the Iraqi program of turning over 75 per cent of the taxes and royalties on oil to the Development Board, provide sources of saving. But oil is not sufficient. In Saudi Arabia, average income is low; development is slow. Much revenue from oil is spent on consumption. Capital assets are built, such as the Damman-Ridyadh railroad or King Saud's third palace costing $176 million,[15] with little view to their future productivity.

Much attention has been given to the resource preconditions for an iron and steel industry.[16] Steel is heavy and therefore difficult and expensive to import. Where coal of the appropriate quality for coking and good-grade iron ore are found in relative juxtaposition to one another, steel can be produced more cheaply than it can be bought from abroad for an equivalent investment of capital and labor in the export commodity; or, what amounts to the same thing, a greater quantity of iron and steel, and hence higher levels of consumption and investment capital formation, can be obtained from the same inputs. Coal and iron ore are not a condition of economic development. Their absence can be compensated for by other inputs, to give the same level of output at greater cost; or by other resources that will enable the developing country to buy expensive steel with its low-cost products in other lines. But, other things being equal, coal and iron ore help. And, lacking coal, it is possible to build a steel industry with iron ore, as in Brazil at Volta Redonda; or, lacking iron ore, one can follow the example of the Ruhr or Pittsburgh. Or, in a few cases, with good loca-

[14] Venezuela enjoys a much higher average income per capita in U. S. dollars than, say, Colombia, which lacks basic energy resources; but Colombian development is making strides. On the other hand, Lebanon, without oil production, is developing at a more rapid rate than Iran and Iraq.

[15] See *New York Times Magazine,* June 10, 1956.

[16] See, for example, *Coal and Iron Ore Resources of Asia and the Far East,* United Nations Economic Commission for Asia and the Far East, Bangkok, 1952; *World Iron Ore Resources,* United Nations Department of Economic Affairs, New York, 1950.

tion close to the market, one can import both iron ore and coal, as at Sparrow's Point in Baltimore or Morrisville, Pennsylvania, and still get steel cheaply in finished form. The impressive recent development of the Japanese steel industry provides another illustration.

The same considerations hold true of energy. It is better to have sources of energy than not; but it is not fatal to development to be obliged to import energy.

Lack of steel-making materials or of energy means that economic development must be accompanied by large-scale exporting; and this, as we shall see in Chapter 14, involves certain risks. But similar risks are involved in the development of domestic resources, as the ghost towns of Colorado and the less romantic hard-coal region of Pennsylvania indicate. The existence of rich resources is not a sufficient condition for developed industry, nor even a necessary one. But it helps.

LAND AS A COMMUNICATION NETWORK

An important aspect of land for economic development is the way it lends itself to transport and communication. Mountains are a barrier to transport. The language boundaries in Europe run along the divides. Rivers are generally highways that speed trade and communication. Plains present few obstacles to transport, whether by road, railroad, or canals connecting rivers. A seacoast cut by frequent natural harbors permits ready and inexpensive communication.

These generalizations and their corollaries require little demonstration. Countries that are badly broken up topographically labor under a serious handicap in economic development. This is illustrated most strikingly perhaps by Colombia,[17] Ecuador, and Peru on the west coast of Latin America where the Andes divide the country into three sections, which can be unified economically only with great cost. The fact that Switzerland manages to overcome this handicap and achieve a high state of development offers some encouragement to countries similarly broken topographically; but the development problems of Yugoslavia, Colombia, and Nepal are different in degree from those of Poland, Argentina, and Ceylon.

Broad rivers, such as those which cut the European plain, offer great assistance to transport, and hence to development. Some rivers are better than others. The Hudson happens to flow from the agricultural regions to the industrial and commercial. The Danube runs from the

[17] International Bank for Reconstruction and Development, *The Basis of a Development Program for Colombia*, Johns Hopkins University Press, Baltimore, 1950, has a relief map as a frontispiece, which conveys some idea of the difficulty of transport in the country.

industrial centers of population to the agricultural bottom lands; this means that bulk cargoes typically have to move against the current. In British Guiana and Surinam, the rivers that punctuate the coast are even a barrier: because of jungle, habitation is limited to a narrow strip along the coast. Lateral movement is impeded by the broad mouths of the rivers, now ferried, and one day, if development continues far enough, to be bridged or tunneled.

Access to the sea is important for cheap transport in international trade. It was a great British advantage that no point in the British Isles lies more than 110 miles from a seaport. But it is important to combine this with interior lines of communication, as on an island.[18] In Libya and Indonesia a long seacoast may inhibit economic development if local producers have little transport advantage over foreign.[19]

As in agriculture and industry, the relation of land to communication is a function of innovation, as well as inputs of capital and labor. Such innovation may be technological—the change from sail to steam, from wooden vessel to ironclad, the railroad, automobile, and airplane; or it may consist in a dramatic change in transport routes, such as those involved in the construction of the Panama and Suez Canals and the Simplon Tunnel. The economic development of California and British Columbia, for example, initiated by the transcontinental railroads, received new and striking stimulation from the completion of the Panama Canal. The French steel industry expects similar dramatic cost-reducing impetus from the canalization of the Moselle River to permit cheaper transport of Ruhr coal to Lorraine.

LAND, LABOR, AND CULTURE

Land and labor can substitute for one another in the production process, within certain limits, and labor skills can substitute for labor numbers. The land/labor ratio indicates very little as to the level of income per capita if we compare Latin American Indians with Danish dairymen or pig and egg producers.

Chinese pre-scientific agriculture, it is said,[20] achieved the most effi-

[18] It is sometimes asserted by Indians that the system of railroad communication constructed by the British connected various parts of the Indian interior with ports, for ease of exports and imports, but not with each other, to the detriment of domestic trade. After World War I, Poland found itself with parts of three railroad systems—Russian, Austrian, and German—connected to the outside world but not to each other.

[19] *Processes and Problems of Industrialization in Underdeveloped Countries,* United Nations, New York, 1955, p. 14.

[20] See G. M. Winfield, *China: The Land and the People,* William Sloane Associates, New York, 1948, p. 60.

cient possible level in terms of wasting nothing of the fertility of the land. Everything, literally everything, was consumed or put back into the soil. The Netherlands, Israel, and Japan have developed the equivalent preoccupation with the conservation of natural resources, but on a scientific basis. The contrast is with Indian fire agriculture in Latin America, where land is cleared by burning,[21] using up much of the fertility of the soil, and then the plot is abandoned in a couple of years to revert to jungle or brush because it will no longer produce an adequate yield.

More significant than the variation in mere numbers, however, is the interaction between the character and amount of land and the culture. On the one hand, purely cultural factors, such as the form of inheritance of land, determine, along with the rate of population increase, the size of the farm unit. On the other hand, the types of crops produced react in turn on the social structure. In most parts of the world, in the past, there has been either a tendency for farms to get smaller and smaller as equal division of land among children or among male children is the ruling family practice, or for farms to get bigger and bigger with primogeniture, under which the oldest son inherits and occasional families die out. The system of inheritance is by no means the sole determinant of farm size. Other factors include the availability of uncleared land, of machinery, and of farm credit, and the nature of the land and the possible crops that can be grown on it, etc. But in Europe, with no uncleared land, and in Asia, with limited amounts of it, farm size became bigger or smaller, with few exceptions. In France farms grew bigger and bigger up to the Revolution, after which, with the abolition of primogeniture, they became smaller and smaller. Only in Denmark, by a series of apparently unconnected and unconscious events, did the middle-sized farm prevail.[22]

The significance of this for economic development is apparent. Large farms tend to produce for export. They specialize in single crops, sold for cash. Consumption by the agricultural worker is limited. It is even possible to form capital, although in many cases this is consumed by the landowner or, in the case of plantations, remitted as profits to another country. In small-scale farming, on the other hand, the principal object is subsistence. Production is diversified among field crops and animal products. If the land is very rich, as in Iowa, or production is very capital- and labor-intensive, as in Iowa and Denmark, there will be exports of animal products.

[21] In China, in the pre-scientific period, straw was burned but only for the purpose of cooking, and then in limited handfuls.

[22] See C. P. Kindleberger, "Group Behavior and International Trade," *Journal of Political Economy*, February, 1951, pp. 30–46.

Moreover, different crops have different impacts on the population. It has been pointed out that in a single country—Cuba—sugar and tobacco develop completely different rhythms of life and social patterns.[23] Sugar is produced on a sizable scale with capital and unskilled labor in a highly seasonal burst of work, followed by a "dead season" of four or five months. Tobacco, on the other hand, calls for skilled labor, working all year round; a worker has a chance to develop his creative powers. In sugar, the land is owned by large companies, and it is impossible for a worker to move up the economic scale through acquiring land.[24]

The impact of urbanization on labor will be discussed later. Here the obverse is in point. In a small country like Denmark, with a labor-intensive agriculture, it is possible to maintain a communicating society by special efforts, such as the Folk High Schools started in the nineteenth century by Bishop Gruntvig,[25] or by a high level of living, which will give farmers radios and television, and automobiles for getting to town. For the most part, agriculture is an isolated occupation.[26] Farm labor is attached to land and immobile, while communication is limited.[27] Farmers are conservative in outlook, and change occurs slowly.

The impact of people on land has a long-run aspect. Land can become worn out through overuse. In the pre-scientific agriculture of China, as much nutriment was being put back into the land as was taken out, but this situation had been reached through necessity, after deforestation, erosion, and overcropping had mined the soil of all its excess productive capacity. Man can make the desert bloom like the rose, but the necessity to do so arises in many cases from the result of neglect and waste.

[23] F. Ortiz, *Cuban Counterpoint*, Alfred A. Knopf, Inc., New York, 1947, part I.

[24] See also R. A. Manners and J. A. Steward, "The Cultural Study of Contemporary Societies: Puerto Rico," *American Journal of Sociology*, September, 1953, pp. 123–130, for a discussion of the subcultural differences among sugar, tobacco, and coffee. Coffee in Puerto Rico (and Brazil) is a high-value product, which, like tobacco, can be brought to market by muleback. Accordingly, the coffee worker can live in isolation far from roads. Bananas, plantains, yams, etc., however, as well as sugar, can be raised for the market only along roads.

[25] For references see Kindleberger, *op. cit.*

[26] There are exceptions, which are a function of land tenure. In Europe there are two types of agriculture, one organized into villages, the other, in which the farmer lives on his land along a road, as in the United States. Where land is owned in large latifundia, as in southern Italy, the "villages" may be very large —occasionally as large as 50,000 inhabitants. They are still called villages rather than cities because of the failure to add new functions such as commerce, transport, etc.

[27] This point was impressed on me in 1945, in observing a team of PW interrogators processing 5,000 prisoners a day. In preparing to ask questions about economic matters, they asked for a show of hands of farmers. These they directed back into the compound, saying that they did not possess information of interest.

Interaction of land and people occurs in agriculture. But the problem is more general. The significant question is that posed by Huntington in his view that climate determines the level of civilization. Huntington attributed the difference in level of civilization between the tropics and the temperate zones to the average temperature, and to moderate changes in temperature from one day to the next, which are a function of storms. Not only do moderate temperatures and storm patterns account for differences in civilization today. He explained further that the path of ancient civilizations, starting in the Middle East and Far East and working westward through the Mediterranean, follows the path of storm peak density. In the Toynbee version, creativity requires a challenge and response. In the tropics the challenge is too weak; in the Arctic zones, too great.

It is argued in opposition to these views that the temperate-zone visitor in the tropics is listless not because of the temperature but because of his inability to adjust culturally. He wears too many clothes, eats the wrong foods. The white man's burden is that of his own culture, which he carries into the alien environment of the tropics. The resources of the tropics are not inadequate; they are culture-bound.[28] Thus the "laziness" of the native is explained as well as the tendency of the visitor to go native. A. J. Brown ascribes much of the "laziness and lack of ambition" to malnutrition and disease, the rest to the "traditional outlook" engendered in other ways by the social setting.[29]

It is impossible for an economist to resolve these issues. The arguments against Huntington are telling, but the fact remains that no tropical country in modern times has achieved a high state of economic development. This establishes some sort of presumptive case—for the end result, if not for the means.

LAND AND CAPITAL

It was noted above that there is some difficulty in distinguishing land and capital, comparing plain with cleared forest. The difficulty, however, goes deeper. Land and capital are substitutes for one another. Land depleted from its original state can be restored to something approaching it through capital formation. Chemicals replace depleted fertility; reforestation restores the capacity of land to hold

[28] M. Bates, *op. cit.* See T. S. Simey, *Welfare and Planning in the West Indies,* Clarendon Press, Oxford, 1946, pp. 112–113, who also disputes the Huntington thesis and attributes part of the deterioration of the white man in the tropics to the negative attitude toward life of men who choose to go to the tropics. This characterization does not apply to missionaries who perform more effectively than government officials.

[29] *Industrialization and Trade,* Oxford University Press, London, 1943, p. 27.

water; irrigation restores desert to cultivation. Capital is a substitute for land. In the limiting case, it would be possible to raise food in factories, by hydroponics, just as poultry products are now being produced with a minimal input of land. It is also possible to find substitutes for scarce land, using capital and abundant labor. Lower-grade iron ore and bauxite can be used, with more capital to reduce them to pig iron and alumina. Staple fiber can replace wool normally produced by large inputs of grazing land. When the most accessible hydroelectric sites are used, as in the Alps, new and more capital-using projects are undertaken, including bringing streams from one side of the watershed to the other through a tunnel in the mountain. Even fresh water, the basic requirement for human life, can be produced from the sea by the use of capital and energy. Land and capital are substitutes for one another.

The fact that capital can be substituted for land does not make land unimportant, however. This substitution is limited by capital availability and by capacity to apply the appropriate technology. The less developed a country, the smaller its supply of capital, and the more important the amount and character of the land it possesses. And vice versa. Contrary to the view widely held in this country, the United States does not confront a problem in the adequacy of its resources, at least in the foreseeable future. Short-run events affecting supply or demand, such as drought or war scares, may give rise to short-run difficulties of economic adjustment. And the social and political questions concerning resources—depletion, public versus private management, etc.—will try our capacities for equitable and efficient solutions. But there is little or no problem of the adequacy of resources in the long run. This country can import the products of land, or substitute capital for them. It has sufficient capital so that no significant resource problems can arise. The more resources we have, the higher our level of living; but no lack of resources, or depletion, given our capital availability, is capable of producing a serious decline in our material well-being. The most difficult problem is that posed by water west of the Mississippi. But water can be produced from energy and sea water, and energy from shale, if not from the sun, and atomic fission is available in considerable abundance at only slightly higher cost than our present sources of energy supply.

With underdeveloped countries, however, resource problems are much more significant in the absence of cheap capital. The most striking case of a country lacking land is Israel, which is substituting capital and labor resourcefulness for it—with difficulty. Irrigation, the ready answer to land scarcity in many countries, requires large amounts of capital, and often diverts this useful factor from other and more productive employments. Agriculture is capital-saving in underdeveloped countries, and capital-intensive in developed. But if land is needed in large measure in underdeveloped countries, the capital required to substitute for land is likely to be on a sizable scale.

LAND AND TECHNOLOGY

A census of the resources of the world or of a country would be valid only in the absence of new discovery and technological change, i.e., in a given state of knowledge and of the arts. Discovery changes land resources in an obvious way. Technological change alters it as surely. The Renaissance was made possible by an enormous change in the productivity of land, equal to an accretion of land resources, whether by the development of hay, which enabled farmers to winter their livestock in good condition, as Simkhovitch thought,[30] or by the horse collar, invented in the tenth century, which enabled horses to pull a plow without choking, as Delaisi believed.[31] The rubber economy of Southeast Asia has been built on the pneumatic tire since 1900; and technological change makes it possible to rework the old slag heaps of the Malayan tin mines to recover wolframite.[32]

It is not appropriate to develop the subject further at this juncture, since a subsequent chapter will be devoted entirely to technological change. It is sufficient to indicate that resources are relative, and this relation runs to discovery, on the one hand, and technology, on the other. In the fourteenth to the eighteenth centuries, the guess may be hazarded, discovery and technology ran each other a close race. With the exploration of the Western Hemisphere, Oceania, and Africa south of the Sahara, and the speedup in technological advance, technology has since probably far outrun discovery. But there is still room for the latter, and not only in oil.[33]

CONCLUSION

We conclude that it is difficult to define land unambiguously, and as distinct from capital on the one hand and technology on the other;

[30] V. G. Simkhovitch, "Hay and History," *Political Science Quarterly*, September, 1913, pp. 385–403.
[31] F. Delaisi, *Les Deux Europes*, Payot, Paris, 1929, p. 29.
[32] L. D. Stamp, *Our Underdeveloped World*, Faber & Faber, Ltd., London, 1953, p. 111.
[33] See *Scientific Conference on the Conservation and Utilization of Resources*, 2 vols., United Nations, New York, 1950.

that it is relatively unimportant for a developed country that has abundant capital to alter the character and capacity of its existing land, and human drive and creativeness to substitute for the niggardliness of nature; but that, other things equal, more and more varied land is better than less and less varied; that land is particularly important to underdeveloped countries with their paucity of capital and innovational skill; and that to ask the question, whether small differences in land, or small differences in social structure, are more significant in boosting or halting economic development, is to outrun the capacity of the discipline for answering questions. Many of us have opinions; no one knows. To the particular question whether France would have behaved like Germany if it had had the Ruhr, one can only reply that partial-equilibrium analysis is not helpful in tracing through long stages of development.

THE ROLE OF CAPITAL

In the view of many economists, capital occupies the central position in the theory of economic development.[1] Development brings with it, as we shall see in detail below, an increase in population and in the labor force. Since land is fixed, barring discovery or a frontier, the land/labor ratio must decline. An increase in output per worker, therefore, would appear to call for an increase in the capital/labor ratio. In this view, the process of economic development is one of replacing shovels with bulldozers, scythes with reapers, three horsepower of machinery per worker with ten horsepower. As we shall note below, this view implies a fixed state of the arts, i.e., no changes in technology.

Capital is regarded not only as central to the process of development but also as strategic. The process of capital formation is interacting and cumulative: capital formation increases income, which makes possible more capital formation. At low stages of development, poverty precludes the saving necessary to form capital. Once the process is started, however, it feeds on itself. "The rich get richer and the poor get children."

[1] See, for example, Walter Heller, "Fiscal Policies for Underdeveloped Countries," in H. Wald (ed.), *Agricultural Taxation and Economic Development*, Harvard University Law School, Cambridge, Mass., 1954, p. 62; he calls it the "main key to economic development." M. Abramowitz puts it in a tie for first place: "It is probably safe to say that only the discovery and exploitation of new knowledge rivals capital formation as a cause of economic progress." See his essay, "Economics of Growth," in B. Haley (ed.), *A Survey of Contemporary Economics*, Richard D. Irwin, Inc., Homewood, Ill., 1952, vol. II, p. 146. Buchanan and Ellis express the point negatively in calling a deficiency of capital the most nearly omnipresent limiting factor, and one that is frequently also the most severe: see N. S. Buchanan and H. S. Ellis, *Approaches to Economic Development*, The Twentieth Century Fund, Inc., New York, 1955, p. 67.

There is another reason, however, why capital occupies such a central position in the theory of economic development today, and this derives from intellectual history. Keynes discussed the dependence of income and employment on investment in the 1930s in static terms. He was interested in capital formation not for what it would produce but for the employment it would give. Harrod saw that the newly created capital itself would be unemployed in a subsequent period unless total spending were expanded to take up its production. His dynamic system, developed to show how much expansion in spending was required to maintain full employment, was later used by Domar and others to indicate how rapidly output could be expanded in a growing economy. The emphasis on investment for employment in the 1930s was readily converted into emphasis on capital formation for economic growth. It is perhaps unnecessary to add that most of this emphasis is warranted.

TYPES OF CAPITAL

Capital can be classified in a variety of ways, depending upon ownership, physical characteristics, and economic function. Many systems of classification use a combination of these schemes of categorization. For present purposes, we distinguish social overhead capital, plant and equipment, and inventories, and occasionally that part of agricultural capital which consists in improvements to land. Social overhead capital is occasionally broken down into economic and purely social overhead capital.

Economic overhead capital consists of public utilities—transport, including ports, roads, railroads; electricity and gas production capacity, pipelines, transmission lines, communication networks, etc.; one can also include the buildings needed for government, fire and police protection, facilities to maintain roads, etc. Strictly social overhead capital includes the plant and equipment required for shelter, education, and public health. Plant and equipment in industry and agriculture need little explanation. This category also includes a large component of fixed capital equipment, sometimes slighted, in office space for business administration, insurance, banking, advertising, selling, wholesale and retail trade. The inventory component of capital is another item that tends to be neglected. Leaving out consumers' inventories, it is important to count the stocks of intermediate goods, and goods in process, as well as finished goods at various stages in distribution from producer to consumer.

In the United States, with an income of $216 billion in 1949, the stock of capital has been estimated at $721 billion, using a definition limited to reproducible tangible assets, including consumers' durable goods.[2] This amount can be broken down as follows:

	Value (In billions of dollars)	*Per cent*
Structures		
Nonfarm		
Residential..................	$195.1	
Nonresidential..............	90.2	
Mining.......................	12.8	
Farm.........................	26.2	
Institutional..................	9.9	
Government..................	74.2	
Total structure....................	$408.4	56.7
Equipment		
Producers' durables............	104.2	
Consumers' durables...........	99.3	
Total equipment....................	$203.5	28.2
Inventories		
Livestock......................	13.2	
Crops.........................	5.9	
Nonfarm......................	58.1	
Public.......................	3.8	
Total inventories....................	$ 81.1	11.2
Monetary gold and silver..............	27.7	3.8
Grand total........................	$720.7	100.0

These categories do not exactly fit those just outlined, either in the definition of capital or in the distinction between social and economic overhead. International comparison along these lines is made everywhere difficult by the fact that categories overlap or do not cover the total population. See, for example, the table of Colin Clark in *The Conditions of Economic Progress*[3] on "Capital in International Units per Head of Persons in Work." Nonetheless, some points may be made. Construction forms a high proportion of total capital, whether housing, overhead capital, or plant, including plant for distribution and administration. If a country is already built up, construction is continuously needed to take care of the increase in population. Actual tools or equipment are likely to be less than half of the plant and equipment item.

Considerable importance attaches to inventories. In the United

[2] R. W. Goldsmith, *A Study of Savings in the United States,* Princeton University Press, Princeton, N.J., 1955, vol. II, pp. 14–15.
[3] Second edition, Macmillan & Co., Ltd., London, 1951, pp. 486–489.

States, these amount to $81 billion, 11 per cent of total capital. In-ventories form a higher percentage of total capital in underdeveloped than developed countries for a variety of reasons. For one thing, as mentioned below in Chapter 6, a larger scale of output enables firms to use inventories more efficiently, whether in production or distribu-tion. In addition, since agricultural output is produced at one time of the year and consumed evenly over the year as a whole, half of output on the average is in inventories at a given time. This is a higher ratio than in industry or services. In consequence, since the proportion of agricultural output in total output declines as income grows, the ratio of inventories to output declines.[4]

The major problems associated with the allocation of investment among the various types of capital will be discussed in Chapter 9.

RATES OF CAPITAL FORMATION

In a stagnant economy where income per capita remains constant or declines gently, savings are likely to run to 5 or 6 per cent of national income per year. How rapidly this rate of savings will increase the stock of capital depends on the relationship between the stock of capital and national income. If the stock of capital typically has a value four times the national income, a rate of capital formation equal to 5 per cent of national income will increase the stock of capital by $1\frac{1}{4}$ per cent. If the rate of growth of the labor force is $1\frac{1}{4}$ per cent per annum, the capital/labor ratio will remain unchanged. To the extent that output per capita depends on the capital/labor ratio, no progress will be made.

Since an increase in income per capita is likely to raise the rate of population increase,[5] possibly to more than 2 per cent, the rate of capital formation must rise sharply to achieve a significant increase in income. How much this rise must be will depend upon the rate of in-come increase required, on the one hand, and the relationship between the increase in capital and the increase in income, on the other. If this

---

[4] This point was made to me by P. N. Rosenstein-Rodan. There is some counter-weight to it in the fact that agricultural workers have a high ratio of savings to income, on the average, since they produce their income at a given point in time and consume evenly over the year.

For a useful discussion of the importance of both construction and inventories in capital, see W. A. Lewis, *The Theory of Economic Growth,* Richard D. Irwin, Inc., Homewood, Ill., 1955, pp. 210ff.

[5] It should be noted that an increase in the population and an increase in the labor force need not be identical, and will not be, except after a considerable lag, when the rate of increase in population changes. The distinction will be empha-sized in Chap. 12. It is neglected here.

relationship or coefficient runs at the same level as that given above, the relation between total capital and total output—i.e., 4:1—an increase in population of 2 per cent per annum will mean that savings must amount to 8 per cent per annum to maintain income per capita, and to 12 per cent per annum to permit a rate of growth in income of 1 per cent yearly.

These relationships among the rate of capital formation, the rate of population change, and the ratio of capital to output are often regarded as the determinants of the rate of economic development. In algebraic terms

$$dY = \frac{s}{k} - dL$$

where dY is the rate of change in national income, s is the rate of savings out of national income, k is the ratio of capital to output per unit of increment in both, and dL is the rate of change in the labor force (sometimes given as the rate of change in population).

This is frequently referred to as a Harrod-Domar type of analysis. Harrod's interest in it was initially limited to the question of how to maintain employment in the long run.[6] He was concerned with the rate of growth in expenditure (dY) needed to absorb the goods produced by past savings. Omitting the change in the labor force, expenditure had to increase, to achieve full employment of the capital, by an amount represented by the savings of an earlier period, divided by the capital/output ratio, which represented the increase in productive capacity. Domar[7] saw that the equation could be used to illuminate the problem of economic growth, with dY becoming not the required increase in expenditure to maintain full employment so much as the growth in output, made possible by the rate of savings, given the capital/output ratio. Singer put the rate of growth in population into the equation to convert dY from the rate of change in total income to the rate of change in income per capita.[8]

[6] R. F. Harrod, *Toward a Dynamic Economics*, Macmillan & Co., Ltd., London, 1949.

[7] E. D. Domar, "Capital Expansion, Rate of Growth, and Employment," *Econometrica*, April, 1946, pp. 137–147.

[8] H. W. Singer, "The Mechanics of Economic Development," *Indian Economic Review*, August, 1952. It is an oversimplification to *subtract* the rate of population increase to get the rate of increase in output per capita, rather than to divide new total output by new total population and compare with the previous period. For year-to-year changes, however, these amount to virtually the same thing, since population increases are limited to 3 per cent per annum at most. For example, $104/102 \times 100 - 100$ is virtually the equivalent of $4 - 2$. For longer periods of time, such as decades, one must do it the long way, since $140/120 \times 100 - 100$ is not $40 - 20$.

THE CAPITAL/OUTPUT RATIO

Two types of capital/output ratio must be distinguished, one from the other and both from the marginal productivity of capital. An effective way of doing so is with a diagrammatic presentation of a production function, which is a mathematical expression of the relationship between inputs of factors of production and outputs of a given good. Figure 3.1 shows a production function in which lines 1, 2, and 3 represent successively higher isoquants, or amounts of equal product which can be produced with varying inputs of capital and labor, assuming only two factors. Every point on line 1 represents the identical

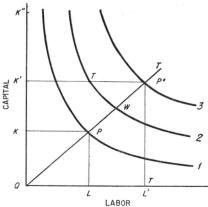

Figure 3.1. The capital/output ratio distinguished from the marginal efficiency of capital.

amount of output, and each point shows a possible combination of capital and labor which can be used to produce that output. Like contour lines, isoquants can be drawn infinitely close together to represent infinitely small differences in output, but are usually portrayed at discrete intervals. In Figure 3.1 with *OK* of capital and *OL* of labor, the optimum or least-cost output occurs at point *P*, which lies on the highest possible isoquant attainable, in this instance, 1.

The *average capital/output ratio* is that between *OK* (capital) and *OP* (output). Now, if capital is increased to *OK'*, output increases. How much this increase will be depends partly on the marginal productivity or efficiency of capital and partly on the efficiency of inputs of other factors. The marginal productivity of capital is the increase in output which is achieved from the application of a given increment in capital with all other inputs unchanged. In the diagram the addition of $K — K'$ of capital will increase output from P to T, or from isoquant 1 to isoquant 2. The incremental or *marginal capital/output ratio*, however, is represented by the relationship between the change in capital and the change that actually occurs in output. If, in this case, the new output after investment of $K — K'$ is OP' because of the availability of extra labor $L — L'$, the marginal capital/output ratio will be KK'/PP', or the slope of PP'. This means that the economy is operating under fixed factor proportions, despite the fact that the isoquants in the production functions show a gentle curvature which indicates a wide range of substitutability between the factors. If less or more additional labor had been available than LL', the capital/output ratio would have changed.

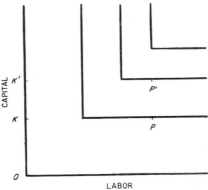

Figure 3.2. The marginal capital/output ratio equal to the marginal efficiency of capital.

If the capital/output ratio is constant, OP is a straight line, and the marginal efficiency of capital differs from the capital/output ratio by the difference between KK'/PW and KK'/PP'. In the real world this difference is likely to be substantial. The net productivity of capital, i.e., the incremental product holding all other inputs constant, less depreciation, is likely to be close to 5 to 10 per cent per annum, while the total productivity of capital, i.e., the inverted capital/output ratio, is likely to vary between 25 and 40 per cent as implied by capital/output ratios of $2\frac{1}{2}$:1 to 4:1.[9]

The marginal productivity of capital and the total productivity of capital would be the same only if the marginal productivity of other factors were already zero and remained zero. Figure 3.2 shows a production function with fixed coefficients, i.e., no possible substitutability

[9] See A. Kervyn, "Le Rapport du capital au revenu: aspects théoriques," *Bulletin de l'Institut de Recherches Économiques et Sociales*, August, 1954, p. 506.

between factors, but where production initially takes place at a point (p), where labor is redundant. If capital is increased from OK to OK', the marginal efficiency of capital is represented by the increase in output from P to P'. If more labor were added, no additional output would be achieved, since the marginal product of labor is already zero. Accordingly, the marginal efficiency of capital and the reciprocal of the capital/output ratio are identical in this case.

Initial fascination with the capital/output ratio arose because of the possibility that it was a strategic variable in economic development. This point of view was illustrated recently in a statement of the Working Party of Problems and Techniques of Planning of the Economic Commission for Asia and the Far East, which said:[10]

The rate of economic growth may be analytically considered as being a function of two factors, (a) the rate of capital formation and (b) the capital/output ratio; accordingly development policies may be described as aiming to increase the former and reduce the latter, or do both.

This statement is qualified at some length in a footnote, but it raises the possibility that the capital/output ratio is subject to manipulation.

The capital/output ratio must not be regarded as identical throughout an economy. Capital is not homogeneous, and capital proportions are not identical in all sectors and industries. A prima facie case can be made that, by investing in those industries with low capital/output ratios, one can maximize total output. The fact of the matter is, however, that the capital/output ratio is not a very useful analytical device. An entire chapter is devoted below to the question of the sectoral allocation of investment. At this point we are interested only in indicating some of the limitations of the capital/output ratio, both over-all, and in the disaggregated sectoral model.

THE LIMITATIONS OF THE CAPITAL/OUTPUT RATIO

There is some significance to the over-all capital/output ratio as an indicator of the necessity for savings and capital formation. But the ratio is of less value for use in prediction and planning. The difficulties are legion and inhere in the ambiguities implicit in the notion of capital, and in imputing a given output to a given input. This last problem is difficult enough through time for the aggregated model in which the capital of an economy is treated as a whole. It is even greater for the disaggregated model where inputs and outputs are identified by sectors.

[10] ECAFE, *Bulletin,* November, 1955, p. 25.

Some of the difficulties of distinguishing capital from land were mentioned in the previous chapter. These are no less when the attempt is made to distinguish capital from labor. A sharp distinction is made between consumption and capital formation, but the line must be drawn for the most part in highly arbitrary fashion. Education, for example, clearly contributes to further production and so in fact does leisure.

Another difficulty is raised by durable goods in the possession of consumers—not only automobiles and washing machines, but also soft goods like clothing, which give off their services over a period longer than some arbitrary short period such as a year.

Even if one takes an arbitrary definition and limits capital to tangible and reproducible assets, excluding those owned by consumers except for housing, there is a considerable question whether one should properly count as the output the gross or the net return, i.e., whether one should count the interest *and* depreciation or interest alone. It makes a substantial difference. An investment in equipment worth $100,000 with a life of ten years costs the same, net, as construction of equal value with a life of fifty years. If each, along with other factors of equal cost, produces $25,000 net each year, the capital/output ratio is 4:1 on a net output basis. But the capital/gross-output ratio is very different in the two cases. Assuming straight-line depreciation, the item with a ten-year life produces $25,000 of net return, plus $10,000 of depreciation, to give a gross output of $35,000 and a capital/gross-output ratio of 2.87, while the fifty-year life construction earns $27,000 for a ratio of 3.7.

The answer to the question which one ought to take, like the answers to so many questions in economics, is, "It depends." In this case it depends on whether the capital structure is likely to be fairly stable, or whether transformations in the structure of the economy, discussed below, are frequent. With stability, it is sufficient to deal with net output, since depreciation allowances are not needed to shift capital to other sectors. If there is a large possibility that capital will be shifted into other industries, however, as transformation occurs, then gross production is the relevant concept.

Another aspect of this distinction is raised by the question whether one ought to consider the capital or the current cost of the capital input in choosing between two competing investments. Assuming a single rate of interest, the initial and the current costs of two capital projects bear the same relation to one another if the current cost is figured net of depreciation. Thus two investments of $50,000, at 6 per cent interest, cost the same whether one uses the capital expense of

$50,000 or the current net cost of $3,000. But if the current cost is gross, this no longer is the case. The longer the life of the capital, the smaller the depreciation charge in any one year and the lower the capital cost, calculated gross. But this type of reasoning may lead into danger, since it favors long-lived capital.

A number of other significant questions are raised by depreciation. For one, there is no fixed scientific basis for calculating depreciation for a given capital asset; in most instances, depreciation is charged fairly uniformly through the life of the assets, either in a straight line or with constant percentage formula. Physically, however, some capital tends to wear out more rapidly at the end of its life than in the beginning. It is possible, therefore, in a growing economy, to reinvest depreciation allowances from recent investments in new capital formation and rely on the greater productivity of the economy later when development has proceeded some distance to make good the physical exhaustion of capital. If an economy is consistently growing, moreover, straight-line depreciation will continuously provide more depreciation allowance than is needed to make good physical wearing out. But this is a simple property of geometric growth.

The production function of the type set out in Figure 3.1 assumes that output occurs in a single instant in time with its input, or in the same period, perhaps with the inputs at the beginning and the outputs at the end. This is a helpful but heroic assumption. Some additional reality can be introduced by a lagged model, in which inputs in period t lead to outputs in period $t + 1$, and inputs in period $t + 1$ produce their outputs in period $t + 2$. To retain the simplicity of this model the period of investment must be constant. The real world, however, is very different. Some inputs, like planted trees and wine to be aged, occur at a point in time and produce their outputs at a considerably later point in time. In other cases, such as inventories, inputs and outputs are both continuous. In still others, illustrated by producers' durable goods, inputs will be made at a point in time and outputs will be continuous. The rate of output may be constant or vary, and may start immediately, or begin only after a lag. In these cases the imputation of a given output to a given input becomes impossible. When an economy undertakes all three types of investment—point-input, point-output; continuous-input, continuous-output; and point-input, continuous-output—the capital/output ratio that relates this year's output to this year's investment is evidently wide of the mark.

In a system of instantaneous production, or with a fixed lag, it is appropriate to take account of the capital/output ratio. When output is received in a different time sequence, however, the investment problem becomes one of comparing the cost of a given input with the present value of its future output. This requires applying a discount to future benefits. Where output is constant and begins immediately, the present benefit can be calculated from the formula

$$V = \frac{Y}{r}$$

where V is the capitalized value of the stream of income, Y, at the rate of interest, r. Where there is a lag in outputs, and variability, it becomes necessary to go back to the underlying series

$$V = \frac{Y_1}{1+r} + \frac{Y_2}{(1+r)^2} + \frac{Y_3}{(1+r)^3} \cdots \frac{Y_n}{(1+r)^n}$$

The longer the delay in receiving the initial outputs, and the smaller they are in relation to the ultimate level of output, the lower the present value (V) of an investment which must be compared with its cost (C). This is because the present value of the nearer outputs is higher than that of those further in the future, which are more heavily discounted. The progression above is a declining series in which the early terms, omitted in an investment with a long gestation period, are higher than the succeeding ones.

There may arise a question whether to use a simple or a compound-interest formula in comparing the present value of two investments with different time profiles of income. Simple interest, as given in the preceding formula, assumes that there is no necessity to calculate the yield on the yield, whereas compound interest allows for interest to be earned on the interest. Professor Rosenstein-Rodan has suggested a compromise.[11] If the marginal rate of savings in the economy is 20 per cent, the compound interest formula should be applied to this much of the income foregone, and simple interest to the rest. This assumes that an investment in which returns are delayed or low in the early years should earn enough later to make up not only for the income actually foregone in the early period, but also that income which one could have expected the economy to earn on the portion of income foregone which would normally have been saved.

When the model is disaggregated, the difficulty of associating inputs with outputs is further increased, and the rule of thumb which advocates investing in those industries with the lowest capital/output ratio loses most of its remaining meaning. This is largely the result of complementaries. It may be true that manufacturing and distribution have capital/output ratios as low as 2:1, as compared with 16:1

[11] In a private communication to the author.

for electricity and railways.[12] But beyond the point of full employment of electrical and transport capacity, the basic industries must be expanded in order to take advantage of the opportunity to invest capital "efficiently" in the low-ratio sectors. The manufacturing sector has a low ratio only if it be assumed that markets have already been linked up by transport, that materials can be cheaply assembled, and that energy is available as needed. To the extent that each sector uses intermediate products and services from other sectors, the sectoral capital/output ratios have limited meaning.

To these theoretical objections, one can add the statistical. The capital/output ratio assumes a given state of the arts, i.e., a given efficiency of production. When the isoquants pull in toward the origin, through technological innovation, so that the same inputs of capital and labor can produce more output, or the same output can be produced with fewer inputs, the meaning of the incremental capital/output ratio is clouded still further. Most recently, the Indian ratio has approached 1.2, as compared with a planning figure of 3, due to considerable increases of output in agriculture which took place in the absence of capital investment. Further, changes in the rate of production through the business cycle will produce declines in output associated with positive capital investment, which makes the ratio negative and uninteresting.

Despite these objections, theoretical and practical, the capital/output ratio is widely used as a planning device. Its predictability as suggested is weak. In the short run it is markedly variable. But over longer periods of time, averaging the annual marginal rate appears to produce meaningful results. This is in large part, no doubt, the result of the law of large numbers in which opposing movements cancel out. The capital/output ratio has in fact been remarkably steady in a number of countries, averaging close to 3.3:1 in the United States, slightly higher than that in Latin America.[13]

Where labor is redundant, the capital/output ratio is appropriate to use and handier than the marginal efficiency of capital which requires attention to the other factors. And for rough-and-ready calculation it

---

[12] These are British figures from the *Economist* (see chart, "Pruning Nationalized Investment," Mar. 17, 1956, p. 621), which are likely to be exaggerated for nationalized industries by the fact that they were running at a loss, so that output was understated. The opposite was true for manufacturing and distribution.

[13] See *Analyses and Projections of Economic Development*, vol. I, *An Introduction to the Technique of Programming*, United Nations Economic Commission for Latin America, New York, 1955, p. 22. The figures are given in product/capital ratios of 0.30 for the United States and 0.43 to 0.46 for Latin America. A considerable part of the difference, however, is due to the exclusion of inventories and consumers' durable goods from capital in Latin America.

has great usefulness. But the experience of underdeveloped countries does not suggest that it is more than a rough indication. It has just been mentioned that the first Indian Five-Year Plan assumed an incremental capital/output ratio of 3:1, and realized 1.2 in practice. Burmese planning uses a ratio of 2:1; the United Nations Economic Commission for Asia and the Far East suggests that a ratio of 2.5:1 would be appropriate for the countries in its area; in Latin America figures of 2.2 to 2.4 are mentioned by the Economic Commission for Latin America, without any planning body able to justify and prove the correctness of a given ratio.

The capital/output ratio, then, is analytically useful in calling attention to the importance of capital in economic growth and handy for many rough computations. But in its present rudimentary stage it is hardly a planning device.

THE MARGINAL EFFICIENCY OF CAPITAL

While most analysis runs in terms of the capital/output ratio in which other inputs are neglected, a recent formulation[14] has made use of the Cobb-Douglas production function which uses the marginal efficiencies of capital and labor.[15] This equation is

$$P = bL^K C^J$$

where P is an index of output, b a constant, different for different economies, L and C indexes of inputs of labor and capital, and K and J exponents of labor and capital, respectively, which indicate the marginal efficiencies of these factors. In the United States these exponents have been calculated for manufacturing as .75 and .25, respectively, indicating that a 1 per cent increase in labor will increase output by .75 per cent, while a 1 per cent increase in capital will lead to a .25 per cent increase in production. The marginal efficiencies of the factor inputs add to 1, which indicates that the production function operates with constant returns to scale; where the exponents add to more than 1, there are increasing returns; where less, decreasing. Belshaw notes that two Indian students have applied the Cobb-Douglas function to Indian manufacturing[16] and found the equation

$$P = bL^{0.402}C^{0.598}$$

[14] H. Belshaw, *Population Growth and Levels of Consumption*, George Allen and Unwin, London, 1956, chap. IV.
[15] Paul Douglas, *The Theory of Wages*, The Macmillan Co., New York, 1934, pp. 131ff.
[16] M. V. Divatia and H. M. Trivedi, *Industrial Capital in India*, N. M. Tripathi, Bombay, 1947, p. 9.

where constant returns either prevail or are assumed. For the rest, however, he uses the Cobb-Douglas formula primarily as a basis for organizing discussion of economic development rather than for empirical research.

The formula has the merit of making explicit a number of variables which are lost in the Harrod-Domar formula, first the productivity of labor; second, the existence of increasing, constant, or decreasing returns. The formula further calls attention to an asymmetry in much of the discussion of development, which discusses the quality of labor and the quantity of capital. The quantity of labor should not be neglected, nor the quality of capital. In the present book the quality of labor is discussed in the next two chapters, the second of which is also concerned with the quality of capital, and economies and diseconomies of scale are dealt with in the sixth chapter, which follows them.

CHANNELS OF INVESTMENT

As a preliminary discussion of sources of saving for capital formation, it is desirable to examine the agencies engaged in making investments. It is generally felt that the limiting factor in capital formation is the volume of savings, and that all the savings accumulated can be readily invested. More recently, however, this view has been disputed. The International Bank for Reconstruction and Development has suggested that the bottleneck is not funds, but projects which are sufficiently advanced in planning to warrant investment consideration. And in a considerable number of countries—Turkey, Mexico, Pakistan—it has been found that the basic lack is businessmen ready and willing to undertake the investment functions of the entrepreneur.

Investment in a developing society is undertaken by farmers, by domestic and foreign entrepreneurs, and by government. Where housing is owned by the occupants, as in the United States, rather than rented from landlords or government, there is another channel of investment—the consumer—who is also responsible, of course, for investment in consumers' durables if these are included in capital.

Farmers are responsible for all but the largest investment projects in agriculture. Government is clearly obligated to furnish social overhead and economic overhead capital except in rare instances. These will occur when a large and rich company, generally foreign, undertakes a big investment in a poor country and wants to raise the efficiency of its workers through investment in education and health—the Arabian American Oil Company in Saudi Arabia, or the United Fruit

Company in many countries of Central America—or when transport and housing facilities are totally absent—particularly likely in mining —in which case the company railroad and the company town may be constructed privately.

Difficult questions arise in the area of productive investment when entrepreneurship is weak and government is inadequately equipped by training and experience to substitute for it. The range of issues involved will be explored in Chapters 5 and 8.

When the private entrepreneur is the channel of investment, it does not follow that he is the sole decision-maker in the process. If he has accumulated his own capital, and obeys the laws, he may be. But in the majority of instances, the entrepreneur employs borrowed or external capital, and the decision to lend to him may be more significant than his readiness to take the risk. While the problem in a number of underdeveloped countries today is to find enough able would-be entrepreneurs, more difficulty was encountered in the history of Western Europe and the United States in deciding which of an unlimited array of potential investors was to be entrusted with capital. In this decision-making, the role of banks has been of great importance historically.

It is a little old-fashioned today to pay much attention to the bank as a director of the flow of capital. Corporations in the United States have largely freed themselves of the dependence on banks characteristic of the three or four centuries before World War I. Reinvestment of corporate profits and sale of securities to the public through investment bankers, or directly to insurance companies, have lessened the extent to which large business in the United States depends on the good will of the commercial banks. In contrast, however, are the banks in Western Europe in all of modern times, and particularly in the nineteenth century. Entrepreneurs proposed; banks disposed.

It appears unlikely that the commercial bank will play the decisive role in channeling capital in economic development in those countries now underdeveloped. This role is probably assigned to government, even though the investment be in the private sector, and with private funds. The foreign entrepreneur with capital must still obtain a license to qualify under laws concerning foreign investment, and to this end he must submit his proposals for government approval. The domestic entrepreneur may be financed by a development bank, using government funds (and perhaps some International Bank capital). Large domestic enterprises which want access to foreign capital must obtain the approval of government to borrow, and in some cases, its guarantee. Whether the capital is privately or publicly owned may make little difference in this respect; government directs investment, in the private as well as the public sector.

SOURCES OF CAPITAL

In a fundamental sense, capital formation is possible only when a society produces a surplus of consumers' goods sufficient to satisfy the wants of the workers engaged in producing capital, i.e., producing goods which are not themselves consumed during the period. In primitive economies this surplus consists largely of food and to a lesser extent of clothing. The problem of capital formation in these societies is seen as one of feeding (and clothing) the labor taken away from the production of food and clothing and put to work to produce capital. In more developed societies, which live further from the margin of subsistence, essentially the same problem presents itself in another form: how to get the savings out of current production to form capital. These savings may be regarded as consumption goods produced but not consumed by their producers; or capital goods produced and offset by the savings of their producers, which reduces their demand for consumers' goods.

Saving may be undertaken by business, by households, or by government in the domestic economy, or may come from abroad. These savings may be voluntary, or may be the involuntary result of inflation. The question of foreign borrowing will be left for later discussion, as will a number of aspects of government capital formation. Here, however, it is appropriate to indicate some of the major factors affecting personal and business savings.

In agriculture, saving frequently takes place in kind. The farmer clears land, repairs buildings, builds fences. This is simultaneously saving and investment. To a limited extent saving in kind can take place in the nonagricultural sector, particularly perhaps in the accumulation of inventories and in owner-constructed housing. For the most part, however, saving takes place through investment of income received in money form.

A variety of influences affects the volume of personal savings. The rate of saving is a function of level of income; its distribution; the prevalence of institutions which make for saving, such as the habit of life insurance, the practice of amortizing mortgages, the horizontal family in which each generation is expected to provide for its own security; and the existence of incentives and opportunities for social advance through economic betterment. A separate item should perhaps be made of the value system of the society which may attach special importance to the accumulation of wealth, whether for religious or secular motives. It is difficult to assign relative priorities to these and other contributing factors, partly because the same factor may be of different significance under different circumstances. In a closed society in which social mobility is impossible, a highly skewed income distribution may not lead to a high level of saving; and such saving as does occur in this situation may take nonproductive form in jewelry, precious metals, and luxurious dwellings. In an open society, however, in which social advance comes from economic success, the more highly skewed the distribution of income, the higher the capital formation. Lewis has pointed out that in a society where 10 per cent of the population receives 40 per cent of the income, as is true of many underdeveloped countries, it should be easy to increase savings to 20 per cent of national income.[17] This would appear to make the level of income less important than its distribution. Figure 3.3 indicates, moreover, that, once a society is saving more than 10 per cent of its income, the connection between the levels of income and savings tends to disappear. Brazil at $100 of income per capita in 1949 and the United States at more than $1,400 save roughly the same percentage of income, and so do a variety of countries between. On this showing, saving is more likely to explain income than vice versa, while the existence of motivation to advance materially in various levels of society is more significant than particular institutions or the distribution of income.

In one or two cases in Figure 3.3 comparison runs between capital formation and domestic product, rather than national product. The difference between domestic and national product arises from the fact that some incomes produced in a country are in fact earned abroad, and so are in domestic geographical, but not in national, product; or some incomes earned by factors in domestic ownership but located abroad are received in the country and so are part of national but not of domestic product. The Burmese ratio of net capital formation to net *domestic* product in 1938 was 7.1 per cent, but domestic capital formation was negative since capital exports amounted to 11.5 per cent of domestic product. The savers and the capital exporters in this case consisted of Indian and European middlemen. Similar reasons explain the very large ratios, again relating to domestic and not national product, which apply to the Belgian Congo and Southern Rhodesia. The former are not given in Figure 3.3 since income data for them were not provided by the study used. But net capital formation to net domestic product ran as high as 21.7 per cent in the Belgian

[17] *Op. cit.,* p. 236.

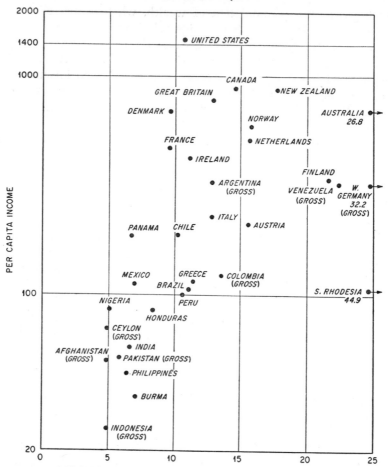

Figure 3.3. Ratio of net capital formation to net domestic product (or in a few cases gross capital formation to gross national product) compared with national income per capita, about 1949. SOURCES: S. Kuznets, "International Differences in Capital Formation and Financing," in *Capital Formation and Economic Growth,* Princeton University Press, Princeton, N.J., 1956, pp. 60–68; and estimates assembled by W. W. Rostow in "The Take-off into Self-sustained Growth," *Economic Journal,* March, 1956, p. 36; income per capita, Table 1.1, Income per Capita in U. S. Dollars.

Congo in 1951; and gross capital formation as high as 45 per cent of gross domestic product in Southern Rhodesia in 1950. These enormous ratios reflect high profits and high rates of reinvestment in the foreign-investment sector of the economies. A similar explanation applies to the high Venezuelan figure.[18] The Norwegian level, on the other hand,

[18] See W. W. Rostow, "The Take-off into Self-sustained Growth," *Economic Journal,* March, 1956, p. 36, n. 3.

reflects investment taking place in shipping and electrical power generation, both of which are capital-intensive, and a government-operated investment plan which raises the over-all level of capital formation to the highest in Europe.

There are few data by which one can compare the shares in total saving of individuals, businesses, and government. Some for the United States, derived by Kuznets[19] from Goldsmith data, suggest that non-agricultural individuals (as distinct from farmers, unincorporated business, business corporations, and government) have been responsible for 50 to 70 per cent of United States savings; business corporations for approximately 25 per cent, over the period from 1897 to 1949, and giving little weight to the depression decade 1930–1939. For the rest, the share of farmers and unincorporated businesses has declined; that of government, risen.

There is no reason, however, to regard these proportions as typical. Nor is it always clear in a country how sharp the distinction is between individuals and businesses.

Business savings come out of profits. Some considerable amount of gross investment, of course, comes from depreciation and depletion allowances. Depreciation is naturally much higher as a percentage of income in a developed country with a large stock of capital than in a country beginning its economic growth. Moreover, depreciation is a source of capital formation in a sense if the capital replacement is more productive than the capital worn out. But net savings come from profits.

W. A. Lewis believes that the secret to the rapid increase from 5 per cent of income saved in a stagnant country to 10 to 15 per cent in a growing economy is to be found in a high rate of profit.[20] High incomes as such are not significant: rich landlords are limited in their capacity to expand, likely to be satisfied with their social status, and are usually high consumers. But high profits, whether retained by businesses, or passed along in dividends to individuals, lead to reinvestment, expansion, development, growth, at least if the economic growth takes place under capitalistic institutions.

Government as an investor may finance its capital formation with internal savings or with external savings acquired from households or

[19] See S. Kuznets, mimeographed supplement to "Towards a Theory of Economic Growth," in R. Lekachman (ed.), *National Policy for Economic Welfare at Home and Abroad*, Doubleday & Company, Inc., New York, 1955.

[20] *Op. cit.*, pp. 234ff. In his earlier article, "Economic Development with Unlimited Supplies of Labour," *The Manchester School*, May, 1954, pp. 139–191, Lewis calls the problem of explaining the increase of saving from 4 to 5 per cent of national income to 12 to 15 per cent the "central problem in the theory of economic development."

business. Internal savings represent the difference between taxes and expenditure for governmental expenditures other than those for capital formation. These savings, of course, can exceed the amount of government investment and become available for investment by private business. If government taxes the economy to finance its investment, it may seem ironic to call the result government saving, but such is the practice. If, on the other hand, government finances its investment through a deficit, the saving is done in other sectors. The saving may be voluntary, and take the form of an expansion of holdings of government debt by households and business, including, it may be well to note, government debt in bank notes. Or, if the deficit is financed in inflationary fashion, the saving is involuntary and represented by the reduction in consumption caused by the rise in prices, as the government bids resources away from the other sectors. The merits, if any, and demerits of deficit financing by governments will be discussed further below. At this point, however, it can be indicated merely that economic development can occur on this basis, as the example of the Soviet Union bears out.

CAPITAL AS A KEY

Is capital formation the key to economic development? Many think so. Capital can substitute for resources; capital can substitute for labor. Given a capital/output ratio of some sort, capital formation leads to more output which provides a surplus for further investment and further increases in output. But there are several reasons for believing that capital formation, while necessary, cannot explain economic development. First is the fact that the take-off, in Rostow's phrase, from 4 to 5 per cent to 12 to 15 per cent, to use Lewis's figures, is often (but not always) abrupt. To explain it, one must go beyond the geometric-growth type of model in which capital leads to growth in income which leads to more capital. Second, the growth takes place at rates which are higher than can be explained on the basis of capital formation alone (see Chapter 5). Third, as economic growth picks up, the rate of capital formation levels off, which requires more explanation than is provided by a theory which gives the central role to capital.

It is true that capital formation is a tender plant. Its germination may be frustrated by poverty, by taboos on lending, by a preference for investment in housing, bidding up the prices of agricultural land and commodity stocks on the part of those with wealth. Once started, its growth may be stunted by hoarding, the export of capital to financial centers, by distortions introduced by inflation, by conspicuous consumption. Or savings available for external financing may not be loaned to investors through the mechanism of the banking system and capital markets. Finally, once investment takes place, there are important problems of ensuring that it finds its way into the most productive lines which will lead to further output and growth. Accordingly, it is appropriate to spend time on problems of capital formation.

But capital formation is not the only ingredient of the growth process.

SUMMARY

Economic growth requires and depends on inputs of capital. The rate of growth implied by a given rate of capital formation is a function of the capital/output ratio and the rate of population increase. The capital/output ratio and the marginal efficiency of capital, identical when other factors are redundant and receive no incomes, normally differ. The capital/output ratio represents the relationship between all or increments of capital with total or incremental output, without regard to other factors, whether unchanged or variable. The marginal efficiency of capital, on the other hand, is the incremental output associated with an increment of investment when all other factors are held constant. The capital/output ratio is widely used in economic-development discussion, but serves principally as a handy, rough measure which is not useful for fine work. Its drawbacks include ambiguity over whether to take output net or gross; the problem of associating given outputs with given investment, whether by sectors or in time; and disassociating simple growth based on capital investment from changes in output produced by changing technology, discoveries of land, etc.

The process of growth involves savings to create a surplus for capital investment. The source of voluntary saving is intricately bound up in social attitudes toward economic mobility; in income distribution, by sectors and factor shares; and in the level of income. Saving can be undertaken by government, and can be forced on households and corporations by inflation. One of the mysteries about economic development is what makes the rate of saving rise in the early stages and decline in the late.

CHAPTER 4 *Labor*

THE IMPORTANCE OF SOCIAL FACTORS

Along with land and capital, labor evidently has a hand in economic development. By labor in this chapter we mean not the numbers of people of the working force. Demographic questions are postponed until Chapter 12. We mean instead the capacity of labor for work, not so much in terms of productive skills, as of its social response to economic opportunity and readiness to undergo economic change. Our subject is thus the social capacity of labor for economic development.

The question may properly be asked whether the capacity of the labor force shapes the character of economic development, vice versa, or a little of both in an interacting system. Assuming that one takes the last and eclectic view, the question arises how to fit the social capacity of the labor force for development into the development model.

Rostow suggests that variations in the behavior of people relevant for economic development can be summed up in a number of propensities—propensities to develop science, to apply science to the world about them, to propagate and rear children, and to strive for material advance.[1] Given these propensities, which are the business of other disciplines such as sociology to study and measure, the economist is in position to investigate economic questions regarding capital formation and foreign trade. Hagen, on the other hand, seems to doubt the soundness or appropriateness of economic analysis on economic development, apart from study of psychological propensities and social structure, and is prepared to undertake a direct investi-

[1] *The Process of Economic Growth*, W. W. Norton & Company, Inc., New York, 1952, chap. II.

gation of the social and psychological factors influencing economic development.[2]

We have noted in Chapter 2 the existence of a difference of view over the relative importance of resources and social attitudes in economic development. Similar differences can be developed between capital and labor capacity. Kuznets has said:[3]

The major capital stock of an industrially advanced nation is not its physical equipment: it is the body of knowledge amassed from tested findings and discoveries of empirical science, and the capacity and training of its population to use this knowledge effectively.

Don Patinkin has said (privately) that the effective asset of Israel which gives it a much higher level of income than the surrounding Arabian states, including those with oil ($389 in 1949, and $500 in 1953, against perhaps $85 and $90, respectively), is not its access to capital and gifts from world Jewry. These hardly sufficed to pay its pre-Suez national defense bill. It is, rather, the attitudes of its population. Into this population, originally largely from Europe, have lately come considerable numbers of Jewish immigrants from Arab countries —from Yemen, Morocco, Algiers, etc. These have been rapidly assimilated. If the United States has been a melting pot, Israel is a pressure cooker.[4]

It is impossible for an economist to explore this vast subject in detail, in a single chapter, and to offer a synthesis of the ways in which people shape and are in turn affected by economic development. The most that can be done is to suggest the aspects of social character which may be significant, and something of the variability which inhibits generalization. It is realized that this is unsatisfactory. The treatment is necessarily scrappy, and overlapping, rather than neatly integrated. But the subject does not as yet lend itself to more systematic and integrated treatment.[5] The various aspects to be touched upon include the orientation of the individual in his society, family, class, race, religion, urban/country, national character, size of the social

[2] In a research project at the Center for International Studies at Massachusetts Institute of Technology, Cambridge, Massachusetts.

[3] In "Toward a Theory of Economic Growth," in R. Lekachman (ed.), *National Policy for Economic Welfare at Home and Abroad*, Doubleday & Company, Inc., New York, 1955, p. 39.

[4] See S. N. Eisenstadt, "Sociological Aspects of the Economic Adaptation of Oriental Immigrants in Israel: A Case Study in the Problem of Modernization," *Economic Development and Cultural Change*, April, 1956, pp. 269–278.

[5] This does not take into account T. Parsons and N. J. Smelser, "A Sociological Model for Economic Development," in *Explorations in Entrepreneurial History*, April, 1956, pp. 181–204, nor their *Economy and Society*, The Free Press, Glencoe, Ill., 1956.

unit, the effect of culture on institutions, and the interaction of cultural values and economic change.

THE INDIVIDUAL AND HIS ENVIRONMENT

Parsons[6] and Levy[7] have indicated that the relations of an individual to his society will differ in a number of dimensions, of which the most significant involve *cognition, membership,* and *substantive relations.* Cognition, or the way the individual interprets the physical world about him, tends to vary from the irrational to the rational, as societies develop, or from superstition to reason. In terms of membership, development brings with it a change from particularism (or, in Parsons' term, ascription) to universalism (or achievement). Under the former, roles in society are chosen on the basis of the individual's family, religion, caste, income; under the latter, the choice is made on the basis of his capacity to fulfill such a role. Substantive relationships range from the diffuse, in which the limits of the obligations of people to one another are vague, to the specific, in which they are spelled out in contractual form.

Development along any one of these dimensions is likely to involve a parallel movement along the others, but there may be considerable variation within any one. A society may have progressed beyond belief in magic, the evil eye, or the power of saints' relics to produce cures, but still believe in luck, lotteries, or extrasensory perception. Levy cites that particularism, which found one of its highest expressions in the Chinese family, was missing from the Chinese civil service, which was open to competitive examination. The converse is occasionally met in developed countries where the principle is accepted that the best man gets the job, but the best man frequently turns out to be the boss's son. In substantive relations, diffuse obligations can run within the family and with neighbors and intimate friends, while contract governs those in a wider circle, or diffuse relations, such as those involved in academic tenure, protect the teacher, while the business employee can be fired on short notice.

For economic development to take place, some considerable rationality in cognition, universalism in membership, and specificity in relations are needed. Rationality is required not only at the highest levels, to further the development of science and productive invention, but throughout the system. It must be understood that identical action by

[6] T. Parsons and E. A. Shils (eds.), *Toward a General Theory of Action,* Harvard University Press, Cambridge, Massachusetts, 1951, pp. 80–91.

[7] M. J. Levy, *The Structure of Society,* Princeton University Press, Princeton, N.J., 1952.

individuals under identical circumstances leads to identical results without the whimsical intervention of irrational forces. People must learn to be goal-oriented, and work to achieve given ends. And systems of thought must be devised, like the invention of accounting by the Italians in the Middle Ages, which permit a rational view of the world.

Universalism is less insistent a requirement than rationality; but nepotism, caste, slavery, and a closed society of classes waste ability and reduce a society's capacity to produce. The degree of universalism is perhaps less significant than its location. The selection of priests, army officers, or social leaders through class and family ties is less important for these purposes than the filling of economic and political roles.

In terms of substantive relations, it is important to know not only the nature of these relations within various groups, but the way they change toward others. Sharp discontinuities can occur. One may have an obligation to assist and share one's belongings with members of a joint or extended family, reaching up and down in terms of generations, and out to cousins and second cousins, without being enjoined even to respect the property of people to whom one is not related. It may be forbidden to charge interest to a fellow Moslem, but encouraged to gouge and cheat an infidel.

FAMILY STRUCTURE

Intimately related to these aspects of the individual's relationship to others is the family structure in a society. Sociologists and anthropologists distinguish many types of family in terms of who lays down the law and where the newly married couple lives—e.g., the patrilineal, matrilocal, etc. For present purposes it is enough to observe that the vertical family, under which young adults continue to live with one set of parents after marriage and contribute earnings to a common pool, has a distinctly inhibiting effect on many of the factors affecting economic development: mobility, savings, risk-taking, even willingness to work more for a higher price. Labor supply curves may bend backward with respect to wage increases because of a limit on economic aspiration, or because the personal incentive is dulled by the necessity to contribute all the work while sharing its fruits. The incentive to take risks in entrepreneurship is blunted in the same way. In the vertical family, as compared with the horizontal, the necessity to save is reduced, since the family provides insurance for dependents and security for old age out of current production, which obviates the necessity to acquire assets. The existence of the vertical family clearly limits mobility, both in space and in occupation. If it is the duty of the son to remain in his father's house, he can shift from agriculture to industry, or from farm to farm, only when he is freed of his filial obligations by his father's death, at which time he is encumbered by dependents. The unmarried son may leave for short stretches of city work, but is bound to return.

The family system affects economic development in many other ways. The alleged French entrepreneurial unwillingness to permit enterprises to grow beyond family size has been mentioned earlier.[8] So, too, has the system of inheritance, which may divide land equally among children, or among male children, or may give it all to the first son. This affects not only the size of the agricultural land input, but also mobility. An extreme form of family relationship to land, mortmain, under which land cannot be alienated outside of the family, restricts efficient use still more.

Closely connected with the family structure is the role of women, which has effects on rate of population increase, proportions of the labor force to total population, demand for household laborsaving devices, and a host of other economic variables. The range runs from some form of purdah in which women are clearly inferior in status to men and subservient to them, to full equality of rights, decision-making, job opportunities, and equal pay.

How significant family structure is by itself is hard to evaluate, since the more primitive and inhibiting forms of family coexist as a rule in a social matrix loaded with other restrictive aspects. Some caution and skepticism are warranted when it is noted that the Hindu joint family in India is not paralleled in Pakistan, where, by Moslem tradition, the horizontal family system prevails.[9] Indian income in 1949 was slightly higher per capita than that of Pakistan. It may be that its advantages in family structure give Pakistan somewhat greater promise in development than India. It is also possible, however, that as economic development proceeds from the force of positive factors, those aspects of family structure which stand in the way—the joint Hindu family, and a residual subjugation of women under Moslem law—will give way and be modified.

CLASS STRUCTURE

It has widely been observed that economic development depends upon an open class structure, in which social mobility is possible, and in particular on the existence of a strong middle class. These may

[8] See above, p. 17.
[9] I. N. Qureshi, *The Pakistan Way of Life,* William Heinemann, Ltd., London, 1956, chap. 2.

amount to different ways of saying the same thing. Where the classes are widely separated, as under feudalism, or today in Spain, the gap is too wide to be bridged. The middle class is weak and ineffectual, and tends to become dependent on and subservient to the ruling class. The oppressed classes seek relief in revolution; the ruling class defends its position with force. With a strong middle class, however, social mobility in both directions is possible. Agricultural and urban workers can rise to the middle class; dispossessed members of the ruling class can find outlets for their energies short of laboring.

In some societies, social advancement for the vigorous and able is possible only through church or army. Given a middle class widely engaged in commerce, industry, and the other professions such as law, medicine, science, teaching, accounting, engineering—and, one must add, government—these energies and abilities can be harnessed to economic growth.

What makes for an open society with a middle class? In this area, as throughout the book, it is never completely clear to what extent the factor under discussion shapes or is affected by development. At an early stage of development, a middle class is favored by the existence of money (which enables slaves to buy their freedom, and wealth to be accumulated in other forms than land), by the secularization of education (to free science from the narrowness of church rule), by the existence of a frontier (either to the west as in the United States or seafaring, as in Britain and Scandinavia) to preserve mobility, and by the critical start in capital formation and mechanical production necessary to overcome initial inertia. Particular circumstances have important effects in particular cases, such as primogeniture in England which produced a crop of younger sons originally for the church and army, but later for commerce and the professions; or, going further back, the enclosures, which destroyed feudal obligations, created a basis for capital formation in agriculture, and developed a working class to encourage entrepreneurs; or, most recently, the readiness of the aristocracy, first, to open their schools and universities in England to the children of successful entrepreneurs, which would give them the necessary external polish for admission to the upper class and, second, to sell them land.

Economic development, of course, has its impact on the class structure. G. D. H. Cole has traced through the distinctive impact on the British class structure of four stages in the Industrial Revolution: the first, in iron manufacturing and coal mining, being highly localized; the second, involving textiles, railways, and the rapid development of banking, emphasizing mobility of human beings, merchandise, and money; the third, mass production, reducing the demand for brawn and calling for higher skills; and, finally, the age of synthetics and automation, which requires highly differentiated, skilled people.[10] Moreover, the growth of the middle class feeds on itself, as the increase in incomes from commerce and industry creates a demand for superior shopkeepers, better attorneys, doctors, teachers.

Of critical importance, frequently, is the value system of the various classes. "In the Middle Ages a gentleman did not engage in economic production . . . . Because we are middle-class minded, America is a society where millionaires go to work as well as everyone else."[11] In many parts of Latin America professional life has a prestige well above that of business;[12] and, while money is more potent than family in making class distinctions, "culture" is more important than money.[13] Or the middle class may be intensely competitive, intensely ambitious, but frustrated, by feeling that it is helpless in the face of the politically powerful upper class.[14] Or the society may confuse the shadow with the substance and educate hundreds of thousands of people to middle-class appetites, without providing them middle-class incomes.[15]

The view has been expressed by E. E. Hagen, and is under investigation by him, that economic development is customarily led by a class or group in the society which has some reason to be dissatisfied. This "out-group," to use an expression from social psychology, must have been brought up to "achieve," and must sublimate its antagonism to the existing elite by pushing forward as entrepreneurs. Examples are abundant in European history: the Dissenters in England; the Calvinists in Switzerland; the Huguenots in France. But the theory, which is not yet thoroughly tested, may have to be stretched somewhat to account for the leadership of the samurai in the economic development of Japan, or the emergence of the Parsees in India as leading entrepreneurs in the textile industry. These leaders have not been subordinate in their own society, although there is a possibility that the same effect can be produced by their recognition of subordination or inferiority as compared with foreigners.

[10] G. D. H. Cole, *Studies in Class Structure*, Routledge and Kegan Paul, Ltd., London, 1955, chap. II.

[11] H. Grayson, *The Crisis of the Middle Class*, Rinehart & Company, New York, 1955, pp. 97, 99.

[12] See Robert Redfield's introduction to J. and M. Biesanz, *Costa Rican Life*, Columbia University Press, New York, 1944, p. viii.

[13] J. and M. Biesanz, *op. cit.*, p. 21.

[14] See J. and M. Biesanz, *The People of Panama*, Columbia University Press, New York, 1955, pp. 211ff.

[15] This is a particularly pressing problem in the Middle East and in India. In the latter it is reported that 500,000 out of 5 million persons who have gone through high school are unemployed. See "India Perplexed by Jobless Youth," *New York Times*, Mar. 25, 1956, p. 28.

CULTURAL DIFFERENCES AMONG RACES

Racial questions are intimately related to class, religion, and to economic development. This is not to say that some races are superior in economic terms to others, although the white races have achieved on the whole a higher material level of living. Modern anthropology has exploded the notion of fundamental physiological differences in race. Race nonetheless enters into the question of the aptitude of a people for development, but as a cultural factor. In what follows, the term race is used very loosely and is hard to separate completely from culture. Religion, social and cultural attitudes, have in the past erected taboos against certain types of essential occupations. On occasion this has led to the subjugation of other races as slaves, as in the Southern United States, the West Indies, and Brazil, to provide cheap labor.[16] At other times taboos against commerce and money lending led to the importation of other races to carry out these functions. The Christian injunction against usury could be ignored by Jewish money lenders, just as the religious taboo on the same subject brought Hindus into the Moslem parts now Pakistan, and into Burma; and Jews, Armenians, and Greeks into Turkey; and lack of interest in trade brought Chinese merchants to Malaya, Indonesia, the Philippines.

Races need not remain separate. The major sociological fact about Brazil is the intermingling of the white and negro races;[17] and everywhere in Latin America, except for Argentina and Uruguay (white), and West Indies (Negro), the majority of the population is mestizo or of Indian origin.[18] Figure 4.1 shows some but not a very high correlation between income per capita and percentage of white people. If

[16] It may be argued that the Negro was needed physiologically to be able to withstand the heat involved in cultivating cotton, sugar, coffee. This view, however, runs contrary to that expressed in Chapter 2 above that the barrier to manual labor of white men in the tropics is cultural rather than physical.

[17] G. de Freyre, *Masters and Slaves*, Alfred A. Knopf, Inc., New York, 1946, p. 83 *et passim*.

[18] See D. B. Brand, "The Present Indian Population of Latin America," in *Some Educational and Anthropological Aspects of Latin America*, Latin-American Studies V, University of Texas Institute of Latin-American Studies, University of Texas Press, Austin, Tex., 1948, p. 51 (quoted by W. E. Moore, *Industrialization and Labor*, Cornell University Press, Ithaca, N.Y., 1951, p. 81). The definition of white is 76 to 100 per cent Caucasian; mestizo is Indian and white breeds with no more than 75 per cent white blood; Indian is 76 per cent or more Indian. Negroid is all persons with perceptible Negro blood. It may be observed that the racial purity of Argentina and Uruguay is due to the fact that the earliest settlers had no need for labor in their land-intensive agriculture, and therefore imported no Negroes and killed off the Indians or drove them into the mountains.

Venezuelan oil and the Panama Canal are taken out, the correlation is somewhat higher, but still not striking. Moreover, race and other bases of social stratification cannot be kept completely separate. "Money whitens" is one slogan in Jamaica which exemplifies this, and there are others.[19]

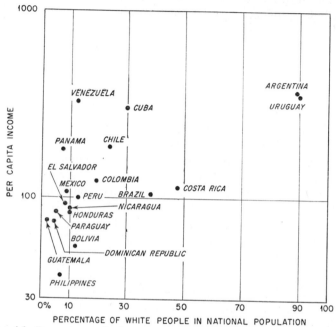

Figure 4.1. Percentage of white people in national population, compared with income per capita, about 1949. SOURCES: Percentage of white people, D. B. Brand, "The Present Indian Population of Latin America," in *Some Educational and Anthropological Aspects of Latin America*, Latin-American Studies V, University of Texas Institute of Latin-American Studies, University of Texas Press, Austin, Tex., 1948, p. 51 (quoted by W. E. Moore, *Industrialization and Labor*, Cornell University Press, Ithaca, N.Y., 1951, p. 81); income per capita, Table 1.1, Income per Capita in U. S. Dollars.

In some societies rigid taboos hold;[20] in others, economic power given over to an alien race in certain occupations can be gained back with great difficulty. In the Philippines, Malaya, and Indonesia, native populations are using political power to force entry into trade and

[19] T. S. Simey, *Welfare and Planning in the West Indies*, Clarendon Press, Oxford, 1946, p. 19. See also J. and M. Biesanz, *The People of Panama*, p. 202, where *campesinos* and peons refer to prosperous townspeople as whites, regardless of color.

[20] It is interesting to observe that the taboo against employment of people of Jewish extraction in the 1930s, now largely broken down, differed between Europe and the United States. Many Jewish refugees coming to the United States from Germany found the United States much more liberal because they could get

commerce where the Chinese merchant has economic control, backed by family ties. In these plural societies, apart from the political tension, there is loss of energy and capacity through the racial particularism. At least two solutions are possible, neither very attractive: one is the melting pot, in which cultural values and racial attributes are fused through intermingling. This is the solution applied among white races and nationalities in the United States, though not to the Negro on any scale; and among all races in Latin America. It necessitates the weakening of racial and national characteristics which is frequently impossible in the light of the tenacity with which they are maintained, and not always desirable. The other solution is expulsion, applied by the Turks to the Jews, Armenians, and Greeks in 1921; by the Hindus and Pakistani to each other in 1947 and thereafter; by the Jews to the Palestinian Arabs. This method is cruel, but it has the advantage of requiring the country expelling its moneylenders, merchants, experts, or other economically useful groups to do its own work, It is likely that in the very long run the capacity of the society to develop is thereby enhanced. But the cost in suffering is very great.

RELIGION

Hand in hand with the roles of family, class, and race in economic development, comes religion. Max Weber and R. H. Tawney have long emphasized the connection between the Protestant Reformation and economic growth, running through the Puritan injunctions to work, save, and to achieve spiritual satisfaction through material reward. The subordinate groups mentioned above under class have in many cases been religious ones. But religious change is far from being the primary factor determining social capacity for development or the level of development itself. The Moslem south of the Sahara—stable, equable, and balanced—is an entirely different social being from his North African coreligionist of Morocco, Algiers, or Tunis, who is described as continuously either "one up" in a maniac state or "one down" in bitter frustration. Northern Italy, the Low Countries, and the Rhineland, largely Catholic, participated as fully in the commercial and industrial revolutions as many parts of Protestant Europe.

Moreover, religion is to a considerable degree malleable. In Burma, a revival of Buddhism is under way, a religion which in its earlier form strongly emphasized asceticism, abstinence, cultivation of the

employment in government, an occupation closed in Germany. On the other hand, German-Jewish engineers were shocked to learn that United States corporations, equivalent to those for which they had worked in Germany, were not then open to them.

spirit. In its present vein, however, closely associated with a revival of Burmese nationalism, and Asian political independence, Buddhism is in process of subtle conversion to a banner of economic advance.

It has been pointed out that economic development has taken place in Europe not only where the Reformation took place but also where the state successfully wrested control of education from the Church, as in France, Belgium, and the Netherlands.[21] This was a necessary prelude to economic development to free science and enable it to be harnessed to the solution of practical questions. Since World War I, of course, the Roman Catholic Church has encouraged the advance of science, and the antithesis between religion and economic growth no longer exists, if it ever did.

CITY/COUNTRY

Robert Redfield, the anthropologist, is responsible for the thesis that there is a gradual change in every society between city and country. The isolation of the country, communion with nature, the inexorable demands of nature tend to stabilize and make rigid social life and values. In the city, on the other hand, the majority of contacts are with man and man-made objects rather than with nature. This increases the need for rationality, universalism, and specificity in the relations of man to his environment; breaks down family, class, racial and religious habits, barriers and taboos; gives plasticity and mobility to social life. Specialization requires the use of money; opportunities for communication build literacy; face-to-face contacts alter the status of women and tend to lower the birth rate. On this showing, the differences between town and country are more significant for development than the differences among towns or among rural societies.

As already noted, this generalization overlooks plantation society, with its rural proletariat living close together in intimate contact.[22] It further neglects an essentially middle-class agriculture, like the Danish, where the Folk High Schools maintained the basis of communication and interchange, or like that of the Middle Western United States, Australia, and New Zealand, where radio, television, the automobile, and rural free delivery of mail, including cheap rates for newspapers and magazines, have kept the farm population in intimate contact with national life.[23] But there may be something to this gen-

[21] F. Delaisi, *Les Deux Europes*, Payot, Paris, 1929.

[22] See p. 30 above; note also that different types of crops produce different social patterns.

[23] There are equally considerable differences among aristocratic farmers, e.g.,

eralization, especially in the Asian village, isolated and remote, in the Middle East, and in Latin America.

The literature abounds in contradictions, even among field investigators in the same situation. For example, R. R. Jay, writing on rural Central Java,[24] asserts that, while the villagers and townspeople regard themselves as different, the existence of distinctions based on city and country is largely mythical, and the real problem in city and village alike is the intensifying bitterness between Moslem and non-Moslem political groups. A Dutch missionary, on the other hand, emphasizes the social, religious, moral, and economic differences between village and town in the same area.[25] The outsider in terms of discipline, culture, and nationality, is unable to judge between such opposing views. Yet there can be little doubt that the agglomeration of cities has an impact on the speed and character of economic development. We shall touch upon this later in Chapter 7 and again in the discussion of community development.

SIZE OF THE SOCIAL UNIT

With economic development, the size of the social unit grows. In the Indonesian village "interest in the affairs of other families, except close kin, for most people extended no further than a radius of 100 to 150 yards."[26] In Greece, Spain, and Italy, regional ties at least until recently have been far stronger than national. In more developed countries the primary social group is the nation; some expect a further move in Europe to the Continent.

The extension of the social unit is of course a necessity in cultivating the characteristics needed for economic development. Nepotism makes excellent sense in a society where honesty is limited to the family circle and intimate friends.[27] To hire a stranger into the firm would

---

the Junkers who were vigorous, close to the soil, hardworking, and at the same time soldiers and government administrators, on the one hand, and the Russian aristocrats who were not really farmers, and exploited the peasant rather than the land.

[24] "Local Government in Rural Central Java," memorandum, Center for International Studies, Massachusetts Institute of Technology, Cambridge, Mass., 1955.

[25] H. Bass, "Village and Town in Indonesia," reprinted from *Panjadar,* a theological monthly from Central Java, in *Background Information for Church and Society,* March, 1956.

[26] Jay, *op. cit.*

[27] See M. Mead, *Cultural Patterns and Technical Change,* UNESCO, Paris, 1953, pp. 87–88: "Greek parents are agreed that the principal thing to teach their children is to be honest and tell the truth; but this of course means to be honest in their dealings with their parents and other relatives, all friends of these, and with people who value them and trust them as people."

be to run the risk of losing its assets the moment one's back was turned.

These generalizations must be modified for particular circumstances, which affect the capacity of a social group to have intercourse with

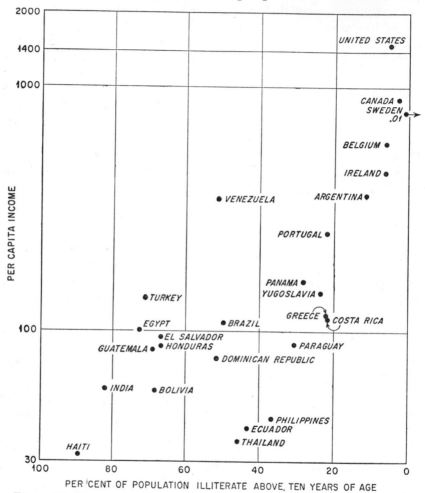

Figure 4.2. Illiterate population as a percentage of total population above ten years of age, compared with income per capita, about 1949. sources: Illiteracy, *Statistical Yearbook, 1955,* United Nations, New York, 1955, pp. 564–568; income per capita, Table 1.1, Income per Capita in U. S. Dollars.

others. Topography, cultural heritage, the communication system, level of education, and a host of other factors play a part. Of these, the aspects which change with development are primarily education and the system of communication. It has long been observed that there is a strong correlation between literacy and the state of development, despite the possibility of overeducation or mal-education mentioned earlier. Figure 4.2 offers some evidence on the point. The relationship is particularly strong up to 5 per cent illiteracy and $350 of per capita income in 1949. H. A. Innis, the distinguished Canadian economic

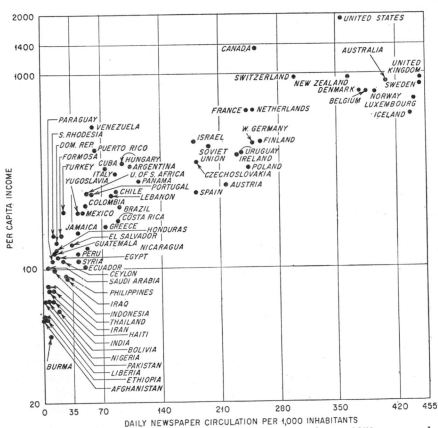

Figure 4.3. Daily newspaper circulation per 1,000 population, 1952, compared with income per capita, 1953. SOURCES: Newspaper circulation, *Statistical Yearbook, 1955*, United Nations, New York, 1955, pp. 593–594; income per capita, Table 1.1, Income per Capita in U. S. Dollars.

historian, has emphasized the role of the communication system in shaping the character, and affecting the rate of development. He regards as great stimuli to British economic growth in the nineteenth century the introduction of the penny post and the penny press. Figure 4.3 conveys less than an exact idea of the amount of communication through the printed word because it is limited to daily

newspapers appearing six times or more per week and ignores differences in size among newspapers. There seems to be little relation between communication and level of income at the lower end of the
scale.

An important aspect of capacity to communicate is language, and
a language may or may not lend itself to ready written use. One of
the disadvantages of the British withdrawal from India has been the
loss of a common language. Urdu in Pakistan and Hindi in India are
not the mother tongues of a majority of the two populations. To substitute them for English as the lingua franca involves a high short-run
cost. An important reform in Turkey to stimulate communication and
interchange was the Latinization of spelling, just as the adoption
of the Arabic system of numbers after the Crusades liberated European calculation. Whether the Chinese will succeed in building a
relatively cheap typewriter or reforming spelling by characters in such
a way as to make communication cheap and efficient will affect the
size of the social unit, its cohesion, and in turn the rate of economic
development.

In Chapter 6 we will pay considerable attention to the linkage of
markets. The social parallel is a widening of the social unit. In a
healthy society the size of the primary unit increases without altogether destroying ties to the lesser ones—the village, metropolitan
area, region. But there are other and complex social situations. French
nationalism has been characterized as unhealthy since it brooks no
loyalties higher or lower than itself, and has found no place in the
social contract for big industry or the working class.[28] The 100 per
cent American or the British jingo is unable to reconcile his patriotism
with wider responsibility. What in the total situation permits a healthy
system of social relations with a large primary group in one situation,
and not in another, lies well outside the scope of this study. Such
differences exist, however, and have importance for the effective functioning of the economy. The creation of a large market, which may be
necessary for economic development, presupposes some degree of
social cohesion, as well as affects it.

NATIONAL CHARACTER

Up to this stage, emphasis has been on the changes in people
needed to enable them to cope with economic growth. Interpersonal

[28] H. Luethy, *France against Herself*, Frederick A. Praeger, New York, 1955,
esp. p. 431.

attitudes, family and class structure, racial and religious views, the size of the social unit, must alter if economic growth takes place, and in adjusting readily and without convulsion, assist the process of development. If in any aspect these changes are blocked, it follows that economic development is impeded or halted.

But the differences in peoples may go deeper than merely their standing on the Parsons-Levy scale, or their evolution in societal change. There is a variety of possible group or national cultures which are ingrained in the society from generation to generation. This national character, according to social psychology, is communicated in the process of child-raising, is largely unconscious, and alters slowly. It may be that the rate of change picks up with development, particularly as fads in child training develop. But to the extent that national characters differ, that some lend themselves in critical fashion to economic advance while others do not, and small differences in cultural practices can produce large differences in character of significance for the economy, the economist is helpless before this development problem.

Spengler divided peoples into the Apollonian and Dionysian types, the even-tempered and those whose tempers exploded. Benedict, in *Patterns of Culture,* traced similar attitudes, particularly in the Zuñi and Kwakiutl Indians, to permissive and authoritarian upbringing, and emphasized the capacity of the Zuñi to work together cooperatively, the competitive hostility of the Kwakiutl Indians leading to conspicuous and wasteful consumption. Modern anthropology has penetrated into these matters to produce a much wider range of differentiation in matters affecting economic behavior—cooperation and competition, the nature of individualism, attitude toward work, etc.[29] Thus far the social psychologist has been unable to establish the relative importance of various characteristics of a culture for development, to indicate rates of substitution among them, or to suggest to what extent they are independent or linked. Danish capacity to cooperate[30] (and Uruguayan and that of New Zealand) is a tremendous national asset for development, as is the German compulsive urge to work.[31]

[29] See especially M. Mead (ed.), *Cultural Patterns and Technical Change,* where the cultures of Burma, Greece, the Tiv tribe in Nigeria, the Palau in New Guinea, and Spanish Americans in New Mexico are studied.

[30] See C. P. Kindleberger, "Group Behavior and International Trade," *Journal of Political Economy,* February, 1951, and the references on Danish character there.

[31] See H. C. Wallich, *Mainsprings of the German Revival,* Yale University Press, New Haven, 1955, chap. 12, "Economic Consequences of German Mentality," and esp. pp. 332ff.

But is Uruguayan character important if its level of living is no different from that of the temperamentally explosive Argentina? How
significant is the attitude toward work as it varies from avoidance,
philosophic resignation, acceptance, idealization, and compulsive de-
votion, or the attitude toward time, or toward friends?[32] Even individualism in a society may take different forms, as for example between Britain and France. In Britain individualism focused on the
sanctity of property, which permitted enclosures, and two centuries
later the pauperization of more than a million agricultural workers
through wheat imports. In France, individualism concentrated on the
inviolability of personal action, which protected the French peasant in
similar circumstances.[33]

There is a possibility that differences in national character are wan-
ing as world culture becomes homogenized—some people would think
Americanized. David Riesman has identified three stages of social development—the traditional, the inner-directed, and the other-directed.[34] Culture is clearly idiosyncratic in the first of these, and tends to
perpetuate itself in the steady state. Differences in national character
also play a major role in the inner-directed period, as people act out the
roles laid down for them in their upbringing, impervious to the effect
they are creating in the world about them. The nineteenth-century
entrepreneur in Victorian Britain is the classic example of the inner-
directed man whose counterpart in the United States was prepared to
let the public be damned. Today, the world over, however, people
have become much more responsive to their peers, aware of the efficacy of the public relations man and advertising, and in consequence
readier to suppress and alter the characteristics acquired in their childhood. Fashions extend to child rearing, changes in which rupture the
continuity of national character. Consumption changes from conspicuous to self-conscious. The demonstration effect, which we shall discuss
in the next chapter, leads people to strive to forsake their traditions

[32] Of great interest in this connection is the study of Oscar Lewis, *Life in a
Mexican Village,* University of Illinois Press, Urbana, Ill., 1951, which suggests
the difficulties of generalization. Work, industry, and thrift for the purpose of
accumulating property (in land and animals) are the highest and most enduring
values—in a Catholic country (p. 296) relations are impersonal and reserved—
though life is rural and not urban (p. 287). There is much hostility in interpersonal relations, although there are no sharp social differences since the revolution,
and no conspicuous consumption or boasting (pp. 292, 54, 177, 297).

[33] See Francis Miller and Helen Hill, *The Giant of the Western World,* William
Morrow & Company, Inc., New York, 1930, p. 188. See also K. Polanyi, *The
Great Transformation,* Farrar & Rinehart, Inc., New York, 1944, which expresses
surprise that British society would permit so complete a domination of social by
economic considerations.

[34] *The Lonely Crowd,* Yale University Press, New Haven, Conn., 1950.

in favor of the consumption standards of others, studied through international communication by press, radio, magazines, books, motion pictures, tourists, including military forces. The desire to conform in consumption standards may be sufficiently strong that, given the minimum of resources and capital, impediments in the national culture will be overcome.

INSTITUTIONS AND CULTURE

Adam Smith believed that economic development would follow if government provided "law, honesty, peace, and easy taxes." John Stuart Mill added to this list "improvement in public intelligence and the introduction of foreign arts." It may be granted that institutions are an expression of culture, in the usual case, that they are critical for economic development, but that the list extends beyond that of Smith and Mill.

Cultural lag, a familiar social expression, is important here. Many institutions have outlived their usefulness, but have strong holds on a culture and are difficult to change or modify. This applies not only to such matters as corruption or squeeze, systems of land tenure, or village family organization, religious or educational practice, but to much imbedded in the habitual patterns of economic production, distribution, and consumption.

Another incongruity, less often noticed, is cultural lead, which occurs when economic institutions are borrowed from a more developed country and grafted onto a society which they do not fit. This is a well-known phenomenon in the political sphere, where constitutions, parliaments, cabinets, and elections abound in countries which are far from democracies. But it is not missing in economics. In the interwar period, money doctors from Britain and the United States traveled to a number of underdeveloped countries and established central banks. Perhaps not too curiously, in countries visited by British experts little Banks of England were established; in those favoring United States experts, little Reserve Systems. One of the basic and devastatingly expensive examples of cultural lead today is the application of Keynesian economic analysis needed for developed countries in periods of unemployment to underdeveloped countries to which the quantity-theory analysis of full employment more truly applies.

To be effective, economic institutions must be adapted to the needs and the culture of the country in question. This adaptation may be undertaken consciously. In the optimal case, however, institutions evolve to fit a country's economic requirements and its national character in a subtle and unconscious way. In Denmark, when the world price of wheat fell, the marketing cooperative was devised to meet the need for large-scale marketing of the products of labor-intensive and hence necessarily small-scale agriculture. The institutions used in a given country at a given stage of its development for production, distribution, allocation of credit, and for associating producers, consumers, and the public in the process are most effective when they fit both the economic needs and the cultural conditions of the country. Borrowed institutions, like hand-me-down clothes, may fit without alteration, but it is not likely that they will.

CULTURE AND DEVELOPMENT

The argument about the role of culture in development, as in the case of resources and capital, has two aspects: first, whether cultural factors may not be critical in shaping an on-going economic development and determining how far it may carry; and second, how far cultural factors are necessary and sufficient for development in the presence or absence of other ingredients. There can be no ready answers to these questions. On the turning points in economic history some student will emphasize one factor, some another, as in the controversy over whether it was French character or French lack of coal which permitted Britain to develop beyond France, or United States social mobility or America's vast resources which account for the wealth of the United States. It seems likely that anything can happen: a hard-working, nose-to-the-grindstone people like the Germans, with rather mediocre resources can achieve developmental success; and so can a classless, consumption-minded society with abundant resources like the Australian. In Japan, lack of resources and capital did not hold back development, given effective leadership and a few other fortuitous circumstances. In Brazil, however, rich resources, a high land/labor ratio, and a series of spurts of foreign investment have, until recently, failed to produce a self-sustaining growth process. Some minimum of social capacity for development is necessary. Japan and Israel may indicate that enough is sufficient.

SUMMARY

Economic development is associated with social changes which pervade the relationships of man to his environment and to his fellows. The individual's interpretation of the world about him, his relations to his and to other families, classes, races, the size of the social unit, etc., all change. Economic development is also associated with certain religions, city rather than rural life, cultural attitudes which emphasize competition rather than contemplation.

Whether the social attitudes lead or follow economic change is impossible to say in general. Instances of each can probably be found; in the usual normal pattern, interaction is likely, with some cultural and social habits which fail to give way under economic pressure serving to block further advance.

CHAPTER 5

Technology and Entrepreneurship

TECHNOLOGY AND DEVELOPMENT

There have been short-run fluctuations in the importance attached to technology and technological change in economic development. Following President Truman's 1949 inaugural address, with its introduction of the Point Four program, many people appeared to think that underdeveloped areas could be made to catch up with developed parts of the world through the simple communication to them of secrets of advanced technology.[1] Longer hoes, row planting, improved seed, and the diffusion of agricultural techniques through extension services were thought to be sufficient. An appropriate reaction against this easy optimism led to the tendency to pay less attention to technology and more to capital. Row planting was fine, but really needed were dams, ports, roads. When technical assistance was useful, it almost invariably called for new equipment or capital. Most recently, however, there has occurred a new intellectual appreciation of the role of technology. It has been emphasized that growth of real income in developed countries has taken place at rates that cannot be explained in terms of capital formation but require increases in productivity, i.e., more net national product per unit of total input.[2]

This attention to productivity is not entirely new. Schumpeter makes it the center of his theory of development:

[1] In what follows, an attempt will be made to abjure use of the monstrous banality know-how.

[2] See M. Abramowitz, "Resource and Output Trends in the United States since 1870," *American Economic Review, Papers and Proceedings,* May, 1956, p. 6; and A. Cairncross, "The Place of Capital in Economic Progress," in L. H. Dupriez (ed.), *Economic Progress,* Institut de Recherches Économiques et Sociales, Louvain, 1955, p. 235. Note that Cairncross in this statement mixes up the net marginal product of capital and the capital/output ratio. See A. Kervyn, "Le Rapport du capital au revenue: aspects theoriques," *Bulletin de l'Institut de Recherches Économiques et Sociales de l'Université de Louvain,* August, 1954, p. 506, n. 1.

The slow and continuous increase in time of the national supply of productive means and savings is obviously an important factor in explaining the course of economic history through the centuries, but it is completely overshadowed by the fact that development consists primarily in employing existing resources in a different way, in doing new things with them, irrespective of whether those resources increase or not.[3]

Dewhurst, referring to the United States, writes: "Technology, in fact, can be thought of as the primary resource."[4]

In terms of the production functions set out in Chapter 3, a technical innovation permits more product for the same resources, or the same amount of product for less resources. This is illustrated in Figures 5.1 to 5.3, where R is an isoquant of the production function before technological change; R_1 represents the same quantities of output after the innovation. In Figure 5.1 the innovation is drawn neutral

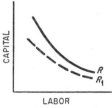

Figure 5.1. Technological innovation.   *Figure* 5.2. Laborsaving innovation.   *Figure* 5.3. Capital-saving innovation.

with respect to the two inputs. It is possible, however, that innovations may be laborsaving or capital-saving, as illustrated by Figures 5.2 and 5.3.

Resources exist only in terms of a particular state of technology. As a rule, moreover, a technological change requires a shift in the character of the inputs which cannot be seen in two-dimensional diagrams with homogeneous factors. With saving of labor in general, there may be demand for special grades of labor skill; capital-saving inventions inevitably demand a different type of physical capital input. Agriculture approaches pure increases in productivity, where the pounds of meat or milk or eggs per pound of feed, or bushels of corn per acre, with labor, machine, and fertilizer inputs held constant, have been going up year after year. Even here, however, there are small changes in inputs, such as the addition of hormones, sulfa drugs, or hybrid seeds. Outside of agriculture, the comparability of production functions is generally upset by the change in character of inputs. Capital

[3] J. A. Schumpeter, *The Theory of Economic Development*, Harvard University Press, Cambridge, Mass., 1949, p. 68.
[4] J. F. Dewhurst, *America's Needs and Resources: A New Survey*, The Twentieth Century Fund, Inc., New York, 1955, chap. 24 and p. 834.

and labor are homogeneous over time, when depreciation allowances can be taken out of an industry and the supply of recruits for training can be cut off. In the long run, therefore, but not in the short, it is appropriate to consider technological change as bringing about an increase in income per head through reducing the inputs required for a given output or giving more output for a given input.

INVENTION AND INNOVATION

Schumpeter made a fundamental distinction between invention, which was the discovery of new technique, and innovation, which consists in the practical application of an invention in production for the market. Somewhat analogously, Rostow distinguishes the propensity to develop pure science, and that to apply science in output for the market. In Schumpeter's view, invention was performed by inventors, innovation was the task of the entrepreneur. In Rostow's version these propensities could exist together or separately in a given country: in the nineteenth century France had a high propensity for pure science, but inventions first reached the market in Britain. Today the British role is largely reversed. British scientists and inventors have no reason to be ashamed of their record in mathematics, physics, chemistry, or in radar, jet propulsion, etc. But mass production in these areas is frequently first reached by the United States. The case of atomic energy is instructive: the bulk of the theoretical work was done by Europeans; the construction of the first pile and first bomb by American teams.

Usher has pointed out that the distinction between invention and innovation is too sharp, and that limiting the field of technological change to the physical sciences and their applications is unduly restrictive. Using modern psychology, he notes that all action can be divided into three types: (1) innate activities, which are unlearned and instinctual; (2) acts of skill, which are learned, whether through formal training or individual imitation; and (3) inventive acts of insight, resulting in new organizations of prior knowledge and experience.[5] Usher insists that inventive acts occur in fields of conceptual activity, involving interpretations of codes, rules for group behavior, and the execution of policies for individual or group activity. He is fearful that Schumpeter's distinction between the inventor and the innovator, and identification of the entrepreneur with the latter, may be misleading, since it suggests that the inventor has a monopoly on in-

[5] A. P. Usher, "Technical Change and Capital Formation," in *Capital Formation and Economic Growth*, Princeton University Press, Princeton, N.J., 1956, pp. 523–550.

ventive acts of insight. This is not the case. It should also be said that acts of skill frequently require abilities of a high order, and that at higher levels, acts of skill and acts of insight become interwoven to an extent that they cannot readily be distinguished.[6]

This emphasis further stands as a corrective to Rostow's narrow view of the propensities in terms of science and its application to production. Usher does separate fundamental science from applications, designating as primary, inventions not carried to the stage of commercial application; secondary, those which open up new practical uses; and tertiary, improvements in a given device which do not extend the field. But inventions can occur well outside physical science—in commerce, industrial administration, government, communication, even advertising. More significant than the presence of discrete classes of inventors and of entrepreneurs is the spirit in a society which is prepared to devise new means to solve problems at all levels, whether by trial and error, intuition, or operational research, and whether in the laboratory or on the shop floor.

Not all inventions are economic to the point where they can use the services of the innovator, to continue to use the Schumpeterian terminology in qualified form. Atomic energy provides one striking example. Here many groups have confidence that the long-run cost curve is bound either to fall or be reduced to the point where it will be able to compete with coal and hydroelectric power in locations of economic significance. But there are others. Modern alchemists can contrive a million chemical and physical miracles which run afoul of the economic disability that the inputs cost more than the output can be sold for. The insight which converts an invention from uneconomic to profitable may be trivial in scientific terms.

That necessity is the mother of invention, like most proverbs, contains an element of truth. The most striking economic development occurs where demand for a new good in consumption meets an innovation which permits it to be satisfied with new efficiency in production. Swedish economic development after 1870, for example, had its roots in the substantial increase in demand for lumber and wood products, including particularly paper, plus a series of peculiarly Swedish inventions in the chemical processing of wood pulp which reduced its price.[7]

[6] One difficulty with Usher's distinction is that, under modern research methods, invention becomes an act of skill rather than an act of insight. It may be necessary to separate out the class of inventions which were produced to order from those which resulted from random insights or from research into fundamental science with no practical applications contemplated.

[7] See E. F. Hechsher, *An Economic History of Sweden,* Harvard University Press, Cambridge, Mass., 1954, pp. 228ff.

The Danish response to the fall in the price of grain after 1870 was not only the marketing cooperative, but also the invention of the mechanical cream separator, which made possible the production of a standardized butter on a large scale for the hearty breakfast of the British middle class.[8] In Canada, opening of the prairie provinces after 1900 required improvement of cultivation techniques, particularly in dry farming and summer fallow, which permitted a profitable harvest where none could be grown before, and appeared as a response to the reduction in freight rates of the Crow's Nest Pass Agreement of 1897.[9] But necessity is not always fruitful in such timely fashion. British industry lost some of its lead in steel production when the Bessemer process, announced in 1854, proved unsuitable to iron ores with high phosphorus content. Not until 1878, with the development of the Thomas process, did it have an opportunity to regain its lead. By this time German competition had gotten well under way. The threat of orlon and dynel to wool in Australia after World War II was met—at least for a time—by an improvement of productivity, reducing costs as much as 30 per cent through myxamytosis, the disease which wiped out the jack rabbit and left more grass for the sheep. But Japanese silk, Chilean nitrates, and similar products needed similar *dei ex machina* and waited in vain. There is an element of luck in whether new inventions will be forthcoming to exploit opportunities or defend economic positions; but beyond this random element there is the capacity of the society to respond to the situation by producing a new insight.

IMITATION

Brozen observes that there is a difference among (*a*) what is technologically possible; (*b*) the technical capacity of the leading firms; and (*c*) the technology used by the economy as a whole.[10] The first exceeds the second; the second, the third. Even in the United States, handicraft firms exist alongside firms using modern machine techniques to a surprising degree in a surprising number of industries and trades. The question arises, why does not imitation—i.e., the learned act of skill—raise the technology of the total to the level of technological possibilities? The existence of technological possibilities better

[8] See C. P. Kindleberger, "Group Behavior and International Trade," *Journal of Political Economy*, February, 1951, p. 36.

[9] P. C. Hartland, "Factors in Economic Growth of Canada," *Journal of Economic History*, 1955, no. 1, p. 19.

[10] Y. Brozen, "Invention, Innovation and Imitation," *American Economic Review, Papers and Proceedings*, May, 1951, pp. 239–257.

than those in use obviates the necessity for a large part of the difficult tasks of invention and innovation.

A wide variety of answers is given to this question—answers which take us into the other ingredients of economic development. There is a cost to changing techniques, a cost involved in the fact that the capital and labor used in the old process are not homogeneous with those needed for the new, so that the old capital, at least, must be written off. Ignorance, legal restriction (patents), standardization (particularly codes in housing), unwillingness to change because of tradition or managerial inertia, lack of market competition—these are among the reasons cited for the technological dispersion in a given country. Between countries (and regions in a given country), there may be the added reason that the factor proportions appropriate to the technology of the leading country or leading firms in the country may be altogether different from those in the lagging.

Brozen lays stress on lack of competition.[11] Where the leading firm is interested in lowering prices, expanding its share of the market, improving product and production efficiency, the industry as a whole is necessarily required to imitate, innovate, or perish. The automobile industry in the United States illustrates this condition fully. But where the leading firms are nonaggressive, secretive, content to live and let live, and where entry into markets is restricted by weight of the product, inadequate transport, lack of large sums of capital needed to make a start, or a class structure which keeps people in their place, imitation languishes. But, as this last list suggests, the character of the competition may lead back into social structure, or into capital formation.

DEMAND-INCREASING AND COST-REDUCING INNOVATION

Innovations are of two types: there are new goods and new ways to produce old goods. The distinction is a loose one. Synthetic rubber is mostly a new way of producing an old good, but partly a new good; equally mixed is the automobile, which is partly horse-and-buggy— i.e., local transport on the former limited scale—and partly an entirely new item of consumption. To the extent that inventions take place in new goods—particularly consumption items—invention is the mother of necessity.

[11] So does H. J. Habakkuk, "The Historical Experience on the Basic Conditions of Economic Progress," in Dupriez (ed.), *op. cit.*, pp. 149–170, although he is disposed to believe that producers who responded to an increase in demand were as important as innovators in the early Industrial Revolution (see *ibid.*, p. 524).

In discussing Brozen's paper, Scoville points out that, while competition may be vital for the spread of imitation in new ways of producing old goods, i.e., cost reductions, it is not equally clear that this holds for new goods, i.e., demand-increasing innovation.[12] It is sometimes charged that large companies slow down the rate of innovation, holding inventions off the market—the perpetual razor blade and the perpetual match are most frequently cited in the folklore. But large companies with records of high profits also have the resources for research and experimental projects and frequently a bias in favor of introducing new products. In part this may be wasteful product differentiation without significant difference, as in oligopolistic competition in gasolines, cigarettes, soaps, etc. Beyond this, however, is the record of new products in chemicals, aluminum, oil, automobiles, where the attempt is made to develop a broad market for a new product.

The appeal of new goods to the consumer has been a powerful factor in economic development, but may currently be even more powerful. Nurkse, in particular, has called attention to the "demonstration effect," following a lead of Duesenberry in domestic trade.[13] Domestically, this effect is used to explain why increases in consumption use up most of the increase in real income and more, and savings tend to remain relatively steady or decline. New goods satisfy new wants; appetite grows with eating. The demonstration effect in the domestic area operates as a stabilizing influence to maintain expenditure and output. With consumption growing continuously, it can be argued that economic development depends on consumers as much as or more than on entrepreneurs.

In the international realm, however, the demonstration effect injects an element of instability and disequilibrium. Classic economic theory operated on the assumption that opening of trade between two countries left tastes unchanged, and had its effects in inducing shifts in production. With the demonstration effect, however, the impact of new trade may be to shift demands even before any impact on the allocation of resources. Before trade, the underdeveloped countries consumed native foodstuffs, local products, and went without the material trappings of the developed country. With trade introduced, there occurs a substantial change in its pattern of tastes and a shift in demand in favor of imported goods, and against the goods produced with a comparative advantage.

[12] *American Economic Review, Papers and Proceedings,* May, 1951, pp. 274–279.
[13] R. Nurkse, *Problems of Capital Formation of Underdeveloped Countries,* Basil Blackwell & Mott, Ltd., Oxford, 1953, pp. 58, 63–67, etc.

There is much dispute about the existence of the demonstration effect. It is possible to adduce evidence on both sides of the question. A distinguished economist visiting Latin America insists that the demonstration effect is a figment of an overdeveloped imagination. A keen observer of the French scene notes that the American way of life has penetrated a certain depth into cities, but that the countryside is unaffected. On the other hand, there is a wealth of testimony to the effect that, especially since World War II, the entire world has been moving toward the adoption of United States and Western European standards of consumption in food, dress, amusements, and even literary and artistic taste, as well as in durable consumer goods. One can find evidence on both sides of the question to prove both that there are places where the demonstration effect exists, and places where it does not. The question is how widely is it prevalent, and how intense. That the effect is spotty is probably undeniable. One can find little trace of it, for example, in Lewis's account of Mexican village life;[14] whereas Simey can say about Jamaica:[15]

It would be relatively easy (given the necessary basis of research) to define standards which are capable of attainment in the West Indies which would allow mankind a reasonable chance of a happy and useful life without fear of "outside" comparisons. But the opportunity to lead their own lives in their own way is a slender one . . . . "Outside" standards are applied through the medium of the middle and upper classes, who in a materialistic and competitive age see no alternatives to the standards of living which have been set by the urban communities of Great Britain and North America. The motor car, the refrigerator, the suburban house of a type quite grotesquely unsuited to a tropic climate, all these are the hallmark of success in the West Indies.

Standards of food consumption are particularly important. The incorporation of milk in the Indonesian diet, the substitution of wheat for rice in Japan, the adoption of the European breakfast in place of fish and soybean soup in Thailand[16] work against comparative advantage, and often reduce dietary levels.

Often the objects of consumption are symbolic rather than useful.

[14] Oscar Lewis, *Life in a Mexican Village,* University of Illinois Press, Urbana, Ill., 1951 (but see the exception in *ibid.,* p. 182).

[15] T. S. Simey, *Welfare and Planning in the West Indies,* Clarendon Press, Oxford, 1946, p. 160.

[16] *New York Times,* July 4, 1955. See also the quotation from J. and M. Biesanz, *Costa Rican Life,* Columbia University Press, New York, 1946, p. 35, from Chacon Trajos, *Tradiciones Costaricenses:* "Our zeal to imitate the foreigner has made us abandon our good food. . . . We have lost our classic more nutritious and savory national cooking."

Grattan observes that the underdeveloped world prizes above all American fountain pens, Swiss watches, and British bicycles.[17] The last has primarily a utilitarian flavor, but the pen is as much a symbol of literacy as an article of writing, and the watch exemplifies a shift from the timeless world of the peasant to the split-second, synchronized universe of the machine. It seems safe to conclude that the spread of interest in the Western standard of living has occurred in many areas of the world, and everywhere among government officials, and that the demonstration effect is to this extent an important factor creating interest in economic development.

Wallich has drawn the contrast between Schumpeterian development in which the leadership is taken by the entrepreneur, imitating or creating new ways of production, and Duesenberry development with its emphasis on consumption.[18] In the one case the leadership comes from supply; in the other demand. In Riesman's terminology, Schumpeterian development is inner-directed; consumption-oriented development produced by the demonstration effect, other-directed. In the former instance, savings and capital formation are fairly readily produced from the fortunes of driven and dedicated men, who have no time for consumption; in the latter, government is called upon to lead investment, and savings are difficult to accumulate because consumption tends to parallel or outdistance increases in productivity.

There is something to this insight. It may be well, however, not to draw too sharp a distinction between production and consumption for this purpose. Part of the imitative effect in production arises from a desire to emulate the attitude rather than the result, and partakes of the nature of consumption. We shall have occasion to discuss this in particular in dealing later with factor proportions. Moreover, some considerable element in the desire for a higher level of living can be accounted for, or at least is consistent with an increase in productive capacity. It is always difficult to determine whether a society works to eat or eats to work, but there can be little doubt that in a number of underdeveloped countries a superior level of consumption may be a requisite of superior production.

Whether innovation is cost-reducing or demand-increasing, it tends to be concentrated in developed countries, and to lag in underdeveloped. This gives rise to problems of international trade, to be discussed later, as underdeveloped countries experience new demands

[17] H. Grattan, "The Things the World Wants," *Harper's Magazine*, November, 1956, pp. 57–60.
[18] See H. C. Wallich, *Mainsprings of the German Revival*, Yale University Press, New Haven, Conn., 1955, chap. 2.

for foreign goods and productive processes, and meet increased competition in existing lines of production. If the imitative urge from entrepreneurs leads the demonstration effect for consumers' goods, the forces of disruption are countered by the expansion of capacity. The first impact, in either event, is increased expenditure.

It is hardly necessary to mention that, whether cost-reducing or demand-increasing, the effects of some innovations are more far-reaching and pervasive than others. Isard has viewed innovations in transport as strategic, and Innes's preoccupation with innovations in communication has been mentioned. These areas are clearly seminal in their effects on the economy as a whole. Reductions in costs and development of new means of transport make possible new combinations of resources to serve new markets. The picture magazine, the motion picture, radio, and television—to take a limited number of innovations in communication—are to a large degree responsible for the demonstration effect, insofar as awareness of Western levels of living has penetrated underdeveloped areas. How extensive the impact of an innovation may be is difficult to determine in advance: too high hopes have been held out for early effects of atomic energy; many other innovations have been underrated.

ENTREPRENEURSHIP

A school of economic history has attempted to apply the insight of Schumpeter to explanations of economic growth which emphasize the role of business enterprise. A leader of this school, Professor Cole, has suggested that entrepreneurs themselves change with the course of development. Originally Professor Cole classified various stages of entrepreneurship into "rule-of-thumb," "informed," and "sophisticated," as business leaders became less intuitive and empirical and more highly rationalized. More recently he has been inclined to substitute systematic change along a different dimension than cognition, and focus on the entrepreneur's consciousness of the impact of his decisions. In the early stages of development, according to this scheme, entrepreneurs are community-oriented—aware, that is, only of their impact on local markets for labor and goods. Later they become conscious of the industry as a whole, and interested in technical progress of the industry, their share of its output, their standing. At some still higher stage, the entrepreneur is nation-oriented.[19]

This evolution of the entrepreneur from local tycoon to trade-

[19] A. H. Cole, "A New Set of Stages," *Explorations in Entrepreneurial History*, December, 1955, pp. 99–107.

association power and finally to business statesman of national importance may be appropriate for some purposes. In more general terms it should be said first that entrepreneurship frequently takes on a highly national or cultural shape, and second, that the degree of specialization in entrepreneurship changes with development. In a number of instances—Britain, the United States, and Turkey—the ranks of industrial entrepreneurs will be filled from commerce: the putting-out system evolves slowly into the factory in the same trade in Britain; the New England merchant who made a killing in rum turned to textiles during the 1806 embargo; the leaders of new industry in Turkey are drawn from the merchants who piled up profits in chrome and dried fruits during World War II. In Japan it was the samurai who turned to industry, and kept their social structure intact by the expedient of adopting vigorous young businessmen, or taking them into the family through marriage.[20] India developed a peculiar institution, the managing agency, through which foreign capitalists not resident in India could have their projects watched over despite the scarcity of entrepreneurial talent. A managing agency would undertake the direction of a series of firms, in the same industry or in different industries.[21] The possibility that French entrepreneurs differ from American in their desire to keep their firms small enough for family control has been referred to in Chapter 2, in connection with the question whether this was more important than resources in shaping the economic development of France. It has been observed that in Germany decision-making was broken down in a highly specialized way in large firms; the cartel worried about price; banks about finance; managers about production; and business executives about investment and plant location.[22] In writing about German entrepreneurs, Parker has suggested that the success of German large enterprise was due to its extensive division of entrepreneurial labor; a high degree of specialist training; sufficient social mobility to permit some matching of talent with job responsibility, despite the prestige accorded to soldiers, state officials, and academic people. He observes, however, that high prestige for German entrepreneurs was limited to those fields in which Germany had a world reputation—exports and armament production —and that there was no kudos in working for the home market or for

[20] M. J. Levy, "Contrasting Factors in the Modernization of China and Japan," in S. Kuznets, W. E. Moore, and J. J. Spengler (eds.), *Economic Growth: Brazil, India, Japan,* Duke University Press, Durham, N.C., 1955, p. 516.

[21] A. F. Brimmer, "The Setting of Entrepreneurship in India," *Quarterly Journal of Economics,* November, 1955, pp. 553–576.

[22] W. N. Parker, "Entrepreneurial Opportunities and Response in the German Economy," *Explorations in Entrepreneurial History,* October, 1954, pp. 28–29.

consumption.[23] Ranis has noted the existence in Japan of a further type of entrepreneur who is community-minded, rather than self-centered, and who seeks to accumulate wealth and power for his neighbors along with himself.[24] On the showing of this sort of evidence, it can be said that the entrepreneur is not a fixed type, whether the "business-like man" emphasized by Phelps Brown,[25] the exploitive or hoarding personality manipulator distinguished by Erich Fromm (from the productive entrepreneur),[26] or the Schumpeterian innovator. National, cultural, and even personal characteristics will intervene to shape the person and through him the business enterprise.

In addition, it may be said that the task of the entrepreneur changes with development, along some such lines as those suggested by Cole. In underdeveloped countries the functions of a given person in entrepreneurial capacity include innovation, promotion, capital provision and risk bearing, management, assembling materials and labor.[27] The entrepreneur must be less stereotyped, and cannot afford to be as professionalized as in developed countries. He lacks the help of markets for components, materials, labor, capital—markets which have already standardized products and trained workers as well as organized them in readiness. He also lacks the communications network—specialized industrial newspapers and magazines, not to mention governmentally collected statistics, which apprise him of availabilities of inputs, outlets for outputs, and technological progress.

Whether the task is more difficult because it is more varied is impossible to say. The entrepreneur in the developed country in a large business frequently has only narrow limits within which to make decisions but their significance may be large. There can be little doubt, however, that traditional societies provide poor hunting ground for entrepreneurs with capacity for "doing new things with resources in different ways." The nature of the entrepreneurial problem, however, is likely to differ from country to country. In one country, imitators may be lacking. It is said that the textile industry is profitable in Brazil, but that there are ten companies there where there ought to be one hundred. Or imitators may be abundant, and innovators scarce, as is claimed to be the case in the textile industry of India. A number

[23] *Ibid.*

[24] G. Ranis, "The Community Centered Entrepreneur in Japanese Development," *Explorations in Entrepreneurial History*, December, 1955, p. 81.

[25] E. H. Phelps Brown, *Economic Growth and Human Welfare*, Ranjit, New Delhi, 1953.

[26] E. Fromm, *Man for Himself*, Rinehart & Co., Inc., New York, 1947, pp. 62ff. Fromm also regards the market orientation as "nonproductive."

[27] *Processes and Problems of Industrialization in Underdeveloped Countries*, United Nations, New York, 1955, pp. 30–31.

of countries—Colombia, Ethiopia, India, Mexico, Pakistan, Turkey—
have organized government-sponsored industrial banks with a view
to seeking out and financing entrepreneurial talent.[28]

Who are the new men needed to lead new combinations of resources and capital as countries develop? Where do they come from?
What is their motivation? These questions have no general answers
good for all economies, and take us in the main back to the cultural
and social differences discussed in the previous chapter. They may be
aristocrats, as in Japan, subordinate groups, as in the Protestant
Reformation and the Dissent from the Church of England, intellectuals
recruited into the civil service and politics in India—or Army officers.

LABOR SKILLS

Leadership requires followership, and entrepreneurs need a labor
force. It is not enough, however, to overcome malnutrition sufficiently
to enable people to work effectively, or to find these members of the
society, more in some cultures than in others, who are clever at
operating and keeping running complex machines.[29] Labor must develop an interest in economic goods, submit to factory discipline; and
there must be developed a series of noncommissioned and junior
officers to stand between the entrepreneur and the man at the
machine.

The backward-bending supply curve is a familiar phenomenon of
cultures to which the demonstration effect has not penetrated. In upper
Burma, rural Mexico of the 1920s, or parts of Africa today, the higher
the rate of pay, the less work was forthcoming, since a fixed set of
wants was more readily satisfied. The manipulative entrepreneur uses
trade goods to bring forth a supply of labor (or ivory or native
rubber). The anthropologist is distressed that the civilization is
spoiled. Living in the world with the communication of today, it may
be asked how long any culture can remain free of contact with the
materialistic civilizations of the West. The backward-bending supply
curve, however, is not a significant factor limiting labor inputs in
many parts of the world, although it, and the difficulty of the work,
may limit voluntary recruitment and increase turnover for work in
African mines. But even where there is no backward-bending supply
curve, material rewards may not be the prime engine of output by

[28] For a discussion of International Bank loans to a number of these, and the
lack of interest in Mexico, see *ibid.*, pp. 95ff.

[29] R. Linton, "Cultural and Personality Factors Affecting Economic Growth," in
B. F. Hoselitz (ed.), *The Progress of Underdeveloped Areas,* University of Chicago Press, Chicago, 1952, p. 77.

labor. Moore's study of Mexico[30] and Rottenberg's work in Puerto Rico[31] have demonstrated that social prestige of a job may be more important than the level of wages. The boredom and impersonality of factory or plantation work may be a stumbling block to the effective utilization of labor. Most cultures are used to hard physical work, but often, in subsistence farming, fishing, or similar tasks, it is varied and interesting, and may give opportunity for social intercourse. A few devices have been developed to modify the Western factory system, where the monotony of work may be alleviated by the development of a team spirit. One is the compradore system, under which labor is recruited in small groups, often from the same village, responsible to a compradore or recruiting agent.

In a number of countries, of which perhaps Cuba is the outstanding example, labor legislation has been adopted to ensure high standards of pay, and many social benefits such as limited hours, security of job tenure, etc. The International Labor Office has been interested in promoting the adoption of standards in this field. Unfortunately, however, labor legislation, like the increase in consumption represented by the demonstration effect, should follow, not precede, the increase in productivity. The International Bank study of Cuba is full of examples of harm done through increasing labor costs by premature raising of labor standards.[32] In Chapter 13, however, we take note of the fact that some raising of labor standards may be necessary to win a commitment of the labor force to the discipline of factory technology.

But beyond a minimum stage of development, the major requirement is for foremen, technicians, supervisors, maintenance and production mechanics, and engineers.[33] The capacity to handle modern technology in the United States does not reside in a small group of business and engineering school graduates, but is diffused throughout the culture. The great majority of employees are interested in productivity, and their early training, formal and informal, is machine, production, and team directed. In underdeveloped countries, therefore, it is not enough to cultivate a handful of entrepreneurs and business executives. Partly the requirement is for vocational education which can succeed only against a background of literacy and elementary schooling; partly it is for in-plant training. In part, however, it requires wide diffusion of the values of industrial society.

[30] W. E. Moore, *Industrialization and Labor*, Cornell University Press, Ithaca, N.Y., 1951.
[31] S. Rottenberg, "Income and Leisure in an Underdeveloped Economy," *Journal of Political Economy*, April, 1952, pp. 95–101.
[32] *A Development Program for Cuba*, International Bank for Reconstruction and Development, Baltimore, 1951, esp. pp. 357ff.
[33] United Nations, *op. cit.*, pp. 41ff.

A special word should be added on the particular problem of governmental administration. This, though not usually thought of as such, is a problem in technological change, since with economic development the nature of the governmental problem and the types of administrative capacity required change. India, and to a much lesser extent Pakistan, found themselves on independence with substantial assets in the form of well-trained and dedicated civil services, developed under British rule. In many countries which have won their independence, the most serious bottleneck is the shortage of capable administrators, competent to handle complex affairs, and instilled with the national interest to the point of ignoring opportunities for personal gain.

DIFFUSION OF TECHNOLOGY

The international spread of technology is not new. British wool was originally sold abroad. A woolen industry was established in the sixteenth century on the basis of skills acquired from immigrants from Flanders. The British Industrial Revolution spread over the Continent originally through workers and master craftsmen, later through British companies organized to build railroads and develop mines, and often to operate them.[34] The United States, evidently, acquired its productive techniques from Europe, but long after this country was a going concern there was a steady infiltration of new industries brought by the technically skilled who, frequently until the 1830s, when prohibitions against export of machinery were repealed, were obliged to smuggle out examples of the machines used in Britain.

The record of United States experience has been briefly summarized by Handlin, who notes that the imported skill was initially highly valued, but later replaced by domestic talent partly because of cost, sometimes because of further innovation, and frequently because of its technological conservatism which resisted further evolutionary change.[35] The speed with which this displacement took place in the United States was of course a function of the country's receptivity to the ideas brought by the technician immigrants and the country's capacity for innovation and adaptive imitation. In other situations the transition to innovation might take place more slowly.

Underlying the receptivity of a country to the diffusion of new technology is the rationality of the culture, the level of literacy and education, the existence of channels of communication and techniques

[34] See, e.g., W. O. Henderson, *Britain and Industrial Europe, 1750–1870,* University Press of Liverpool, Liverpool, 1954.
[35] See O. Handlin, "International Migration and the Acquisition of New Skills," *The Progress of Underdeveloped Areas,* pp. 54–59.

of demonstration. If illiteracy is prevalent, there may be a long way to go, especially in certain cases, as Simey points out, because it is not worthwhile to provide education for people who are hungry.[36] Basic to speed of learning is the desire to learn.

A special problem exists in agriculture because of the lack of communication in most countries, especially when compared with urban life. Peasants and farmers are more tradition-minded, especially in the Middle East, Africa, and Asia, which means more resistant to change; more illiterate; and more difficult to reach by communication. On the first two scores, it is believed that demonstration techniques hold more promise than the written or spoken word. Because of the last, experience in technical cooperation suggests the wisdom, in countries like Brazil, of combining the usual type of technical assistance in health, education, and agriculture with credit in a single package.[37]

Developed countries have on the whole institutionalized research to the point where changes in techniques are produced as acts of skill rather than inventive acts of insight. The resulting improvement in technology is probably taking place faster than imitation in underdeveloped areas, and the technological gap is widening, not narrowing.

SUMMARY

Technological change is a prime mover in the course of economic development. Historically, invention and innovation have led the process of growth in advanced countries. Imitation by less advanced countries affords them a short cut to higher levels of living.

Technological change consists in devising new goods and new ways of producing existing goods and services. The introduction of new goods in developed countries creates a problem in lagging countries to the extent that demand grows faster than capacity to satisfy wants.

The entrepreneur has been the disseminator of technological change. New men have come forward, interested in new goods and prepared to attempt new ways of doing things. In historical development, the process of technological advance has taken place without conscious direction as entrepreneurs found it profitable to devise new techniques and to borrow those developed abroad. Today there is awareness of the importance of technology and conscious attempts are being made by governments to close the technological gap between countries. Systematized invention in developed countries, however, may maintain it.

[36] Simey, *op. cit.*, p. 92.
[37] A. T. Mosher, "The Agricultural Program of ACAR in Brazil," pamphlet in series on *Technical Cooperation in Latin America*, National Planning Association, Washington, 1955.

THE SIZE OF THE MARKET

The engine of economic development before the days of governmental planning was the market. Some economic historians describe the process of growth as one of increasing the size of the market. Adam Smith believed that the core of increased productivity was specialization, which in turn was limited by the size of the market. In primitive stages of development, households were largely self-sufficient and did little trading in the village. Thereafter village trade picked up, possibly with markets on special days in special places, but with most produce local, and little but salt, kerosene, matches, or iron pots, machetes, and axes bought from outside.[1] At a further stage of development, the village was joined to the metropolitan system. The market moved in from village square to stores, which were open regularly. Barter and exchange of gifts gave way to use of money. And increased specialization in production made possible more output and required exchange. At a final stage, goods which are valuable and transportable in some appropriate combination, in which a low mark on one score is compensated by a high grade on the other, are traded all over the world. But there are still countries where rural life is self-sufficient. The higher the stage of development, the higher the proportion of consumption represented by purchases—with appropriate qualification for owner-occupied houses and a few hobbies such as gardening. Wisconsin farmers can no longer afford to eat butter produced in their dairies, buying instead margarine made from cottonseed oil originating

[1] Under conditions of highly skewed income distribution, trade may be needed to provide items of consumption for the upper-income group. Such was the case in pre-Communist China, for example, where trading activity took place within a complex, inefficient, and highly fragmented market system characterized by a marked proliferation of middle men.

more than 500 miles away; and Italian peasants buy and sell olive oil, exchanging their high-quality product for the inexpensive variety they consume.

With widening of the market, and in part a result of it, comes the spread of the money habit. The more developed a country, the larger the proportion of its income earned in money form, which is the simple obverse of the statement made in the previous paragraph. And the more it needs monetary institutions. The major factor initially separating markets is the cost of overcoming distance between them. Investment and technological change in transport and communication reduce this cost and are a prime cause of linking and enlarging markets. Finally, fusion of markets has significant repercussions on entrepreneurs and labor. It is perhaps not too much to say that commercial revolution is a vital and almost a necessary step on the way to industrial revolution as it sets the preconditions for rapid economic growth.

ECONOMIES OF SCALE[2]

Economic theorists debate at length questions of economies of scale. Much in this debate need not concern us, since under the conditions of markets in underdeveloped countries the existence and importance of economies are hard to doubt. But it is appropriate to recapitulate the categories of economies and diseconomies of scale.

The first distinction is between external and internal economies; the second, between pecuniary and technological. Internal economies are those within the firm; external economies are external to the firm but available to all firms in the industry. Pecuniary economies arise from a change in the price of a factor or intermediate good, or a cost of marketing. Technological economies are realized when a higher scale of output permits a lower input per unit of output to be realized in physical terms.

Much of the emphasis in economic development is on external economies, on the ground that internal economies cannot exist under competitive conditions. Moreover, there is the tendency of some theorists to go further and to dismiss external technological economies as bucolic in character—the classic example is beekeeping and the growing of fruit, where the two industries provide external economies for each other—of little importance under modern conditions. Finally, it is suggested that external pecuniary economies are typically the result of internal economies in another industry where the increased efficiency is passed along in the form of lower prices for intermediate

[2] This discussion relies heavily on a manuscript of R. L. Bishop.

goods. If this be so, and if internal economies due to monopoly are ruled out, economies of scale would seem to be pretty well disposed of.

But this is inappropriate in economic development. Internal economies of scale are important in this area, since markets are frequently monopolistic rather than purely competitive. Even if it is necessary to dismiss external technological economies as idyllic, and internal pecuniary economies which occur when a firm can buy factor and material inputs more cheaply as its scale of output increases, as rare, internal technological and external pecuniary economies have real importance. So does the irreversible downward shift of supply curves, which theoretically differ from reversible economies of scale but which resemble them in the real world. Costs and prices decline as the scale of output increases with development. The monopolistic character of the market in underdeveloped countries, which makes possible internal economies of scale, is the result of difficulties of new entry into profitable industry and limitations on the expansion of production due to high costs of transport, ignorance of market opportunities, lack of capital, unavailability of inputs, etc.

Internal technological economies are those resulting from the division of labor, the use of specialized machinery and other capital equipment with considerable capacity, the opportunity for using the insurance principle in massing inventories, and certain once-for-all contributions, like new design. The division of labor was extolled by Adam Smith in his classic example of how ten men can make more than ten times as many pins as one man. The savings inherent in the division of labor derive from the increased physical efficiency in work that comes with repetition; increased knowledge of the job, and avoidance of waste of time and motion in moving from one task to another, as required of the generalist. If enough can be sold to keep men and machines fully employed at the appropriate scale determined by the lowest common multiple of their separate individual efficiency rates, considerable gains in efficiency and lower costs can be achieved.

Offsetting technological economies, in some part, are technological diseconomies. These are largely a function of the increased difficulty of organizing, administering, and supervising work as its scale increases. One man can keep himself busy and active. With division of labor, administrative personnel is needed to keep the work flowing smoothly, and to see that the workers stay up with their tasks.

Division of labor can take place within and between firms. Within the firm, various sets of individuals or shops may concentrate on various stages of production and achieve efficiency in the production of components. If, however, the organizational problem leads to diseconomy, there is the possibility of vertical disintegration and exchange of components through the market mechanism. Buying and selling of standardized components at prices determined by the market may be easier to organize than the administration of the necessary men in one unit to produce them locally.

One important external pecuniary economy in underdeveloped countries arises from the improved organization of the market itself. When markets are fragmented and small, it is necessary to incur marketing costs to move production. Marketing costs can be regarded either as an input or as the reduction of an output, i.e., a subtraction from price. As marketing facilities grow, some markets become organized on a formal basis with a building where buyers and sellers gather, and with rules for trading. In other goods and services firms in different industries selling to similar customers gather to assist the buyer, whether in insurance, entertainment, garments, cloth, securities, or diamonds, to indicate some of the market areas in New York City. The external economy is realized through reducing marketing costs or, what is the same thing, an increased selling price realized by the producer. The organization of formal and informal markets in cities —for factors and intermediate goods as well as final product—plays an important role in the achievement of scale. In the opinion of some economists, however, reduction in cost to the consumer is not a true economy of scale but an irreversible downward shift of the supply curve arising from the breaking down of monopoly with new entry. It has the same effect.

GROWTH OF MARKETS

Markets may grow through increases in real income of the people of an area which enable them to buy more. Where markets are now world-wide, this and taste changes are the only means of expanding demand. But, short of those commodities where the market is already the world, and historically of greatest importance, markets grow because of improvements in transport and communication. The market is originally local and small. Demand is restricted by the cost of getting goods out of the village and ignorance of whether they can be sold outside; supply is limited by the cost of getting goods into the village, and ignorance of how much they can be bought for outside. In these circumstances, markets grow through increases in transport and communication. The expansion becomes cumulative. Increased outlets for a commodity give rise to increased real income which in turn raises the demand for other products. As new supplies of these come on the market, in turn, incomes grow further. The linkage of markets by an improvement in transportation, or by the improvement in a product which makes it lighter and more readily transported, becomes part of a developmental process.

In these circumstances, it is not surprising that economic development is correlated positively with transport facilities. Figures 6.1 and

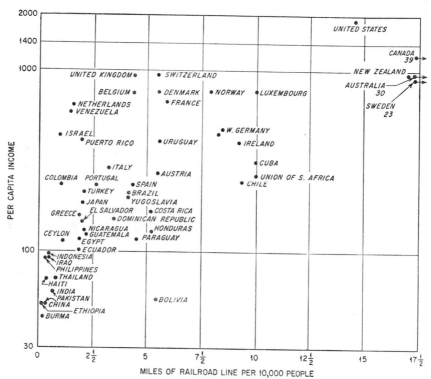

Figure 6.1. Density of railroad lines compared with income per capita, about 1953. SOURCES: Railroad density, i.e., miles of railroad per 10,000 people, and length of railroad lines, *The Statesman's Yearbook, 1956,* Macmillan & Co., Ltd., London, 1956, pp. 511–521; population, *Demographic Yearbook, 1954,* United Nations, New York, 1954, pp. 116–127; income per capita, Table 1.1, Income per Capita in U. S. Dollars.

6.2 relating railroad and highway construction per capita to income per capita give only a rough approximation of this, since qualification is needed for the density of population by area, responsible for the outstanding results in the case of Australia and Canada, and for other means of transport such as canal boat, seagoing vessel, etc.

It is unnecessary to dwell upon the means by which changes in transport link markets and produce their expansion. These changes may be simple extensions or transport innovation. A striking example of extension is the recent spur given to economic development in Turkey by road-building. In 1947 the Truman Doctrine of military support for Greece and Turkey included in Turkey a major program of building military roads to render troops mobile. To these trunk lines

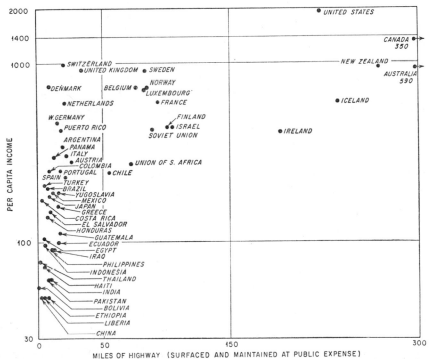

Figure 6.2. Density of highways compared with income per capita, about 1953. SOURCES: Highway density, i.e., miles of roads surfaced and maintained at public expense per 10,000 people, and length of highways, *Statesman's Yearbook, 1956,* Macmillan & Co., Ltd., London, 1956, pp. 511–521; population, *Demographic Yearbook, 1954,* United Nations, New York, 1954, pp. 116–127; income per capita, Table 1.1, Income per Capita in U. S. Dollars.

were joined feeders, a good many built under Point Four assistance. The results were startling, in social terms[3] and in the linkage of markets for wheat produced in the interior and manufactures and imports available in the towns.

Development literature is full of such examples of the impact of

[3] See D. Lerner, "The Grocer and the Chief," *Harper's Magazine,* September, 1955, pp. 47–56.

roads. In some cases the emphasis is on the social changes; in others, on the possibilities provided for expansion of production, and economies of scale in the division of labor, through access to a new market. The significant handicap in southern Italy has been lack of communication. *Christ Stopped at Eboli*[4] on His way south from Rome because the road network petered out. In Brazil the subsistence farmer has great difficulty in bringing his coffee to market, and the technical assistance mission, visiting the farmer, has to use jeep, boat, mule, and shank's mare.[5] In Oscar Lewis's account of *Life in a Mexican Village* frequent reference is made to the changes introduced when the road was built.[6]

In the history of developed countries, great impact has been made by technological change in transport, particularly innovations of railroad, ironclad vessel, automobile and truck, and most recently the airplane, as well as cost-reducing investments like the Suez and Panama Canals and the Simplon Tunnel. The rise of the world economy is generally dated from 1870 after transcontinental railroad construction in the United States and similar construction in other areas combined with the general transoceanic haulage by ironclad steam vessel to bring the produce of the Western Hemisphere, India, and Africa to European ports on a substantial scale.

Too little attention is generally paid in these accounts to the spread of communication needed to link markets. Face-to-face trading in which the producer or his agent must deal directly with the buyer or his agent imposes a considerable limitation on the extent of the market. The peddler is an inefficient marketer compared with the traveling salesman who follows up leads derived from direct mail advertising, telephone canvas, or records of previous sales. Provision must be made especially for communication of price information so that the village trader can tell whether and when he chooses to take his plums to which city. In modern markets there has grown up a paraphernalia of market quotations in the general and specialized press, telephonic and telegraph communication, including ticker tapes, avalanches of discussion by mail of specifications, price, and delivery dates. Along with transport, or rather some distance in advance of capacity to transport, there must be a network of communication which is vital to market operation.

[4] This is the title of the book by Carlo Levi (Farrar, Straus & Company, New York, 1947) which gives a vivid account of life in southern Italy in the 1930s.

[5] See A. T. Mosher, "The Agricultural Program of ACAR in Brazil," pamphlet in series on *Technical Cooperation in Latin America*, National Planning Association, Washington, 1955.

[6] University of Illinois Press, Urbana, Ill., 1951, pp. xv, 36, 165, etc.

A quantitative impression of the growth in numbers of people engaged in the distribution of goods, which is positively correlated with economic growth generally, is given in the next chapter, and particularly in Figures 7.4 and 7.6. That chapter also suggests some reasons why the figures of occupational distribution should be treated skeptically in very underdeveloped countries. Nonetheless, there can be no doubt that, as development proceeds, it takes more and more people to distribute goods, and less and less, proportionately, to make them. Production may be less significant than marketing, and the services of transport and communication which spring up around it.[7]

THE CHANGE IN CHARACTER OF MARKETS

With the growth in numbers of people in a market comes an inevitable change in its character. The major change is in the elasticities of demand and supply. It is a familiar observation in economics that, whereas the demand of an individual for a given commodity may be low, or the supply of a given producer, when linkage of markets takes place under competitive conditions, the elasticities of demand and supply facing the individual seller or buyer increase manyfold, and under pure competition, become infinite. The buyer in the village learns about alternative sources of supply. The seller is conscious of alternative outlets. For labor there are alternative occupations into which it becomes possible to move. The landowner cannot move his land but can contemplate its use in other than the traditional ways.

This increase in elasticity of demand and supply is vital to the effective working of the price system, discussed in Chapter 8 below. Here it may be said, however, that a number of economists consider that a primary distinction between developed and underdeveloped economies lies in the efficacy of their price systems. In underdeveloped economies, it is sometimes said, the price system is ineffective. An increase in the demand for a given product elicits no response because supply is inelastic, frequently at zero output. A decrease in price, moreover, produces no increased consumption because the limited number of buyers does not extend consumption at lower prices and no

[7] T. A. F. Noble, in "Economic Progress in Underdeveloped Areas," *Scottish Journal of Political Economy*, June, 1956, pp. 97–114, gives the central places in development to (1) the adaptation of economic and social institutions to give the operations of economic incentives full play; (2) capital formation; and (3) the widening market "with the improvement in economic organization and the extended division of labor it involves." In his view, however, the "widening of the market begins under the influence of new forms of demand" (p. 100).

more buyers are added to their number. All changes are structural; the marginal analysis associated with the price system is incapable of producing changes on the needed scale. In this circumstance, the nature of the economic analysis applicable to underdeveloped countries differs sharply from that of developed.[8]

There may be differences in elasticities of demand and supply between developed and underdeveloped countries which are not solely a function of the size of markets as determined by transport and communication networks. Lack of interest in increased material well-being, so that consumption is unchanged at all levels of income, is one such feature which may be found in some underdeveloped countries. The existence of economies of scale external to the firm which cannot be turned into profit opportunities and therefore do not lead to private investment undertakings, may be another. Still other factors play an important part, such as lack of capital, information, and skill which inhibits entry into new industries and reduces elasticity of supply, and the low level of income which inhibits demand. But a significant part of the difference in the character of developed and underdeveloped markets lies in the number of buyers and sellers, which again is frequently a function of their physical extent in space. The linking of local into regional and regional into national and world markets through the spread of transport and communications is a step in the direction of a more effective price system.

THE GROWTH IN MARKETS AND NATIONAL INCOME PER CAPITA

It should not be forgotten that growth of markets and the increased division of labor made possible thereby also directly increase income. Kuznets has pointed out that income in currently developed countries was higher prior to the Industrial Revolution than levels existing today in the underdeveloped parts of the world.[9] Using Colin Clark's crude figures of International Units (dollars of United States purchasing power during 1925–1934) per occupied worker (not per capita), he notes that in Britain the level was more than 300 in 1800 and even in 1688, as compared with 230 to 250 for British India in the 1930s and

[8] If lower price does not bring increased volume, it is sensible for producers and distributors to maintain the highest possible markup. See J. J. Spengler, "IBRD Mission Economic Growth Theory," *American Economic Review, Papers and Proceedings,* May, 1954, p. 590.

[9] S. Kuznets, "Toward a Theory of Economic Growth," in R. Lekachman (ed.), *National Policy for Economic Welfare at Home and Abroad,* Doubleday & Company, Inc., New York, 1955, p. 27.

1940s. Other countries which achieved levels of more than 300 I.U. prior to intensive industrialization were the United States in 1830, France in the 1840s, Belgium in 1854, Germany in 1854, Sweden in 1860. By contrast, Brazil was scored at 153 in 1928 and rose rapidly to 297 only by 1946.[10]

Kuznets forbears to attribute these relatively high levels of income to any particular cause. He is not even certain that they came from increases in output per worker, although this is regarded as probable. But, while the data which prove the point conclusively have not been gathered, it is a foregone conclusion that the answer was that to which Adam Smith attached so much importance—the division of labor. British agriculture benefited from technological improvement as well, but in part this depended again on the merging of markets, the concentration on cash crops instead of general-purpose subsistence or mixed farming, and production on a basis involving scale.

MARKETS AND MONEY

Specialization and exchange require the parallel growth of the money mechanism. With the commercial revolution inevitably come the development of paper money and checking instead of specie and coin, the evolution of credit instruments to finance roundabout production and the holding of stocks, and finally techniques for regulating the amount of money in the system. As the subsistence economy shrinks and the proportion of total income exchanged against money enlarges, a concomitant expansion in the money supply must take place. This expansion is indicated in the correlation between income per capita and money supply per capita given in Figure 6.3. This figure, it should be noted, plots money supply as a percentage of national income against national income per capita in dollars (in 1952, not 1953, as usual, because the underlying data relate to the earlier year). If the percentage were to remain constant, the money supply would grow with income. The fact that the percentage rises substantially with growth, however, underlines the faster growth of the money supply than of income.

A sharp discussion has centered on the question of whether management of the money supply should take into account the requirements of economic growth.[11] Whittlesey suggests that it should;

[10] *Ibid.*
[11] C. R. Whittlesey, "Relation of Money to Economic Growth," *American Economic Review, Papers and Proceedings,* May, 1956, pp. 188–201, with discussion by E. S. Shaw, P. W. McCracken, H. S. Ellis, and I. O. Scott.

others, especially Ellis, argue that it should not. For the most part, the argument turns on whether monetary expansion and some measure of price inflation are stimulating to economic growth—a question we have reserved until Chapter 11. But there can be no doubt that the

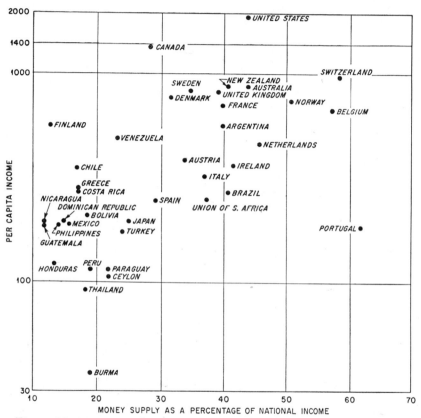

Figure 6.3. Money supply as a percentage of national income compared with income per capita, 1952. sources: *International Financial Statistics,,* International Monetary Fund, July, 1953, p. vii; income per capita in 1952, computed by dividing money supply per capita in dollars in the original source by money supply as a per cent of national income.

monetary mechanism must be developed in parallel with linkage of markets and expanded use of money. At an early stage moneylenders become commercial banks. Later a central bank is needed and central bank technique. And the money supply must grow in some relation to the growth of markets. In the ordinary case, in the closed economy, this requirement will not be very different from the requirement of stability measured in terms of prices and/or employment. In an open economy, however, there may be failure of articulation between the monetary policy which would maintain the foreign-exchange value of the currency, and the appropriate rate of monetary expansion, having in mind the rate of economic growth. In a number of such instances, however, the conflict between external and internal stability, including within the latter the requirements of growth, goes much deeper than any conflict between growth alone and external or internal requirements.[12]

Considerable debate has occurred historically over the appropriate rate of monetary expansion in the course of development. In addition to the over-all rate of inflation or deflation, the sectoral distribution of income has been at issue. In caricature, Wall Street has been for deflation; mortgaged farmers and producers of commodities, for inflation, or for a more rapid rate of monetary expansion.

IMPACT OF THE MARKET ON ENTREPRENEURS, LABOR, CAPITAL FORMATION

In some societies, trade is regarded as contributing to lower status and is handed over to foreign groups. Where this is not the case, however, the growth of markets performs an important role in preparing members of the society for economic development. Part of this preparation consists in training potential entrepreneurs. Traders develop capacity to maximize, sufficient literacy to calculate. More than this, however, the expansion of trading is preparatory for the degree of rationality, universalism, and functional specificity required of a developed economy.

In underdeveloped economies, trade is frequently partly a test of skill and partly an experience in social intercourse. The initial asking price is not "the price" but a stylized opening in an act or game. The rules of the game are few and far between, but the game is played partly for its own sake, as well as to be won, which explains the disappointment of some sellers when a Western tourist buys an article at the asking price. *Caveat emptor* applies—let the buyer beware. If he is cheated, it is his own fault. The seller expects no retribution, no repeat sales, has no interest in building a reputation, or good will.

It is a condition of markets which spread beyond face-to-face contacts, however, that these rules of the game be modified. Standardiza-

[12] See H. C. Wallich, *Monetary Problems of an Export Economy*, Harvard University Press, Cambridge, Mass., 1950.

tion of product and grading make possible the sale of goods halfway around the world, without the danger that the seller will misrepresent. In some commodities like wool and furs, it is impossible to grade and standardize, so world markets are operated by auction with buyers present. But to sell its wheat without discount, Turkey finds itself obliged to standardize and grade, to clean it of stones and mice. Before Denmark could sell butter on a large scale to Britain, the flavorful but frequently surprising "peasant butter" had to be brought to the standard consistency of "manor butter." And so on with native and estate rubber, and a host of other products. At a later stage entrepreneurial talent is expended in differentiating products, to increase the demand for the product of the firm. In an early stage the requirement of market standards, spread by wholesalers and jobbers back to producers, inculcates some of the training for mass production needed as a precondition of the industrial revolution.

Not only does the growth of markets train the entrepreneur: it eases his tasks. As the labor market grows, he can call upon it rather than beat the bushes for his workers. The same for capital, and for intermediate goods. His need to hold large inventories of materials is reduced if these can be readily acquired in organized markets. His incentive to standardize, moreover, is that he can reduce his marketing problem, the task of showing the ultimate consumer exactly what his wares are. Production to the specifications of the market simplifies his task in another of its myriad facets.

The commercial revolution does more. It starts the accumulation of capital. Inventories and ships are two early objects of and outlets for capital accumulation. The productivity of capital becomes evident, the habit of saving spreads, and accumulations of capital capable of being converted to industrial use come gradually into existence.

The impact of commerce extends beyond the entrepreneur. Markets are located in cities, which are breeders of a different attitude toward tradition and material rewards. Production for the market requires division and organization of labor, whether in the small shop or on the plantation, which begin the inculcation of the submission of the individual to the spirit of the enterprise necessary for factory production. As was mentioned in the previous chapter, the introduction of money leads to the breakdown of traditional ways of life as wealth can be accumulated in other ways than land; as wealth acquires mobility payments in kind become converted into money payments, etc.

On this showing there is a strong argument to be made for the proposition that economic development through industrialization should be preceded by commercialization, and the industrial by the commercial revolution. To short-cut the evolutionary process and attempt forthwith to turn a subsistence into an industrial economy finds the society badly equipped. It may well be possible to abbreviate greatly the commercial period in the West, which lasted perhaps 300 or 400 years, but whether the process can be eliminated altogether is open to question. Especially is this the case in those countries which have relied on foreign traders to perform the necessary commerce over long periods of time: the Chinese merchant of the Philippines, Malaya, and Indonesia; the Armenian, Jew, and Greek in Turkey. A powerful case can be made that the rapid rate of growth in Turkey in recent years depended not only on the construction of trunk military and farm-to-market roads, but on the fact that Turkish citizens were forced, after the great transfers of population in 1921, to perform trading functions, and so were prepared for their later increased responsibilities.

The Japanese example may be put in the balance on the other side. Industrialization moved very rapidly and capacity at marketing increased *pari passu* rather than in advance. Government preserved order, provided the necessary expansion of money, but marketing grew up along with capacity at administering production, without the necessity for prior conditioning. This is a remarkable case. In my judgment, however, it provides the exception rather than the pattern. Attention to commerce and marketing is an important element in a design for development.

BLOCKS TO DEVELOPMENT IN MARKET ECONOMIES

It must not be thought that the linkage of markets which ultimately connects the interior village with the world economy is a cumulative process, which, well started, leads inevitably to industrialization. Many economies, for reasons not always clear, make an effective start along the commercial revolution and reach a stage at which further progress of a spontaneous character seems impossible. At least two elements in such situations can be observed: undue concern with the profit rate, and the widespread adoption of the speculative psychology.

A number of countries in Europe have remained blocked essentially at a mercantilist stage of development. Markets have developed and are traded in. But marketers become bemused by their rate of profit, per unit sold, rather than by the total profit per capital invested or some other rational criterion. High profits per unit tend to keep turnover small and are maintained only by limiting entry. Where it is impossible to limit entry, the combination of free entry and price fixing leads to overcapacity and underutilization, the affliction which besets retail trade particularly in Belgium and France.

What seems to be missing from this scene is the entrepreneur's interest in innovation for the sake of increasing his profits. The *petit bourgeoisie* runs its tiny café or *épicerie* (small corner grocery store) much the same way today as it did in 1870. As a member of the *bourgeoisie,* the owner has status. He is content. He grumbles that his level of living is no higher, and in France he may be beguiled by the Poujade movement into taking political action. But these countries have failed to pass the stage of mercantilism largely because the pattern of trade has become frozen. This suggests that, while commercial revolution may be a necessary prelude to industrial development, it may not be sufficient.

A second form of marketing pathology is speculative fever. In Western Europe and the United States this disability has not been unknown, but its incidence has been sharp and short. The South Sea Bubble, Crédit Mobilier, and the Ponzi scheme, are part of the economic history of the West, but they do not dominate it.

In the Middle East and in many parts of Latin America, however, social status is accorded to wealth, but wealth appears to be the result of luck rather than work. A corner on the Alexandria cotton market, a squeeze in wheat, or a relatively small movement in the price of coffee, rubber, sugar, or tin, can produce sizable fortunes from trading on organized commodity markets. In Western Europe and the United States, such speculation has by no means been unknown, but a considerable part of speculative interest has attached to corporation securities, and the speculative position of the owner of a block of shares can be improved by effective production on the part of the corporation, and effective innovation.

Stabilizing speculation performs a useful economic function in providing additional demand when supplies are heavy, and additional supply when this is needed. Speculation, however, may be destabilizing, exaggerating the swing of prices, and interfering with orderly production and distribution. More significant, perhaps, for economic development in the long run, it creates a speculative psychology which tends to denigrate success through work and thrift, and to elevate the role of luck. Western development has never been free of predation, but it has been based on work. Where fortunes can be made far more readily, and with less effort, through speculative excesses, interest in horse races, football pools, and the national lottery increases and the incentive to continuous application diminishes. The authors of the International Bank study on Cuba refer to speculative interest in sugar in that country as economic diabetes.

DISTRIBUTION AND DEVELOPMENT

The emphasis on markets in spontaneous or private enterprise development must not lead anyone to believe that no comparable set of problems exists in, say, the Soviet Union. There the allocation of resources to distribution is clear: apart from private marketing arrangements, there must be transport, workers, and administrators, plus the state stores, whose task it is to distribute goods. In spontaneous development, growth of size of market through linkages, with improved transport and communication, has been an engine assisting in the process of development. One is obliged to say an engine, rather than the engine, since there are cases on record of development and no substantial linkage of markets (Japan) and commercial revolutions which did not roll forward into industrial development.

But whether markets pull development or lag behind it, it is evident that much planning in the area of economic development today neglects distribution. The lessons concerning transport and communication have been learned in the ordinary planning effort, as discussed below in Chapter 9. But marketing means more than this. Storage facilities in particular tend to be neglected, and encouragement to middlemen, wholesalers, jobbers, who are too often regarded as parasites because of the distasteful record of the market manipulator. Product standardization may also be an outlet for energy and resources with a high payout in terms of permitting more effective scales of production and reducing costs of distribution.

Distribution is inescapable. The Western economist has always been fascinated with how swiftly, efficiently, and with how little direction free markets can perform this function. Whether the linkage of local into larger markets be encouraged for its transforming function, or the movement of goods and services into consumption and investment be tackled directly according to plan, distribution takes resources. It cannot be overlooked.

SUMMARY

Efficiency of production is partly a function of its scale, which in turn is limited by the size of the market. The larger the scale, the cheaper the cost of the product when there exist economies external to the firm. In economic development, moreover, one expects to meet opportunities for internal economies of scale blocked by the existence of monopolies where entry is limited by lack of knowledge, capital, skill, etc.

The growth process can be led by a widening of the market, which in turn may result from increased efficiency in transport or communications. Cheapening transport fuses markets, bringing additional buyers and sellers into contact one with another, increasing elasticities of demand and supply. Or markets can grow through an increase in efficiency and income in any commodity, which increases the effective demand for other products and spreads in cumulative fashion. Even where the growth process is led by efficiency in production, however, the requirements of distribution are inescapable.

CHAPTER 7 *Transformation*

THE SCOPE OF THE TERM

In writing of the economic growth of Europe in the interwar period, I. Svennilson uses the term *transformation* in a broad sense to include:[1]

1. Capital deepening
2. Cost-reducing innovation
3. Demand-increasing innovation
4. Changes in exports and imports in relation to domestic industry
5. Redistribution of manpower among industries

Here the term is used in a narrower meaning, limited to the last in this list, but including other inputs along with manpower and without excluding changes in the next to last. Unlike resources, capital, people, technology, and scale, which are ingredients of increased income per capita, transformation in the sense used here does not make the economy grow; but there must be transformation or growth will halt. Anything that grows changes; and anything that has lost its capacity to change has stopped growing.

It is not very polite to borrow a man's word and alter its meaning. But transformation is a useful term, and it would be well to have its content streamlined.

Transformation can occur only in the disaggregated model. In a one-commodity, two-factor world, economic growth can occur through capital deepening, and innovation (of the cost-reducing type only, to be sure). But transformation is required because of the physiological and psychological limits on increased consumption in any one good. The one-commodity, two-factor world does not take one very far because it requires for development a unit income-elasticity of de-

[1] T. Svennilson, *Growth and Stagnation in the European Economy,* United Nations, Economic Commission for Europe, Geneva, 1954, p. 7.

mand for the one commodity: demand for the product increases with capacity to turn it out. If there is more than one good, it would be arbitrary to assume that income-elasticity for each was unitary. Even in the one-good model, one is tempted to admit diminishing returns in consumption, which requires the introduction of a second good— savings, or leisure. Moreover, enough is known about the behavior of demand to enable one to make some fairly realistic assumptions. Transformation occurs because, with increased output and income, the demand for some products increases less than proportionately, and the demand for others, including in this category leisure and savings, more than proportionately. While the demand for all goods and services excluding savings and leisure can be less than unity, it cannot if these are included.

ENGEL'S LAW

It is well known that the Prussian statistician Engel discovered the uniformity that, with the growth of income above a certain minimum, consumption of food decreases as a percentage of income, even though the absolute amount of food consumption increases. A considerable difference is made, to be sure, whether one counts food as it leaves the farm in its rudimentary state, or food served on the table at home or in a restaurant. Engel's law applies to both, but to basic food more than to food plus services embodied in it in the finished state. Moreover, the demand for simple food energy in calories responds more quickly to the law than protein or protective foods.

Unfortunately the data on income-elasticities of demand for various types of food are not sufficiently extensive to enable us to furnish measurements of income-elasticity for food for countries at various stages of growth. It is believed that the income-elasticity of demand for food is close to unity in a number of densely populated and underdeveloped countries: this would mean that most or all of an increase in income would be spent for increased consumption of food. And it is known that in the United States only a small proportion of an increase in income is spent in ways which increase the sales of farmers.[2] But adequate comparative studies are lacking. The best that can be done is to use budget studies for given countries to illustrate how demand alters with rising income within a given culture. Figure 7.1 furnishes a regression of expenditure on food on income per capita derived by Colin Clark from limited data for a few countries. The

[2] For particular (inferior) goods, income-elasticity can of course be negative. But no class of consumption such as food is inferior as a whole.

income figures are in International Units (dollars of 1925–1934 purchasing power) rather than postwar dollars.

Generalizing from Engel's law, Bruton suggests that consumption, as well as production in many instances, follows a Gompertz curve of growth. The physical demand for any product will have an upper limit, so that no matter what happens to per capita income, the rate of growth of demand for a given product will not expand faster than the rate of population increase when this limit has been reached.[3]

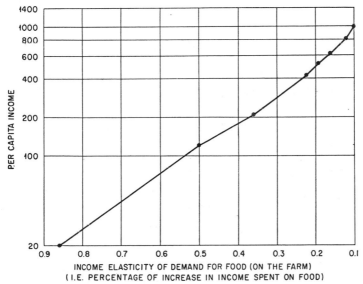

Figure 7.1. Income-elasticity of demand for food compared with income per capita (in 1925–1934 dollars—International Units). SOURCE: Colin Clark, "World Supply and Requirements of Farm Products," *Journal of the Royal Statistical Society* (series A), 1954, part 3, p. 278.

Moreover, the limit is approached asymptotically, so that the demand pattern for any new good which wins public acceptance is likely to show a slow rate of increase as this acceptance is being won, a high income-elasticity in the middle stages, and thereafter a decline in income-elasticity as the physical limit of consumption is approached.

This law of consumption has great importance for economic growth. To illustrate with a closed economy, if transformation is impossible, economic growth will fail at some stage because of lack of demand. Without new goods, and without new entrepreneurs to arrange the

[3] H. J. Bruton, "A Survey of Recent Contributions to the Theory of Economic Growth," Massachusetts Institute of Technology, Center for International Studies, Cambridge, Mass., April, 1956.

transfer of capital and labor into their production, economic development must slow down with the decline of demand for old products.

PRIMARY, SECONDARY, AND TERTIARY PRODUCTION

An early contributor to the modern discussion of economic development was A. G. B. Fisher, who introduced the concept of primary, secondary, and tertiary occupations.[4] Fisher observed that countries could be classified with respect to the proportions of their total labor force engaged in these sectors. Primary production was defined originally to include agricultural and pastoral production, and, in some versions, mining. Secondary production comprised manufacturing, generally mining, and, as a rule, construction. Tertiary industry consisted in transport and communications, trade, government, and personal and domestic service.

Fisher's insight was supported by a host of statistics assembled by Colin Clark.[5] Figures 7.2 to 7.4 show the correlation of employment by sectors with income per capita, and bear out in general Fisher's view. The proportion engaged in agriculture declines from roughly 70 to 80 per cent of total population in underdeveloped countries to the level of 12 or even 6 per cent in the most highly developed countries such as the United States and Britain.

The statistics bearing on this transformation will be criticized in a minute. Here, however, it is important to indicate that the total allocation of resources by sectors should not be measured by the single factor, labor. Factor proportions not only may differ by sectors; they must do so, since secondary industry uses much less land than primary, and tertiary industry virtually none. Even if the marginal products of land, labor, and capital are identical in all three sectors, resource allocation is inadequately measured by a single factor, and presents an index-number problem if the attempt is made to measure the total resource input. The more of a given factor input, the lower its marginal product, and the lower weight its quantity input is accorded. The higher the marginal product, the higher the price weight of the scarce factor. This index-number difficulty brings it about that in measuring capital/labor ratios between countries it is hard to obtain meaningful results. The country with abundant capital and scarce labor has a low

---

[4] A. G. B. Fisher, "Economic Implications of Material Progress," *International Labour Review*, July, 1935, pp. 5–18; and "Primary, Secondary and Tertiary Production," *Economic Record*, June, 1939, pp. 24–38.

[5] C. Clark, *The Conditions of Economic Progress*, 1st ed., Macmillan & Co., Ltd., London, 1940, chap. V; 2d ed. (completely rewritten), Macmillan & Co., Ltd., London, 1951, chap. IX.

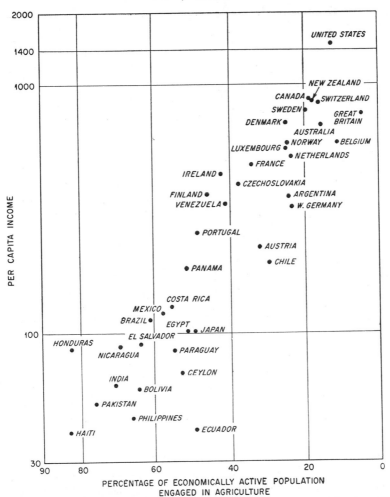

Figure 7.2. Percentage of labor force engaged in primary production, 1947–1952, compared with income per capita in 1949. sources: Percentage of actively engaged population in agriculture, forestry, hunting, and fishing, *Demographic Yearbook, 1955*, United Nations, New York, 1955, pp. 510–573; income per capita, Table 1.1, Income per Capita in U. S. Dollars.

value for the one and a high for the other; and vice versa for the underdeveloped country with little capital. Unless the measure is put in physical terms, such as horsepower or acres per head, international comparison of factor proportions and of total factor inputs is a blind alley.

These difficulties apply where the marginal product of each factor is identical among sectors. But this is more nearly approached in de-

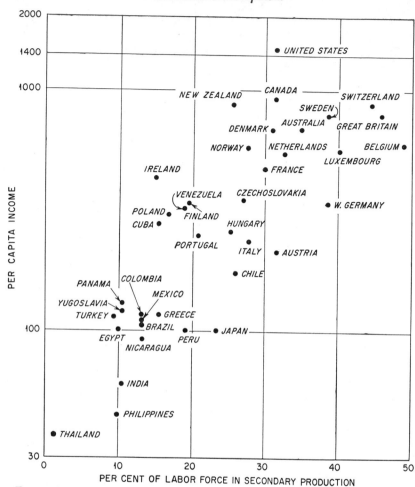

Figure 7.3. Percentage of labor force engaged in secondary production, various dates, compared with income per capita, about 1949. SOURCES: Percentage of labor force in secondary production, W. S. Woytinsky and E. S. Woytinsky, *World Population and Production,* The Twentieth Century Fund, New York, 1953, p. 424; income per capita, Table 1.1, Income per Capita in U. S. Dollars.

veloped than in underdeveloped countries. In underdeveloped countries factor as well as goods markets are localized, separate, monopolistically competitive. Perroux has called underdeveloped economies "disarticulated" with this aspect in mind, and Myrdal approaches the same concept from a different direction when he suggests that economic development is a precondition of "economic integration." In his sense, integration means equalization of factor prices with the elimination of all noncompeting groups (or quasi rents) except those based on physical attributes of factors, including in labor, intelligence as well as dexterity, mechanical aptitude, etc.[6] If labor can earn more in industry than in agriculture, but does not move, there is a presump-

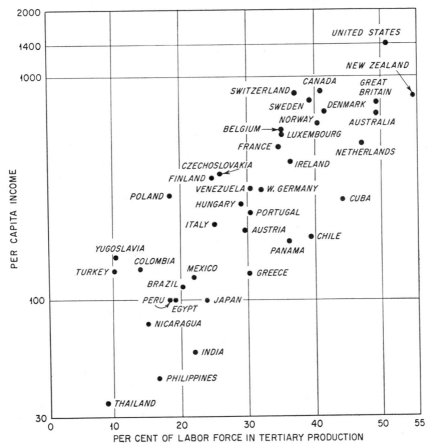

Figure 7.4. Percentage of labor force engaged in tertiary production, various dates, compared with income per capita, about 1949. SOURCES: Percentage of labor force in tertiary production, W. S. Woytinsky and E. S. Woytinsky, *World Population and Production*, The Twentieth Century Fund, New York, 1953, p. 424; income per capita, Table 1.1, Income per Capita in U. S. Dollars.

tive case for reallocation. This is equally the case if capital can earn more in agriculture than in industry.

It has been maintained in some cases that the marginal product of

[6] G. Myrdal, "Toward a More Closely Integrated Free-world Economy," in R. Lekachman (ed.), *National Policy for Economic Welfare at Home and Abroad*, Doubleday & Company, Inc., New York, 1955, pp. 235–292; and *An International Economy*, Harper & Brothers, New York, 1956, esp. chaps. 1–4.

labor in agriculture in some underdeveloped countries is zero, that labor in fact suffers from "disguised unemployment" in this sector. It is not universally agreed that the term should be reserved for those cases where marginal product is exactly zero—illustrated for labor in Figure 3.2 by the point p. When marginal product is positive but lower than in another industry, an element of disguised unemployment is present, and the term is sometimes used in this sense. If too much labor has been moved from Yugoslav farms to factories, and marginal productivity of labor is higher in agriculture, which has unused land, than in industry, where workers get in each other's way, this is disguised unemployment in industry only in the less strict sense. But it is probably better to regard this and instances where labor earns a positive wage in agriculture, though lower than in industry, as instances of underemployment.

Transformation, then, may have two aspects in the course of economic development: first, resource reallocation as a consequence of the improved functioning of factor markets, even without any increase of inputs or increased efficiency of existing inputs; and second, as demand changes, resource reallocation with the growth of income for whatever reason. The equalization of marginal product of factors has gone further in Britain than in the United States, it may be observed. In Britain, net labor productivity is as high in agriculture as in industry. In the United States this is not the case. This country has in fact not one agriculture but two: an efficient, capital-intensive, commercial agriculture, located for the most part in the Middle West, Texas, and California, together with parts of the South; and a subsistence, labor-intensive, impoverished agriculture, largely in the South, in the hills of the border states, and in parts of New England.[7] In this respect, development has not brought about economic articulation.

MEASUREMENT OF PRIMARY, SECONDARY, AND TERTIARY PRODUCTION

The data on the allocation of resources in Figures 7.2 to 7.4 are an approximation only, for a variety of reasons. Some of these have been referred to obliquely already. Where labor productivity is lower in agriculture than in industry, a choice is presented between using income generated by sectors, and numbers of gainfully employed. In an average underdeveloped country, 80 per cent of the working popula-

[7] See T. W. Schultz, "Reflections on Poverty within Agriculture," *Journal of Political Economy*, February, 1950, pp. 1–15.

tion may be engaged in agriculture; but, since their productivity on the average is as little as one-third that of people engaged in secondary and tertiary production, the proportion of income generated in that sector will amount to less than that. With the numbers chosen, this proportion will be 56 per cent, since $[80 + (20 \times 3)]/80 = 56\%$.[8]

A second qualification is needed for foreign trade. The allocation of resources adequately measures the state of demand in a closed economy, since production and consumption are identical, except for changes in stocks which differ from one sector to another. But in an open economy, primary products may be exchanged for manufactures in foreign trade, or vice versa, with the result that the allocation of resources by sectors does not reflect the state of demand. Resources which are engaged in primary production which is exported, as in Turkey, are really engaged in satisfying the demand for secondary products, while contrariwise in Britain manufacturing industry is needed to feed the population through the exchange of exports of secondary products for imports of primary.

A third difficulty is due to the nature of the data and the fact that they, like other statistical measures developed by mature economies, do not neatly fit underdeveloped countries. Bauer and Yamey have pointed out that occupational differentiation is carried much less distance in underdeveloped countries than in developed.[9] Specialization is imperfect. People reported to be engaged in agriculture spend time in trading, and are partly idle for lack of complementary resources, or during the dead season. The assignment of whole men to specific sectors presupposes a division of labor which has not been attained, with the result that the figures for tertiary industry are vastly understated and those for agriculture overstated. Nor is imperfect specialization confined to agriculture: entrepreneurs in underdeveloped countries double in brass in a dozen capacities. And Bauer and Yamey note that even "doctors, lawyers, and leading chiefs (in Nigeria) have extensive trading interests."

Finally, it should be mentioned that Fisher's generalization lumps under tertiary production a variety of services, and that the demand for these is by no means uniform from service to service. This of course is not surprising. Demand for various foods differs widely, from

[8] For figures on the comparative productivity in agriculture and the rest of the economy, see E. M. Ojala, *Agriculture and Economic Progress*, Oxford University Press, London, 1952, Table LI.

[9] See P. T. Bauer and E. S. Yamey, "Economic Progress and Occupational Distribution," *Economic Journal*, December, 1951, pp. 74–85; A. G. B. Fisher, "A Note on Tertiary Production," *Economic Journal*, December, 1952, pp. 830–834; S. Rottenberg, "Note on 'Economic Progress and Occupational Distribution,'" *Review of Economics and Statistics*, May, 1953, pp. 168–170.

negative income-elasticities in potatoes and rye bread to very high ones in lobster and champagne. Similarly with secondary production, which includes both necessities of low income-elasticity, such as work clothing, and luxury products, like sports cars. But tertiary production seems even more disparate in its behavior. Most services—education,

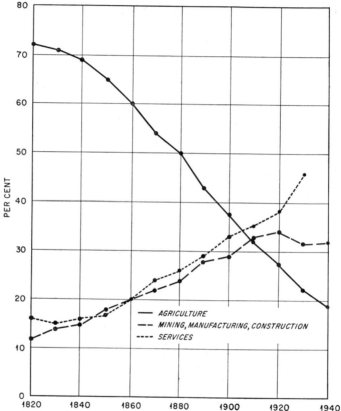

Figure 7.5. Percentage of United States labor force engaged in primary, secondary, and tertiary production, 1820–1940. SOURCE: S. Kuznets, appendix to "Toward a Theory of Economic Growth," in R. Lekachman (ed.), *National Policy for Economic Welfare at Home and Abroad*, Doubleday & Company, New York, 1955, based on Colin Clark, *The Conditions of Economic Progress*, Macmillan & Co., Ltd., London, 1951, chap. IX.

government, entertainment, transport and communication, commerce —have high income-elasticities at early stages of economic development, and grow faster than total output. But others, particularly domestic service, follow mixed trends, depending upon the level of income, its distribution, and social attitudes toward the occupation. Domestic service in households is not separated in the statistics from hotel services, although both tend to follow different patterns of demand with respect to income. In Britain the composite group declines sharply with development, from 17 per cent of the gainfully occupied in 1880 to 11 per cent in 1940. In Belgium from 1880 to 1930, the decline was from 20 to 5 per cent. In the United States, on the other hand, the total fell from 10 per cent in 1870 to 9 per cent in 1900 and the same in 1920, before rising to 12 per cent in 1940. And in India

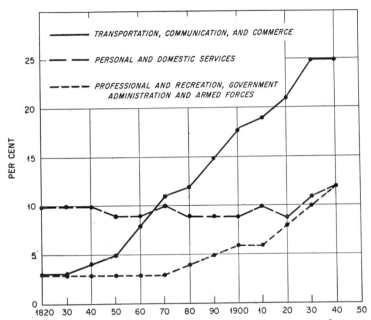

Figure 7.6. Percentage of United States labor force engaged in various branches of tertiary production, 1820–1940. SOURCE: S. Kuznets, appendix to "Toward a Theory of Economic Growth," in R. Lekachman (ed.), *National Policy for Economic Welfare at Home and Abroad*, Doubleday & Company, New York, 1955, based on Colin Clark, *The Conditions of Economic Progress*, Macmillan & Co., Ltd., London, 1951, chap. IX.

the level was 8 per cent in 1880, and appears to have risen between 1910 and 1930 from 7 to 10 per cent.[10] This suggests that demand patterns, at least in the field of tertiary production, are by no means identical from country to country, and that, even if all countries experience the same growth in income per capita, their requirements as to transformation may significantly differ. The data for the United States for all sectors, and for separate activities within the tertiary sector, are shown in Figures 7.5 and 7.6.

[10] All figures are from C. Clark, *The Conditions of Economic Progress*, 2d ed., Macmillan & Co., Ltd., London, 1951, chap. IX.

SYSTEMATIC PRODUCTIVITY DIFFERENCES BY SECTORS

The French statistician, J. Fourastié, who is much interested in productivity, has suggested a model of economic development which combines systematic differences in productivity by sectors with the pattern of income-elasticity of demand implied by Engel's law.[11] In his exposition, potatoes are chosen as an example of a primary good, bicycles of secondary, and a hotel room of tertiary output. Labor productivity in the first is said to have increased from 100 in 1800 to 130 in 1950. Consumption rose continuously throughout the period to the 1920s, but has recently developed negative income-elasticity with per capita consumption 250 per cent of the 1800 level. In bicycles, it is necessary to take 1900 as a base year, since the product is relatively new: productivity increased from 100 in 1900 to 700 in 1950, and is still increasing. Consumption has gone up nine times in the same period, but is beginning to level off. In the hotel room, labor productivity has remained practically unchanged from 1800 to 1950, but demand has brought about an increase in consumption from 100 in 1800 to 10,000 in 1950. Fourastié uses these systematic differences in productivity and demand by sectors to project systematic changes in the terms of trade which favor tertiary industry over primary, and both over secondary.

It is by no means clear that the productivity differences between sectors are everywhere as sharp as in this example. In the United States, labor productivity has been rising as rapidly in agriculture as in industry in recent years—or more rapidly—due partly to increased investment of capital, and partly to higher real productivity. Moreover, productivity in tertiary industry is not stationary. Many tertiary occupations are labor-intensive, with a given state of the arts; and, with only small amounts of capital, limits of productivity of labor are quickly reached. But in the United States substantial changes in production functions have occurred in retailing and administration, to say nothing of transport and communication. Economies of scale are being achieved in the large-scale shopping center, with a substantial investment in land for parking as well as area of building; automation is increasing capital-intensity in administration, and improving the productivity of labor and of total resources.

Without commitment to any values of systematic changes in productivity by sectors, therefore, it may still be possible to suggest broadly that, on balance, labor productivity tends to be higher in secondary

[11] See J. Fourastié, *La Productivité*, Presses Universitaires de France, Paris, 1952.

than in primary production, and higher in primary production than in tertiary production as a whole, though not in the capital-intensive branches of transport and communication. This, of course, is gross productivity, or the inverse of the labor/output ratio, and differs from the marginal product. To the extent that this is true, and demand for tertiary production is more income-elastic than that for manufactured products turned out by secondary industry, transformation requires first a fairly slow transfer of labor from agriculture to industry, and then a much faster movement to tertiary production. Since much of the demand for tertiary production, however, in commerce as in transport and communication, is complementary to secondary production, the movement of labor into secondary and tertiary production is not sequential but simultaneous, which smooths out the process. This complementarity, it may be noted, further undermines the notion of systematic differences in productivity between sectors.

THE DIMINISHING IMPORTANCE OF FOREIGN TRADE

As economic development progresses, there is a tendency for foreign trade to decline as a proportion of national or domestic product. The tendency is perhaps not strong, since it is compounded of several conflicting effects of various strengths. In the United States, imports of merchandise have declined from 15 per cent of national income in 1870 to 10 per cent in 1913 and to approximately 3 per cent today. Britain has experienced a similar trend. Exceptions exist in some small countries, as the Netherlands; but Sweden, where exports as a percentage of national income have declined fairly steadily—29 per cent in 1872, 20 per cent in 1900, 24 per cent in 1913, 19 per cent in 1928, 15 per cent in 1938, and 17 per cent in 1952—perhaps well exemplifies the rule.[12]

The basis for this decline in importance is the fact that services are traded internationally much less than goods, primarily because they must be consumed on the spot. As the proportion of services in national income grows, national income almost certainly grows more rapidly than imports. There will be occasions when a country introduces a commodity of high income-elasticity abroad, where the foreign sales, and in turn, imports, may rise more than national income. The ratio of trade to income may then temporarily increase. But this is

[12] See C. P. Kindleberger, *The Terms of Trade,* The Technology Press of Massachusetts Institute of Technology and John Wiley & Sons, Inc., New York, 1956, p. 301, for similar percentages for exports for the countries of Western Europe, including both merchandise trade and an approximation of the current account in the balance of payments as a whole.

unlikely, since the greater the gains from specialization and foreign sales, the higher the income rise, and the greater the tendency for income to spill over into domestic service. Again, temporary increases in this proportion may occur because the income-elasticity of demand for imports may be greater than one; the country may finance investment with foreign capital used to purchase foreign equipment.

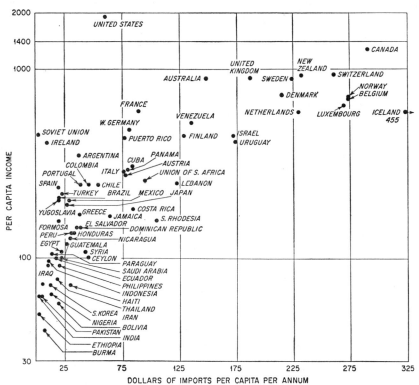

Figure 7.7. Imports per capita compared with income per capita in 1953. SOURCES: Imports, *Direction of International Trade* (Statistical Papers, series T, vol. VI, no. 10), United Nations, pp. 83–328; population, *Demographic Yearbook, 1955,* United Nations, New York, 1955, pp. 116–127; income per capita, Table 1.1, Income per Capita in U. S. Dollars.

By and large, however, it may be said that foreign trade tends to decline with the growth of income. This is a general tendency, and one to be distinguished from the tendency observed in Latin American economic circles for the "capacity to import," i.e., the quantity and price of exports, to lag behind the need for imported capital equipment for development purposes. This subject is reserved for Chapter 14. Nor does it follow, if the trend in foreign trade as a proportion of income is downward, that there is a warrant for limiting international specialization.

Figures 7.7 and 7.8 illustrate, however, that the tendency for the proportion of the foreign trade of a given country to decline with growth does not produce a strong correlation between the proportion of total income spent on imports and per capita income. Per capita expenditure on imports rises with per capita income, particularly after

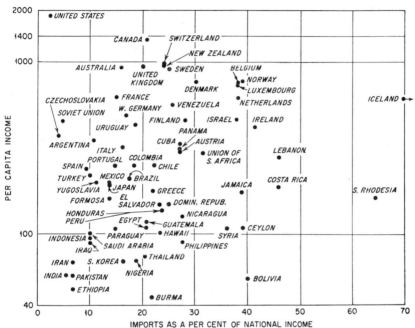

Figure 7.8. Imports as a proportion of national income, compared with income per capita, 1953. SOURCES: Imports per capita from Figure 7.7 divided into national; income per capita, Table 1.1, Income per Capita in U. S. Dollars.

the level of about $150 per capita of income, but since there is little or no correlation between total income and population, the connection between income per capita and imports as a percentage of total income is weak.[13]

THE REALLOCATION PROCESS

There seems to be no consistent sequence in transformation. Productivity may grow throughout the economy. This results in an increase

[13] If M/P varies with Y/P, it does not follow that M/Y varies with Y/P unless Y varies with P, where M is imports, P population, and Y income.

in income, which in turn requires a different set of outputs. Commodities and services experiencing a reduced relative demand also experience relative price declines. The returns to factors engaged in such industries undergo a relative fall. Where possible, such factors seek other occupations to earn higher rates. Transformation is thus led by general productivity increase. Or the increase in productivity can be restricted to a given sector. If output can be sold at home or abroad without producing a disproportionate fall in price, income in increased and the income-elasticity of demand requires a new allocation of resources as in the general productivity case. But another possibility is that demand is inelastic; increased productivity results in a fall in the value of product; resources are pushed out into other industries in accordance with price elasticities.

Or the original initiative may come from the side of demand. In the open economy, foreign demand may impinge on domestic production, raise prices, attract resources, and bring about increased productivity through economies of scale; and the process starts off in this fashion. Or it can even happen that a domestic decision is taken to transform the economy, and resources are shifted from one industry to another.

One advocate of action along these latter lines has been the Romanian economist, Manoilescu, who has argued that the marginal private net product of labor in underdeveloped economies is frequently lower in agriculture than in industry. It may happen that labor receives a wage in both sectors, whether it has a positive private marginal product in agriculture or not. The payment may involve transfers from productive workers. But social net product is understated by market prices and returns in industry, and overstated in agriculture. Manoilescu uses the possibility of such under- and overstatement as an argument for imposing tariffs on manufactured imports to shift labor out of agriculture into industry, and hence to increase total social product.

We shall have occasion later to examine this model, and in particular to investigate first, whether the net productivity of capital is equally understated in agriculture and overstated in industry; and, second, how to arrange that workers transferred from agriculture to industry continue to consume the food which had been available to them in agriculture.

A less subtle form of the Manoilescu argument is involved in the proposal to use the disguised unemployed workers from agriculture anywhere else in the economy where they can be productive. Frequently this suggestion ignores complementarities among inputs.

Another source of transformation from the side of demand is simply development programs, the conscious decision of government to raise productivity and to transform the society.

To a considerable extent, Clark's emphasis on changing proportions of primary, secondary, and tertiary production brought by economic growth has led to the fallacy of *post hoc, ergo propter hoc:* developed countries have large sectors of secondary and tertiary production; our country will be developed by expanding secondary and tertiary production. Frequently tertiary production is ignored altogether and development is identified with industrialization. It is the corrective to this attitude which has led to the emphasis on "balanced growth" discussed in Chapter 9.

But whether the increase in productivity leads and stimulates demand, or an increase in demand induces a rise in productivity—or whether the two are nearly simultaneous as in the examples of Sweden and Denmark referred to in early chapters, certain requirements must be met. There must be a new group of entrepreneurs, or entry by old entrepreneurs into new lines of activity and exit from the old. The flow of capital must be redirected into new lines. New labor skills must be developed, or old converted. Occupational and possibly spatial mobility must permit recruitment of the new labor force. Innovation is needed, or effective and frequently adaptive imitation of examples already extant. It may be necessary, as indicated earlier, to undertake some innovation in the field of economic and social institutions.

BARRIERS TO TRANSFORMATION

A variety of barriers to transformation is suggested by the last paragraph. Lack of entrepreneurship, labor immobility, rigid and inappropriate institutions pose obstacles to the evolution of the structure of the economy in the direction required by the shifting of demand. The prices of old outputs decline; those of new rise. But nothing happens. Supply is inelastic in the face of falling prices in the first case, despite rising prices in the second. Monopoly profits elicit no expansion of old firms, nor any entry of new. The system becomes inured to high returns in one area, low in another.

Some special obstacles to transformation, discussed in Chapter 9, are encountered where investment programs are designed to alter the economic structure and reallocate resources.

In Svennilson's view, the slowing down of European economic growth between the two world wars resulted from a temporary incapacity to transform the economic structure in line with the increased economic potential made possible by the higher technology, and to fit the changes in world structure which had taken place during the war. The rest of the world had developed capacity in textiles, matches, basic steel, and energy. Europe insisted on continuing to produce and sell to the world textiles, matches, basic steel, and coal. The new industries of automobiles, engineering, chemicals, and electrical equipment were slow in developing; textiles and coal were slow in transferring their resources into other occupations. Management in iron and steel, matches, and similar industries clung to old methods and tried to hold their position by organizing world cartels. After World War II, Europe achieved a more effective reorganization of the economic structure; textile and coal industries were permitted to shrink. The modernized engineering, chemical, and electrical industries expanded their employment. Increased supplies of Middle East oil and heightened investment in hydroelectric facilities permitted a substitution of new sources of energy for the coal.

In underdeveloped countries, lack of capital, unskilled labor, absence of entrepreneurship, and social structure which emphasizes traditional irrationality, particularism, and diffuse functional relationships are all barriers to transformation. There is also a danger that a governmental program will plan too drastic a restructuring of capital investment, which will fail for lack of the social capacity to carry it out. Economic development is a product of many interlocking and articulated changes. Construction of a hundred factories, together with connecting transport and public utilities, will not by itself convert an agricultural to an industrial state.

SOCIAL TRANSFORMATION—URBANIZATION

It is appropriate to tie discussion of change in economic structure to the parallel social change, and in particular to the growth of cities in development. The two movements are interconnected in a variety of ways. Specialization and exchange based on markets give the first impetus to increased production. Markets require cities. Pirenne explains that by the ninth century the earlier cities of Europe virtually disappeared. Their revival was initially due to the requirements of defense and of administration, particularly ecclesiastical, with its requirement of cathedrals. But beyond this, and more significant, the city was the home of the merchant and of the rising middle class which he represented.[14]

Cities have been classified as eotechnic, paleotechnic, and neo-

[14] Henri Pirenne, *Medieval Cities*, Princeton University Press, Princeton, N.J., 1923, chaps. 2 and 3.

technic—the first preindustrial, the second industrial, and the third the modern metropolitan city.[15] Perhaps the more important distinction is that between the first two, the mercantile city and the industrial city; the former growing up around markets and developing services ancillary to its original functions and to meet needs of merchants buying from and selling to the wider community; the latter springing up around factories and evolving services of repair, maintenance, equipment, supplies, and research needed by factories as external division of labor takes place or internal division followed by vertical disintegration. Manchester is cited as the classic example of an industrial city, rising out of mere villages, to rival or outstrip in size longstanding commercial towns. The Ruhr, where industrial communities reach out to merge into one another, Pittsburgh, Cleveland, and Cincinnati provide later examples.

In some metropolitan cities—London, Paris, Berlin—administration and commerce are combined. In others specialization takes place, as between Washington and New York, Ottawa and Montreal (and Toronto), Rome and Milan, the Hague and Amsterdam, Bern and Zurich. Higher education may be combined in the metropolitan city or separated out in an Oxford or Cambridge.

The distinction between the industrial and the mercantile, administrative, and education city is regarded as important by some writers. Hoselitz started with the view that "one may therefore look to the cities as the crucial places in underdeveloped countries in which the adaptation to new ways, new technologies, new consumption and production patterns, and new social institutions is achieved."[16] In a later article he is disposed to believe that industrial cities perform these functions less effectively in underdeveloped countries than cities as a whole, including industrial cities, have done in developed areas.[17] In developed countries, cities have evolved self-government, with some political activity and consciousness on the part of their inhabitants. In addition, there has developed attachment to urban life, while in underdeveloped countries a sense of community is generally lacking. Various quarters of the city form self-contained villages spiritually connected to the rural area from which the migrants came. Cities with a strong sense of unity, such as Mecca, resist industrialization rather than promote it. The rapid urbanization now taking place all over the under-

---

[15] P. Geddes, *Cities in Evolution,* London, 1915, cited by E. E. Lampard, "The History of Cities in Economically Advanced Areas," *Economic Development and Cultural Change,* January, 1955, pp. 81–136.

[16] B. F. Hoselitz, "The Role of Cities in the Economic Growth of Underdeveloped Countries," *Journal of Political Economy,* June, 1953, pp. 195–208.

[17] B. F. Hoselitz, "The City, the Factory and Economic Growth," *American Economic Review, Papers and Proceedings,* May, 1955, pp. 166–184.

developed world has its origin in the push of the insecurity and economic turmoil of the country rather than the pull of the economic
opportunities of the city. Life in the city is precarious, demoralizing,
incapable of training its inhabitants for roles in industrial output or
inculcating in them the appropriate values. Hoselitz concludes that the

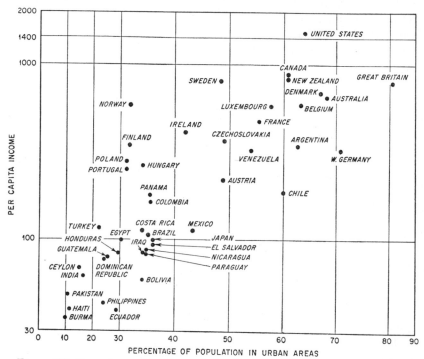

Figure 7.9. Percentage of total population living in urban areas, compared with
income per capita, about 1949. sources: Percentage of population in urban areas
(generally incorporated townships or similar entities of more than 1,000, but
frequently some higher number, up to 5,000), *Demographic Yearbook, 1955*,
United Nations, New York, 1955, pp. 185–198; income per capita, Table 1.1, Income per Capita in U. S. Dollars.

factory has to inculcate these values itself without the help that urbanization previously afforded.

Whether cities are effective means of diffusing the values needed
for economic development or not, there is no doubt that there is a high
correlation of development with urbanization, and that development
requires heavy investment in urban construction. Data on the first
point suffer from the variety of definitions; and, if population size is
the criterion, the critical value must be arbitrarily chosen. National
statistics, in fact, classify as urban localities, somehow defined in space

or by political considerations, those varying from more than 1,000 in the case of New Zealand to more than 20,000 for the Netherlands and 30,000 for Japan. Nonetheless, the data furnish a fairly good correlation between population living in "urban" localities and income per capita, as Figure 7.9 shows.

In Western economic development a rapid rate of growth involved a rapid expansion of city construction. Figure 7.10 shows this in a most

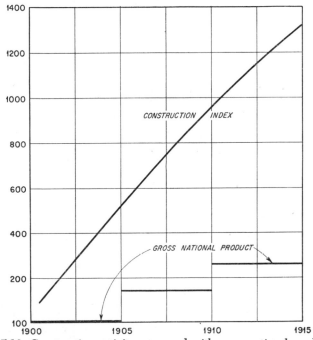

Figure 7.10. Construction activity compared with gross national product, Canada, 1900–1915. SOURCES: Construction index, K. Buckley, *Capital Formation in Canada, 1896–1930*, University of Toronto Press, Toronto, 1955, p. 141; gross national product, K. Buckley, "Capital Formation in Canada," in National Bureau of Economic Research, *Problems of Capital Formation*, Princeton University Press, Princeton, N.J., 1957, p. 128.

striking way for Canada, where national income from 1900 to 1913 more than doubled, and income per capita rose by more than 50 per cent—an impressive performance—but urban building activity octupled.

THE PROCESS OF ECONOMIC GROWTH

This, then, completes our introductory discussion of economic development, including its ingredients and the changes it involves. We have suggested that there is a wide range of substitutability among resources, capital, technological advance, and social capacity for material advance. With enough resources, a country can live well without half trying. On the other hand, a high-pressure society can, starting from a low level of income and capital resources, and, without much in the way of resources, get the process under way. No one ingredient is sufficient. A minimum of each is necessary. We have encountered theories which have laid special stress on resources (Huntington, Toynbee), capital formation (Harrod, Domar), technology (Schumpeter), and social capacity (Hagen). For ourselves, we have chosen the timid course of eclecticism, suggesting that each of these effects may be dominant in particular cases; none is the universal solvent. An Innes can focus on written communication, an Isard on transport, a Kardiner on basic personality; each has part of the truth, none all.

The substitution ratios among these ingredients of growth raise an interesting point. In the first chapter it was suggested that income per capita provides an approximation of growth, but that some writers wanted to discuss growth in relation to capacity for higher incomes rather than in absolute terms. Height is an inappropriate measure of relative growth if a Californian is compared with a Pygmy.

But this assumes that the capacity for development has some definitive meaning, as would be the case if there were a finite limit to it imposed by resources, or by some total of inputs, including resources, capital formation, quality of population, optimum technology (assumed not to change), and optimum scale. The difficulty, however, is that capacity for development has meaning only with respect to the minimum amount of resources needed. If this minimum is present, there is no basis for determining when returns to capital formation become negative, or when further economic development is impossible as a result of qualitative changes in population. An economy, unlike a student with a fixed IQ, cannot be measured in performance against a capacity standard, since in a multidimensional system, with most if not all of the inputs variable, there is no meaning to capacity.

We proceed to deal with a more manageable series of topics—issues in economic development. These are chosen particularly from the problems confronting countries which are underdeveloped today, rather than from economic history, and can follow, unfortunately, no very sensible order. Domestic issues, however, are gathered together; international ones separately.

CHAPTER 8

Planning Versus Prices

THE ROLE OF THE PRICE SYSTEM IN
ECONOMIC DEVELOPMENT

There is a considerable area of disagreement over the proper role of the price system in economic development—how much should be left to its inscrutable outcome at the hands of private enterprise, and how much the government should enter the economic arena and perform basic functions of ownership, production, and distribution. A distinguished Western economist with long interest in and experience of development discussion says that he "doesn't believe in the price system for underdeveloped countries." Prices function after a fashion in developed countries, but not in underdeveloped areas. A parallel view is that the price system is capable of producing changes at the margin; the changes required in underdeveloped countries are structural, not marginal; ergo, the price system is inadequate to cope with the problems of underdeveloped countries.

These opinions are open to controversy. Western Europe and the United States developed with private enterprise and market prices— more or less. The process took time, longer than underdeveloped countries today may choose to give it. Nor was the private nature of enterprise as pure as some commentators now choose to think. Governments built considerable overhead capital in roads, education, administration, and subsidized canals and railroads. Neither is the authoritarian system of the Soviet Union pure in its way; not only is some room left for private production in agriculture and for private distribution in response to profit opportunities dictated by free prices, but nationalized production itself uses a system of prices in reaching decisions respecting output and distribution. An indication of the controversial nature of the subject is furnished by the fact that in parallel reviews of United Nations and International Bank studies on economic development, Mikesell attacked the former for relying too much on government,[1] Spengler the latter for undue dependence on private enterprise.[2] A further dimension is added to the discussion in that one critic of the International Bank, thought by Spengler to rely unduly on private entrepreneurship, finds fault with its study on Nigeria for not once mentioning the price system.[3] In this chapter we shall discuss these issues, the nature of development planning, and the possibility, raised by Abramowitz, that government should be regarded as a factor of production in underdeveloped countries.[4]

THE DEFECTS OF THE PRICE SYSTEM

The objections to the use of the market mechanism to achieve development are several: *laissez faire* can't produce development, or won't, or costs too much.

The argument that the market mechanism can't achieve development rests on the relevance of external economies and complementarities. Where economies are external to the firm, and to the industry, the private and the social benefits differ.[5] Government may use cost-and-benefit calculations, using a shadow price which differs from that charged or paid in the private market, to determine whether various types of activity are worthwhile. It is pointed out that industry does not in fact take advantage of cheap wages in the short run if the complementary facilities are lacking. Capital was slow moving to the South of the United States; still slower moving from northern to southern Italy, in both cases within the same country. Equally neglected have been northern Brazil and northern Norway. In part it was because labor was not educated, and therefore not cheap, despite low wages, because of inefficiency. In part it was due to the fact that in the North of the United States and of Italy, and southern Brazil and Norway,

---

[1] R. F. Mikesell, "Economic Doctrines Reflected in United Nations Reports," *American Economic Review, Papers and Proceedings,* May, 1954, pp. 570–582.

[2] J. J. Spengler, "IBRD Mission Economic Growth Theory," *American Economic Review, Papers and Proceedings,* May, 1954, pp. 583–599.

[3] P. T. Bauer's review of International Bank for Reconstruction and Development, "The Economic Development of Nigeria," in *Journal of Political Economy,* October, 1955, pp. 398–411.

[4] See his comment on the Kuznets essay in R. Lekachman (ed.), *National Policy for Economic Welfare at Home and Abroad,* Doubleday & Company, New York, 1955, p. 81.

[5] The path-breaking essay expressing this view is P. N. Rosenstein-Rodan's "Problems of Industrialization of Eastern and Southeastern Europe," *Economic Journal,* June–September, 1943, pp. 202–211.

there was no need for private enterprise to build ports, houses, roads to make productive investment possible.

This suggests a division of labor: let government concentrate on overhead capital—economic and social—and leave the field of productive investment in agriculture and industry to private hands. Rosenstein-Rodan anticipated this. He agrees that where lack of transport facilities is a flagrant obstacle to economic progress, as in China and parts of Latin America, government investment is warranted. But in southeastern Europe there was no such shortage. "The quality of 'basic industries' is not confined to . . . some public utilities . . . . Complementarity makes to some extent all industries 'basic.' "[6]

While the argument that the price system cannot produce economic growth depends on external economies, the argument that it will not rests rather on internal economies and monopoly. The number of entrepreneurs is limited, with new entrants kept out by rigidity of the social structure. Existing firms maintain high rates of profit on low turnover:[7]

Indian capitalists, with a few exceptions, remain merchants by temperament and inclination. They are interested in buying and selling, in quick turnover, however small. As a class they would rather sink their profits below ground, in gold, than reinvest them in expansion and modernization of their enterprise. They would rather obtain oblique control of a business through the managing agency system . . . than risk their capital in a straight deal.[8]

The economy rests on dead center with private enterprise and free markets. Some new source of energy is needed to break out of the vicious circles pinning it down.

Finally, there may be occasions when government intervention in the growth process is required to lower the real cost of development to the society—another instance of divergence between private and social return, but this time a case of external diseconomies. Private enterprise may be willing to develop a country's mineral resources or timber, but only if it can appropriate the capital represented by the natural resource for its own. Or agriculture clears acreage by burning

[6] *Ibid.*, p. 208.
[7] See P. Franck, "Economic Planners in Afghanistan," *Economic Development and Cultural Change,* February, 1953, pp. 323–340. This article states that investment has a mercantile odor about it, that the entrepreneur is a monopolist, and that he wants 20 per cent per annum rate of profit. The quotation from the *Christian Science Monitor* is exceptional in its mention of "small" turnover.
[8] "India's Growing Solid Industrial Base Attracts Foreign Investors," *Christian Science Monitor,* May 4, 1956.

off timber, thereby disturbing the ecological balance, wasting timber,
fuel, water, and mining soil fertility.

Where profits are high, but spent on lavish consumption instead of
reinvested in productive enterprise, there may be little to be said for
free enterprise on the ground of either equity or growth; but where
some amount of profits is reinvested, and some amount—small or
large—is frittered away in ostentatious consumption, considerations of
equity and growth conflict and require choices. This argument becomes most powerful when economic progress requires social retrogression: enclosures which uproot a large agricultural population, or
a response to price changes which drives peasants into urban slums.
Karl Polanyi, in a powerful book, has suggested that only a society as
individualistic and obtuse as Britain in the nineteenth century could
permit the outcome of a highly artificial economic system to dictate
its social destinies.[9] Indians have accused British government officials
of destroying the native hand-woven textile industry in the nineteenth
century by ripping down tariff barriers which protected it. At the
present time a sharp debate is taking place in India whether to tax
machine-made textiles in order to keep alive cottage industry. In these
terms, however, the question is clear: is economic development worth
the candle? In the majority of cases government, and the consumers it
represents, have already decided that it is.

ADVANTAGES OF PRIVATE ENTERPRISE

While private enterprise and the market mechanism have their drawbacks, they are not without certain, possibly limited, advantages. These
relate to capital formation, the dispersal of decision and risk, and the
incentive for innovation.

The desirability of a high rate of profits as a source of capital formation has been discussed. To some this is the primary advantage of
private enterprise. Government is the creature of the people. In some
countries, such as Norway, people are willing to save collectively but
not personally, since they have a close to classless society in which the
desire to rise in the social scale has been exhausted. But in less sophisticated societies it may be more painful to pay taxes to government
for capital formation because of the element of compulsion than to
allow entrepreneurs to drain off a comparable amount as profit for reinvestment. Though physiological need and social pressure may render
it largely illusory, the consumer appears to have the option of not
contributing to this capital formation, by refraining from the con-

[9] *The Great Transformation,* Farrar & Rinehart, Inc., New York, 1947.

sumption concerned. The entrepreneur typically makes a better collector for capital formation than government.

The dispersal of decisions introduced by private enterprise is a more debatable effect. Mistakes are made in development, inevitably. Many are called; few chosen. Bankruptcy purges the system of a deadweight load of debt unsupported by productive assets. Given uncertainty as to the exact nature of blocks to development, probing along a broad front in reconnaissance strength may make more sense than committing all one's forces to a single salient which may prove unyielding.

But it is equally true that a light reconnaissance may be unable to make the initial breakthrough which can later be so profitably exploited, when an adequate force can. If increasing returns to scale are available, it is a waste to commit too little. The strong believer in external economies of scale is unmoved by the mention of too many eggs in one basket, or of the grand failure of the groundnut scheme.

Finally, some feel that the basic defense of capitalism rests on its capacity for innovation.[10] Bureaucracies become bureaucratic, pass the buck, dodge responsibility, cling to proved methods. This argument may be applicable in developed countries, more in some than in others, and more in some industries which are committed to change, and less in others which have sunk into private bureaucratization. In underdeveloped countries each situation probably requires separate evaluation. It may be that government is a more probable innovator than private enterprise; it may indeed be that government is unduly receptive to new ideas, with business too little willing to depart from tradition.

DEFECTS OF GOVERNMENT AS A DEVELOPMENT AGENT

The weaknesses of government as a prime mover in economic development have been touched upon in passing. Politicians and civil servants may attempt too much, interest themselves unduly in the showy and monumental venture, neglect fruitful but unspectacular tasks, and even turn irrational.

The possibility that economic development is too important to leave to civil servants is increasingly recognized. The International Bank for Reconstruction and Development has frequently pointed out that its operations are held up not by lack of finance but by insufficient effective demand, i.e., requests for loans buttressed by carefully engineered

[10] See D. McC. Wright, *Capitalism,* McGraw-Hill Book Company, Inc., New York, 1951.

and economically analyzed projects. In announcing the first Five-Year plan of Pakistan, Mohammed Ali indicated that the chief bottleneck in executing the plan is the dearth of skilled manpower and shortage of technical and administrative talent. In 1954 and 1955 only $160 million of $230 million earmarked for various developmental programs had been spent because of "our inability to pursue several projects through to completion primarily because of a lack of qualified personnel to carry them out."[11] It is likely that the society as a whole lacks qualified personnel in these circumstances. The question then comes down to whether private or public sponsorship is the more effective way to train and employ them.

Some aspects of development, such as elimination of waste and adequate attention to the New England virtues of repair, maintain, and make-do, fail to come naturally to government officials. The pay-off in government is votes, or consent, or absence of trouble. It is easy to neglect petty economies which in depth can produce resources for development. The incentive system is rather geared the other way. It is charged with justification that neglect of agriculture in a number of countries—chief among them perhaps the Soviet Union, Yugoslavia, and China—has its origin in contempt for the familiar and fascination with the spectacular.

It is natural and inevitable that government should be interested in the showpiece. Hirschman regards this as the weakness particularly of "strong" governments. Democratic governments, on the other hand, in his view have a bias for undue dispersion of investment in all regions of a country, in the effort to mend fences. And all governments are likely to show a preference for projects which can be started with fanfare.[12] Hirschman goes on to observe that the biases of foreign experts and even international lending agencies frequently work in the same direction as those of the government. The former are in the country for only a short time, and therefore try to change the face of the country rather than its people. The latter look for short cuts, and permit themselves to be persuaded that they may be found in this or that project.

There are wide differences, of course, in the extent of government involvement in the development process. Government may direct and lead, undertake substantial amount of the actual investment, and even

---

[11] "Pakistan Issues First 5-Year Plan," *New York Times*, May 15, 1956, direct quotation in original.

[12] A. O. Hirschman, "Economic and Investment Planning, Reflections Based on Experience in Colombia," in *Investment Criteria and Economic Growth*, Massachusetts Institute of Technology, Center for International Studies, Cambridge, Mass., 1955, p. 43.

operate business enterprises. In Ceylon, government investment continues to increase as a proportion of total capital formation, at the same time that industries constructed with government capital either closed down or were handed over to cooperatives or private enterprise for operation.[13] There is less debate over the role of government in planning and even in investment than there is in government operation of business. The latter issue is probably most acute in India, where certain industries—diamonds and life insurance—are being nationalized; others, such as oil refining, are more or less reserved for private enterprise; while in still other fields, such as steel, private domestic, private foreign, and domestic government-owned plants seem likely to exist side by side, in some sort of competition. In Turkey a very high degree of government operation, called *étatism*, has been reversed, at least until lately, under the pressure of advice from abroad, and with the development of entrepreneurial talent after World War II. The Turkish experience is referred to as an example of the inadequacy of governmental domination.

ADVANTAGES OF GOVERNMENTAL INTERVENTION

I find it difficult to discuss the role of government in economic growth in the abstract. Government responds to politically perceived needs not otherwise filled. Where entrepreneurship is weak because the middle-class basis for it is missing, reluctance on the part of government to innovate and imitate means no development. Where no savings are forthcoming, government is obliged to produce savings if productive investment is to be undertaken. Where there are no investment or commercial bankers to direct the flow of investment, and even in some instances where there are, government machinery is needed to allocate capital.

Government's role is not confined to filling the vacuums left by the private market and its institutions. At a minimum there is need for social and economic overhead capital, the "basic facilities" which must be provided and whose benefits are diffused so widely that it is impossible equitably to collect all of the costs by charging direct users. There may be a particular argument in particular circumstances for replacing private with public management in areas where private and

[13] See *Economic Survey of Asia and the Far East, 1954,* New York, 1955, pp. 49, 82. Between 1947 and 1953, while gross capital formation was rising from 5 per cent to 12 per cent of gross national product, the private share of gross capital formation declined from 75 per cent to 44 per cent. In Pakistan, while the share of total capital in private ownership is 75 per cent, the proportion of current annual investments undertaken privately is only 25 per cent.

social benefits diverge in the other direction, i.e., in the case of external diseconomies where private gain is higher than social, because of losses associated with depletion, erosion, pollution, etc., introduced by private enterprise and borne by society. The more usual remedy is regulation, where the natural resources are renewable or maintainable at extra cost, or recapture through taxation of some of the benefit for wasting assets to replace them. This is the policy of Venezuela in "sowing the petroleum," now widely emulated in the Middle East.

This vacuum theory of government, which can be applied to developed countries as well as to underdeveloped, leaves little room for generalization. Circumstances alter cases, and governments will have different functions in different countries. It is well to remember that the absence of a middle class capable of entrepreneurial leadership by no means guarantees that the government will be capable of fulfilling these functions. In fact, there is a strong probability that the factors which inhibit the private sector will also limit the capacity of the public. It may still be true that it governs best which governs least.

Monopoly profits raise still another issue. Where the monopoly is a natural one, the choice is between government operation and regulation. Where the profits result from supplying less than the quantities demanded at a price which would produce a normal return, a dilemma is encountered. Doctrinaire Socialists generally have this case in mind, though they often end up socializing an industry because of its losses. At least two courses are open: to break down the monopoly by encouraging new entry, and possibly in a few cases by horizontal disintegration (Standard Oil trust busting); or government ownership. These may even be combined, as in the Indian steel industry. But clearly the lesson is to work in the direction of expanding output. High profits, far from indicating exploitation in the usual instance, are a sign of need for further output. Where entry is free already, and the monopoly profits simply indicate a firm which is ahead of its competition in introducing new goods or cheapening methods of producing old, there is much to be said for a leisurely course of governmental action to expand output, since this sort of innovation should be rewarded. Where entry is limited, however, more output is the answer, whether through breaking down artificial barriers to entry, encouraging and even subsidizing new firms (as the United States has done with Reynolds and Kaiser in aluminum), or even, possibly as a last resort, government entry. Price reduction by fiat, which creates the need for rationing and discourages expansion of output, has little to recommend it.

With all that needs to be done in underdeveloped countries, and in the light of the limited resources available outside government to do it, it might be thought that the role of government would decline as countries developed, along the lines of the Marxist doctrine of the "withering away of the state." Such, however, does not appear to be the case. There is a variety of conceptual and practical problems encountered in measuring the importance of government in national income;[14] but one such measure indicates clearly that in the middle of the twentieth century, development and the extent of governmental

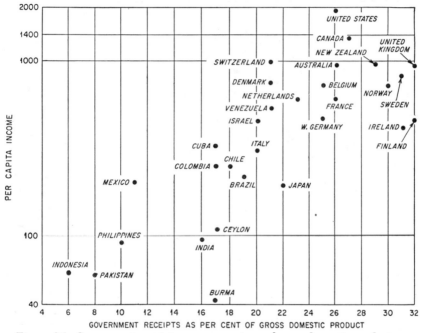

Figure 8.1. Government receipts as a percentage of gross domestic product compared with income per capita, about 1953. SOURCES: Government receipts, H. Oshima, "Share of Governments in Gross National Product of Various Countries," *American Economic Review*, June, 1957, pp. 381–390; income per capita, Table 1.1, Income per Capita in U. S. Dollars.

participation in economic life were positively, not negatively, correlated. The evidence is presented in Figure 8.1. But these data, it should

[14] It makes a considerable difference for a single country whether one measures the role of government by comparing total expenditure, expenditure on final product, or expenditure on factor services with output. The second measures the effect of government on resource allocation; the first, including transfers, relates to government's influence on income distribution; and the last refers to income originating in the governmental sector. It is likely, however, though not a foregone conclusion, that international comparisons made on these separate bases would show much the same result. The statistical problems are of course myriad. For some, see H. Oshima, "Share of Governments in Gross National Product of Various Countries," *American Economic Review*, June, 1957, pp. 381–390.

be observed, provide no warrant for the belief that expanding the role of government is the road to development. A great deal of the necessity for high governmental receipts in developed countries is associated with the destructive tasks of wars, whether interest on war debts, pensions for veterans, or defense programs. A further element represents the revenue going to redistribution expenditures which underdeveloped economies may be too poor to afford. The data do not exist in finished form to establish whether the role of government in positive peacetime production and direction of the resources of an economy expands or contracts as development proceeds.[15]

TYPES OF GOVERNMENTAL PLANNING

Although there is little opposition to all forms of governmental planning—there is some, to be sure, and it is vocal—it is possible to differentiate governmental planning from less to more—and there is likely to be a difference in warmth of reception to the different grades. At the minimum, a government can plan the environment in which business enterprise operates, lay down the rules, build the necessary institutions, and preserve law and order.[16] At the next level, represented today by Indonesia, the government may plan a series of investments for the public sector, including some projects which in other countries might be regarded as falling within the scope of the private sector, and leave the rest of the private sector strictly alone. Beyond this, there is a series of possible gradations of interference in the private sector, ranging from simple projections or estimates of its behavior, included in plans such as the Italian Ten-Year Plan for southern Italy, to priorities laid down for the private sector, as in India, to complete absorption, as for a time was the case in Ceylon. At a minimum there will be some degree of government regulation. Following from that, there is some degree of government planning in the public sector, if only for a year at a time through the budget mechanism, and then separately by national, provincial, and local ad-

[15] G. Colm, in "Comments on Samuelson's Theory of Public Finance," *Review of Economics and Statistics*, November, 1956, p. 410, refers in passing to "Adolph Wagner's 'law' of the growing importance of the public sector in the process of industrialization."

[16] E. O. Reichshauer's review of W. W. Lockwood's *The Economic Development of Japan: Growth and Structural Change, 1868–1938*, Princeton University Press, Princeton, N.J., 1954, states that Lockwood's most interesting and significant interpretations concern the relation of the state to economic development: "Its chief contribution was in providing unity and stability, a system of universal education and specific institutions such as modern currency and banking systems." See *Journal of Economic History*, September, 1955, p. 308.

ministrative bodies. There remain for decision the scope of the planning in the public sector, the extent of the public sector vis-à-vis the private, if any, and the nature of government direction, if any, in the sector left for private enterprise.

THE PLANNING PROCESS

An economic development plan may start with resources and work to goals, or the other way around; it may emphasize the financial aspects of growth, rates of saving, and capital/output ratios, over-all and by sectors, or concentrate on physical requirements, or both; it may consist merely in a sketch of what the economy might look like if it were developed, indicate what it is at the time of the sketch, and subtract the capital requirements of the latter from the former; it may represent a handful of projects; it may consist of a discussion of the blocks to development and how they can be overcome, and leave to the imagination where and how fast removal of the bottlenecks will take the economy.

The most widely discussed aspect of economic plans currently is their balance. This topic has been reserved for discussion in the next chapter. Here it is proposed only to consider the various types of plans and the criteria of excellence among them.

Most usual are financial plans. Starting from a given level of income and capital, planners project rates of capital formation and income growth, based on a rate of investment in relation to national income and a capital/output ratio for the economy as a whole and frequently by sectors. Marginal propensities to save and to import are used to develop the multiplier, and prospective values for income, imports, and domestic savings. The volume and price of exports are projected from past trends. If planned imports exceed anticipated exports after investment has been pared down and sources of domestic savings thoroughly explored, the amount of foreign borrowing is calculated, if the country has access to credit. If, on the other hand, the amount of foreign loans is fixed, the rate of capital formation and possibly the permitted level of imports must be adjusted to it.

Questions relating to the amount and character of foreign borrowing are reserved until Chapter 14. Here it may be observed that both the Indian second Five-Year Plan and the Pakistan first leave uncovered foreign-trade gaps. The level of investment is set at a value which, given the forecast marginal propensities to save and import and projected foreign sales, leaves large uncovered foreign deficits. In both cases, it seems, the plan has been added up, found not to come out right, but embarked on notwithstanding. Considerable uncertainty attaches, of course, to the availability of foreign loans, and loans in hand or capable of being reckoned on by past experience may turn out to be small. Uncertainty equally attaches to other features, especially to the character of the harvest. The first Indian Five-Year Plan left the country with a positive balance of trade in each year, owing to an underestimation of the harvests, which, as a result of several excellent monsoons, reduced the necessity to import food. A plan based on long-term average yields will provide too little capital formation or too much, depending upon whether the actual harvests are above or below average.[17]

Integral parts of an over-all financial plan are the distribution of income among factors of production, the level of taxes as well as government expenditure, the amounts of savings generated in the personal, business, and government sectors of the economy, and the means by which net investors at home acquire the external funds made available to them by sectors producing net savings or by foreign capitalists. The financial plan is a model of income receipts and expenditures. While net receipts of all saving sectors, including foreign borrowing, must equal net expenditures of all investing sectors, the provision of this credit requires capital markets capable of making the requisite transfers.

The over-all model may be modified by breaking investment, capital/output ratios, exports, and import spillover into industrial sectors, and in particular by indicating the interconnections among sectors. This begins to approach physical planning. In its developed state, this method starts from an input-output table and applies methods of linear programming to show how to maximize domestic production, given limited capital inputs and foreign-exchange proceeds of exports, and how to choose between domestic production and imports and production for export and the home market.[18]

The input-output table for a country presents a picture of the interrelations among industries. Sectors or industries are listed across the

----

[17] Variability in harvest results plays a much larger role in disturbing the balance of payments of most countries than economists are apt to allow. In India, with a highly variable yield, this is especially true; but even in Europe the structural disequilibrium of 1947 and the recovery due to the Marshall Plan in 1948 were both exaggerated, failing to take account of a bad harvest in 1947 and a good one the following year.

It is worth recalling that the basic limitation to capital formation in an underdeveloped country is its capacity to obtain an agricultural surplus to feed the labor engaged in constructing capital, and this limitation varies with crop yields.

[18] See H. B. Chenery, "The Role of Industrialization in Development Programs," *American Economic Review, Papers and Proceedings,* May, 1955, pp. 40–57.

top of the columns, and down the left-hand tab of the rows, indications reading down, whence each industry gets its inputs, and across, whither each industry sends its outputs. Extra columns on the right indicate final demand, including consumption, investment, and exports. Extra rows may be used, or separate tables, to indicate the initial inputs of labor, capital, land, and imports. The capital/labor and hence the capital/output and the labor/output ratios in each sector, excluding intermediate goods, are derived from as intensive as possible—but frequently very slight—statistical investigation. The breakdown of increases in final product by sectors is derived from budget and other studies.

Input-output tables have advanced professional understanding of the intricacies of economies. One of their initial purposes was to show how much additional demand for intermediate products—materials and components—would be generated by a given demand for final product. Thus defense planners could tell the increases in capacity, direct and indirect, needed to increase the size of the airforce by 10,000 airplanes, or to equip fifteen armored divisions. Airplanes are related to steel, aluminum, power, labor, and buildings in a series of simultaneous equations which can be expressed in an input-output table. But these tables assume fixed coefficients. Part of the process of economic development expressly involves capital deepening; another aspect requires the alteration of production functions. A method relying, in the usual case, on fixed coefficients of capital and labor to output, and between inputs and outputs in various sectors, cannot go all the way to solve the planning program. It is clearly superior, however, to partial-equilibrium planning, in which the output of steel is projected, as if the supply of electricity were fixed, and the need for electricity is worked out as if the supply of steel were unchanged. As a first approximation of where to invest a given increment of capital, given the requirements of the foreign balance and the desire to maximize output, it may be a long step forward, provided the data are available to construct the table in the first place.

Input-output tables are expressed in value, but assume fixed prices. They can therefore be translated back into the physical quantities of steel, turbines, transformers, combines, and tractors from which they were built up to begin with. In some cases, planning commissions find it useful to work with the physical requirements in parallel to a broad financial plan only roughly broken down into sectors. Thus the requirements of social overhead, economic overhead, and plant, together with agricultural investment in marketing facilities, must be compared with the capacity of the construction industry, the availability of cement, domestic or imported, and supplies of furniture, electric fixtures, etc. This physical planning can be plain or fancy, depending upon the capacity of the private sector to respond to demands placed upon it. If this is minimal, as in the Kariba development of Northern Rhodesia, the physical planning must go to the full length that is required of a contractor, where there are no subcontractors. But if the economy is fairly flexible in response to incentives, it may be sufficient to check that steel, cement, electrical equipment, and such major items are available or can be ordered from abroad.

Thus far we have been discussing operational plans, that is, projections of the year-by-year course an economy is expected to take, along with, in the majority of cases, lists of investment projects phased in time which are expected to get it there. Another looser type of planning is represented by the studies of the International Bank for Reconstruction and Development. These are made by outsiders, not servants of a responsible government. They are not intended to be operational, except in a very general way, and they are made in a brief period by a group of experts. For the most part, these studies survey the level and types of output in the country, indicate a number of investments the country might have were it developed, and the character of industrial or agricultural output these imply. The effect is one of two snapshots, before and after, rarely with a step-by-step account of the process of change, or with priorities among various investments in the event that they cannot all be undertaken at once. While the letters exchanged between the Bank and the government in question invariably agree that the study mission shall recommend priorities, this is seldom carried out in practice. Moreover, the missions contain a variety of experts, the composition of whom in some part determines the character of the final report. It is inevitable that a specialist attaches importance to his line of interest; at a minimum he is prepared to recommend what ought to be done in his field, even though in a candid moment he would agree that it had less importance than other types of activity. In the nature of the social structure of such missions, something gets into the report for each expert. There are thus few surprises; and, if the group of experts is chosen with perfect foresight, the appropriate attention may be given to each field. It may be observed, finally, that there is never an expert in people as a member of the mission, who may have insight into how economic growth is blocked by what the people are like, rather than by the inadequacy of their natural resources and capital.

These difficulties in planning in its present rudimentary state have led some observers to suggest that the major contribution of planning should be to locate and break bottlenecks impeding that economic development which would take place through the normal operation of the price system. To the extent that the bottleneck is lack of overhead capital, the bottleneck approach may differ in no respect from what is normally understood by planning. But, if other blocks are in fact operative, and are amenable to treatment, it may be that the system can be made to take off by itself.

Hirschman on the basis of his Colombian experience believes that planning has very little to contribute once a country has begun the process of development, since bottlenecks stand out for all the world to see.[19] In these circumstances, the value of planning, as he views it, is to push a few projects further along toward realization.

Where an economy is stagnant, planning makes much more sense; but it remains uncertain that the kind of planning needed is investment planning, which is generally what is meant by the term. The temptation is strong to analogize on the experience of developed countries in which investment projects, added in a social and cultural milieu where everything else was present, achieved development. The Tennessee Valley Authority investments in flood control, electric power, and navigation took place in a pocket of underdevelopment left behind in a totally developed situation. The social setting was favorable to development; outside capital quickly moved in to take advantage of the opportunities uncovered by the investment. The projects sparked a tinderbox long ready.

Multipurpose projects in really underdeveloped countries, by way of contrast, may lack every precondition for success except the high hopes of politicians and the public. In Afghanistan the recent completion of the Helmand Dam—with irrigation, electric power, and flood control—found local tribes incapable of readapting their ways from nomadic to settled cultivation, inadequate administrative provision for the division of the waters, and few potential users for the electric power.[20] To extrapolate the galvanizing effects of the TVA to other underdeveloped countries requires a similar social and economic setting; and this is almost invariably missing.[21] Investment planning,

[19] "The most superficial observer of the Colombian economy will realize that transportation and electric power are key factors conditioning further growth." *Op. cit.*, p. 43.

[20] P. and P. Streit, "U. S. Sponsored Helmand Valley Irrigation Project Failure Discussed," *New York Times Magazine*, Mar. 18, 1956.

[21] Such would not perhaps be the case in Israel, with its Westernized population, or even in southern Italy, with the highly developed economic and social structure of northern Italy behind it. Compare the comment on the Iranian program of assistance by the Hoover Commission Task Force, *Report on Overseas Operations*, Washington, 1955, p. 668: "Much money unwisely spent . . . Many of these physical assets have become liabilities to Iran, due to the fact that there are not enough men trained in the required skills, knowledge and ability to maintain and use the machinery and equipment in an efficient and economic manner."

and particularly the planning of large-scale, multipurpose projects which dramatize intended changes in the way of life, must go deeper into the social and economic matrix before they can be confident of success.

The question of planning for agriculture is reserved for the next chapter on sectoral and other types of balance.

One rather sterile question in planning asks whether one should start with resources and evolve optimum output, or start with requirements and calculate what resources, including foreign loans, will be needed to fill them. Evidently one must do both. In the European Recovery Program, the Committee on European Economic Cooperation began by building up a set of requirements, which turned out to cost $30 billion of outside funds in four years. Messrs. Clayton and Douglas suggested that this was well beyond the resources which the United States was likely to make available. Accordingly, a new and less ambitious plan was drawn. The fact that Pakistan and India have Five-Year Plans which call for more domestic and foreign resources than they can count on suggests that they have started with requirements. But of course the deficit in resources is not so large as to be impossible of fulfillment. It is possible that any good planning board, like a good college treasurer, should come out at the end of the period with a small deficit, big enough to make clear to the world the need for help, but not so large as to discourage potential supporters.

OTHER CRITERIA OF GOOD PLANNING

It has been suggested that planning for economic development should cover both the financial and physical aspects of the economy, over-all and by sectors; it should take into account the social situation in which physical capital is to be formed, and should avoid the pessimism which may come from undue concentration on resources available or the optimism which derives from focusing on requirements. Dean Mason has put the major criteria of effective planning, beyond these considerations, as those of consistency, administrative feasibility, and optimal allocation of resources.[22] He is disposed to view the last, discussed in the next chapter, as least in importance.

Consistency means financial consistency, in terms of domestic and foreign-exchange sources, but also physical consistency in having components available for production and outlets for what is produced. In a developed society with private enterprise, this consistency is obtained

[22] In a seminar on the planning process in Pakistan, given at the Center for International Studies, Massachusetts Institute of Technology, Jan. 11, 1956.

by the entrepreneur, who does not undertake an investment unless he is fairly certain he can get what he needs for the purpose and make a profit in selling what he produces. If he is sadly wrong, he fails. Where the price system flourishes, moreover, he may be able to evoke sources of supply by offering to pay somewhat higher prices than he originally intended, or sell more of his final product by lowering prices slightly, thereby falling short of his intended profits, but not necessarily failing.

In underdeveloped countries, however, little can be left to the market process, and most must be foreseen. Foreign components of domestic projects must be ordered in advance, and foreign exchange must be allocated to their purchase. To overlook an item may slow down the project by six months or more. Moreover, gross planning errors abound. The Hoover Commission cites cases of ordering electrical equipment where no power connections exist.[23] More subtle errors can be corrected when the gross mistakes have been eliminated.[24] In the Soviet Union it appears that the capacity of the transport system has been continuously overestimated. But road-building programs have been undertaken in French Equatorial Africa from Libreville to Brazzaville, which managed to make two miles at one end and twenty miles at the other against the rain forest. In some areas, such as ensuring that supplies of steel and cement are sufficient to sustain a given program of construction, headway has been made. In other respects, however, physical nature has been underestimated, and human nature overestimated, with the result that consistency in planning programs falls short of the needed level.

The administrative feasibility of a plan turns on one limited but important aspect of its consistency. Most plans require governmental administration. Effective, honest administrators are one of the scarcest resources in underdeveloped countries; and too many of these, for reasons of national prestige and to secure the representation of underdeveloped countries, are made available to international agencies. Jöhr and Singer point out that the weakness of many planning reports is that they produce a group of undertakings, each desirable by itself, but together assuming an unlimited supply of high-level administrative talent.[25]

Whatever degree of development planning may be adopted, there

[23] *Op. cit.*, p. 818, in a catalogue of United States technical assistance errors in the Philippines.
[24] Cf. Hirschman, *op. cit.*, p. 39, who states that poor planning, a phrase often used in Colombia, never refers to alternative uses of resources, but to highways built where there is no traffic, irrigation in areas with adequate rainfall, eight-story buildings in areas with no electricity to run an elevator, etc.
[25] W. A. Jöhr and H. W. Singer, *The Role of the Economist as Economic Adviser*, George Allen & Unwin, Ltd., London, 1955, pp. 84–85.

is reason to contemplate the maximum dispersal of decision-making. The reason for this is the internal diseconomy of scale in administrative decision, plus the shortage of governmental administrative talent. It is true that administrative capacity is likely to increase along with the capacity of the price system to achieve the necessary allocative changes.[26] In the early stages of development, moreover, the former capacity may grow faster than the latter. But, over time, the outcome is likely to be the other way.

In the intermediate period, some attention may be given to dispersal of decision-making or concentration of the available supply. Rosenstein-Rodan has suggested that the centralized planning agency should lay out priorities by sectors, but that decisions on projects within sectors should be undertaken by others.[27] In the longer run, a more tolerable system might evolve into leaving questions involving external economies and diseconomies to governmental decision and gradually turning other investment decisions over to the decentralized action of the increasingly effective private market.

[26] The argument that development calls for structural changes which the price system is incapable of bringing about, while ordinarily the requisite changes are merely marginal, seems neither logical nor historically realistic. Any marginal change is a change in structure: the difference is one of degree, not kind. Historically, moreover, vast structural changes have been effected by price movements in developed and underdeveloped countries alike.

The real difference runs between the elasticities in demand and supply curves, particularly the latter, and here the difference in degree between developed and underdeveloped countries may be so wide as to constitute a difference in kind. But as a country develops, resources acquire mobility, entry is easier and exit less traumatic, and higher supply elasticities permit the price system to undertake marginal changes and all structural changes not dependent on external economies. Since many structural changes cannot initially be undertaken because of internal economies of scale, this last qualification is not as sweeping as it sounds.

[27] P. N. Rosenstein-Rodan, "Programming in Theory and Italian Practice," in *Investment Criteria and Economic Growth*, Massachusetts Institute of Technology, Center for International Studies, Cambridge, Mass., 1955, p. 26.

CHAPTER 9

Balance Versus Priorities

A SEMANTIC WARNING

The allocation of investment, and in particular the question of the appropriate *balance* among industries or sectors, are the subjects of this chapter. First, however, it must be emphasized that the balance or balanced growth has so many meanings that it is in danger of losing them all. At one extreme, it represents in pure theory the mathematically optimum expansion path in a production function in a world where every kind of capital stock grows at constant rates.[1] At the other, the word has purely rhetorical meaning, like "well-conceived plans" or "carefully integrated projects," and means little more than "successful."[2] Between, however, the term is used in a number of ways. Occasionally balance is used to refer to the expansion of consumption appropriate to match the over-all growth in productive capacity, and hence to maintain full employment of capital and the incentive to invest.[3] More usually, and in the sense of this chapter, it refers not to levels of over-all consumption and investment, but to their composi-

[1] P. A. Samuelson and R. M. Solow, "Balanced Growth under Constant Returns to Scale," *Econometrica*, July, 1953, pp. 412–424.
[2] See, for example, the title of the American Economic Association's discussion of the role of monetary policy in economic development, *American Economic Review, Papers and Proceedings*, May, 1955, p. iv, "The Monetary Role in Balanced Economic Growth." Only Ellis referred to the word "balanced" and this in an oblique way: "But economic growth, even balanced economic growth, as an objective of monetary policy is extraneous and potentially pernicious" (p. 208).
[3] See *Economic Survey of Europe in 1955*, Economic Commission for Europe, United Nations, Geneva, 1956, p. 76. In this context, balance further requires that the real wage be such that consumption and investment together do not prejudice external balance in the balance of payments. In short, balance is equivalent to equilibrium.

tion. And in whatever sense it is used, many writers regard balance as critical to growth.[4]

Apart from pure theory, there is little agreement as to what balanced growth means or implies. To some it means investing in a laggard sector or industry so as to bring it abreast of the others.[5] To others, it implies that investment takes place simultaneously in all sectors or industries at once, more or less along the lines of the slogan, "You can't do anything until you can do everything."[6] In still other meanings, balance is a motto opposed to the even simpler slogan of development through the establishment of manufacturing industries, and serves primarily as a salutary reminder not to neglect agriculture. Other writers veer among these and other meanings.[7] Whether balance has any particular significance depends on the context.

The present chapter, which explores the concept of balance, is largely a discussion of investment criteria in economic development. This is a subject which we began in Chapter 3 on capital and continued in Chapter 8 in the discussion of planning. In the present context, we shall pursue the investment criteria into one further stage. Many economists insist that capital must be invested so as to provide balance. The question which we address is whether this exhortation has meaning.

BALANCE IN SUPPLY

For working analytical purposes, it is useful to distinguish two broad classes of balance discussed in the literature: balance in supply and

[4] W. A. Lewis, *The Theory of Economic Growth*, Richard D. Irwin, Inc., Homewood, Ill., 1955, p. 141: "The secret of most development problems is to maintain a proper balance among sectors." See also *Processes and Problems of Industrialization*, United Nations, New York, 1955, p. 2: " . . . manufacturing, agriculture, power and transport and export activities . . . upon whose balanced growth integrated economic development depends."

[5] *Taxes and Fiscal Policy in Under-developed Countries*, United Nations, New York, 1954, p. 5: "Balanced economic development depends on assigning priorities to projects according to their contribution to the productivity of the economy . . . ."

[6] See, e.g., "India's Crucial Plan," *Economist*, Feb. 25, 1956, pp. 516–517: "In an undeveloped economy everything has to be got going at once, so that the various sections can provide each other with markets and complementing facilities; a lag in any part destroys the balance of the plan." See also J. J. Spengler, "IBRD Mission Economic Growth Theory," *American Economic Review, Papers and Proceedings*, May, 1954, p. 590; he refers to "simultaneous expansion on all or most subsector fronts."

[7] A prize example collected for me by a student is found in an account of a lecture in the Philippines by an economist from Cambridge University, which states (*Manila Daily Bulletin*, Feb. 23, 1956): "The first major difficulty, the professor pointed out, was the fact that the Philippine economy, being neither agricultural nor industrial, was 'unbalanced.' "

balance in demand. The first emphasizes complementarities and external economies among industries and vertical sectors in the economy; the importance of higher stages, producing energy, raw materials, intermediate products and services such as transport, to the lower industries which produce for the consumer. (The distinction between the vertical and horizontal orderings of industry is exactly parallel to that between vertical integration, among firms at different stages of production, and horizontal integration, or mergers between companies producing the same product with the same purchased materials.) The second refers to complementarities among industries, particularly consumer-goods industries, and horizontal sectors, especially agriculture and manufacturing industry.

Like many distinctions in economics, that between the horizontal and vertical ordering of industry breaks down in practice. It becomes impossible to order all industries in a vertical array, so that the output of the higher ones would be sold only to those below it. In an input-output table this would mean that there would be no figures in the half of the table below a diagonal line running from upper left to lower right. In fact, electricity is sold to steel mills and steel to power plants, to take but one illustration, so that it is impossible to arrange industries in descending order where an industry can be said to be uniquely vertical or horizontal to all others. Nonetheless, the rough distinction is worth keeping.

The desirability of balance in supply arises from external economies. Social and economic overhead investment, themselves requiring large capital investment and producing a low rate of return, may be justified because of the fact that they make possible profitable investment in industries using skilled workers produced by education, or industries drawing on the electricity produced. In a vertically integrated industry, low rates of return in one or more branches are tolerated if they are necessary to high profits in others. In some underdeveloped countries, where large foreign companies are operating, it pays the latter to construct ports, railroads, workers' housing, etc., in order to be able to get at the primary undertaking. This problem has already been discussed above in connection with the difficulties of imputing particular returns to particular capital investments. Rosenstein-Rodan in his 1943 article pointed out that if a "sufficiently large investment unit" is established to include "all the new industries in a region, the external economies become internal profits, out of which dividends may be paid easily."[8]

An important point must reluctantly be made by the economist

---

[8] P. N. Rosenstein-Rodan, "Problems of Industrialization of Eastern and Southeastern Europe," *Economic Journal*, June–September, 1943, p. 207.

against the city planner and the educator. Much of what these and other social planners have to contribute to economic development is economical only in the too-long run, or makes its contribution to income directly, rather than to the increase of further production. The case may be illustrated with both housing and education. New housing may be needed, both to make possible production in a new location and to rehouse slum dwellers who by any social standard are entitled to more salubrious accommodation. The first has clear complementarity for other investment: new production in the new location depends on it. The second may have ancillary benefits, increasing the productivity of the rehoused workers through raising their level of health. Its main effect, however, is to increase their level of living. Education may similarly focus either on productivity—technology plus a minimum of literacy—or it may address itself to the enrichment of lives through literature, history, art, and the humanities. The first is productive and alone has significance for further production. The second is consumption.

Planners point out that in the long run it is economical to build cities along well-planned lines rather than to let them grow up to slums which are ultimately torn down and replaced. This is perfectly true in a partial-equilibrium setting, i.e., if other things are equal. But if savings for capital formation are limited, as they are, and if adequate city planning absorbs considerable savings, the recommended investment involves external diseconomies in other investment projects which must be foregone. It is cheaper to buy $120 suits rather than $40 suits—they last more than three times as long and give much more satisfaction; but not everyone can afford to take advantage of these economies, and the extra $80, invested in something else, may bring advantages much greater than the extra value of the better suit.[9]

In an open economy foreign trade may provide an opportunity for escaping internal balance in supply. Components can be purchased abroad, and technical assistance obtained to meet some needs for skilled labor. To the extent that imports can be substituted for domestic production, balance can be obviated. But there are some services, like power, which are required to give industry a start and which cannot be imported. Some components are too expensive. Accordingly, there is a strong argument for investing in social and economic overhead industries where these have large external economies.

[9] City planners will disagree with these remarks. For a vigorous statement of dissent, see Catherine Bauer, "The Case for Regional Planning and Urban Dispersal," in B. Kelly (ed.), *Housing and Economic Development*, Massachusetts Institute of Technology, School of Architecture and Planning, Cambridge, Mass., January, 1955, pp. 39–51.

A semantic question can be raised, however, whether this calls for balance or priorities. The existence of external economies in supply clearly leads to priority for investment in those areas—generally transport, communication, education, and sometimes electric power— where external economies are largest and most potent. This differs distinctly from "getting everything going at once." Social overhead investments of low payout directly and indirectly get postponed until the marginal efficiency of capital has been reduced by increased supply. Where existing overhead facilities have excess capacity, they are left alone.

Moreover, it is important to avoid one particular fallacy which lies in wait for underdeveloped countries: the construction of an overhead facility to give rise to external economies, and subsequent investment which barely becomes worthwhile if it exploits all the advantages offered by the initial project. The initial investment with low output is justified by the fat profits anticipated at lower stages of production, while the subsequent construction is designed to rescue capital now regarded as sunk.

An example may be furnished by the Assan hydroelectric power project in north Sumatra, to which aluminum production was to be added to use up the cheap power. The combined project is highly capital-intensive, and would make sense only at a low rate of interest. If Indonesia were to be offered capital available only for this combined project, and for no other purpose, the opportunity cost of the capital may be said to be low, and a capital-intensive project possibly economic. But if using capital in this way limits other investments in the country, it would seem, on the basis of limited information, that the project affords an example of fallacious planning, in which power is undertaken for the sake of other projects and a single other project is undertaken for the sake of using up power.

Rosenstein-Rodan's view, referred to in the previous chapter, that all industries are basic because of external economies, is impossible to accept if it means that all are equally basic. Analytically, perhaps, it is possible to conceive of a situation in which every industry is equally endowed with external economies at a diminishing rate, so that the optimum investment path is to divide investment among them all. In the real world, however, some industries and sectors have greater external economies than others. These may not always be the same industries in all countries; but transport, communication, education, and perhaps electric power are the most obvious candidates for examination.

BALANCED CONSUMER DEMAND

Nurkse has made much of the point that a single manufacturer cannot undertake an investment on a large and efficient scale because only a very small amount of the income paid to productive factors will be spent on the output. He quotes Adam Smith that the division of labor is limited by the extent of the market, observes that price elasticity of demand in underdeveloped countries is low, and concludes that the only chance of starting efficient consumer-goods industries in an underdeveloped country is if a large number of industries are started at once. In this eventuality, the increase in income to the factors working in each industry will be spent among them and make them all profitable.[10]

This view is based upon a breakdown or disaggregation of the Malthusian underconsumption model. It is true, of course, that final demand of producers in the consumer-goods industries will be insufficient to buy their total output if they attempt to save any part of their income. Demand from producers in the investment industries is needed to offset that part of the output of consumption goods which is not disposed of in that sector. Put another way, this surplus of consumer goods, including food, is needed to make investment possible by supporting the producers of investment goods. Underconsumption is not a problem in underdeveloped countries: on the contrary.

The model, moreover, fails to take account of foreign markets. If the output of new investment cannot be sold at home, it may, in certain circumstances, be marketed abroad.

The more fundamental difficulties with Nurkse's model, however, as it relates to separate consumer-goods industries, are first, it ignores price elasticity which may be fairly high in one or more products because of existing producers; second, it pays no attention to the possibility of starting with cost reductions instead of with new industries. On a practical basis, if it were true that one had to start everywhere before one could start anywhere, it would be necessary to abandon all hope of development, since the capital requirements necessary to do everything at once are beyond all dream of realization.

Suppose the new investment occurs in a good where existing consumption takes place on a substantial scale from high-cost sources. Room will be made for the investment by displacing other producers. Technological and transitional unemployment will result. If any and

[10] R. Nurkse, *Problems of Capital Formation in Underdeveloped Countries,* Basil Blackwell & Mott, Ltd., Oxford, 1953, pp. 11ff.

all unemployment are ruled out by hypothesis or political restraint on the solution to the problem, Nurkse's model may be applicable again, and no investment in any single industry can be made. But under more normal circumstances, existing resources are displaced in the market by new investments at the same time that real income is increased generally throughout the system by the resulting lower prices. This increased income, if saved, holds out the possibility of expansion in investment industries and the transfer of the displaced resources thither. If spent in accordance with the income-elasticities, it creates further employment opportunities in those industries. When the displaced resources have found new employment in industries as dictated by the income-elasticities, the result is balanced growth. But it is not necessary in this, the normal case, to undertake simultaneous investment everywhere at once.

As an alternative to the foregoing case of a single investment in an existing industry, there is the possibility of cost reduction in general. Assume full employment, and balanced expenditure and production by industries: a cost-reducing innovation occurs, or a decline in the interest rate. (Assume the latter.) It now becomes profitable to expand output in a variety of industries, but particularly in those which use capital in substantial amounts. This expansion takes place. Where demand is price-inelastic, this expansion will go only a limited distance, lowering price and increasing consumers' real income. Where demand is price-elastic because of competition of existing production, production will be expanded, to raise producers' real incomes, rendering some resources unemployed (as in the example in the previous paragraph). Incomes are raised, however, and will be spent or saved, whether one starts with an increase in demand, a single new investment, or a reduction in costs.

It remains true, however, that it would be foolhardy to undertake a substantial investment in an income-elastic and high-standard-of-living item—automobiles, refrigerators, electrical equipment—in a poor country. There will, nonetheless, always be some industries which offer investment opportunities which can be taken up one at a time.

BALANCE BY SECTORS

When consumer-goods and investment industries are aggregated horizontally into sectors, particularly industry and agriculture, a large-scale program of investment in one sector which is out of line with the income elasticity of demand may put too great a burden on the price system. Suppose the income-elasticity of demand for food is still very high. To undertake investment in industry, possibly with resources taken from agriculture, will increase the demand for food while reducing the supply; increase the supply of industrial products when the income-elasticity of demand for them is low. The price of food rises relative to that of industrial products. If the economy is an open one, the terms of trade may be held steady by imports of food and exports of industrial products. This possibility is discussed in Chapter 14. In a closed economy, however, the rise in agricultural prices may not produce any more food; the fall in industrial prices may not tempt farmers to buy more consumer goods (a restatement of what has just been said). In these circumstances, it would have been more appropriate to increase investment in food along with that in industry, so that additional food would have been forthcoming to hold the terms of trade steady.

A special and particularly difficult example of this sectoral problem is furnished by those instances in which the attempt is made to use the disguised unemployed from agricultural areas for purposes of investment in other sectors. If the marginal productivity of these workers in agriculture has been zero or close to it, removing them from the land raises per capita income in the agricultural sector. Output is unchanged, but it is shared by fewer people. If the increased per capita income of farmers is spent now on the goods newly produced by the previously unemployed workers, these latter will be able to buy food, as the surplus food on the farms is sold for cash. Their only gain is the dubious one of becoming self-supporting. They eat as before, but now are obliged to work for it.

On the other hand, if the farmers decide that they would like to use their additional income to increase their consumption of food, i.e., have a high income-elasticity for food, the formerly unemployed do not even do this well. Their appetites may grow because of working, but less food is available to them. (It is assumed that a change in the terms of trade between food and industrial output does not correct the situation through producing increased offers of food and bids for industrial products. It may in fact make it worse by increasing still further the incomes of peasants, and lowering those of pre-existing industrial workers.) The disguised unemployed were better off when they lived on the farm. There they had a seat at the table and received transfers of income in kind from the producers, or the work was spread evenly so that there was underemployment rather than disguised unemployment. Once they leave the farm, however, and are put to work in industry, the lack of balance in the new output is compounded by the distributional problem of ensuring that they eat regularly.

Other means are available, of course, than simply balancing output by stepping up agricultural investment. One remedy is reliance on foreign trade to hold prices steady—exporting industrial products and importing food. This was the method followed by Britain in the nineteenth century. Another is to hire the disguised unemployed for governmental investment and to levy on the agricultural sector the taxes to pay them. This appears to have been the traditional Chinese method, developed still further by Mao-Tse Tung, despite his insistence that the revolution is in the name of the peasants. It was also used in Japan where the big campaign to increase agricultural productivity was accompanied by a 3 per cent land tax, payable in money, which provided 65 to 80 per cent of government revenue in the 1870s and required the farmer to use 25 to 30 per cent of the proceeds of his crop to pay his taxes.[11] Finally, there is the Soviet (and Communist Chinese) technique of limiting investment in agriculture to tractors, and attempting to achieve the bulk of the increased productivity in agriculture needed to hold steady the terms of trade between agriculture and industry by a reorganization of production methods, and principally the substitution of large-scale farming for small. The purpose of the collective farm was partly to increase output but also to limit consumption in the agricultural sector.

The distributional problem of bringing food to workers moved off the farm from disguised unemployment may be analytically separated from the question of the income-elasticity for the outputs of the various sectors. There is a distribution problem, even where there is no increase in output in any sector, but agricultural workers of low or zero productivity are shifted to new locations; the old arrangements under which they were fed by transfers no longer hold. But considerations of distribution and income-elasticity can merge, as when the previously unemployed or underemployed workers are set to producing consumption goods for which the demand of the farmers turns out to be income-inelastic. To the extent that the two problems are separate, however, it is well to recall that the distributional question can be handled by taxes and transfers, and does not of itself require that planning new investment with underemployed workers from agriculture be limited to high income-elastic industries.

[11] See E. H. Norman, *Japan's Emergence as a Modern State*, Institute of Pacific Relations, New York, 1940, pp. 77, 143. For an account of the effort to increase agricultural productivity, see B. F. Johnston, "Agricultural Productivity and Economic Development in Japan," *Journal of Political Economy*, December, 1951, pp. 498–513.

BALANCE AND THE PRICE SYSTEM

Emphasis on balance by sectors or by industries of final consumption implies that consumption paths are fixed as income increases, without reference to the relative prices of consumption goods or to the distribution of income. It assumes that a change in the terms of trade between foodstuffs and industrial commodities will change neither patterns of consumption nor the allocation of resources on the supply side. Price elasticities are close to zero.

If this is an accurate description of the price system in underdeveloped countries, it is true that one should disregard the signals transmitted by present prices, and attempt to balance output by reference to existing knowledge of income-elasticities, in which price can be ignored. With elasticities low, present prices are no indication of what future prices will be, when demand has been changed by the growth of income, and its redistribution, and supply altered by resource reallocation. Present prices, in short, are no indication of prospective prices, and cannot serve as a guide to investment decisions. The marginal efficiency of capital in various uses calculated from present prices must be disregarded, since it will be substantially altered by small changes in demand or supply, which will entail large changes in price. The allocation of resources, and particularly of increments of capital, must then be guided by the dictates of balance.[12]

If, on the other hand, there is responsiveness to price, more attention can be paid to shortages as revealed by current high prices. Prices will not change a great deal as a result of increments and decrements in demand and supply. It then becomes possible to calculate investment criteria not on the basis of sectoral balance, but in terms of the marginal efficiency of capital in various uses, regardless of sector. Any diversion in the composition of the increments in production from

[12] For an interesting example under planning, see the interview with Oskar Lang of the Polish State Planning Commission in the *New York Times*, July 18, 1956: "Professor Lange gave a frank review of the shortcomings of the First Five-Year Plan. He said that the plan had been 'basically carried out' with the development of heavy industry but not with the expected rise in living standards. This he attributed to the lag in the development of agriculture and of smaller industries and handicrafts.

"'Disproportions,' he said, 'have developed between agriculture and industry, between investment in fixed capital and availability of raw materials. Owing to a shortage of the latter, fixed capital investments have not been fully utilized,' he continued.

"Dr. Lange noted that there had also been a lack of balance between quality and quantity . . . . "

The entire interview, too long to be reproduced here, is worth reading as an indication of the problems of planning for development.

that dictated by income-elasticities of demand will be offset by shifts in consumption and production brought about by the price system.

This seems to be the implication of Rostow's remark that when economic growth is blocked by the "propensities," i.e., when the social and cultural conditions of growth have not been met, "concentrated action is inappropriate,"[13] i.e., an investment program for a stagnant economy should be balanced. The bulk of Rostow's paper, however, is designed to emphasize strategic sectors of economic development in which concentrated investment and other inputs lead to rapid growth. He makes a distinction between primary growth and other sectors. The former is stimulated by increases in demand perhaps, but also frequently by innovations. A rapid rate of output expansion requires the parallel growth of "supplementary growth sectors," needed to supply the intermediate products and factor inputs for the primary sector. Finally, the increase in income produced by these sectors spills over into derived-growth sectors, selected by the dictates of income-elasticity. This pattern, Rostow believes, fits the experience of Western Europe and the United States—first, the cotton-textile industry in Britain, and then railroads, steel, electric power, chemicals, and automobiles have been the prime stimulant of growth.[14] This pattern, moreover, is sharply at variance with the requirement of balance as the secret of most development problems.

Singer suggests a compromise between balance and priorities.[15] One should look not to industry or agriculture as entire sectors, but to separate capital-scarce projects in each. He suggests that the criterion for investment should be projects with a high marginal efficiency of capital in whatever sector. His analysis contains a hint that industry will be favored as a whole in densely populated countries, and agriculture where land is abundant. This is because where land is scarce, investment in agriculture requires enormous amounts of capital for such projects as irrigation, whereas industry offers opportunity for investment in a plethora of capital-scarce, labor-intensive projects in industry (though not in cities). Where population is relatively sparse and land abundant, on the other hand, high returns to capital are likely to be available in agriculture.

But this compromise at basis rests on the assumption that prices will not change in a very wide range, i.e., that price elasticities are greater

[13] W. W. Rostow, "Trends in the Allocation of Resources in Secular Growth," in L. H. Dupriez (ed.), *Economic Progress,* Institut de Recherches Économiques et Sociales, Louvain, 1955, p. 382.

[14] *Ibid.*

[15] H. W. Singer, "Problems of Industrialization of Underdeveloped Countries," in Dupriez (ed.), *op. cit.,* pp. 171–192.

than zero, and that the marginal efficiency of capital calculated on the basis of, say, the discounted value of the stream of benefits, less the discounted value of the cost of other inputs, has a sufficient basis in forecast prices to be meaningful. It is accordingly a vote for priorities and against balance. If price elasticities are close to zero, on the other hand, it will be impossible to forecast prices and hence the value of benefits, except within a wide range of error.

If one had complete knowledge of all aspects of the economy—price elasticities, income-elasticities, capital/output ratios, marginal efficiencies, etc.—the distinction between balance and priorities would fade into nothing. One could feed the information to a computer, give it a few additional instructions as to what to maximize, e.g., output or employment, indicate what income distribution was wanted from the welfare point of view, and the machine would produce a balanced program of investment priorities. Information, however, is woefully incomplete. In particular, it is difficult or impossible in a closed system to forecast price changes when the elasticities are low. Accordingly, it is necessary to decide how much to rely on prices and how far to assume that the price system is ineffective so that the planning authority must ensure that the economy will produce what is demanded at whatever prices. If the price system works to an extent, investment can concentrate on the most profitable enterprises and expect the trimming and balancing to be undertaken by the economy itself. If not, the plan itself must provide balance.

BOTTLENECKS

Hirschman's view, that bottlenecks are obvious in a developing economy, has already been mentioned. A bottleneck can perhaps be defined as a shortage which the price system is not remedying. The case for balanced growth assumes that bottlenecks are fairly evenly spread throughout the economy, that to break one would advance the economy only a short distance before a new one was encountered, and that bottlenecks must therefore be attacked on a broad front. Support of investment priorities rests implicitly on a different view of bottlenecks, that these bind deeply but are widely spaced. After breaking through a bottleneck, the economy will develop momentum of its own which will carry it a considerable distance until the next one is encountered. Incapacity to forecast leaves the economist with little knowledge of the form the next bottleneck is likely to take. Accordingly, it is appropriate to take on current bottlenecks, one by one, as they appear. A bottleneck is recognizable either because of a shortage at existing prices or a high price and high quasi rents for the limited factors engaged in its output. New investment is needed where capital earns the highest return, or where shortages at existing prices are the most serious.

GROWING POINTS

A special form of the belief in priorities emphasizes *growing points*, or investment projects which have a high potential for development because their effects ramify in a wide area. A search of the literature on development reveals a wide use of the term growing points, which I have traced back to A. G. B. Fisher,[16] but never a definition. It may be associated with external economies and particularly the impact of industrial areas in training labor, agglomerating markets, etc. It may be related to bottlenecks, although the concept is less one of breaking through a restraint than of fastening on something which will give a forward impetus. To the extent that importance is attached to growing points, however, a clear case can be made for priorities, rather than balance.

In the Plan Chillan in Chile, 70 per cent of the technical assistance rendered to that country under United States bilateral technical assistance is being concentrated in one region. The pamphlet of the National Planning Association describing this rather primly states: "The advantages of dispersing bilateral programs and projects throughout a country must be weighed against those of concentration within a more limited area."[17] A similar view was expressed by Winfield in discussing the introduction of Western medicine into China. He suggested that, instead of applying the available resources at the points in the system where the most lives could be saved—probably delivery of infants with a limited amount of prenatal care—more progress could be made faster over the long run by bringing public health and hygiene in depth to a limited number of Chinese women who would be invited to undertake an extensive program of prenatal instruction, followed by a month or more of hospital care and instruction in infant health care and feeding.[18]

In my own view, the two major growing points, and possibly, though not necessarily, the major bottlenecks of an economy, are transport (and communications) and education. Some part of the gain is external economies, pure and simple. But more is likely to be the

[16] Production: Primary, Secondary and Tertiary," *Economic Record*, June, 1939, pp. 24–38.

[17] "Administration of Bilateral Technical Cooperation," National Planning Association, Washington, January, 1956, p. 15.

[18] G. M. Winfield, *China: The Land and the People*, William Sloane Associates, New York, 1948, chap. XIV, esp. pp. 344ff.

joining of markets, the development of a distribution system, and the spread of communication with its impetus to change in the social structure, which causes development to become a self-sustaining, cumulative process. In a stagnant economy there may be as much need for priorities as in a growing one, where bottleneck breaking is called for. Priority should be given to those industries which lend themselves to classification as growing points, since they have capacity for training and reshaping the society in such a way as to make it develop itself.

It is perhaps unnecessary to add that the distinction between investment for further production and investment for direct consumption of the output is appropriate here. Education for an appreciation of philosophy or literature falls into the second category and is not regarded as a growing point. The same strictures apply to personal travel, though this has value in fusing the larger social unit so as to make the price system more effective in goods and factor markets—and especially to unduly luxurious forms of transport, such as the Venezuelan six-lane divided highway with a limit of 5 per cent grade between Caracas and the port. Making low the mountain and hill and exalting the valley is a capital-intensive occupation. As such it is barely appropriate to rich societies which put high values on timesaving and on individual life (to the limited extent that these highways are in fact safer) and in which capital is cheap. For underdeveloped countries, roads can more properly follow the contours.

Cities typically become growing points in a physical sense. They train entrepreneurs and laborers; they make beginnings of occupational mobility; markets cluster in them; communication spreads, and ideas disseminate.

Emphasis on growing points raises complex questions. Should the investment program back an area where progress is being made, or is it necessary to get a stagnant area to move? The answer in theory, which is difficult to apply in actuality, is that effort should be concentrated on the moving program if in fact the stimulus will spread regionally, whereas if the other areas are blocked, stagnant, and impervious to the stimulation from economic advance in neighboring regions, balance is called for.

THE SHAPE OF INVESTMENT PROGRAMS

Comparison of investment programs in given countries is difficult because of differences in definition and overlapping of categories.

Some programs refer to the public sector only; some to investment as a whole; public utilities may include railroads, or they may not, etc. It may nonetheless be useful to glance at the composition of a variety of recent programs, as set forth in Table 9.1. Some of these percentages are produced from mission surveys of the International Bank for Reconstruction and Development (IBRD); some have emerged from five-year plans. None is accurate within a few per cent because of uncertainty as to the whole and the definition of the part. The divergence among countries, however, is not without interest.

The sharpest distinction perhaps is that which runs between Red China and the Joint Brazilian-American Commission Plan of 1954, which relies on private enterprise. The high figures for transport and power in Brazil, and the low investment in everything else, are results of the private enterprise system, operating both in agriculture and in industry, the land-intensive, labor-scarce structure of the economy, and the fact that development is under way. In this circumstance, it is clear that transport and power are the main bottlenecks, and that bottleneck breaking, plus restraint of inflation, constitute the formula for development.

In stagnant economies, with heavy population/land ratios, the interesting contrast runs between the current Chinese Five-Year Plan and the Indian first Five-Year Plan, and between the first and second Indian plans.[19] Much has been made of the Indian-Chinese contrast, with the former concentrating on agriculture, the latter on industry. In the first Five-Year Plan, India stood for balance; China for skewed emphasis on heavy industry. In the second Five-Year Plan, announced in 1955, India shifted the emphasis away from agriculture and irrigation in favor of industry and mining. The proportion of industry and mining was still fairly small—19 per cent—compared with 58 per cent for the Red China program or even the 25 per cent allocated to this field in Indonesia; but it is concentrated on heavy, rather than light, industry and in the more capital-intensive branches such as steel and chemicals.

Which is the more certain road to development? Time will give a general-equilibrium answer in which other factors beside the isolated variables will intervene to shape the outcome. If economic growth is thought of as a self-sustaining process, there is little doubt that investment in transport, communication, and education have most to do with changing people—which is likely to be the critical ingredient in the growth process. If development is regarded, however, not as a

[19] See W. Malenbaum, "India and China: Development Contrasts," *Journal of Political Economy*, February, 1956, pp. 1–24.

Table 9.1. Rough Percentage Breakdown of Public Investment under Government Plans

	Nicaragua	Guatemala	Colombia	Jamaica	Surinam	Iraq	Turkey	Ceylon	Ceylon	Nigeria	Brazil	Brazil	India	India	Pakistan	Indonesia	China
	IBRD	IBRD	IBRD	IBRD	IBRD	IBRD	IBRD	IBRD	1955	IBRD	SALTE 1949	1954	1951	1956	1956	1956	1952
	1	2	3	4	5	6	7	8	9	10	11	12	13	14	15	16	17
Agriculture	36	16	11	41	53	37	15	25	36	18	20	[a]	16[b]	12[b]	11	16	17
Irrigation	}	}											17	9	32[d]	13[c]	} 8
Transportation	30	44	39	6	16	18	36	26	} 33	46	44	61	} 24	29	20	25[d]	19
Communications	2	5	3				4	7								25	
Public works			14			15	16	12									
Power	6	20	16	16	3	22	12	5	5	12	18	33	11	9	13[e]	25	58
Industry and mining	5			16	11		15	3				[a]	7	19	10		
Housing and building	16	14	} 18	16	14	3		11		13	14		23	} 20	4	25	
Health	}	}		} 21		4		10	16	8			}		7	} 12	
Education	6					1	4	1									
Administration													2	2			
Miscellaneous					3					3	4	6[a]		2	4		15

[a] Included under miscellaneous.
[b] Including community development.
[c] Including community development and transmigration.
[d] Irrigation and power included under irrigation.
[e] Research undertaken for industry.

SOURCES: Columns 1 to 8 from J. J. Spengler, "IBRD Mission Growth Theory," *American Economic Review, Papers and Proceedings,* May, 1954, p. 591.

9. *The Times,* Aug. 5, 1955.

10. IBRD, *Economic Development of Nigeria,* Johns Hopkins University Press, Baltimore, 1953.

11. George Wythe, *Brazil, an Expanding Economy,* The Twentieth Century Fund, New York, 1949, p. 353.

12. Joint Brazil–United States Economic Development Commission, *The Development of Brazil,* Institute of Inter-American Affairs, Washington, 1954, p. 79.

13, 14. *The Asian Recorder,* 1956, p. 658.

15. Government of Pakistan, Planning Board, *The First Five-Year Plan, 1955–60* (Karachi, Manager of Publications, 1956), p. 9.

16. Speech of Dr. Ali Budiardjo, Deputy Director General, National Planning Bureau, Indonesia, at MIT, Dec. 14, 1955.

17. W. Malenbaum, "India and China: Development Contrasts," *Journal of Political Economy,* February, 1956, p. 13.

process but as a condition, the Soviet and Chinese method of building steel to make more steel to make more steel may have something to recommend it. Capital formation spreads fastest in this fashion, provided the planning is careful, and provided the lack of proportionality between output and consumer demand can be repressed in some fashion. But the possibility that it cannot calls for balance, unless indeed it calls for regarding economic growth as a self-cumulative process again. Among the three attitudes, assuming everything else equal, emphasis on balance advances the claim for investment of agriculture; emphasis on building a developed economy calls for industry and mining; emphasis on the process of growth, for transport and education.

BALANCE VERSUS PRIORITIES

As a warning against large-scale investment in industry, and the kinds of imbalance problems which seem to have been met in the Soviet Union, Poland, and Yugoslavia, balance has much to recommend it. Imbalance had been carried so far in Yugoslavia, it seems, that disguised unemployment appeared in industry and land became idle in the countryside.[20] In a stagnant economy, with the price system not functioning effectively, and without access to foreign outlets for excess production, or foreign sources of supply for income-elastic products of consumption as income grows, balance may be a vital consideration.

But balance is a most discouraging operational slogan. To say that one cannot do anything until one can do everything, or that economic development can be started only on a broad front, or in almost all sectors and subsectors, is to suggest that it is well-nigh hopeless. The administrative machinery will be overloaded. Mistakes will be made.

On an earlier occasion I suggested that national character made the British emphasize a broad attack, Americans the concentrated thrust.[21] During the war, in the aerial bombardment of Germany, strategies divided along national lines in this way; the British were for destroying cities or, later, railroad centers, while the United States forces were interested in a separate industry, like aircraft or oil, and in halting transport by destroying a selected system of railroad bridges. After the

[20] See, among other accounts in the press, "Reversal by Tito on Economy Seen," *New York Times*, Jan. 21, 1956. Apparently the marginal product of some industrial workers sank to zero: "Civil engineering enterprises in Bosnia and Herzegovina decided recently to reduce their industrial work force by 30 to 35 per cent. About 15,000 workers were transferred to villages for employment in agriculture. It was asserted that production would not be influenced."
[21] *Review of Economics and Statistics*, November, 1952, pp. 391–394.

war, in the reconstruction of Germany (before monetary reform, when the issue solved itself), the British authorities wanted to allocate coal and building materials thinly over the economy as a whole, the United States to establish overriding priorities to get coal, which would be used to get more coal, and more coal, until the economy was pulled to its feet.

In the present debate, however, national lines seem no longer to apply. In growing economies, moreover, or planned economies with perfect knowledge, the dispute between skewed investment, balance, or priorities to investments which change people does not arise. But in the ordinary case, where knowledge is far from perfect, and it is not clear whether the economy is advancing or not, so slow is the rate of progress, my own predilection for transport and education as top priorities rests on the belief, or possibly the feeling, that the road to balance is through priorities for investments which change people. Balance, in this view, can be more surely achieved by concentrating on those places which will let the energy of the society achieve it for itself.

But it is necessary to return to investment criteria. Assuming that the overriding consideration is increased output at the fastest possible pace, and not some maximum employment or some redistribution of income which accords with welfare, resources should be invested where they will earn the highest possible return, direct and indirect, including imputed external economies and correcting where necessary for differences between private and social costs. This means equalizing the return in various occupations for each factor. The return, of course, is the discounted present value of future output less the discounted present value of the future cost of other inputs. If the marginal social return of labor and all other inputs is zero, the total value of output can be imputed to capital, and it will be appropriate to use the capital/output ratio instead of the marginal efficiency of capital, or rather as a measure of the marginal efficiency of capital, since in these circumstances they are identical.

The proponent of skewed investment may or may not go through this process. Sometimes his instinct merely tells him that the rapid expansion of heavy industry is the road to development. Sometimes he even entertains noneconomic thoughts, such as the notion that prestige in the world is distributed in accordance with heavy industrial capacity.

The proponent of balance and the proponent of priorities for transport and education basically differ in what they think the outcome of the examination will be. Where there are agricultural investments of high payout—particularly in research, in demonstration, in storage and marketing facilities—an economist urging priorities in transport would suggest that they by all means be included in the program. His essential feeling in the matter, however, is that the more interesting external economies and opportunities, particularly those of reshaping behavior in ways which will make it advance development, but which are perhaps hard to incorporate in the calculation of extra benefits, will lie in economic overhead capital. To devote large amounts of scarce capital to capital-intensive projects such as irrigation dams, in order to produce more food, to prevent a prospective change in price some distance in the future, strikes him as risky. He would rather bet his chips on so altering the character of people and establishing institutions that, if this rise in price occurred, the shifting of consumption and the reallocation of resources would restore equilibrium. And in this chapter he gets the last word.

CHAPTER 10 *Labor-Intensive Versus Up-To-Date Technology*

FACTOR PROPORTIONS

Economic development through time involves an increase in the capital/labor ratio and permits capital deepening. A significant question, over which some dispute has arisen in economic discussion, is whether a developing country should use the technology appropriate to its existing factor proportions, including especially its capital/labor ratio, or whether it should anticipate the relative growth of capital and begin the use of capital-intensive methods of production before its capital endowment is really suitable for this. In particular, the question is whether countries at early stages of development, with capital scarce and often with labor abundant, should take advantage of the modern technology developed by advanced countries, where capital is abundant and labor scarce, or whether they should devise a technology of their own or use production methods which are obsolete in countries abroad.

The dispute has many facets. It can be argued on a priori grounds, by appeals to history, and by reference to empirical data and current practice.

The theoretical argument for using a technology appropriate to existing factor proportions has been tartly put by Hayek:[1]

I am profoundly convinced that we should be doing more good to the underdeveloped countries if we succeeded in spreading the understanding

[1] F. A. Hayek, comment on S. Kuznets, "Toward a Theory of Economic Growth," in R. Lekachman (ed.), *National Policy for Economic Welfare at Home and Abroad,* Doubleday & Company, New York, 1955, p. 89.

of elementary economics than by elaborating sophisticated theories of economic growth. If, for example, we could merely gain understanding of the simple and obvious fact that a country which cannot hope to reach within foreseeable time a capital supply equal per head to that of the United States will not use its limited resources best by imitating American production techniques, but ought to develop techniques appropriate to a thinner and wider spreading of the available capital . . .

This is evidently a static argument. Maximization of the return on capital is achieved by equalizing its return in every use. If there are two possible ways to produce a commodity, represented by production functions in Figure 10.1, of which R_1, R_2, R_3, and R_4 are the isoquants

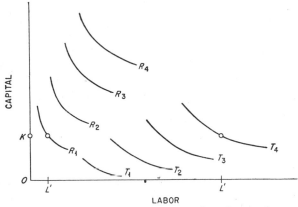

Figure 10.1. Alternative technological means of producing the same good.

of one, and T_1, T_2, T_3, and T_4 are the isoquants of the other, and $R_1 = T_1$, $R_2 = T_2$, etc., a country with OK capital and OL' labor would do well to use the process represented by T. To use the capital-intentive method R would reduce output from T_4 (or R_4) to R_1 and would leave unemployed at positive wages $L - L'$ of labor.

On this showing, much of the adoption of modern technology is mere demonstration effect on the side of production, the attempt to run before one can walk. Such technology wastes capital, since it uses it too intensively in a narrow sector, and requires ignoring opportunities for profitable investment. If a bulldozer costs $5,000 and shovels $2.50 each, if 1,500 men can shovel in a day as much as one man can move with a bulldozer, and if manpower is abundant, capital can be saved by buying $3,750 worth of shovels, and disguised or open unemployment avoided.

Kuznets' objection to Hayek's argument ran largely along empirical lines, discussed below.[2] But a theoretical argument may be made against it. For one thing, capital-saving technology may involve substantial innovations of a neutral variety. Suppose, for example, that isoquant R_1 was equivalent in terms of output not to T_1, but to T_5 or T_6 (not shown). To change from T_4 to R_1 would disemploy some labor but increase over-all output.

In dynamic terms, Bruton has suggested that the industries which embody external economies are frequently capital-intensive. These capital-intensive investments must be undertaken before one can take advantage of opportunities for investment in labor-intensive industries. When industries are linked together in complementary interacting fashion, the capital intensity of a single industry is not an appropriate index of its suitability for investment until one has traced through and imputed to it its total return, with all the difficulties this involves.[3] This is only mildly persuasive, however, and appears to concede that in industries producing final output, a country should on theoretical grounds adopt the technology appropriate to its factor proportions after subtraction of those considerable lumps of capital needed for the overhead industries. This article further implies that labor productivity is higher in capital-intensive than in labor-intensive industries, and that this is an argument for the former. But this is not true with a competitive market for labor; nor, if true, is it relevant. The investment criterion is net capital productivity or gross, if labor is redundant.

Another quasi economic and institutional argument relates to savings. It is believed that capital-intensive industries are more effective producers of savings than labor-intensive, and hence likely to speed development faster despite a possibly lower static level of output.[4] To the extent that rising and ambitious entrepreneurs are found in new industries, and these are capital intensive, there may be something to

[2] "Brief consideration suggests a much less certain diagnosis. The United States technique may be particularly well adapted to the use of large numbers of workers with relatively low levels of individual skills, unlike the less capital-intensive technologies of some European countries. American machinery may be more suitable because of an assured supply of spare parts and better servicing arrangements. In short, the validity of the principle is contingent upon a large number of items impounded in *ceteris paribus,* many of which are not casual disturbances but are integrally connected with processes of economic growth." Kuznets, *op. cit.,* p. 98.

[3] H. J. Bruton, "Growth Models and Underdeveloped Countries," *Journal of Political Economy,* August, 1955, pp. 322–336.

[4] W. Galenson and H. Leibenstein, "Investment Criteria, Productivity and Economic Development," *Quarterly Journal of Economics,* August, 1955, pp. 343–370.

it. There are no data to support or deny the assertion. But it is not compelling.

The theoretical case which an economic historian such as Gerschenkron has in mind urges the use of the latest technology in general:[5]

Industrialization always seemed the more promising the greater the backlog of technological innovations which the backward country could take over from the more advanced country. Borrowed technology, so much and so rightly stressed by Veblen, was one of the primary factors assuring a high speed of development in a backward country entering the stage of industrialization . . . .

. . . to the extent that industrialization took place, it was largely by application of the most modern and efficient techniques that backward countries could hope to achieve success . . . . The advantages inherent in the use of technologically superior equipment were not counteracted but enhanced by its labor-saving effect.

Gerschenkron uses in part an argument discussed below, that abundant labor may be expensive rather than cheap in underdeveloped countries. But his argument appears to rest mainly on growing points. He points out that growth in countries of Europe embarking on industrialization frequently took place in those industries where technological progress has been the most rapid. The use of modern technology in a limited and rapidly moving primary sector of the economy, to use Rostow's phrase, has dynamic effects in attracting entrepreneurs, developing profits from which savings produced capital, and training labor. Once development is under way, as a result of the removal of large social blocks, the existence of sufficient resources, and presumably some capital formation, most rapid progress is made by using late technology.

We shall suggest below that the crux of the question is the capacity to distinguish between two situations, of very little objective difference. In one, modern technology will lead to rapid growth, and constitute an effective short cut. In the other, the use of the latest technology fails to produce rapid development and creates no capital for use in other occupations which have been rationed on capital to make possible the capital-intensive investment. In the latter situation, an economy should make haste slowly.

[5] A. Gerschenkron, "Economic Backwardness in Historical Perspective," in B. F. Hoselitz (ed.), *The Progress of Underdeveloped Areas*, University of Chicago Press, Chicago, 1952, pp. 6–7.

FACTOR PRICES AND FACTOR EFFICIENCY

An important element in the arguments of Kuznets and Gerschenkron in favor of modern technology in underdeveloped countries is that abundant labor may not be cheap labor. Two reasons may explain this. Labor may be low in price, but lower in efficiency. Or the price of labor may have been artificially bid up or raised by one or another means.

Low-priced labor may not be cheap because of malnutrition, incapacity to stand up to factory discipline, or high rates of absenteeism (possibly at a period of harvest or of religious festival). In many countries there may be not only a backward-bending supply curve of labor but also, in terms of costs, a forward-falling one, as higher wages enable a worker to raise his consumption to the physiological minimum needed for efficient factory work. But even where nutrition is not a problem, the uneducated, undisciplined worker will not be readily used in large-scale production with simple machinery, since his efficiency is too low to compensate for his low wages. In these circumstances there is an argument for laborsaving technology.

Saving one type of labor requires the assistance of another. The more automatic the machinery, the higher the training required of skilled maintenance staff, production engineers, etc. At low levels of training, and in the absence of capacity to recruit maintenance personnel abroad, neither labor-intensive nor laborsaving production may be possible.

It is possible to illustrate disparity between factor price and factor cost outside the field of labor. Hirschman calls attention to the fact that underdeveloped countries are weak on maintenance, and that it may be useful to invest in industries where maintenance is less necessary, or where failure to maintain becomes more immediately evident or carries with it a more obvious penalty. In Colombia, airplanes function better than railroads, which perform at a mediocre standard but above that of roads. The penalty for postponing maintenance of airplanes is dramatically evident. A highway engineer recommends using bituminous surfacing on low-traveled routes instead of dirt, because holes in the road would more quickly attract attention and maintenance and retreatment would be less long delayed.[6]

In addition to low price but lower efficiency, another obstacle to

[6] A. O. Hirschman, "Economics and Investment Planning: Reflections Based on Experience in Colombia," in *Investment Criteria and Economic Growth*, Massachusetts Institute of Technology, Center for International Studies, Cambridge, Mass., 1955, pp. 48–49.

labor-intensive technology is inefficient but high priced workers.
Where the demonstration effect has extended into the field of social
services and collective bargaining, the price of labor, including wages
and benefits, will be high despite low productivity. Italy provides an
example of this: small-scale industry must ignore the social security
system, with its heavy exactions in unemployment insurance, old-age
pensions, severance pay, etc., or be unable to function. Large-scale
industry can afford to hire labor, but the numbers are limited, and new
workers are hired with reluctance because of the difficulty of dis-
missing them should they not be needed. A labor-intensive industry
such as shipbuilding is priced out of the market and subsidized back
in again. The consequence is that there grow up, side by side, two
separate sets of factor proportions—one, a small-scale, labor-intensive
industry, in which employer and employee alike disregard the laws;
the other, a capital-intensive industry, where large amounts of capital
are combined with small amounts of labor, in some considerable part
due to the high price of the latter.

It has already been mentioned that trade union control in Cuba has
made labor costs very high in that country and has discouraged the
employment of redundant and seasonally available workers.

Even apart from social security and high wages, labor may be expensive in the domestic market because of domestic inflation, and
foreign capital equipment cheap because of the overvaluation of the
exchange. This combination in Israel gave entrepreneurs every incentive to substitute machinery for labor.[7]

The disparity between factor prices and factor efficiency may extend
beyond labor, and particularly into the field of capital. Capital is
frequently underpriced and overused, in a limited sector, with the
result that it is not available for high-earning occupations outside.
This may occur as a consequence of government concentration of investment in industry; but even where no government interference has
occurred, the capital market may be imperfect and split into segments
within which demand and supply for loanable funds yield different
rates of return. The credit system frequently slights agriculture and
small-scale industry. Or the noncompeting groups may be regional, as
the South in the United States before World War I and in southern
Italy.

It is sometimes argued that prices of factor inputs correctly reflect
factor efficiency, but that entrepreneurs adopt the wrong factor proportions because of their unwillingness or incapacity to maximize

[7] See M. E. Kreinin, "Controlled Inflation in Israel, 1949–1954," *Journal of
Political Economy*, April, 1956, p. 117.

their return. On occasion this may reflect ignorance, although competitive elements should ensure that a Darwinian survival value is attached to finding the right combination, if only by trial and error. At other times, however, it may reflect a more systematic bias, such as a predilection for modern laborsaving technology, despite cheap labor and expensive capital. If so, this is demonstration effect in production.[8]

Or factor prices in various parts of the economy fail to reflect social marginal product, even though they may accurately represent efficiency in the private sense. This was the basis for the Manoilescu recommendation of shifts of workers out of agriculture, where its private return overstated its social efficiency, into industry, where its social return was understated by the market.[9] Manoilescu failed to consider that the opposite was likely to be the case in the capital market, nor did he contemplate the possibility that the shift of labor into, and of capital out of, industry called for different sets of factor proportions in industry as well as in agriculture. He was, however, one of the first to recognize that different factor proportions, or rather different combinations of factors involving labor, might exist side by side in the same economy, and that this situation offered a potentiality for increasing output by factor redistribution. His interest was in increasing tariffs on industrial products to bring private marginal products more nearly into line with social, and to move labor from underemployment in agriculture into employment in industry. Like many who use the capital/output ratio as the criterion of investment, on the ground that the marginal productivity of labor is zero and the total value of the product can be imputed to capital, he worked only with labor, and appeared to assume a limitless supply of capital of zero marginal efficiency.

One final source of confusion arises with foreign investment. What are the relevant factor proportions, and hence technology—those of the country of origin of the capital, those where the investment is taking place, or those where land and labor of the latter are combined with the capital of the former? To the country in which investment is taking place, all but the second will involve factor proportions different from those of purely domestic industry; but for the investing firm or country, only factor proportions consonant with those of the

[8] A Chinese student has mentioned as an example of the demonstration effect in production, the building of two-story factories on cheap land to emulate foreign practices, and the purchase of the latest machinery in textiles while neglecting maintenance and repair. The Chinese source cited was dated June, 1937.

[9] See M. Manoilescu, *The Theory of Protection*, P. S. King & Staples, Ltd., London, 1932.

country of investment represent maximization of return. It is convenient to use the same technology as in the home country, and to pay high wages, despite the fact that labor is abundant. In addition to managerial inertia, it is possible to justify the practice in terms of earning good will in the local population. But this is not the outcome under competitive conditions, or conditions of short-run income maximization.

For the country of investment, capital invested in this way can be regarded as cheap because its opportunity cost may be zero. An oil company may put in a refinery, an aluminum company a reduction plant, a chemical company a fertilizer installation; but the alternative to these investments is no capital. If capital is available for a given project and for nothing else, its opportunity cost is zero, and from an economic point of view it may be properly used in most capital-intensive fashion. This is the basis for the original 1952 encouragement to the construction of hydroelectric installations of great capital intensity at Kariba in Northern Rhodesia, and of electric and aluminum installations on the lower Volta River on the Gold Coast.[10] With the increase in cost estimates of 60 per cent, and the necessity for the Gold Coast to invest its own savings in the project if it is to go through, the wisdom of such capital-intensive investment as aluminum becomes more debatable. Nonetheless, according to the *New York Times*, the Gold Coast appears to be prepared to "sacrifice other types of development to find the needed money."[11]

The result of the introduction of modern or even reasonably efficient technology in some cases may be to develop what has come to be called a dual economy, i.e., an economy with different marginal efficiencies of identical factors in different parts of the economy. Different factor proportions and equal marginal factor product can exist side by side, of course, if production functions have different shapes in different sectors and industries. But in dual economy the marginal efficiency of labor and capital will be different in different sectors,

[10] Hydroelectric power and alumina reduction are of course highly capital-intensive. Bauxite mining presumably could be undertaken on a labor-intensive or on a capital-intensive basis. In Jamaica three bauxite firms have $70 million of capital and only 3,000 workers, or a capital/labor ratio of some $23,000 per head.
  In the construction stages, hydroelectric dams and aluminum plants can be built with a high or a low capital/labor ratio, depending upon whether one uses modern construction equipment or not. In many parts of India highly labor-intensive methods are used. But where manpower is used for simple energy, in traditional methods of construction, the ramifying effects of training and discipline may not be large.
[11] "Cost Rise Perils African Project," *New York Times*, July 28, 1956.

different industries, and frequently, as the examples of native and plantation rubber and bananas show, in the same industry.

A dual society may be distinguished from a plural society or economy, and not in the numbers of different markets for identical factors. A plural economy is generally also a dual economy in the foregoing sense of having more than one factor market for a factor, but the differences in factor markets are based on race, such as characterize a plural society. The major literature in this field has developed over Indonesia.[12]

It is sometimes argued that the difficulty of a dual society is that, even where the gap is not based on a social difference, too wide a gap in the return to labor in the two-factor markets will paralyze rather than stimulate development. It is claimed, and denied, that high rates of wages paid by oil companies in Venezuela discourage work, thrift, and innovation. It is easier to take one's chances of getting a job with the oil company. Like speculative psychology in market economies, which undermines ambition to advance through socially productive channels, the modern sector of a dual economy may cause people to queue up for good jobs rather than demonstrate the advantages of capital accumulation and modern technology for diffusion throughout the society. Where the dual economy is also a plural society, more rigid barriers to enter the high-priced labor market are likely to be accompanied by less incentive to the lower-priced factor to contemplate change.

Apart from significant social influences, it seems likely that small differences in the spread of wage rates in a dual market may result in opposite effects—in one case, stimulating the lower-priced factor to catch up, in the other, leading it to sink back. The degree of stimulation arising from foreign investment is subject to influence through policy, as discussed below. But, just as the existence of a middle class stimulates social mobility through narrowing the gap between the aristocrats and the workers, giving the former somewhere to go short of sinking to the lowest class and the latter a steppingstone up, so a narrow gap in factor proportions between the leading and lagging sectors in development may stimulate growth, whereas too wide a gap, above a critical level, may slow it down. Research is needed to ascertain whether this is the case, and what the critical levels for stagnation or progress may be from country to country.

[12] See B. Higgins, "The 'Dualistic Theory' of Underdeveloped Areas," *Economic Development and Cultural Change,* January, 1956, pp. 99–115; J. H. Boeke, *Economics and Economic Policy in Dual Societies,* Institute of Pacific Relations, New York, 1953; and J. S. Furnivall, *Netherlands India, a Study of Plural Economy,* Cambridge University Press, London, 1939.

OBJECTIVE: OUTPUT OR EMPLOYMENT

When unemployment exists, disguised or obvious, the choice of factor proportions may be complicated by a confusion, or merging of objectives, between maximum rate of advance in output and maximum employment.[13] With constant returns to scale, two factors and one output, the problem does not arise: the maximum output can be obtained by using capital in such a way as to employ the most labor. But if there are variable returns, with two factors and one output, there may be a conflict, and with more than one output and external economies, there is almost certain to be one.

Increasing returns to scale from capital investment which involves capital deepening puts the problem for a single output. In two or more industries, investment in one may give more income, in the other, more employment. This may be true in each case, both directly and with external economies under which income and employment prospects created in other industries are imputed back to the original investment. In making these calculations the cost of distribution involved in getting consumption goods to the locus of the investment outlay should be taken into account. It may be that this cost would be borne by the workers in the form of higher prices of consumption goods than they anticipated when they accepted employment, or by the employing agency in the form of subsidies to commissariat or other means of distributing goods. As our discussion of planning balance emphasized, however, moving the under- or unemployed to new lines of work may give rise to substantial distributional costs.

Much depends on the nature of the unemployment and the long-run prospects of its correction. It is assumed that it is structural and arises from employing capital in part of the economy with a technology that requires capital/labor ratios which cannot be generalized. The range of choice includes capital deepening in the capital-intensive sector, capital widening which would enlarge that sector relative to the labor-intensive, and improving the capital/labor ratio in the labor-intensive sector. Which is undertaken may turn on whether the capital/labor ratio in the capital-intensive sector is one which would be too capital-intensive in any prospective pattern of the economy's development. In this situation, it makes little sense to widen or deepen capital in this sector, even if this should give greater output.

In the final analysis, the choice between maximum output and maximum employment is not one which the economist can make, although

[13] See R. S. Eckaus, "The Factor Proportions Problem in Underdeveloped Areas," *American Economic Review*, September, 1955, esp. p. 553.

he may be able to tell the political decision-makers how much of one must be given up for a fixed amount of the other. Where unemployment is destroying morale and undermining the society, a strong argument can be made for modifying the usual goal of economic development, which is highest possible output. But if the institutions of the society have adjusted themselves so as to make the problem uncritical, there may be much to be said for undertaking development first and solving the unemployment second.

Where employment becomes a primary and output a secondary objective, it is still necessary to use capital as efficiently as possible. The experience of the United States during the days of the Works Progress Administration has been studied in this connection, and demonstrates that the modifications in technology necessary to maximize employment may call for some significant large-scale units of capital which can be intensively used, such as the trucks to haul men and their shovels to work on the construction site.

COMMUNITY DEVELOPMENT AND COTTAGE INDUSTRY

One solution which compromises the objectives of employment and output is that of community development and cottage industry. This has been tried primarily in Southeast Asia, which is highly labor-intensive. The effort is made to keep underemployed workers in the village (and avoid the distribution problem), rather than transfer them to the city, but nonetheless to give them useful, labor-intensive tasks to perform. In community development the emphasis is on local public works, such as roads and schools. In some cases this is designed as a counterweight to seasonal unemployment in agriculture, and represents an introduction, or frequently an extension, of taxes in the form of services. Elsewhere an attempt is made to build a new community spirit and to let it choose the direction and character of the community works. Where the necessary community enthusiasm exists or can be developed, this sort of development has much to recommend it. It involves no fiscal or inflationary problems, since the investment and saving take place simultaneously. It invokes widespread local participation in a national movement, with the effects both of enlisting support and of training. And insofar as it concentrates on roads and schools, it contributes to the growth process at its core.[14]

[14] T. S. Simey, *Welfare and Planning in the West Indies,* Clarendon Press, Oxford, 1946, opposes reliance on any one social institution such as schools or orphanages, emphasizes the importance of local decisions on objectives of com-

Community development takes place outside the market. Cottage industry, on the other hand, represents production for the market which takes place in the village, instead of in the factory. Cottage industry represents a return to the putting-out system from which the factory originated, a system in Britain in the sixteenth and seventeenth centuries under which middlemen bought supplies and put them out to be worked up into yarn and cloth in cottages. The modern descendant of the putting-out system may be said to be the watch industry of Switzerland.[15] Here there are many small and highly specialized "factories" in mountain towns, which supply parts through highly organized markets to assemblers. This characterization, which has produced objection, may be somewhat exaggerated, but it serves to indicate the essence of the cottage system—small producing units and efficient distribution through organized markets and middlemen.

The most interesting and major issue over cottage industry is that in India. In the second Five-Year Plan, provision has been made for restraining factory production of cloth, through taxation, in order to enlarge the area of cottage production. It is pointed out by a distinguished Indian economist that capital investment runs 100,000 rupees (roughly $20,000) per person employed in the steel industry; about $4,000 to $5,000 in other heavy industries; $2,000 to $2,500 in consumer-goods factories; but only $120 to $140 per artisan family in cottage industry.[16] It is not clear whether this figure contemplates the investment before or after the introduction of the "Ambar Charkha" or improved hand-spinning wheel, with four spindles, recently invented by a follower of Gandhi who thought that the way of salvation for India lay through hand-woven textiles. This spinning wheel, now being tested under a pilot scheme and reported to cost $4.80, will, it is hoped, employ 300,000 to 2,500,000 Indians directly, and enlarge the scope of the hand-weaving industry from its present numbers of 2,000,000 to 2,500,000.[17]

In its early stages, and perhaps for all its life, the hand-spun and

---

munity effort, and warns that food, clothing, and shelter are the primary concerns of people (pp. 192, 200). "It is absolutely no use . . . providing educational services for adults whose chief thought is of food" (p. 92).

[15] *Processes and Problems of Industrialization,* United Nations, New York, 1955, p. 50, notes that Danish efficient small-scale industry evolves only a short distance from cottage industry.

[16] P. C. Mahalanobis, "Role of Household and Small Industries," *Indian Finance,* Sept. 24, 1955, p. 626.

[17] See "Spinning Wheel Splits India in Fiscal Struggle," *Christian Science Monitor,* Mar. 1, 1956; "Local Handicrafts Are Stressed in Indian and Israeli Economies," *New York Times,* Jan. 23, 1956.

woven cloth, khadi, will not be able to compete in price with the machine-made product. Moreover, its quality is uneven—something which makes it attractive as a luxury product, like the products of the handicraft industries of Europe—but which stands as an obstacle to its large-scale use as an intermediate product in, say, the clothing industry. Whether it will ultimately become inexpensive enough to compete with the machine product is doubtful. Mahalanobis envisages a gradual improvement of efficiency of home production through the spread of electricity, small motors, and efficient small machines. Meanwhile, factories would produce for export, but factories which are competitive with cottage industry in the home market would be subjected to production quotas or taxes. To make a place for cottage industry, factories have been limited to an output of 5 to 5.5 billion yards in the second Five-Year Plan, while the output of handlooms and small power looms is expected to rise from 1.6 billion yards to 3.2 billion.[18]

It would be possible to emphasize hand methods of production throughout industry insofar as this is technologically feasible. In the prevailing thought in India, however, capital-intensive efficient production is required for the capital-goods industries, and for export; but labor-intensive methods would be applied in the field of home consumption. This is contrived dual economy. It makes some sense if there is an initial division of capital between that for capital-goods industries, for use in further expansion of capital, and a smaller sum available for home production, combined with a decision to employ only "modern technology" in the capital-goods industries and a desire for optimum employment in consumption goods. The capital-goods industries are important. No risks can be taken with them. If there is any risk in adopting a labor-intensive technology for the sake of employment and to reduce the amount of building needed in cities, by all means let such risk be taken in the area of consumption.

MODERN TECHNOLOGY

The observation has frequently been made that the technology developed in the most advanced countries is not suited to the factor proportions of the underdeveloped. By the time a country is devel-

[18] It should be noted that labor in the factory textile industry is strongly opposed to the rationalization of the industry with more laborsaving machinery, despite the fact that many industrialists and some economists believe that this is necessary if India is going to maintain its recently won place in the export market. See C. A. Myers, "Labour Problems of Rationalization: The Experience of India," in *International Labour Review*, January, 1956, pp. 1–20.

oped, its capital/labor ratio means that capital is cheap and labor expensive, and its inventions and innovations proceed in an awareness of this situation.[19] But laborsaving, capital-using inventions are not appropriate to the factor proportions of underdeveloped countries. They have the choice of ignoring this fact, adopting an obsolete technology already abandoned in the leading country, or devising a new capital-saving, labor-using technology of their own.

In some areas obsolete technologies are used, frequently coupled, indeed, with obsolete equipment. The Japanese textile industry grew to power on secondhand British machines; the Burmese industry has had a faltering start after World War II with the most modern. Kaiser-Frazer automotive equipment dismantled in Willow Run has been set up in Tel Aviv and in Argentina.

But the availability of obsolescent equipment at low prices is not the essence. Obsolete techniques are less capital-intensive. Even if the equipment must be constructed *de novo*, it will frequently pay to do so rather than to buy the latest product on the market. The technique is tested, even though there may be some difficulty in finding manufacturers with experience in producing the equipment. A current example is the windmill, long abandoned for pumping water and generating electricity in the United States and Western Europe, but under current study for adoption in India in the second Five-Year Plan. In Iran a jump has been made straight to diesels from pumping with bullocks and the water wheel. The cheapness of fuel may justify this decision, and possibly the absence of winds of the requisite velocity. An imported windmill now costs $600 to $800 in India. According to the newspaper account, it would be necessary to cut this by two-thirds by the use of bamboo and local woods.[20]

The notion that underdeveloped countries should fashion their own technology has been widely advocated, and widely condemned. The introduction of new techniques is risky, and underdeveloped countries cannot afford to take the risks. As the quotation from Kuznets, page 170 above, indicates, the user would not be assured of parts and servicing arrangements. More significant, however, is whether the actual performance of the machine bears out the promise of pilot studies. The experimentation necessary to develop a process through its *Kinderkrankheiten* (teething troubles) is appropriate to a very large company

---

[19] W. Fellner seems to feel that there is something fortuitous in the capital-using character of United States innovations which have prevented the marginal productivity of capital from falling to zero. See, e.g., his essay in *Investment Criteria and Economic Growth*, Massachusetts Institute of Technology, Center for International Studies, Cambridge, Mass., 1955.

[20] See "India Is Planning to Reap the Wind," *New York Times*, July 18, 1955.

or a small and dogged innovator trying to win a place for himself. There seems to be fairly general agreement that, while in theory it would be useful to develop a special technology for under-developed countries,[21] in practice there are strong resistances which prevent this.

Several compromise solutions are available. In some industries the developed countries may offer a variety of technologies. Side by side with the integrated steel mill with linked stages of smelting, refining, and rolling, the United States is also producing steel in various parts of the country in separate stages which more nearly fit the conditions of some underdeveloped countries.[22] One such stage is rerolling, where semifinished steel shapes—slabs, blooms, or billets—are rerolled, after heating, into rods or light structural shapes. This operation can be undertaken efficiently on a small scale. From this stage it is an easy step to actual production of steel from scrap or pig iron in small furnaces of no more than 100,000 tons of annual capacity, fired by gas, oil, or electricity. This type of furnace has become widely popular in the United States because of costs of transport, both of scrap to the integrated mill and of finished product to the consumer. Scrap is scarce in underdeveloped countries, to be sure, but some is available or purchasable and the smaller efficient scale may make this steel operation more desirable than the more dramatic, modern prestige-conveying integrated mill. In Colombia, the International Bank mission recommended a small mill for treating scrap, but the Colombian government turned down this recommendation in favor of the integrated mill.

Another compromise is to separate technology and factor proportions by stages, and to use capital-intensive methods when increasing returns to scale are available in any stage, but to cling to labor-intensive elsewhere, even in the same industry. Machinery to cut metal makes more sense than machinery to move it. The expensive capital involved in in-plant conveyor systems has little merit in light engineering in underdeveloped countries. Whether it would pay to break down the steps in continuous-process, integrated steel, chemical, or oil re-

---

[21] An interesting question is when in the development process countries begin to go off on their own. Japan was initially a slavish imitator. A recent study of industrial techniques concludes that it is still ten years behind other industrial countries and adds: "The defect of Japan is that it relies too much on foreign techniques. Japanese industries must develop their own techniques with their own efforts and rid themselves of the present reliance on foreign techniques." From "Japan's Research Declared to Lag," *New York Times*, Dec. 20, 1955.

[22] From an unpublished memorandum by Kenneth Bohr of the International Bank for Reconstruction and Development.

fining operations is a difficult question. In general, however, these industries seem unusually capital-intensive to have a prominent role in the plans of underdeveloped countries.[23]

Unfortunately, too many instances exist of no thought being given to the existence of variable factor proportions between countries. The Hoover Commission Task Force Report, *Overseas Economic Operation*[24] argues that large industry cannot provide employment in underdeveloped countries because in the United States an investment of $100,000,000 is needed to provide 10,000 jobs ($10,000 per job). This is half of the Mahalanobis figure for steel for India cited above, but double his figure for other heavy industry. More fundamentally, the statement ignores the possibility of modifications of technique to take advantage of lower rates for labor and to economize on higher-priced capital. A more extraordinary example is furnished by a "Report on Utilization of Waste Gases in Saudi Arabia."[25] This study calculates the costs of an Arabian venture to produce synthetic fertilizer by using American processes and converting to Arabian costs. In capital requirements, conversion uses a factor of 2 to take account of the average added expenses of *American* companies doing business in Saudi Arabia. In labor charges, a factor of $1\frac{1}{2}$ is used, again based on the experience of United States firms in the area. Identical rates of interest on capital were assumed, and identical depreciation. To an economist, these elaborate calculations overlook the essential problem, which is whether, given cheap labor and high capital costs for an Arabian concern, it would be possible to modify American capital-intensive methods of producing synthetic fertilizer from waste gases, substituting labor for capital. All too frequently it is the technologically culture-bound expert from the developed country, rather than the politicians of the underdeveloped, who needs to receive Hayek's understanding of elementary economics.

TECHNICAL ASSISTANCE

These lessons have been learned, albeit often painfully, in the spread of technical assistance in economic development which started with President Truman's Inaugural Speech of January, 1949, with its Point

[23] But note the Soviet Union, Red China, and the second Indian Five-Year Plan.
[24] Government Printing Office, Washington, June, 1955, p. 50.
[25] By a Special Panel of the Advisory Committee on International Technical Assistance, published by the Division of Engineering and Industrial Research, National Academy of Science, National Research Council, Washington, July 14, 1954.

Four program. Initially conceived of as the sole engine of development, it was quickly appreciated that the expert from the developed country has to be malleable to be of use in backward areas. Capital is not available to take advantage of all, or even many, opportunities for increased output, and what capital is available must be used with great economy and spread thinly. Public health, education, and agriculture absorb more than 80 per cent of the United States' and probably a similar proportion of the United Nations' efforts in Latin America. In these areas the expert has been obliged to recall obsolete techniques, which use little equipment, and where he could, to concentrate attention on methods which involve little or no equipment but only changed ways of doing things, even at the expense of some effort.

The initial tendency of the expert to be bemused by the technology and factor proportions of his own country has led recently in the United Nations and in the Colombo Plan area to an attempt to narrow the technological gap between giver and receiver of technical assistance. In India the Japanese technique of rice planting is taught instead of the American. It is more effort to plant rice in rows rather than to scatter the seed broadside in the paddies; but it pays off in a way that the American, less-effort way of broadcasting it from an airplane would not. Similarly in public health in rural Brazil, the need is for privies, not tiled bathrooms.

When it comes to direct investment by developed countries, the merit of modifying advanced technology is not so obvious, if indeed it is evident at all. Inertia, habit, and a sense of the proper way to do things lead foreign direct investment to bring its own technology with it unmodified. The prestige of the underdeveloped country pushes in the same direction: its politicians want to be able to point with pride to the modernity of the foreign plants. As a symbol, capital-intensive foreign industry may have value in encouraging dissatisfaction with old ways and interest in change. But the lesson is directly applied on a narrow front.

FACTOR PROPORTIONS AND DEVELOPMENT—A SUMMARY

If a country were doomed not to develop or to experience a change in its capital/labor ratio, it would maximize its existing income over time, or more probably minimize the rate of decline in income per capita, by equating the marginal efficiency of capital in every occupation. The marginal efficiency of capital is high in a really underdeveloped country, although perhaps not as high as in one which has started its development.[26] It is uneconomical, therefore, to use capital anywhere where it cannot earn the high return.

When a country is successfully developing, it makes sense to employ capital more intensively in a leading sector than elsewhere (taking into account the differences in production functions). But the gap should not be too wide or the educative effect may not take hold, and dual economy may even turn into a block.

Finally, where growth is not yet started or has barely begun, the possibility of direct foreign investment in highly capital-intensive industries requires a weighing of two considerations: the opportunity cost of the capital, i.e., whether it would be available at all if it were not used where it was going; and the possibility of dual economy. If the foreign capital would not be available for any other use with a higher return, its opportunity cost is zero, which would justify investment in any industry at any set of factor proportions above the prevailing level. The prospect of dual economy, on the other hand, may be favorable or unfavorable, depending upon whether the up-to-date technology serves as a source of training and stimulation to labor— a growing point—or inhibits productive effort because the gap is too wide.

[26] It is difficult to get representative figures, free of risk, inflation, and the downward bias imparted by governments. But it should be noted that the private marginal efficiency of capital is low, even where labor is cheap, if complementary facilities of overhead capital are not available. This is the basis for the frequent statement that the profitability of investments is higher in the United States and Canada than anywhere else in the world, and that North America is the most underdeveloped area.

CHAPTER 11   *Active or Passive Monetary*
              and Fiscal Policies

INTRODUCTION

In the short space of a chapter it is impossible to cover in detail the myriad financial questions which arise in the course of economic development. Equally is it inappropriate to select one from their number which is of outstanding importance and worthy of extended treatment. Books have been written on how to collect taxes from the agricultural sector, or the extent to which the quantity theory of money applies in early stages of growth. Here we are posing the general question of how much monetary and fiscal policies can lead development, and to what extent they must follow and consolidate ground won by other weapons. Within this framework, however, a number of specific questions arises and requires discussion of particular points of financial theory and institutions. Among these are whether monetary and fiscal policy should concern itself with growth at all, as contrasted with day-to-day stability, and whether conflict or harmony exists between external and internal stability in economies which are wide open, as are many of the underdeveloped countries engaged in exporting raw materials.

The discussion must proceed on two levels: the technical and the real. Too frequently the latter is neglected. But finance is by no means all technical, and extreme deflation and inflation may have their origin not in superficial errors of analysis or policy on the part of monetary and fiscal authorities. The financial problem in economic development arises from the necessity to divert resources from the production of consumption goods to the formation of capital, and at the same time to see to it that these producers of capital are enabled to consume. Without a change in prices or income, this may be done by inducing producers in both sectors to save and lend their savings to the government, which spends them for capital formation; or the savers may undertake the capital formation themselves, whether directly or through financial intermediaries in the capital market; or the government can acquire the funds by taxation. If voluntary savings are low, and taxation is difficult, moreover, the government can undertake capital formation by bidding away resources from the consumer-goods sector by creating money. This will involve an increase in wages and the price of other factors; and it will result in an increase in the price of consumption goods as the recipients of the new increased incomes bid for a smaller supply of consumption goods.

But beneath the reactions of lenders and taxpayers, on the one hand, and of borrowers, government, and monetary authorities, on the other, lie real forces; the poverty of income recipients, or their unwillingness to restrict their consumption, either at all or so long as they are the only social group forced to do so; the ambition of borrowers and government in investing more resources than the economy will provide, or than can be borrowed from abroad, no matter how much the rate of interest and periods of borrowing be juggled. Finance may operate efficiently and neatly, or finance may be inept and slow down the rate of growth. The range in which financial skill can accelerate the growth process will differ from situation to situation, but may, on the average, not be very wide. No more than anyone else can a central banker make a silk purse out of a sow's ear. Moreover, neither central banking nor fiscal skill is likely to prevent a deterioration of the position when a country of several sectors is determined, group by group, to undertake some expenditure, whether defense or developmental, but no group is willing to accept any share of paying for it. And it is easy in many but not in all circumstances for a governor of the central bank, or a secretary of the treasury, to make a botch out of a sound situation, through elementary errors.

THE CASE AGAINST POSITIVE MONETARY POLICY IN GROWTH

The essence of the argument against the attempt to use monetary policy to accelerate growth is that all roads lead to inflation anyhow; positive policy is likely to be expansive; the contribution which central banks can make in situations of economic growth is to maintain stability from day to day, to ignore an opportunity to affect the trend.

Inflationary tendencies lie in the demonstration effect which makes the economy likely to consume too much and to overinvest in the private sector; in the grandiose development plans, using too capital-intensive projects of governments on too wide a front; and in the cultural lead, which borrows institutions and ideas from developed countries that are too expansionist in underdeveloped. The institutions frequently include a fractional reserve for commercial banks or for the central and commercial banks in tandem; authority to lend to the government or to buy government bonds which makes it possible to expand the money base if the government runs a deficit, or if banks invest in government obligations, and other expansionary means. The ideas will vary widely, but may include some of considerable sophistication, such as liquidity preference, which suggests that the rate of interest can be low if large amounts of money represent assets held in liquid form rather than income in the process of being spent. They are almost certain to include the view that the sovereign power is never inhibited from a task on which its mind is set by lack of finance. Money can be created by printing, borrowing from the central bank, or lowering reserve requirements and selling bonds to the commercial banks.

If these real and institutional factors press in the expansionary direction, there is cause for the authorities to lean the other way. The dangers of inflation in economic development have been recited frequently so that they can be summarized here. Inflation reduces the level of voluntary savings, as income recipients are unwilling to hold money or claims payable in money of declining value. It distorts the pattern of investment by substituting for the criterion of productivity that of capacity to resist depreciation: real estate, and especially luxury housing, hoards of specie and jewelry, and stocks of standardized commodities become prime objects of investment in contrast to industrial plant and equipment. And inflation tends to become cumulative as income recipients exercise what Walker calls extra-market power and strike for higher wages, demand governmental stabilization of farm prices or subsidies to farmers and industry, etc., to protect their incomes in real terms and to push the burden of the extra spending onto others.[1] In addition to these considerations in a closed economy, an open economy faces added disabilities of distorting incentives in favor of imports and against exports, and in favor of the use of foreign capital instead of high-priced domestic labor.[2] It serves at the same

[1] See C. Iversen, *Monetary Policy in Iraq,* Munksgaard, Copenhagen, 1954, chap. 9. The reference on extra-market power is to E. R. Walker, *From Economic Theory to Policy,* University of Chicago Press, Chicago, 1943, chap. VI.

[2] See M. E. Kreinin, "Controlled Inflation in Israel, 1949–54," *Journal of Political Economy,* April, 1956, p. 117. This reflects, of course, overvaluation. If inflation is followed by depreciation, the distortion does not occur.

time to repel foreign capital, and to encourage domestic savers to safeguard their wealth abroad.

An important part of this argument is that the loss of savings from inflation is more significant than the increment of inflationary investment. In Latin America, Chile under inflation has achieved a lower rate of capital formation than stable Colombia or Cuba.[3] In Southeast Asia, inflationary Indonesia has the lowest rate of a number of countries measured.[4] There is, however, the exception that proves the rule. In Mexico, inflation is fairly persistent, but development takes place on an impressive scale. Some distortion of investment may occur, and in particular some projects may be undertaken sooner than they otherwise would. But the underlying economy is growing, and the inflation, though it undoubtedly causes some stresses which it would be well to be rid of, does make the system march.

Inflation may be superficial. An astute French observer once suggested that in the Middle East and Africa it was frequently necessary to make a distinction between the "façade economy" and the real economy. When oil royalty and tax payments by the Anglo-Iranian Oil Company to the Iranian government ceased, the Western world waited breathless for the ensuing collapse. Nothing happened. The impact of the throughput of oil, foreign exchange, and imported consumer goods had affected only a small layer of the economy. Their collapse, when payments were cut off, went virtually unnoticed as the modernized sector returned to the ways of its forebears and contemporaries in the subsistence economy. Similarly, the story is told of Paul Van Zeeland visiting Lebanon to discuss the combination of persistent inflation in the surface economy and persistent growth and vitality in the real economy below. He is reported to have said that he did not know how the economy could function, given the many violations of the rules of sound finance, but since he observed that the economy was fundamentally growing at effective rates, he suggested that nothing be altered.

Institutions and appetites which make for inflation, and inflation's

[3] See F. Pazos, "Economic Development and Financial Stability," *Staff Papers,* October, 1953, p. 235, where net capital formation to GNP is given as approximately 5 to 7 per cent for Chile, 10 to 12 per cent for Colombia, and 10 to 15 per cent for Cuba in the late 1940s and early 1950s. The figures, to be sure, are only roughly comparable.

[4] In an unpublished paper D. Avramovic notes that the postwar average net capital formation to net national product has been 0.5 per cent for Indonesia, 5 per cent for Ceylon, 5.5 to 6 per cent for Malaya, 6 per cent for India, and 7.1 per cent for Burma. The annual increases in prices for the countries in the same order were 15, 8, 3.5, 1, and 0 per cent. To the extent that the figures can be trusted, the rank correlation is perfect. Professor B. Higgins regards the 0.5 figure for Indonesia as a gross understatement.

bad effects on development, have led monetary authorities to emphasize stability rather than growth. The achievement of stability, it is
thought, brings growth as a by-product. The duty of the authorities,
therefore, is to ignore, or pay only slight attention to, the requirements
of growth, and to concentrate attention on stability.[5]

Before getting into details, it must be noted that inflation is by no
means homogeneous, and that some kinds of inflation may be salubrious, others noxious. Much depends on the source of the stimulation
and the reaction of various agents in the economy at the first round of
spending. Profit inflation, stimulated perhaps by bank credit to private
entrepreneurs introducing new goods, may be highly desirable. It
stimulates transformation, encourages savings and reinvestment by
entrepreneurs, produces tax revenue, and leads to growth. Cost-of-
living inflation, on the other hand, where the pressure comes from
wage rates with profits squeezed, is likely to go higher and produce
less capital formation and in the long run less consumption. Where
government starts inflationary spending in an equilibrium situation,
however, there is likelihood that factor prices will be bid up to lead
to cost-of-living inflation. But part of the reason that some economists
favor inflation while the majority are so adamantly opposed is related
to the efficacy of profit inflation in stimulating cumulative growth.

THE CASE FOR POSITIVE POLICY

The opposite side of the debate argues that the monetary requirements of development present a problem—that of avoiding cumulative
inflation—but also a task and an opportunity. The task is to provide
the correct amount of money, since the money supply must change
during the growth process. This was noted in Chapter 6 and demonstrated in Figure 6.3. The challenge is to use monetary policy as a
whole, and the increased requirements for money in particular, as the
basis for capital formation which would otherwise not take place.

The increased demand for money comes from a number of sources.
In the first place, the extension of the money economy at the expense
of the subsistence sector requires a stock of money to satisfy the
transactions demand for money on the part of new entrants. To acquire these balances, the newcomers to specialization and exchange
through markets must save out of current production, and not hoard
precious metals, jewelry, or stocks. In any event, the counterparts are

[5] See especially the views of H. S. Ellis, commenting on C. R. Whittlesey, "Relation of Money to Economic Growth," *American Economic Review, Papers and
Proceedings*, May, 1956, pp. 206ff.

available to the government or monetary authorities for capital formation. This is a once-and-for-all contribution of savings, and in countries
any distance along the development path, it is probably no longer
available. But in many countries, particularly in Asia and Africa, its
significance can easily be underrated.

Next is the increase in the demand for money for ordinary transactions, as income per capita and the numbers of people rise. With no
change in sophistication, this demand will grow proportionately with
total income. After a certain stage of monetary sophistication has been
reached, it will increase at a slower rate. The use of coins gives way
to notes; in their turn notes are displaced by checks. The cost and the
efficiency of the monetary system improve. But some expansion of
coins, fiduciary money, or bank money is possible. This is a source of
available savings. If coins contract, moreover, their replacement by
notes adds another small item.

Thirdly, in the later stages of development, a diversification demand
for money will arise. Growth brings an increase in financial assets, as
deficit-spending units (which invest) issue debt or equity securities
to surplus-spending units (which save). One of the major tasks of the
monetary authorities in development is to support the gradual expansion and proliferation of the machinery—commercial banks, savings banks, investment banking, insurance companies, government
bond market, private bond and share markets, etc.—which link surplus-
and deficit-spending units. Some investment by government and business (and in housing by consumers) will be internally financed. This
will not lead to the accumulation of financial assets. But some considerable part of investment is likely to be financed externally. Government and business, typically, will borrow from household units, either
directly or, more typically, through financial intermediaries. As financial assets grow in this fashion, their composition is important. A
diversification demand for money is likely to develop.[6]

Not much of a counterweight exists on the other side. At some
stage, with the growth of confidence in other financial assets, dis-
hoarding of coins and notes will take place. And ultimately, increased
efficiency of the clearing system will reduce the ratio of money to
national income. But financial assets as a whole will rise with growth,
and that part of the increase which takes the form of money, and, in

[6] See J. G. Gurley and E. S. Shaw, "Financial Aspects of Economic Development," *American Economic Review*, September, 1955, pp. 515–538. These writers
stress the similarities between money and other financial assets in the growth
process, without, however, adequately noting the fact that increases in money
permit investment to take place in advance of saving, whereas those in other
financial assets do not.

the case of bank money, the debt by which the increased bank money is backed, permits and in fact requires government deficit spending, or business deficit spending financed through bank credit.

There is not likely to be much disagreement this far. Money does not lead. In fact, money is not likely to be much of an asset until economic growth is fairly well established and has become a normal expectation; but money and the expansion of government debt or bank credit must follow closely. And in the absence of this expansion, whether because of too low reserve ratios, lack of gold and foreign-exchange reserves, or excessive central-bank regard for stability, economic growth may be held down by deflation. This danger may not seem very real today, when it would be hard to find a country whose development was checked by deflation. Even in the period of deflation from 1873 to 1896 in the United States, the rate of economic growth at 24 per cent per decade was higher than later.[7] Deflation during this period went further in the agricultural sector than in industry. This may be close to an optimal pattern for rapid development: rising prices in the industrial sector and falling in agricultural (because of productivity increases). Where large increases in productivity in transport occur, a country may even have increases in agricultural prices on the farm and falling prices at consuming centers, which make the measurement of price changes difficult. Some of the deflation in the United States down to 1896 partook of this character, which was hardly harmful to growth. But general deflation, with falling prices in industry as well as in agriculture, is generally regarded as a threat to growth.

Can deficit financing go beyond this close support, which takes advantage of the opportunities for increasing money required to meet demands? It is generally agreed that the underemployment or disguised unemployment in the agricultural sector or elsewhere in the economy does not constitute an adequate basis for noninflationary deficit financing.[8] Structural unemployment results from lack of complementary resources or wrong factor proportions, not from dearth of effective demand. The opportunity lies rather in the possibility of limited inflation, which permits limited deficit financing.

At the most modest level there is something to be said for a change

---

[7] From 1869–1888 to 1889–1908, the total rate of growth in the United States was 52 per cent per decade, and the per capita rate 24 per cent. From the latter period to 1909–1928, the over-all rate was 40 per cent, the per capita rate 18. From 1909–1928 to 1929–1948, with depression, the over-all rate was 23, the per capita figure 9. From the mimeographed statistical appendix to S. Kuznets, "Towards a Theory of Economic Growth," in R. Lekachman (ed.), *National Measures for Economic Welfare at Home and Abroad,* Doubleday & Company, Inc., New York, 1955.

[8] See R. Nurkse, *Problems of Capital Formation in Underdeveloped Countries,* Basil Blackwell & Mott, Ltd., Oxford, 1953, p. 17.

in relative prices in the development process which somewhat advances the general price level. To the purist, it is possible to change relative prices while keeping the general price level stable. Where any one price goes up, another can come down. Deflation expels resources, while inflation attracts. In reality, however, there is likely to be some asymmetry. Price deflation is strongly resisted, and takes a long time to drive resources out of a given sector. More than asymmetry of response is involved, however. Deficit spending for a given item will raise the price. To tax for the purpose of financing the spending is difficult in the first place, and may result in decreased savings or reduction in socially useful consumption. One-shot deficit spending as a carrot to move the donkey in a given direction, without hitting him with the directionless stick, has something to recommend it.

Government deficit spending is, of course, warranted when foreign assets are drawn down or foreign aid is received. If these assets are sterling balances owned by the government in the first place, they can be used to buy goods—the goods sold in the domestic market—and the proceeds spent in turn without danger of inflation. In the case of aid, counterpart funds must be spent to avoid deflation, unless they are deliberately sought to mop up an outstanding inflation. Where a long time lag runs between the receipt of aid and the ultimate bureaucratic approval to spend the counterpart, as in Pakistan, central banks must bestir themselves not to permit unnecessary and unwarranted monetary changes which might flow from the aid arrangements.

Beyond these limited instances, V. K. R. V. Rao, with the use of a mathematical model, has made a case in which a limited but continuous deficit will produce a once-and-for-all rise in prices so long as some part of the newly created money consistently comes back to the government in taxes or savings.[9] This, of course, is merely a multiplier model. The higher the marginal propensities to pay taxes and save—the latter influenced by inelastic price expectations and the price rise—the higher the possible deficit or the lower the price increase resulting.[10] But the possibility of continuous deficit financing rests, of

[9] V. K. R. V. Rao, *Deficit Financing, Capital Formation and Price Behaviour in an Under-developed Economy,* Eastern Economist Pamphlets, Delhi, 1953. See also W. A. Lewis, "Financing Economic Development with Unlimited Supplies of Labor," *Manchester School,* May, 1954, pp. 162 and 165; he calls inflation for the purpose of capital formation "self-destructive as prices are sooner or later overtaken by rising output" and states that voluntary savings out of profits grow to the level of investment.

[10] Two forces of opposing directions will be at work over long periods of time: an attempt to maintain the value of cash balances by increased savings, and an attempt to maintain real consumption. Inelastic price expectations permit consumption to decline in the short run.

course, on the stability of the marginal rate of tax, which is dependent on the extent and rates of income tax, and on the stability of the elastic expectations which induce saving. If the fickle public gets the idea that the price rise is permanent or likely to continue, and therefore responds to higher prices by more rather than less spending, the model breaks down. Inflation results from deficit financing rather than from stable prices at a higher plateau.

When is inflation stimulating and when distortionary? Brazil's postwar experience furnishes an interesting case. From 1945 to 1952 Brazilian private investment borrowed heavily from banks, leading to an expansion of the money supply, rising profits, shifts of resources, big increases in productivity, and rising prices, including a shift of the terms of trade against the industrial sector. During this period inflation produced growth. After 1952, however, the economy moved sideways rather than upward for a time, as speculative investment, bottlenecks in production, and social tension resulting in demand for wage increases blocked further real expansion.[11] In 1956 and 1957 the real expansion seems to have been resumed.

Beyond the Rao model there is the possibility of capital formation through the disequilibrium system. Deficit spending creates capital; price control and rationing are invoked to prevent the inflation from becoming cumulative, to minimize the social unrest which inflationary skewness in income distribution produces, and to make the forced savings generally acceptable. During the war, it is argued, the disequilibrium system proved very effective in mobilizing resources for war. In peacetime, why should it not be turned to do battle with underdevelopment by mobilizing resources for capital formation? The Soviet Union, between monetary reforms, exemplifies the disequilibrium system in extreme form but in an economy with only limited resources under private control. Money becomes redundant. Interest rates have no effect in rationing credit; incomes have no effect in rationing consumption goods.

Deficit financing of this sort evidently interests the countries of Asia. The United Nations Economic Commission for Asia and the Far East is aware that there are limits on the capacity of a country to use this method, and warns against operating an "excessive 'disequilibrium system.' "[12] It is perhaps not as aware as Western economists are of the

[11] See *Economic Survey of Latin America, 1951–52*, United Nations, Economic Commission for Latin America, New York, 1953, pp. 51ff; and, by the same organization, *Economic Survey of Latin America, 1953*, New York, 1954, pp. 15, 79–80, 211.

[12] "Problems and Techniques of Planning for Economic Development," *Economic Bulletin for Asia and the Far East*, United Nations, New York, November,

fact, or impressed by it, that the disequilibrium system requires more administrative inputs to be effective than a well-run monetary equilibrium, and the chances of its becoming excessive are ever present and dangerous. Controlled inflation in Israel illustrates this,[13] if a recent illustration is needed. Much of the effort of Western economists has been to warn against what they believe is the illusion that the disequilibrium system can be used for capital formation on a substantial scale.[14]

Finally, some attention is being paid to the sectoral impact of monetary policy. Monetary policy has an incidence, no less than taxation,[15] and the question is sometimes put whether monetary expansion cannot be used to turn the terms of trade against the agricultural sector which tends to benefit, as we saw in Chapter 9, from expanded production in the secondary or tertiary sector. If the prices of industrial goods can be raised through inflation, without spreading to foodstuffs and raw materials, with a resultant change in the terms of trade between the two sectors, there may be an opportunity to offset the strong opposite pressures.

We have already seen how relative inflation for industrial products in over-all deflation may be beneficial, but it is hard to see how monetary policy can make a positive contribution here. There is much to be done on a sectoral basis in the perfection of the monetary machinery to make credit available to agriculture through some more economical institution than the money lender and to ensure that it is used productively. This may benefit the terms of trade between country and town in behalf of the latter by expanding agricultural production. It may also be possible, through the extension of banking, to gather rural savings for urban investment, although the more likely direction of the flow is the opposite. But the notion of inflation as hurting the country and helping the city sounds strange to the student of American financial history. Here the sectoral disputes ran between Wall Street and the farm, to be sure, but with opposite sides: the country wanted more

---

1955, p. 27. See also "Deficit Financing for Economic Development with Special Reference to ECAFE Countries," *Economic Bulletin for Asia and the Far East,* United Nations, New York, November, 1954, pp. 1–19.

[13] Kreinin, *op. cit.*

[14] See E. M. Bernstein et al., *Economic Development with Stability: A Report to the Government of India by a Mission of the International Monetary Fund,* Washington, October, 1953, especially pp. 41ff. In general, this mission appears to have been somewhat too fearful of inflation in India during the first Five-Year Plan, perhaps through underestimating the importance of new saving through the extension of the monetary sector, and because of the favorable influence of unpredictable good monsoons.

[15] As Richard Musgrave has said.

and cheaper credit and an expansion of money supply to raise its prices. So long as agricultural supplies are inelastic, inflation is likely to hurt the town, and hurt private capital formation, which is primarily an urban occupation. The sectoral incidence of inflation would seem to be lined up against the desired solution rather than in favor of it. More effective results will probably have to be sought in shaping directly the incidence of taxation.

THE LIMITS OF INDEPENDENT MONETARY POLICY

These considerations suggest that there is little that the monetary authorities can do to stimulate capital formation beyond sustaining or increasing domestic confidence in the currency. Another limiting factor is, of course, external. This is partly a matter of confidence, and turns on the extent to which development plans or hopes revolve around foreign private capital. It goes further, however. In an export economy, Wallich has pointed out, exports are likely to be larger in relation to net geographical product than either private investment or government expenditure.[16] Moreover, investment and government expenditure are linked to exports through some sort of acceleration principle. The connection in investment is clear, and follows the normal accelerator model. In government expenditure there are two connections. Increased exports give rise to the demand for increased government expenditures to improve ports, transport, and marketing facilities associated with sales abroad. In addition, they bring in revenue through export taxes and, somewhat more slowly, through their general income-multiplier effect. Lacking a developed capital market, government must delay its expenditure—unless it is prepared to undertake purely inflationary finance through bank credit—until it has the funds in hand.

In places where the marginal propensity to import is high, whether because people are hungry and the country imports food or because Western-style items have been added to their standard of living, as in Latin America, independence of monetary policy is narrowly circumscribed. Monetary expansion results in increased imports, an unfavorable balance, loss of gold reserves, etc.

Monetary stability in an export economy requires heroic measures. A country must save all the increase in income from expanded exports in periods of world prosperity, in order to have foreign exchange on hand to maintain imports during periods of world depression. This

---

[16] H. C. Wallich, "Underdeveloped Countries and the International Monetary Mechanism," in *Money, Trade and Economic Growth* (Essays in Honor of John H. Williams), The Macmillan Company, New York, 1951, pp. 15–32.

means anticyclical measures of some considerable proportions.[17] The difficulties are many. Incomes expand in the export sector, and normally the expansion would spread throughout the economy through the influence of the multiplier. To use monetary measures, however, will involve the contraction of some other sector, which must cut spending in response to the contraction of monetary reserves through central bank action to offset the expansion of exports. This is virtually certain to meet resistance. In addition, one must be careful to distinguish sharply cycle from trend, and make sure that cyclical borrowings are not spent through secular inflation.

Apparent independence can be gained by the introduction of the disequilibrium system in international transactions, rationing foreign exchange for expenditure on imports, and insisting on the collection of the exchange proceeds of exports. But this independence is more apparent than real. As in the domestic disequilibrium system, it requires the substitution of strong incentives like patriotism or compulsion to operate the system, plus an incorruptible civil service. Even where these ingredients happen to be present, the system will limp because of the ease of evasion.

The rediscovery of monetary policy in developed countries, which is a phenomenon of the return of full employment in postwar years, is not paralleled in underdeveloped countries. There money has always been more of a problem than an opportunity. That the underdeveloped countries should try to find opportunities in it is understandable. In the early stages of development, the changeover from a specie to a fiduciary coinage gives a once-and-for-all opportunity for spending, and this is followed as the monetary base grows with further opportunities. As shown earlier in Figure 6.3, the money supply grows with economic development, not only proportionately but at a rate faster than that. It must not be thought, however, that monetary manipulation offers a royal road to development. Judiciously used, it helps. Unfortunately, the difficulties of financing government capital formation through taxation induce many countries to use monetary manipulation to excess.

MARSHALLING SAVINGS FOR GOVERNMENTAL CAPITAL FORMATION

Government capital formation can be backed by personal (or business) savings, or by government savings, which are a surplus of tax

[17] S. N. Sen, *Central Banking in Underdeveloped Money Markets*, Bookland, Calcutta, 1952, pp. 76–84, discusses the Argentine attempt to stabilize through monetary measures to offset balance-of-payment fluctuations.

revenue over government current expenditure. Private savings may be forced, by inflation. They may be voluntary, but made in money form and therefore available indirectly to government, as in the deficit-financing possibilities discussed in the previous section; or voluntary and made directly, in the form of purchase of government securities.

Possibilities of capital formation by means of inflation and by voluntary savings indirectly available have been found to be limited. Equally limited is the possibility of mopping up private savings by selling securities to investors. Capital markets for the most part are undeveloped. Private demand for savings for investment is inelastic with respect to increases in the interest rate which might shrink competitive demand. The private supply schedule of savings is equally inelastic with respect to interest rate changes. If capital from abroad is not forthcoming, major reliance must be placed on increasing governmental revenue and decreasing government expenditure for consumption. Since the latter is likely to be low and difficult to reduce, the opportunities at home for capital formation reduce themselves, in large part, to the capacity to tax.

Discussion of fiscal policy in developed countries focuses attention largely on ability to pay, the problem of equity. In underdeveloped countries, however, the relevant ability is that of the government to collect—that is, the administrative convenience and even feasibility of raising the requisite revenue. A secondary consideration, but a vital one, is to raise the revenue with the least possible hurt to productive investment. Taxation to support government capital formation and prevent inflation must restrain consumption, particularly luxury and wasteful consumption, and limit unproductive investment. But it must not at the same time discourage investment which fits into the desired growth pattern.

These considerations imply a tax program heavily weighted on the side of consumption taxes and against imposts on income. The objection to the income tax is partly its discouragement of the new men from rapid accumulation of capital and plowing back of profits, and partly administrative convenience. Personal and business income taxes require a money economy, high standards of literacy among taxpayers, the prevalence of accounting records honestly and reliably maintained, a large degree of voluntary compliance, and an honest and efficient administration.[18] Moreover, where incomes are low, cost of collection is high. Social cohesion which may be important in gathering support

[18] R. Goode, "Reconstruction of Foreign Tax Systems," *Proceedings of the 44th Annual Conference,* National Tax Association, 1951, pp. 212–222.

for the development program might be enhanced by instituting a steeply progressive income tax; and where there is skewed income distribution with the rich indulging in luxury consumption, there is something to be said for an income tax as a diverter of resources from consumption to investment. But the tax runs the risk of weakening the incentive to invest in productive uses in the private sector, unless it be hedged with provision for accelerated depreciation on new investment and similar exemptions. Here the difficulty is to distinguish between productive and unproductive investment. A further point which argues against major reliance on a general business income tax is that where goods and factor markets are monopolistic, as is typical of not a few underdeveloped economics, the tax is likely to be passed forward or backward. It then becomes an indiscriminate tax on consumption and intermediate-goods production or on employment. While the business income tax has certain advantages of administration, it may be desirable to convert it to a direct consumption tax which can be more selective in incidence and in allocative effect.

Real estate taxes are widely used in underdeveloped countries and have much to recommend them in the abstract.[19] An effective tax would be progressive where land was owned by the wealthy; it would stimulate optimal use of land for production, and rates could be adjusted to penalize luxury housing. In practice, these ideals are difficult to realize. Politically powerful landowners resist the changes necessary to keep valuations and rates abreast of the price level. Delinquencies are high. The opportunity presented by taxation of real estate fails to be seized because of the difficulties of administration in the face of interests.

The difficulty of administering the tax is indicated in Indonesia by the fact that the percentage of total taxes provided by the rural portions of the country has fallen from 7 per cent in 1939 to 1 per cent in 1952, despite the fact that the rural areas had expanded more in income than the towns and in 1952 accounted for 81 per cent of national income.[20] Part of the change was due to the substitution of the weaker Indonesian administration for the Dutch. The local nature of the administration of land taxes in Indonesia is used by Paauw as an argument for diverting governmental capital formation from the national to the local level, to increase efficiency in collection and to stimulate participation. Where the land tax is high, as in China, and

---

[19] Douglas S. Paauw, "Financing Economic Development in Indonesia," *Economic Development and Cultural Change*, January, 1956, pp. 171–185.

[20] *Ibid.;* see also "Belgrade Raises Tax on Farmers," *New York Times*, Mar. 12, 1956, in which the increase in tax rates is said to be designed to stimulate production.

can be collected in kind, it makes a contribution to capital formation at the national level by freeing resources and stabilizing the terms of trade between industrial products and foodstuffs.

The unsuitability of income taxes and the weakness of taxes on land leave most of the task of raising revenue to taxes on consumption. That part raised domestically runs between one-fifth and one-third of total revenue, as a rule. Another considerable fraction represents taxes on foreign trade. Import taxes are generally paid by consumers: the tariff to improve the terms of trade plays only a small role in the imports of underdeveloped countries which buy at world prices. But export taxes may be shifted by exporters, whether forward to purchasers in sellers' markets or backward to employees through reducing wages. When they are in fact paid by the producer, which is frequently, they are a selective income tax levied against a particular sector.

Consumption taxes can be made progressive, particularly if they are heavy on luxury goods. It is sometimes claimed that their incidence on consumption and production is moderate, given the inelasticities of demand and supply as dictated by tradition and lack of mobility. But consumption taxes are likely to be regressive; they impede the development of wider markets and the extension of the money economy. When levied against imports, they encourage production of luxury goods at home. They distort the optimal allocation of resources, at least insofar as the market is permitted to dictate it. Nonetheless, they raise revenue.

Using the fiscal system to raise funds for capital formation runs afoul not only of the objectives of progressive redistribution of income, and of efficient allocation (in the international sphere at least); it also conflicts with the objective of stabilization. As we have noticed under the earlier discussion of monetary policy, an export economy has little autonomy in income stabilization, at best. Fluctuations in the supply or demand for its raw-material exports impart sizable swings in the volume and price of its exports, which impart wider swings to money and real income throughout the economy. Export taxes, or income taxes levied on the exporting sector, can effect some stability in national income, but at the expense of substantial variability in governmental revenue. The more the country succeeds in stabilizing its national income, through taxing exports on an increasing scale when prices rise and on a declining scale when they fall, the more it is likely to accentuate the fluctuations in its revenue and balance of payments.

This conflict could be reduced if the raised export taxes were not shifted forward and if foreign-exchange proceeds were hoarded by the central authorities for disbursement as subsidies to producers in slack times. This assumes that the fluctuations take place about a long-run equilibrium level which the fiscal authorities somehow estimate. It is akin to stabilization of the export economy through monetary contraction when exports rise and expansion when they fall, but superior since the dampening occurs in the sector where the expansion and contraction originate. But, in this situation, the proceeds of export taxes above the minimum level are not available for economic development, but must be devoted entirely to stabilization. Such a standard of fiscal self-denial would be high for developed countries. In actuality, cyclical instability of export prices is inflationary in underdeveloped countries because expenditures are tied to revenues which fluctuate with export proceeds, and because projects started in the expansion phase of the cycle are pushed to completion in contraction, despite the decline of revenue.

Taxation of income (or of export proceeds) of foreign concerns with an incidence on the exporter adds to net national income of the country and provides a clear addition to possible capital formation. In Iraq, 75 per cent of taxes and royalties received from the Iraq Petroleum Company are made available for financing the Five-Year Investment Program which went into operation in April, 1955. In Venezuela, taxes on profits from foreign oil exploitation are regarded as a national depletion allowance reinvested in productive assets. An early and rudimentary rule of thumb in Bahrein involved the division by the British resident of the local oil royalty and tax paid by the Bahrein Petroleum Company into three equal portions: one for the administration of the protectorate, one for the support of the Sheik and his extensive entourage, and one for developmental projects.

Multiple-exchange-rate systems can achieve the same effects as combinations of export and import taxes and subsidies. Typically, too, they have a revenue effect, as the state exchange monopoly sells foreign exchange at a higher average price than it pays. A special study of these systems.[21] in connection with economic development emphasized the extent to which special rates charged and paid to foreign investors may be used to increase revenue.

THE DEFICIT AS A SYMPTOM

A wide-ranging review of the inflationary problem in underdevel oped countries produces the simple and evident conclusion that the

[21] E. R. Schlesinger, *Multiple Exchange Rates and Economic Development*, Princeton University Press, Princeton, N.J., 1952.

difficulties are not technical, but come from attempting too much. A United Nations study which summarizes the work of a number of missions proposes many small technical changes for a variety of countries in Latin America, the Middle East, and Asia. But the basic problem would seem to be that deficits run consistently 10 to 20 per cent of total expenditure.[22] The data in this study relate for the most part to 1950 or 1951. In 1956 inflation was still acute in Bolivia, Brazil, Chile, Indonesia, Korea, the Philippines, and Turkey, and began to make an appearance in India. Each case is readily explained by the attempt to undertake some large combination of reconstruction, development, defense, and subsidy expenditures, or to hold up prices, wages, or incomes generally in the face of markets which will not pay them. In Turkey, agriculture is paid a subsidy and taxes on agriculture are voted down by the Assembly, despite crop failures and shrinking markets. In the Philippines,[23]

. . . many intelligent Filipinos are inclined to blame the United States for creating appetites they cannot afford as an independent nation. Others no less intelligent wish to perpetuate the standards of Western living to which they have become accustomed during the last half century. The result has been something of a "great debate" between one school which advocates spending and borrowing to greater limits, and another . . . which holds with conservative hard money economic thinking . . . .

In India, the accelerated investment program of the second Five-Year Plan, begun in April, 1956, coincided with a reduction in the harvest and gave rise to expansions in money supply, increases in the cost of living, especially for food, and an increase in output. Imports of capital equipment in anticipation of use in the investment program overloaded the transport system and played a role in the rapid reduction of sterling balances and other exchange reserves. A supplementary set of taxes was voted, but the plan still called for too much spending.[24]

Discussion of monetary and fiscal policy of underdeveloped countries by American and European economists almost always takes on a patronizing air. Inflation would be cured if the country would cut back on expenditure, or tax more heavily. Suggestions for new taxes occasionally involve elaborate new devices to eliminate tax inequities,

---

[22] See *Taxes and Fiscal Policy in Under-developed Countries,* United Nations, New York, 1954, part III. An exception is Nicaragua with a surplus.

[23] "Philippines Face Austerity Period," *New York Times,* Mar. 6, 1956.

[24] See "India's Pause for Breath," *Economist,* Jan. 5, 1957, pp. 12–13. " . . . the Indian economy cannot escape the consequences of allowing demand to run so far ahead of resources."

like income averaging or expenditure taxation, which have not been tried in developed countries. But it is not so frequently recognized that the fiscal problem is more difficult in underdeveloped countries. The average rate of saving is small, the marginal rate low. Demonstration effect implies that consumption leads production or rapidly catches up with it. There is always need for further overhead capital investments to create opportunities for increasing productivity. Duesenberry asymmetry in the responses of consumers to increases and declines of income—the former being accepted, the latter resisted—and the political power of the masses, even under dictatorship, make the fiscal problem much more difficult. The difference in the intellectual and administrative capacities of the men operating the system are smaller, and certainly less important, than the difference in the difficulty of restraining inflation in a developed and an underdeveloped country.[25]

In this circumstance inflation is more to be pitied than scorned. Not exactly inevitable, since the inflationary push is much harder in some countries than others by reason of circumstances, national character, and essentially surface phenomena, the task of consciously preventing inflation when the pressure mounts is much harder in underdeveloped countries than in countries with higher marginal propensities to save, widely spread overhead capital, and social and occupational mobility.

In these circumstances an underdeveloped country with luck or virtue can avoid inflation; but it needs more of either or both than a developed country. To try to push its luck or risk its virtue in positive programs of accelerating development through a disequilibrium system is likely to end in disaster.

[25] This remark applies less to Britain, and still less to France, than to the United States.

CHAPTER 12 *The Population Issue*

INTRODUCTION

For the last 125 years, since Malthus, the world has been conscious of the race between output and number of people. Optimists emphasize the increase in output, and can point as a demonstration of their view to the experience of Western Europe and the United States, where population has grown rapidly but output has gone ahead faster. Pessimists, on the other hand, point to many other parts of the world, where income per capita has been steady or falling because population increase has outstripped the growth of total income. They may no longer agree with Malthus that output grows at an arithmetic rate, while population expansion is geometric. But they have new worries—the cheap cost of controlling malaria and other epidemic and endemic man-killers with present-day chemicals and drugs which bring down death rates, expand population, and increase the pressure of population on resources. And in the view of some, present exploitation of natural resources is close to ultimate limits, so that Malthusian concern for diminishing returns is not altogether unwarranted.

Too little attention has been given to the fact that the population problem is not encountered everywhere. Some countries which are growing at rates in excess of 3 per cent per year, a high rate, are not densely populated—Mexico and Venezuela, for example. In fact, apart from a number of Caribbean islands, Latin America is not overpopulated, and Africa and substantial parts of Asia—Burma, Siam, Malaya, Sumatra and Borneo—are not.[1] Moreover, in some areas, such as India, East Pakistan, and China, the density of present population is more significant than rates of increase, which are moderate. Nonetheless, in

[1] See W. A. Lewis, comment on J. Viner, "The Role of the United States in the World Economy," in R. Lekachman (ed.), *National Policy for Economic Welfare at Home and Abroad*, Doubleday & Company, Inc., New York, 1955, p. 211.

one way or another, population does represent a barrier to development in many countries.

We may return to the significance of the rate of population increase for income per capita, which we touched on in Chapter 3. At a capital/output ratio of 4:1, a 1 per cent per annum increase in output per capita requires 4 per cent of income saved if population is stable; 8 per cent at a 1 per cent per annum rate of population growth; 12 per cent at a 2 per cent rate of population growth; and 16 per cent at a 3 per cent rate of population increase. Starting with a 4 per cent rate of saving, a 1 per cent per annum population increase, and zero increase in income per capita, a program of investment which leads to increased income is likely to compound its difficulties by reducing the death rate and raising the rate of population increase.

These simple models suggest even more pessimistic conclusions if they are disaggregated by sectors. The agricultural sector is likely to have the faster rate of population growth, the higher capital/output ratio, and the lower rate of investment. In these circumstances, disguised unemployment may grow at a rapid rate.

This chapter has little to add to the general discussion of a well-worn topic and will attempt succinctly to recapitulate the familiar. It will treat, in order, the death rate, birth rate and resultant rate of increase, the change in age distribution of the population, the role of migration, the impact of population change in demand and supply for goods and services, and population density.

DEATH RATES

Figure 12.1 gives crude death rates for a number of countries correlated with income per capita. The data relate to about 1953. The correlation is not nearly so high as one would suppose, if in fact it is positive, and this for a variety of reasons. In many underdeveloped countries, particularly Lebanon, statistics are incomplete. In some others, such as the Gold Coast with a death rate of 21 per thousand, income per capita figures are missing. But the major reason is that the figures by 1953 already reflect the impact of the major postwar reduction in death rates due to the spread of scientific understanding of disease and its treatment, medical cooperation, and inexpensive public health programs. K. Davis has calculated the decline in the crude death rate for eighteen underdeveloped countries by five-year periods showing the striking impact of the years after World War II:[2]

[2] K. Davis, "The Amazing Decline of Mortality in Underdeveloped Areas," *American Economic Review, Papers and Proceedings,* May, 1956, p. 307.

	Per cent of decline in
Years compared	crude death rate
1935 with 1940.............	8.3
1940 with 1945.............................	5.6
1945 with 1950.............................	24.2
1950 with latest·date (1954 or 1953)............	14.0

While the years from 1940 to 1945 were perhaps not representative in these countries, few of which were in war areas, the threefold in-

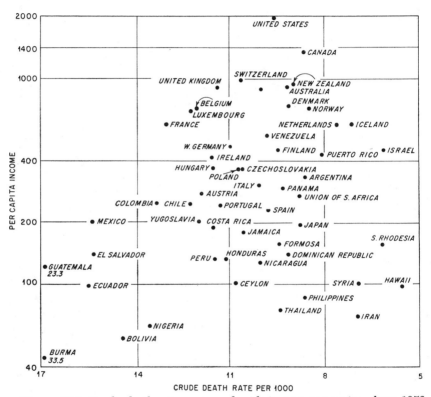

Figure 12.1. Crude death rates compared with income per capita, about 1953. sources: Crude death rates per 1,000 persons of population, *Demographic Yearbook, 1955,* United Nations, New York, 1955, pp. 650–659; income per capita, Table 1.1, Income per Capita in U.S. Dollars.

crease in the rate of decline between 1935–1940 and 1945–1950 is eloquent. In Ceylon, the crude death rate fell by 34 per cent in one year, from 1946 to 1947, as a result of the use of DDT against endemic malaria. Over a period of nine years the death rate fell from 22.2 per thousand to 10.4, or 53 per cent. During the 1940–1950 decade the death rate declined by 46 per cent in Puerto Rico, 43 per cent in Formosa, and 23 per cent in Jamaica. The result of these spectacular changes has been to bring recorded crude death rates in underde-

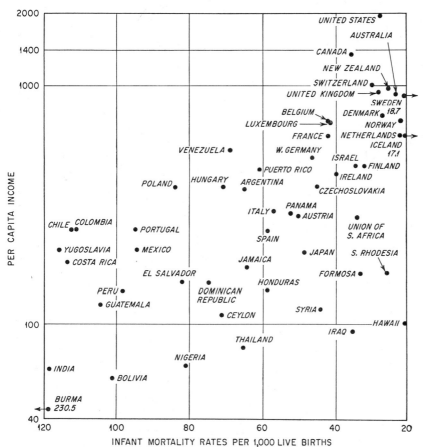

Figure 12.2. Infant mortality rates compared with income per capita, about 1953. SOURCES: Infant mortality (deaths of infants under one year of age per 1,000 live births), *Demographic Yearbook, 1955*, United Nations, New York, 1955, pp. 698–708; income per capita, Table 1.1, Income per Capita in U.S. Dollars.

veloped countries down to the level of those in urban developed countries.

The crude death rate, it should be noticed, does not adequately reflect differences in mortality experience, because of the different average-age composition of population. With identical age-specific death rates, the country with the younger average population—the underdeveloped country—would show a lower crude death rate than the older country.[3] Conversely, the somewhat higher crude death rates of underdeveloped countries with populations which are younger on the average reflect higher mortality rates at a given age.

This is true of certain crude death rates which remain correlated with income per capita, and in particular of the infant-mortality rate. While data are scanty and unreporting is widespread in underdeveloped countries, so that the figures are minimal, it is clear from Figure 12.2 that the correlation is high. In some countries with good statistics —such as Burma, with 231 deaths of children under a year of age per thousand live births; or the British colony, Aden, with 158; or Gold Coast, with 125—very high rates are reached. At the other extreme are Sweden and New Zealand, with figures under 25 per 1,000. (Note that the crude death rate runs in terms of 1,000 people, the infant-mortality rate in terms of 1,000 live births.)

In nonepidemic, nonfamine, nonwar years, the premodern death rate was somewhat higher than 25 per 1,000,[4] which is just about double the central tendency of the rates shown on Figure 12.1. The inclusion of epidemics, wars, and famines raised the *average* death rate to something nearer 30 per thousand. In modern society, however, whether industrialized or underdeveloped, the rate is approach-- ing its long-term limit, which is not far from 9 or 10 per thousand.[5]

BIRTH RATES

Birth rates are much more closely connected with the state of economic development. Figure 12.3 shows the position for a number of countries for which data are available near 1953. Some exceptional figures appear on Figure 12.3, but for the most part the correlation between birth rate and income per capita is a close one.

The connection, of course, is highly complex. In developed countries it may become direct: family limitation is frequently undertaken in order to increase income per capita. But in some instances among developed countries and in underdeveloped countries as a whole, the

[3] *Ibid.,* p. 310.
[4] Kuznets, "Toward a Theory of Economic Growth," in R. Lekachman (ed.), *op. cit.,* p. 20.
[5] Ten per 1,000 would be the limit if everyone lived to be 100 years old and the population were stable. The fact that life expectancies are lower than 100 years raises this rate somewhat less than it is lowered by the fact that the population is growing.

linkage between birth rates and economic growth runs to the cultural pattern—age of marriage, status of women, urban/rural position, and nature of the family system. With agricultural production, ancestor worship, and the extended family, a man begets children to increase output currently (after a five- or six-year lag), to add social security

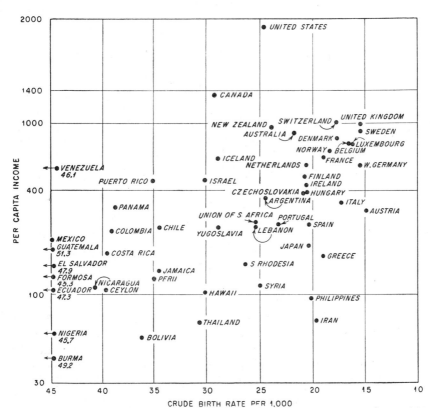

Figure 12.3. Crude birth rates compared with income per capita, about 1953. SOURCES: Crude birth rates per 1,000 persons of population, *Demographic Yearbook, 1955*, United Nations, New York, 1955, pp. 608–620; income per capita, Table 1.1, Income per Capita in U.S. Dollars.

in his old age, and to enhance his standing in the afterworld. Where population pressure on resources grows high, such practices as abortion, exposure of girl infants, taboo against remarriage of Hindu widows, or delayed marriages, as in Ireland, may slow down population increase.

Most cultures set a high store on children in the abstract, and hold infertility in low esteem.[6] As the culture becomes urbanized and increases in economic development, however, emphasis shifts from quantity to quality of children. In Britain, the decline in the birth rate has been linked in the upper classes to primogeniture; in the middle class, to the increase in education.[7] The reasons underlying the halt in the rate of French population growth in the nineteenth century—in what was a Catholic rural society—are not clear. In the view of some, the shortage of land, French distaste for emigration, and the abandonment of primogeniture in favor of equal inheritance slowly brought about an interest in family limitation. To others, the enormous bloodletting of the Napoleonic wars induced the women of France to produce fewer soldiers. The population explosion in Egypt, which currently threatens the economic prospects of that country, had its beginning in the first half of the nineteenth century simultaneously with the introduction of cotton culture. But, whether the added income from growing cotton on irrigated land enabled the prolific workers to afford larger families, or whether the spurt in population was a response to the increased demand for field hands for a labor-intensive crop is an unanswered question.[8]

More surprising than unexplained declines in the birth rate, perhaps, is the demographic counterrevolution which occurred during and after World War II. In the 1930s, demographers in developed countries worried lest they be overtaken by population decline, as birth rates threatened to slide below death rates and the net reproduction rate below 1. As Figures 12.6a and 12.6b below indicate, however, birth rates in the United States and Britain turned sharply upward after the war. In part, the increase made up for the postponements of marriages which occurred during the depression, and of births during the war. For a time, demographers were inclined to dismiss it on these counts. But in the United States at least, and elsewhere in Western Europe if not so clearly in the United Kingdom, it seems that what has occurred is an increase in family size, a return from the modal two-plus children per family during the 1930s to something more

[6] See M. Mead (ed.), *Cultural Patterns and Technical Change*, UNESCO, Paris, 1953, p. 125: "A Tiv married to get children. The production of numerous children was the main function in life." Also, *ibid.*, pp. 57, 96. See also J. and M. Biesanz, *Costa Rican Life*, Columbia University Press, New York, 1944, p. 75: " . . . blessing to have a large family." And T. S. Simey, *Welfare and Planning in the West Indies*, Clarendon Press, Oxford, 1946, p. 15: "Children are highly prized and warmly loved."

[7] K. B. Smellie, *The British Way of Life*, William Heinemann, Ltd., London, 1955, chap. 2.

[8] See C. Issawi, *Egypt at Mid-Century*, Oxford University Press, London, 1954, chap. IV: "The high birth rate in Egypt now seems to be built into the culture. While the divorce rate in 1947 was 31 per cent of the marriages, less than 1 per cent of the divorces occurred where women had three or more children" (p. 56).

nearly approaching four. Rather than raise fewer children to a higher standard of living, the family began to include more children as part of its standard of living. But the reasons behind the change have not been definitively set forth.

One interesting hypothesis has been advanced to explain some part of the decline in birth rates in economic development on physiological

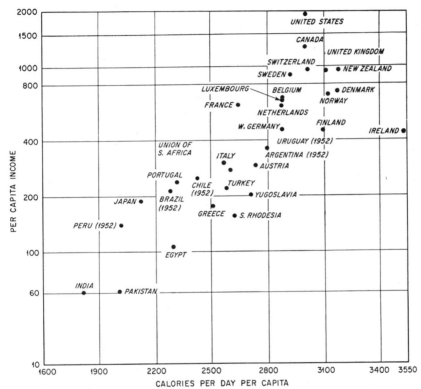

Figure 12.4. Food consumption compared with income per capita, about 1953. SOURCES: Calorie intake per day, *Yearbook of Food and Agricultural Statistics, 1954, Production,* FAO, Rome, 1955, p. 201; income per capita, Table 1.1, Income per Capita in U.S. Dollars.

rather than cultural grounds. J. de Castro, chairman of the Executive Council of the Food and Agriculture Organization, states that the response of nature, when a species is threatened, is to increase the reproduction rate.[9] Fertility, he asserts, is inversely related to protein consumption—a thesis propounded by Thomas Doubleday in 1853. Chronic (but not acute) hunger leads not to depopulation but to over-population. He offers a correlation (page 72) which shows the highest birth rates connected with the lowest rates of daily consumption of

[9] See *The Geography of Hunger,* Little, Brown & Company, Boston, 1952.

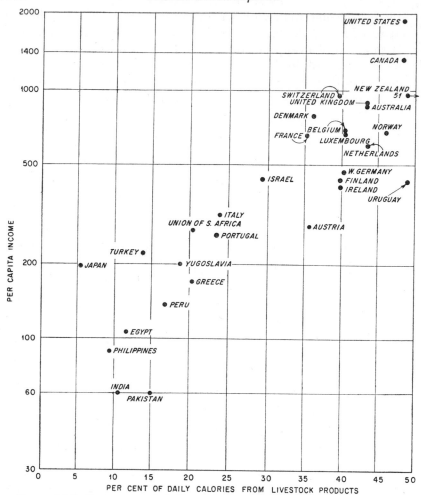

Figure 12.5. Percentage of daily calorie consumption from livestock products compared with income per capita, about 1953. SOURCES: Percentage of consumption in livestock products (meat, eggs, fish, milk, cheese, butter, slaughter fats, and marine oils), *Yearbook of Food and Agricultural Statistics, 1954, Production,* FAO, Rome, 1955, pp. 205–207; income per capita, Table 1.1, Income per Capita in U.S. Dollars.

animal protein measured in grams.[10] Figures 12.4 and 12.5 show the strong correlations between income per capita and calorie consumption per day on the one hand and per cent of daily calorie consump-

[10] Protein deficiency inhibits the functioning of the liver. The liver accordingly is unable to inactivate estrogens, and an excess of estrogens increases fertility (*ibid.*, p. 164).

tion from animal protein on the other. As far as they go, they bear out De Castro. But protein consumption and the birth rate may be unrelated to each other except for their mutual dependence on poverty.

One aspect of the De Castro thesis which must be borne in mind is that diet frequently declines with the early stages of development, which would account for an increase in birth rate. Under the planta-

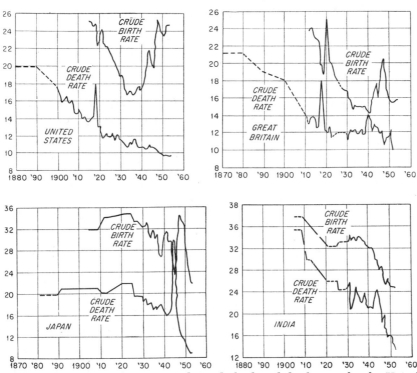

Figures 12.6*a*, 12.6*b*, 12.6*c*, 12.6*d*. Crude birth and death rates for the United States, the United Kingdom, Japan, and India. SOURCES: *Demographic Yearbook, 1950, 1951, 1954*, United Nations, New York; *Statistical Abstract of the United States*, 1936; W. S. Woytinsky and E. S. Woytinsky, *World Population and Production*.

tion system or collectivization of agriculture, obstacles are put in the way of growing food for local consumption, and reliance is necessarily put on imported cereals. With this change, dietary balance is undone, which may stimulate fertility.

While crude death rates have declined from 25 to 10, crude birth rates have followed a somewhat different pattern, declining less and more slowly. In a number of countries an early upward movement in

the birth rate as economic growth makes a start has been followed by
a decline which proceeds more slowly than the decline in deaths. The
position is illustrated in Figure 12.6*d* for India, and the following table
of averages:

Table 12.1. Indian Vital Statistics†

Years	Crude birth rate (per 1,000)	Crude death rate (per 1,000)	Population increase (per cent)
1905–1909	37.7	35.4	0.2
1911–1913	32.7	29.9	0.3
1921–1925	33.3	25.0	0.8
1926–1930	33.2	24.3	0.9
1931–1935	34.3	23.4	1.1
1936–1940	33.3	22.1	1.1
1941–1945	28.3	22.8	0.6
1946–1950	26.3	17.4	0.7
1951–1952	24.8	14.0	1.0

† Data to 1940 for British India; 1930–1946 for British Provinces; beginning
1947, Republic of India.

SOURCE: *Demographic Yearbook, 1951*, United Nations, New York, pp. 146, 160,
161, 188, 200, 201; *Demographic Yearbook, 1954*, pp. 256, 257, 521.

These data are grossly underreported, but the degree of underestimation is likely to have been constant or declining, and roughly
the same in both, so that the changes give an appropriate picture.[11]

One important point on the side of the pessimists is that the birth
rates in underdeveloped countries have started down from levels far
higher than any experienced in Western Europe and the United States
when family limitation began there about 1880. Birth rates higher than
60 per thousand are virtually impossible, and 50 per thousand cannot
long be sustained. A birth rate which stays in the 40s is very high, e.g.,
Singapore, 47; Mauritius, 45; Malaya, 44; Venezuela, 43; Costa Rica,
41; British Guiana, 42; Honduras, 40. These for 1949 and nine in Figure 12.3 for 1953 are the only ones over 40 in countries for which income and birth rate data are available. More of the underdeveloped
countries are in the 30s. But the 30s were high for Western Europe in
the eighteenth century.[12] For the most part, these countries now have
rates in the high teens or the low 20s.

[11] See K. Davis, *The Population of India and Pakistan*, Princeton University
Press, Princeton, N.J., 1951, and S. Chadrasekhar, *India's Population: Fact and
Policy*, rev. ed., Chidambaram, 1950.

[12] Kingsley Davis, *American Economic Review*, May, 1956, p. 315.

RATES OF POPULATION INCREASE

Birth rates and death rates are given per thousand. When the resultant rate of population increase is calculated, the decimal point is moved over one place, and the result expressed per hundred, or in per cent. A birth rate of 40 per 1,000, which is high, and a death rate of 10 per 1,000, which is low, will lead to a rate of increase of 3 per cent, which is about as high as a country is likely to go. Three per cent is the figure reached by Ceylon, Venezuela, Puerto Rico, and El Salvador.[13] Costa Rica has indeed reached 3.7 per cent;[14] but the figure for India has been hovering at about 1 per cent, and Pakistan at about 1.4 (thus far without benefit of an intensive drive on malaria, now under way).

The Malthusian model can be illustrated by comparing curves representing population growth and income growth, plotted as rates of change, each against levels of per capita income. The higher the rate of income per capita, the higher the rate of increase of income. This is because savings vary positively with income per capita, and serve as a basis for capital formation and increments in output. At some level of income per capita, gross savings are just enough to keep the economy stable. At lower rates, capital would be used up and the rate of growth of income would be negative. For convenience, the curve representing the rate of growth of income in per cent (dY/Y) is shown in Figure 12.7 largely as a straight line. In fact, however, above a certain income it will tend to level out to give a constant percentage rate of increase as a limit is reached to increases in savings.[15]

The rate of population increase can also be plotted in terms of income per capita. At some low level the rate of population change will be nil. Population is then stagnant. But higher incomes will bring about an increase in population under the pressure of falling death rates. This increase may well be faster than the rate of income change at the relevant income per capita. Beyond a certain rate of population increase, however, given in Figure 12.7 as 3 per cent, the rate levels off. With still higher incomes it may be expected to decline as the birth rate falls.

In Figure 12.7, the curves are drawn so that they intercept one an-

[13] See *Processes and Problems of Industrialization in Underdeveloped Countries,* United Nations, New York, 1955, p. 15.

[14] Davis, *op. cit.,* p. 316. This table assembles statistics for the eighteen fastest growing countries for which the data are reliable, which condition excludes the Philippines, Egypt, and Thailand.

[15] See above, p. 51.

other twice, at T and at W; T, which happens to be drawn at a positive rate of population increase and income increase, is a stable equilibrium. A small impetus, such as a foreign loan which increased income, would bring about a faster increase in population so that income per capita would decline again to the equilibrium level. At W, however, the equilibrium is unstable. A decrease in income will be cumulative as far as T; an increase will perpetuate itself. T is what has been called a low-level equilibrium trap, which illustrates the Malthusian thesis.[16] If the rate of income increase and the rate of population increase represent functions of per capita income which intersect in this fashion, population and income can grow at the same rate, but income per capita will be fixed.

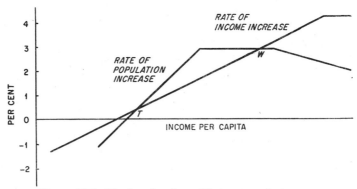

Figure 12.7. The low-level equilibrium population trap.

Whether a country will be caught in the Malthusian trap depends, of course, on the absolute and relative positions of the income and population growth schedules. A change in the sociopolitical outlook can shift the population schedule which, of course, can move only horizontally, i.e., to the right or to the left. Such a shift in either direction may occur from a reevaluation of the desirability of having children; or a technological change in public health may displace the schedule to the left. A technological change or a crash investment program could produce a shift of the income-growth schedule, either horizontally or vertically. There is no need, indeed, for the two schedules to intersect at all, if the income schedule lies originally left and up, and the population schedule lies far to the right. In this case, the trap is not escaped but avoided.

[16] See H. Leibenstein, *A Theory of Economic-Demographic Development,* Princeton University Press, Princeton, N.J., 1954; R. N. Nelson, "The Low-Level Equilibrium Population Trap," *American Economic Review,* December, 1956, pp. 894–908.

This model is based on the assumption that income per capita is a function of the capital/labor ratio, which means that growth is cumulative, since higher income means more savings and therefore a higher ratio. But attention must also be given to the ratio of land to labor. On these assumptions, if income per capita is growing at 1.5 per cent per year, with a 3 per cent annual growth in total income and a 1.5 per cent growth in population, the level of living will rise forever. But a 1.5 per cent rate of growth in population will double the population in fifty years, and this will halve the land/labor ratio. The capital/output ratio, which is good for short periods of time in which the land/labor ratio undergoes little change, is not applicable over long periods. Diminishing returns may reappear in the longer run to which the model does not apply.[17] But it is rash to apply geometric growth rates to long periods. Trees grow for a while at geometric rates but, as Churchill has pointed out, never reach the sky. It may be true that, if the world continues to increase in population at 1.5 per cent a year, the weight of the population would equal the weight of the earth by A.D. 4250.[18] But this is small cause for present alarm, since rates of growth do not hold constant. Apart from some inherent tendency for growth to conform to a Gompertz or S curve, the changes which come with a rise in income per capita—urbanization, education, change of occupation, and frequently the weakening of religious ties—are associated with lower fertility.[19] The significant question is not whether population growth will come to a stop, but at what level of population will the decline of birth rates catch up with the leveling out of death rates. It seems clear that the increase will be sizable in all countries, including those now densely populated. There is little means of determining how much.

AGE DISTRIBUTION

The initial spurt in population encountered by a country in the early stage of development increases total numbers, but not the number of workers. Both a rapidly growing population and one which has stabilized in numbers suffer from the same disability—a high proportion of dependents to actively engaged population. In a rapidly growing population, this is the result of large numbers of youth. In a

[17] H. H. Villard, "Some Notes on Population and Living Levels," *Review of Economics and Statistics*, May, 1955, p. 189.

[18] *Ibid.*

[19] See J. J. Spengler, "Population Theory," in B. F. Haley (ed.), *A Survey of Contemporary Economics*, Richard D. Irwin, Inc., Homewood, Ill., 1952, vol. II, p. 103.

stabilized population, the dependents are to a much greater extent old people.

The age pyramids of populations at different stages in the demographic revolution (and counterrevolution) are illustrated in Figure 12.8, which gives the population distribution by age for the United States, France, Venezuela, and India. If the proportion of the popula-

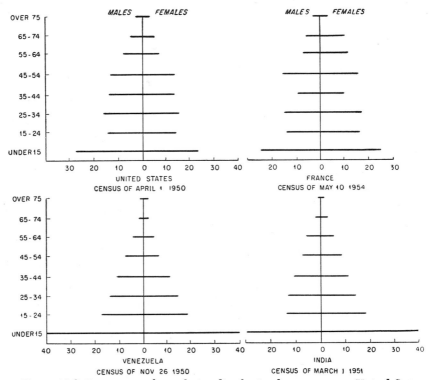

Figure 12.8. Percentage of population distribution by age groups, United States, France, Venezuela, and India, about 1950. SOURCE: *Demographic Yearbook, 1955*, United Nations, New York, 1955, pp. 402–405, 414–415, 490–492.

tion between the ages of fifteen and sixty-four is regarded as economically productive, this varies between something like 55 per cent for underdeveloped countries and 65 per cent for developed. By itself, and apart from differences in average income per gainfully occupied worker, this fact reduces the capacity of underdeveloped countries to save and form capital. The major effect of improved public health methods is to increase the number of children who survive to adulthood. This does not change the proportion of economically active to total population, however, unless the birth rate changes, since the initial increase in number of adults is followed by a further increase in number of children.

Improved public health is not therefore an unalloyed blessing for underdeveloped countries. One of its major effects is to increase the dependent population. But it is equally not a curse. The control or elimination of malaria, smallpox, plague, cholera, syphilis, yaws, and trachoma does improve the quality of living, reducing debility as well as mortality, and increasing vitality and productivity.

MIGRATION

External migration is no longer a cure for overpopulation of under-developed areas. There are some countries whose development would be furthered by immigration. Australia, Rhodesia, and Surinam, where land/labor ratios are very high, fall in this group. But these countries are unwilling to accept immigrants from most densely populated areas, due to the difficulty of social integration on the one hand, and lack of appropriate skills on the other. In Brazil, where relatively indiscriminate immigration has been encouraged to maintain a cheap supply of labor for plantations, a change has been recommended to selective policies designed to settle independent proprietors engaged in mixed farming around the major industrial centers to assist in bringing down the price of food and thus to speed industrialization.[20]

Emigration is still sought as an outlet for surplus population in Italy, and encouraged in the United Kingdom within the Commonwealth. But emigration appears to offer little prospect for alleviating the population surpluses of Asia and the Caribbean (except for Puerto Rican migration to New York). And it is actively opposed in some countries—Ireland and Mexico—since it tends to deprive the country of its most active members.

Emigration from a poor country to a well-to-do one, like capital exports in the same direction, is inappropriate from a welfare point of view. The poor country raises and educates a young man and then ships him off. It knows him only as a dependent, whereas the country of immigration receives him as a member of the labor force. It is true that the country of immigration may be obliged to undertake some complementary capital formation as it receives new arrivals, in order to house, transport, educate, and govern them. If immigrants in all cases sent back remittances to the country of their origin, the capital

[20] F. Bastos de Avila, *Economic Impacts of Immigration: The Brazilian Immigration Problem,* Martinus Nijhoff, The Hague, 1954.

export of a type which the country was well fitted to undertake might pay a high return. More and more, however, in the pressure of today's conformist age, the immigrant quickly shifts his level of living from that of his country of origin to his new homeland, with the result that the benefit accrues to him.

Internal migration offers fewer social barriers, and some considerable opportunities not unassociated, however, with capital requirements of the sort just mentioned. Indonesia's population problem is limited to Java. Sumatra, Borneo, and Celebes have substantial room for settlement. The Indonesian Five-Year Plan provides for some considerable "transmigration" from Java to the islands. Unfortunately, the expense of building roads, clearing land, and constructing houses and villages means that the scale of migration makes little or no dent in the problem. In India nearly half the people live in one-seventh of the area.[21] It is true that the densely settled eastern district is the most fertile because of the monsoon, but as technological change is introduced into agriculture, and as village ties weaken, some resettlement may be possible.

One form of migration which has occurred everywhere is from the village to the city, as already discussed in Chapter 7. In India the percentage of urban population was 9.3 in 1881, grew slowly until 1921, and then began to accelerate. By 1941 it reached 12.8 and by 1951, 17.3. Similar movements appear to have taken place everywhere in the world.

In Brazil the rate of population increase in the cities is much faster than in the country as a whole, despite a much lower birth rate, because of inward migration from the country. This migration is only one of four in the country. The others include a general movement from north to south, i.e., from the slower- to the faster-growing section of the country, a movement into certain frontier districts, and a churning around in rather tragic fashion of a number of seminomads.[22]

The distinction between positive migration, which is attracted by opportunities for economic improvement, and negative migration, which is driven away from a village by lack of opportunity, is an important one. The former requires a feeling of social cohesion which extends beyond the village, and a certain amount of capital, enterprise, and interest in improving one's social and economic condition. The latter is a product of economic distress and is likely to lead to social and political unrest.

[21] K. Davis, *The Population of India and Pakistan,* p. 19.
[22] T. Lynn Smith, "Demographic Factors Related to Economic Growth in Brazil," in S. Kuznets, W. Moore, and J. J. Spengler (eds.), *Economic Growth: Brazil, India, Japan,* Duke University Press, Durham, N.C., 1955, pp. 241–262.

POPULATION POLICY

In the 1930s in Western Europe, population policy was directed to the maintenance of birth rates which were sliding downward. Part of the interest in higher fertility had its origin in eugenics: the quality of population was believed to be deteriorating as reproduction rates were higher among lower-income and less educated groups than among the middle- and upper-income and educated groups. Part was a function of the depression: a slower rate of population growth reduced the demand for housing and overhead capital, and intensified what was regarded as a dearth of investment opportunities.

Population does have supply, as well as demand, effects; but these are slower to be realized except in the event of migration. As already noted, there are a number of countries which want to increase immigration as a matter of national policy[23] to improve the land/labor ratio. A more densely populated area would make for more economical construction and use of "railroads, roads, water supplies and electric power, not to speak of schools, hospitals and social services."[24] But for the most part the population problem consists today of limiting the rise and bringing it to a halt as rapidly as possible.

The only country in the world which has officially adopted family limitation as a national policy is India. Unofficial groups elsewhere have urged dissemination of knowledge of and devices for reducing fertility. These are frequently opposed by the teachings of religion and by the cultural pattern in certain countries, and are impeded, to be sure, by difficulty of communication.

Until recent efforts in India, there had been some doubt whether failure to practice family limitation had its origin in nonacceptance of the goal, ignorance or unavailability of the means, or the fact that the means are complex, difficult of operation, expensive, and uncertain. Recent Indian experience, and the postwar widespread practice of abortion in Japan, even in rural districts, has shifted opinion away from the first of these possibilities.[25] There is still great desire for children in most societies, and opposition to birth control in many

[23] The possibility that one income group in the society should be interested in increased immigration is discussed in the next chapter.

[24] W. A. Lewis, *The Theory of Economic Growth*, Richard D. Irwin, Inc., Homewood, Ill., 1955, p. 211.

[25] See "Overpopulation Held War Peril," *New York Times*, Oct. 25, 1955, which reports that a Japanese doctor addressing the International Conference on Planned Parenthood, held in Tokyo, stated that the number of abortions in Japan, which became legal in 1948, is rapidly rising and approaching the annual number of births.

quarters. But a growing awareness of the possibilities of increasing the level of living has heightened interest in limiting the number of children. The major difficulties in India and Japan, at least, appear to be those of disseminating information. It is generally believed, however, that this would proceed much more rapidly if a cheap, effective, and simple means of reducing fertility, preferably a pill taken orally, could be devised. The complexity of existing methods inhibits learning and practice, even in the face of a strong desire.

Apart from birth control, there seems to be little of a positive nature that can be done. Suggestions have been numerous that expenditures for public health be limited, or postponed, or that economic development programs should focus on social overhead capital and secondary industry, leaving the food supply untouched as long as possible so as not to support higher numbers of people. Still another suggestion is that public health programs emphasize quality, not quantity, and be applied very narrowly in great depth.[26] But none of these suggestions is of any great practicality. Humanitarian considerations suggest that no democratic society can ignore opportunities for inexpensive improvements in public health on a wide scale. A policy of restricting improvements in health to a narrow group for educative purposes is almost certain to run afoul of public opinion. Finally, there is the practical argument that increased output requires improved public health, which is difficult or impossible to dissociate from reduced mortality. In breeding livestock, perhaps, it would be possible to leave high mortality rates unchanged for the mass of the herd, while investing in complementary resources and reserving an investment in general health for the final stage. The clinical detachment necessary to achieve this, together with the passivity of the experimental group, are probably unattainable in people.

Where positive steps are not taken to reduce fertility, and development programs are effective in raising income per capita despite population growth, the concomitants of increased income—city life, higher education, increasing rationality, higher status for women, and interest in material advance will all ultimately reduce the level of fertility. The big questions are how soon and how much. In their answers optimists and pessimists differ.

[26] See above, p. 161.

CHAPTER 13

Evolutionary or Revolutionary Social Change

EVOLUTION OR REVOLUTION

Most feudal societies change only in response to violence from up-thrusting social groups. The aristocrats or elite may give way grace-fully, but this is rare. The new elite is likely to meet resistance from landed nobility, from the established church if this should be eco-nomically powerful, or from the army. Or, if the middle class is weak and parasitical, the proletariat may rise and seize power, as in the Soviet Union and China, and as unsuccessfully attempted in Spain. The social change which is inevitably associated with economic de-velopment, whether as prelude or result, seems, more often than not, to be convulsive. Only where free social institutions have long existed, as in a peasant or a frontier society, is revolution avoidable.[1] And here, as Latin American experience shows, it need not be. Revolution may represent simply a dynastic struggle among various groups in the army or among landowners; or it may go deeper, as in the Argentine revolu-tion, and reflect the clash of interests between *hacendados* and agri-cultural and industrial workers.

The paradox is that the breakup of the traditional pattern and the emergence of a new elite are likely to lead to eruption and violence, but violence, when it occurs, is wasteful of resources and therefore harmful to economic growth.

Social development may be effected short of violence. Sociology has a concept of anomie, which reflects lack of integration of social

[1] W. A. Lewis questions whether it is possible to expect development where peasants hold political power, since they are unlikely to tax away the increase in agricultural output. But Swiss economic development has proceeded far, though leisurely, in spite of peasant political control. See his *The Theory of Economic Growth*, Richard D. Irwin, Inc., Homewood, Ill., 1955, p. 231.

and cultural values. This appears to be a widespread phenomenon in forced-draft programs of economic development. Rural and urban classes become restless and dissatisfied, as old cultural patterns are discarded before new value systems are acquired. The middle class may suffer from anxiety, hostility, guilt, fear, and frustration.[2] It is a short step to give vent to these feelings in violence, rioting, and particularly in xenophobia. Crowding in cities and increasing density of agriculture lead to crime, delinquency, social turbulence, and receptive followers for the political agitator.

ECONOMIC DEVELOPMENT AND SOCIAL STABILITY

In the early days of United States aid to European reconstruction and overseas development, there was a tendency to equate the level of living with political and social stability. Economic assistance was designed to thwart the expansion of communism by raising the level of living. Hunger and poverty were thought to bring about communism; the elimination of hunger and poverty, it followed, would dispel it.[3]

Experience has shown, however, that social stability is a function not of the stage of economic development but of the relation between economic and social aspirations, and the rate at which they are being fulfilled. In stagnant feudal societies, before the prospect of economic development has aroused hopes of dispelling hunger and poverty, stability reigns. Once development is under way, it may bring quiet or turbulence, depending upon whether or not the increased level of living is accompanied by a sense of participation and worth. In the January, 1956, election in France, half the workers of the modern and efficient Michelin tire plant at Clermont-Ferrand, which has high rates of pay, voted the Communist ballot "because the workers, although well paid, were treated about like machines, if not rather worse."[4] In Italy the highest Communist vote was not in the poorest regions in the south but in the richer province of Emilia where income fell short of aspiration.

Development brings with it a rise of the level of aspiration. What is vital to social and political stability is that this be accompanied by a sense of participation on the part of the individual, and a feeling that

[2] See T. S. Simey, *Welfare and Planning in the West Indies*, Clarendon Press, Oxford, 1946, pp. 103–104; J. and M. Biesanz, *The People of Panama*, Columbia University Press, New York, 1955, pp. 211ff.

[3] See M. F. Millikan and W. W. Rostow, *A Proposal: Key to an Effective Foreign Policy*, Harper & Brothers, New York, 1957, pp. 19ff.

[4] "The Red Vote in France," *New York Times*, Jan. 9, 1956.

the aspirations have some prospect of realization. In this it is most important that aspirations not be raised to impossible levels. Premier Nasser, who relied on a single investment such as the High Dam at Aswan to convert a life of poverty into the Garden of Eden, reaped the whirlwind because of aiming too high.

The sense of participation in national economic development is likely to be awakened by a number of institutions which reach down and affect the individual directly. Many of these institutions raise problems, however, since their economic and social objectives are in partial or complete conflict. Land reform, labor unions, social legislation, the cooperative movement, and progressive taxation may have high potentiality for stimulating identification with economic development. In one way or another, however, they have economic drawbacks. Contrariwise, immigration of foreign workers and enterprise may be stimulating in an economic sense, but weaken the tightness of the national feeling on which social stability in part rests. The greater part of this chapter will be devoted to a discussion of these separate institutions and their ambivalent effects.

LAND REFORM

As a general rule, land reform cuts down production, increases consumption, reduces supplies available for shipment to the city and for export, uses up capital, and cuts down capital formation. These are the major economic arguments in favor of retaining land in large blocks. But land reform is a political necessity in many areas where land is held in great latifundia and where the aspirations of the peasantry have become identified with the ownership and cultivation of a separate plot of land. In Mexico in 1911, Russia in 1917, Eastern Europe after World Wars I and II, and in Italy after World War II, the peasant price for participation in political activity, or the bribe paid for peasant support, was the breakup of large estates and distribution of land to peasants.

The splitting up of large estates into small holdings is generally uneconomic. The majority of holders receive plots smaller than optimum size. Small holdings limit the application of capital to land and, through the low incomes of peasants, hold down the accumulation of capital. Lack of capital restricts capacity to shift among crops.[5] But the demand for capital increases. As the labor/land ratio increases, housing is needed. On the latifundia, the peasant may move from the

[5] W. E. Moore, *Economic Demography of Eastern and Southeastern Europe,* Princeton University Press, Princeton, N.J., 1945, pp. 77ff.

village (in Sicily often as large as 50,000 souls) to live on his small plot. Along with new housing, increased numbers of tools must be acquired, only to be used less efficiently.

But there is another side to land reform. It is not always true that the breakup of large estates shifts production to a less efficient scale, and requires more capital for the same output as well as increases farmer consumption. Absentee owners of latifundia on occasion have consistently undercapitalized their holdings. Thrifty peasants may then build up the capital/land ratio even outside the money and market mechanism. In addition, land reform may furnish the spark to economic development, or release the energy needed to make it effective. The theme of S. A. Mosk's *Industrial Revolution in Mexico*[6] is that the rapid rate of growth in income after World War II had its origin in the breakup of the feudal pattern of society in the 1911 revolution. In Italy, land reform appears to be a necessary, if not a sufficient, condition of the development of the south.

Whether land reform will assist or hinder economic development is, then, difficult to predict. In the Soviet Union and in Eastern Europe after World War II, promise of a share of the landed estates was used by the urban Communist group to win peasant support, but was followed by collectivization, which increased large land holdings. The net effect of the double shift was capital consumption, for purely doctrinal reasons, as the peasants slaughtered and ate their livestock prior to merging their assets in the commonwealth. It remains to be seen whether the expropriation of the large estates of the zamindari in India, with compensation, will be permanent, and if so, whether it will release sufficient energy for development to offset the loss of production for the market and the increase in demand for capital.

LABOR UNIONS

Labor unions evolved late in Western industrial society as a reaction and protest against industrial capitalism and to redress the discrepancy of bargaining power in the labor market between workers and employers.[7] In underdeveloped countries, however, imitation of labor unions occurred early in a variety of patterns and with a variety of effects. Development has followed patterns which diverged from private capitalism. More speedily than in Western society, labor has

[6] University of California Press, Berkeley, 1950.
[7] See C. Kerr, F. H. Harbison, J. T. Dunlop, and C. A. Myers, "The Labour Problem in Economic Development," *International Labour Review*, March, 1955, p. 6.

become embroiled in national problems extending beyond wages and conditions of work in separate factories. These unions have gone beyond concern for wages and conditions of work on the local level to protest against the evils of industrialization more generally, but at the same time to recruit, train, and elicit from labor a "commitment to industrial work." They have relations with government administrators, political figures, military cliques, and religious leaders, as well as with employers; and they are concerned with social security, investment decisions, and ownership of enterprise. Some unions go further, like the national Histadrut in Israel which owns and operates a variety of housing and community services, and invests in business enterprises as well as playing a major role in the nation's political life.

The demonstration effect in labor unions may have useful effects. Recruitment of labor is eased when institutions are available to replace the solidarity of the village and assuage the anxieties of the industrial system for the individual. The union in particular can assist in modifying the "partial commitment" of much of the labor force in underdeveloped countries, and the unwillingness permanently to accept industrial life which is demonstrated in arbitrary quitting, absenteeism, or participating in sporadic, guerrilla-like strikes.[8] The union can serve not only as a muffler of protest but as a director of it, channeling it into constructive lines and away from futile anomie.

At the same time, however, there are things that the union cannot do effectively in an underdeveloped society, and other actions which can be positively harmful. The move for higher wages is likely to have adverse consequences for development unless it is accompanied by increases in productivity, and even then this is not the optimal development path. Higher wages may limit the demand for labor in the growing parts of the economy by stimulating the introduction of labor-saving machinery, and thus lead to dual economy.[9] And, as the Cuban experience illustrates, higher wages unsupported by productivity can stifle development.[10] The optimal path may involve low wages in money terms, high profits, and a rapid rate of reinvestment of profits (or, as an alternative, low wages, high taxes, and a high rate of investment of tax revenues). Even where unions consciously teach productivity along with performing their protest function, there is a danger that their success at raising wages will outstrip that at enlarging output, which will increase consumption at the expense of capital formation and reduce the long-run prospects for growth. The weak

[8] *Ibid.*, p. 11.
[9] See above, p. 173.
[10] International Bank for Reconstruction and Development, *The Economic Development of Cuba*, Johns Hopkins University Press, Baltimore, 1951, chap. 16.

unions in West Germany after 1948 may paradoxically have contributed more to the incomes of their members in the long run by their ineffectuality on the issue of wages, since investment of corporate profits at a high rate raised output and consumption higher over time than would have been possible with increased money wages. The less the unions believe in productivity and the more they believe in redistribution of exorbitant profits, the less they aid the development program. It may be true that exorbitant profits are being made, and used wastefully in consumption; the corrective, however, is not redistribution into consumption for different spenders, but redirection into productive capital formation.

Control over labor relations may be in the hands of one group— employers (as in France before the Popular Front), unions (as in some closed shops), or in government (as in the Soviet Union). It may be shared by two groups—employers and unions in the United States, employers and government in Latin America, and unions and government in Scandinavia and Britain. Or the responsibility may involve all three, which seems to be the pattern in India. The path of mature and responsible unionism seems to require that relations be dualistic and between employers and unions. For unions to bypass the employer, and continuously to enlist the aid of the state in the settlement of bargaining issues without accepting the responsibility involved in strike threats and strikes, leads to immature labor relations.

Research is currently required, and some is under way, as to the ways in which the labor movement in underdeveloped countries can contribute to the welfare of its members and of society. A labor movement with strong reformist goals is tolerable primarily where the mass of the workers has already acquired habits of productivity, and does not slough them off as income rises. Where productivity is not ingrained, the movement for higher welfare may end merely in inflation. The difficulty is that where workers are trained to be productive, as in Germany, they are frequently also docile and resistant to militant movements.

The economist interested in development and in labor is therefore faced with a dilemma. If he could use the labor movement to recruit workers, give them a sense of participation in industry, replace village ties, and induce them to accept a commitment to industrial life and productivity, it would be the most valuable instrument of development imaginable. But this is to convert unionism into an overseer, and to undermine its appeal to workers which is based on protest against the worker's loss of freedom and leisure, his lack of security, and his inability to satisfy his wants.

The unionism that a society is likely to achieve will vary over an infinite spectrum, partly dictated by random elements and partly by national character. If the society is inherently cooperative, unions may be the most effective means of organizing labor. But if life in the society is a form of gamesmanship in which a man is either one up or one down, as is said to be the case in Morocco, unionism is a Pandora's box of social unrest, and more likely to hinder than to help economic growth.

SOCIAL LEGISLATION

The same considerations apply to social legislation as to labor unions. Unemployment insurance, old-age pensions, minimum-wage legislation, compulsory annual vacations, maternity leaves, severance pay—all convey to the individual the impression that the government is concerned for his interests, and they increase his sense of belonging and participation. Thus they are useful in stabilizing the social position. But the underdeveloped economy is unable, as a rule, to afford them. To load the cost on employers is to increase labor costs, reduce employment, and distort factor proportions. Foreign investment is repelled. Capital formation and development are slowed down.

Not all social legislation is of this kind, however. Some measures, like the eight-hour day, health insurance, workmen's compensation, and decent working conditions, pay off directly in increased productivity. Concern with full employment, as contrasted with the maximum pace of growth of total output, may also be socially desirable but economically expensive. Unemployment is a peculiarly subversive social phenomenon, even when its effect on consumption is offset by transfers, since it contributes to the individual's sense of insecurity and failure to belong. Where unemployment is heavily concentrated in the group of "passed Senior School certificate holders," it is a strong breeder of revolutionary discontent. As Chapter 10 indicated, maximum employment and maximum output may proceed along different lines. And to hire high-school graduates as clerks in the government in large numbers in order to reduce social discontent worsens the budgetary position.

PROGRESSIVE TAXATION

A further clash between economic growth and social stability may arise over the source of capital formation. The alternatives are two: the business sector and the government. If investment is undertaken significantly by the business sector, maximum growth requires gently rising prices of industrial products, but not of agricultural, and lagging wages. The result is high profits which must then be reinvested. Progressive income taxation would contribute to social stability, which may be threatened by the regressive shift in income distribution as industrial workers and farmers suffer a decline in real income while entrepreneurs pile up fortunes. But it would slow down growth.

If, on the other hand, the government is the major source of capital formation, the conflict is brought out into the open. For popular democratic support, some political leaders will insist on primarily progressive taxation. But, as we have seen in Chapter 11, the difficulties of tax administration require that any substantial program of government capital formation involve taxes levied heavily on consumption and land. Progressive taxation, where it prevents lavish consumption, is both socially and economically useful if in practice it is possible to distinguish between taxes which fall on wealthy landowners who spend their incomes, and those affecting reinvesting entrepreneurs. But large-scale capital formation must imply some austerity for the mass of the people. It makes a considerable difference whether this is brought about through an initial reduction in real consumption or through an increase in productivity, which is diverted to capital formation and unavailable for increases in consumption. But even in the latter case, hopes for betterment are frustrated, and social equilibrium rendered more difficult because of incomprehensible delay.

COOPERATIVE MOVEMENT AND COMMUNITY DEVELOPMENT

The major devices for enlisting participation in the process of development are the cooperative movement and community development. The importance of participation by the rank and file is hard to overestimate. Not only is economic development imposed from above likely to fail to accomplish its objectives in production;[11] it is a threat to existing social stability.

Cooperatives and community development differ from the other institutions discussed above in that they are more rather than less harmonious with economic objectives. They tend to encourage additional capital formation outside the market economy, and in the subsistence sector where capital is formed only with difficulty; further, they save

[11] See A. R. Holmberg, "The Wells That Failed: An Attempt to Establish a Stable Water Supply in the Viru Valley, Peru," in E. H. Spicer (ed.), *Human Problems in Technological Change*, Russell Sage Foundation, New York, 1952, pp. 113–123.

capital by utilizing existing social overheads, such as housing, and avoid the redistribution problem which arises when underemployed workers move to the city from rural areas and have to have their food brought along too; finally, they tend to use factor proportions suitable to the society. In agricultural cooperatives, moreover, it is sometimes possible to perpetuate large-scale agricultural production on an efficient basis and avoid the paralyzing effect of small holdings.

But cooperatives, and possibly community development, are not possible in all human situations. Where a high degree of individualism is present—in Britain, in Mexico, and in a number of Arab countries— the producers' cooperative is not likely to develop far.[12] To spend much time in the attempt to instill the spirit of cooperation in such a society would hardly seem worthwhile. The competitive market mechanism is likely to be more effective.

FOREIGN ENTERPRISE

Foreign enterprise also has conflicting impacts, but of a contrary sort: it is likely to be good for economic development, and occasionally subversive of long-run social stability. On the economic side, foreign entrepreneurs organize production on an effective scale, provide capital, direct goods to markets, and elaborate more efficient techniques. Taxes and royalties paid by them provide a source of savings for capital formation in the domestic sector. In the social area large companies have latterly undertaken investments in education and health in addition to overhead capital such as transport facilities. But there is another side to the case.

Hla Myint, a Burmese economist, contends that foreign investment tends to fossilize the efficiency and earnings of the "domestic" factors of production at their initial low level.[13] Instead of serving as a growing point, foreign investment, he claims, produces an initial change in the efficiency of production and then frustrates further growth in the capacity of the labor force. Plantations or mining replace a primi-

---

[12] See H. Faber, *Cooperation in Danish Agriculture*, 2d ed., Longmans, Green & Co., Ltd., London, 1931, p. vii (foreword by E. J. Russell): "The English farmer is so confirmed an individualist and so imbued with running his own farm in his own way that he cannot cooperate with his neighbor." And O. Lewis, *Life in a Mexican Village*, University of Illinois Press, Urbana, Ill., 1951, pp. 111, 127: "The Mexicans need the stimulus of drink to work together, and are highly individualistic despite the existence of communal land (*ejido*) set up in the revolution . . . . It may be noted that Mexicans have difficulty playing together at soccer whereas British reserve in cooperation is limited to work" (p. 211).

[13] Hla Myint, "The Gains from International Trade and the Backward Countries," *Review of Economic Studies*, 1954–1955, no. 58, pp. 129–142.

tive society with a highly structured one in which foreigners occupy the few positions of responsibility and authority and native workers are left to wield the shovel, pick, or hoe—tools which have little training or civilizing value.

In Latin America, foreign enterprise is said to be a prop for an ineffective entrepreneurial class concerned not to challenge the leadership and status of the landowning elite, but to share it.[14] This small group of industrialists is content with limited economic development, with its shocking gap between the levels of living of the privileged minority, to which it belongs or aspires, and the masses condemned permanently to substandard consumption. It favors monopolistic markets with profits of 50 to 150 per cent a year on invested capital, and increased immigration for the purpose of holding down wages. It insists that foreign enterprise must permit the participation of domestic capital so that competition from abroad cannot upset its local domination. This indictment is certainly too sweeping. Yet the suggestion that local interests may push for imports of foreign capital and immigration to strengthen their position in preparation for a forthcoming showdown between landowners and capitalists on the one hand and the broad mass of agricultural and urban workers on the other has an element of truth, as recent events in Guatemala and Argentina make clear.

ECONOMIC DEVELOPMENT AND NATIONALISM

There is an interaction between development and nationalism. The glorification of the nation requires more economic production. Nationalism is also a spur to the sacrifice needed for capital formation.

Nationalism is of two kinds, hard to tell apart. There is the positive variety in which love of country and willingness to make sacrifices in the national interest are reconciled with loyalty to greater and lesser social units—the village, region, province, or state on a lower political scale and Western or Eastern or Middle Eastern civilization and the United Nations on the higher. Opposed to this is the negative brand, in which patriotism is antithetical to interest in and respect for other countries. A number of countries may be able to cooperate only in their dislike for and opposition to a single country or group. Basically competitive with one another, the Arab countries can unite against

[14] S. G. Hanson, *Economic Development in Latin America*, Inter-American Affairs Press, Washington, 1951, pp. 9, 15ff. For a further expression of Hanson's acid views on development, see "Case Study in Futility: United Nations Economic Commission for Latin America," *Inter-American Economic Affairs*, Autumn, 1948, pp. 81–99.

Israel or the West, and Arab, Asian, and Latin American countries cooperate in the United Nations as an anticolonial bloc.

Opposition to outsiders is a powerful cohesive force. The need for defense gave an important element of stability to feudalism. Another was provided by the view of salvation as deferred until the after-life.[15] With the world increasingly secularized and interested in material salvation in the here and now, xenophobia furnishes a readily available counterweight to centrifugal tendencies in society. The latent antipathy between East and West Pakistan is held in check by the Kashmir dispute. Indian rioting over local issues, e.g., the choice of official language and administrative boundaries where different cultural groups overlap in an area such as Bombay, seems less significant in the light of the Kashmir disagreement at one level and Indian aspirations for a world role on another.

There is little doubt that the cohesion which arises from opposition to outsiders is economically productive. Danish success in converting its agriculture in the 1880s was not unconnected with the increase in cohesion which came from its defeat by Germany over Schleswig-Holstein in 1866. The United States start in development fed on political independence.[16] The development drive in Asia, the Middle East, Africa, and Latin America has given rise to and feeds on increasing independence. The shift from colony to independence or dominion status is particularly stimulating to development aspirations on the part of government; it also enlarges capacities as reflected in general willingness to sacrifice consumption for national advance.

This is not to suggest that metropolitan areas have exploited colonies and limited development in the interest of the mother country—although this has happened. Imperial countries have increased output in their colonies, by establishing law and order; have undertaken investments and social services, not exclusively for the sake of protecting imperial investments; and, particularly in the late colonial period when the perils of neglecting the native interest have been more and more

[15] The World Council of Churches in Geneva is undertaking a study of the "Common Christian Responsibility toward Areas of Rapid Social Change" (see statement of this name dated September, 1955), emphasizing the contribution which the Christian ethic of brotherhood can make to "responsible emancipation." The study will cover "responsible citizenship," "village and rural life," "problems of urbanization," and "the impact of foreign enterprise and international assistance."

[16] An economic historian once suggested privately that the War of Independence was an economic mistake, and that if the United States had remained part of the British Empire, later the Commonwealth, it would have advanced faster because it would have received from Britain a more sustained capital flow on a higher level. The remark was probably not intended seriously. But the counterweight to any possible increased capital inflow was the increase in social cohesion from independence, which far outweighed any possible investment effect.

sharply manifest, have undertaken positive measures of economic development, including the provision of overhead capital. In a few instances, particularly France, colonization has brought civilization.[17]

Anticolonialism and anti-imperialism can thus go too far. They also fail altogether to offset mistakes and weaknesses of developing countries on the home front. Peron's anti-Yanqui crusade could not hide the fact that his domestic revolution had backfired on economic development.[18] The Guatemalan revolution of 1944 involved the middle- and lower-class Ladinos (who speak Spanish in contrast to the illiterate and antipathetic Indians) on the one hand, against church, army, and landowners, on the other, until it was seized by a small Communist group and directed against the United States and the United Fruit Company. Mossadegh's wildly popular expropriation of the Anglo-Iranian Oil Company set back Iranian development between 1952 and 1956, and permanently lost for his country a portion of the world oil market by the stimulus it gave to development in Arabia and Kuwait. In 1956 Premier Nasser's attempt to finance the construction of the High Dam at Aswan by his seizure of the Suez Canal was the desperate act of a frustrated man whose overly ambitious plan was doomed to failure even if the United States and the Soviet Union had together undertaken to carry it through.

With frustration and the development of xenophobia, the temptation to confiscate the wealth of an elite class or of foreigners frequently proves irresistible. Bronfenbrenner argues that where 15 per cent of national income has gone to a wealthy elite or to foreign investors and been used for consumption or remittance abroad to the extent of 12.5 per cent, with only 2.5 per cent for capital formation, confiscation is an irresistible means of increasing the level of investment. The new level of capital formation will be 15 per cent in the Soviet type of development where the development gets it all; 12.5 per cent where, in Red Chinese style, something is allowed to spill over to increase general consumption. Except where special ties of consanguinity exist, as

[17] See "How Strong Are Algeria's Rebels?" *Economist,* Mar. 17, 1956, p. 617: "France means a wide gate to a world of ideas without which self-government would be nothing but an empty fabric. France has known how to make its colonial subjects love it as well as hate it, and perhaps it is unique in this among colonial powers. That is why the rebels insist they do not fight against France or French culture, but only against French control."

[18] It is argued by George Pendle in *Argentina,* Royal Institute of International Affairs, London, 1955, that Peron did not initiate the revolution of the rural proletariat and urban worker against the "entrenched oligarchy" on the land. Already by 1941 only ten of the highest-income recipients were landowners, the others being manufacturers, financiers, mine operators, etc. (p. 75). During six years before the 1943 revolution, the percentage of the labor force employed in industry rose from 12.8 to 17.1, while in the next six years it rose only to 20.1.

in the Commonwealth, or in oil, where underdeveloped countries are dependent upon their foreign partners for markets, or where geographic proximity dominates, as in Cuba and Puerto Rico, Bronfenbrenner expects confiscation to spread over the world.[19]

A later chapter discusses technical questions of foreign investment, and whether the rate of production of golden eggs justifies the slaughter of the goose or argues for a reprieve. Here the issue is the likelihood of confiscation largely on noneconomic grounds, to give vent to years of pent-up protest over confinement to a status of inferiority, and of frustration because economic development does not automatically spring full blown from the brow of the local leader when "exploitation" ends with independence. Nationalism can be a positive force in much economic development. But it is difficult to keep it from degenerating into sterile antagonism.[20]

PLURAL SOCIETIES

It was widely believed in Asia (and in the United States) that the British worries about strife between Moslem and Hindu at the time of the liberation of India were basically a mask for reluctance to part with the sovereignty of the subcontinent. It has been learned this was not so. Independence, despite partition, led to a most cruel and wasteful struggle of cultures, necessitating the exchange of populations, with great suffering and losses, and giving rise to the dispute over Kashmir which requires sizable armies and directly substracts from development resources. But even within India, Pakistan, and Indonesia, sharp cultural and religious differences exist, giving rise to acute political issues.

A similar problem now faces Malaya, from which the British withdrew on August 1, 1957, leaving behind a population 45 per cent Chinese, 43.5 per cent Malayan, and 10.5 per cent Indians and Pakistani. The Chinese dominate Singapore, the Malays the Federation. The Chinese are the merchants or white-collar workers; the Malays, the paddy farmers and fishermen. Prior to World War II, there was almost no contact between the two groups. There was no personal friendliness, no sympathy or understanding, no participation in common ideas or purposes. On the surface, there was complete indiffer-

[19] M. Bronfenbrenner, "The Appeal of Confiscation in Economic Development," *Economic Development and Cultural Change*, April, 1955, pp. 201–218.

[20] Even in Turkey, which long since has halted the humiliating capitulations under which foreigners collected her customs to pay off their obligations and decided to welcome foreign assistance and investment in the development process, sensitivity and pride have led to a ban on foreigners who offer unwelcome advice.

ence. But since World War II each group feels aggrieved at the other: the Chinese in that their economic power is not accompanied by a voice in political life, and that Chinese is not an official language; the Malays that their level of income is inferior to the Chinese. The Chinese have given some support to Communist guerrillas; the Malays threaten *jihad* or holy war, when British withdrawal unhinges the precarious balance.

In these circumstances, which are reproduced on a less acute scale in many parts of the world, development plans offer little hope of fulfillment, pending the achievement of a degree of common purpose among the several groups. The design for economic growth may provide part of the basis of commonality; and more may be derived from xenophobic exercises. Where the cultural differences are not wide, participation in a common experience can, over time, reduce cultural difference to a level of the Yale-Harvard or California-Florida competition within a cooperative frame. More, however, may be needed.

Independence of the totality brings with it demands for autonomy of the parts at a time when the cohesion of the whole is anyway threatened. The English language, which bound the several cultures of the Indian subcontinent in a single communications network, is being deposed in favor of Hindi in India and Urdu and Bengali in Pakistan, both of which are unknown to millions who already know their native tongue and English. A long-run gain in cohesion will pay a short-run price in confusion.

THE CHANCES FOR AVOIDING VIOLENCE

Increasing dissatisfaction with economic and political status in the world seems likely to lead to violent changes in the structure of political, social, and economic relations within countries which have remained feudal, and to forceful change in the relations of many of these underdeveloped countries with the outside world. The chances of avoiding internal outbreaks are positively correlated with the degree of national cohesion achieved, which in turn is partly a function of antipathy for foreigners and partly of successful economic development. Since relations with foreigners and the availability of loan and grant assistance for development are themselves interrelated, the position becomes complex and delicate. The maximum chance of avoiding violence may be given by domestic programs of economic development which rely on the widest possible participation through institutions like land reform, unions, progressive taxation, etc., together with a strong and independent attitude toward foreigners which falls short, however, of that level of intransigence which would cut off all assistance and foreign loans.

How such a formula will apply to different cases must be determined in the light of the separate facts. Some countries seem doomed to sanguinary conflict. In others, the pace of successful development, already established, puts them into the class of satisfied powers which steady, rather than rock, the international boat.

That this is the crucial question in economic development is hard to doubt. But it may be well to let the last word go to an Indian scholar:[21]

The spirit of the Indian people is aflame; the labor and mass unrest which characterize India even after its independence bear testimony to it . . . . Since any quick economic development programs necessitate a breach in age-old customs and practices, and a revolutionary change in social institutions, the present mood of the Indian masses is an invaluable asset. But, unless it is properly channelled, and prospects of rapid betterment created, it may seek avenues which may lead to political chaos and anarchy, making all economic progress impossible. The divine spark of discontent may, if intensified and frustrated, develop into the conflagration which may engulf us and perhaps the whole of Asia.

[21] D. T. Lakdawala, *International Aspects of Indian Economic Development,* Oxford University Press, London, 1951, p. 20.

THE CASE FOR COMPARATIVE ADVANTAGE

The classic case for specialization and trade, based on comparative advantage, is a static one: with two countries, two commodities, two factors (fixed in quantity and mobile within but not between the two countries), identical production functions in both countries, full employment, perfect competition, and a few other assumptions, it has been easy to demonstrate that both countries will be better off with free trade than with restrictions on trade, or at least that one country can be better off and the other no worse off. Comparative advantage will generally arise from differences in factor endowments in the two countries, and each country will export the commodity which is produced with a high proportion of the factor which it possesses in abundance.

The static nature of comparative advantage does not make it inapplicable to countries engaged in economic development, in the view of many economists. If a country is pulled into world trade for the first time by the opening up of transport, or if new opportunities for trade are created by reductions in transport cost, the country can and should maximize its real income by specialization along lines of comparative advantage. If factors should be changed by discovery or population growth, a new basis of comparative advantage is reached, but the same reasoning applies. Resources should be readjusted so as to give a new maximum.

The law of comparative advantage establishes a presumption that an incremental balanced unit of resources should be invested in the export industry rather than in the import-competing industry, to stick to two commodities. The country is more efficient in the production of the export good. Even where demand is strongly biased in favor of the import good, the presumption holds. More of the import good is acquired by producing the export item and exchanging it for the desired one. This is the presumption in favor of comparative advantage which its opponents must overcome.

While land and labor remain relatively unchanged in the short and intermediate run, capital accumulation proceeds at a steady pace. The theory is readily adjusted to accommodate this change.[1] As capital accumulation proceeds faster in one country than another, the factor endowments underlying comparative advantage, and comparative advantage itself, change. The basis for trade is altered. But a new basis exists.

THE OPPOSITION TO COMPARATIVE ADVANTAGE

Exception is taken to this view along a wide front. The earliest argument invoked increasing returns. A long line of economists, from the German and early American protectionists to Allyn Young and John H. Williams, have insisted on leaving room for the possibility that static free trade will give less than an optimum position for the world because of increasing returns to scale available in an industry but unrealizable at the low prices maintained under free trade. With protection and higher prices, an increase in scale will make possible an ultimately lower price than that which prevailed with free imports.

For a long time the infant-industry argument was the only exception to the free-trade case which commanded respectable support. Recently, however, a host of new arguments has been put forth, at a variety of different levels. Dynamic counterweights to static comparative advantage have been found in short-run instability, in long-run behavior in the terms of trade, in disparity between social and private costs, and, more fundamental, in the relevance of the two-country, two-factor, two-commodity world to the world of factor movements, capital accumulation, changing technology, and intermediate goods. There are other arguments, but these are the principal ones.

Short-run instability in export markets is an argument against specialization, insofar as, in the short run, investments are lumpy, resources are immobile, and wants are incompressible. A country might do well to specialize in a food item, an agricultural raw material, or a mineral at the long-run average price, if this were steady; but wide short-run fluctuations in price around the average slow down development. In the first place, it is not possible to vary domestic consumption

---

[1] D. M. Bensusan-Butt, "A Model of Trade and Accumulation," *American Economic Review*, September, 1954, pp. 511–529.

or investment over the range required by large annual changes in export proceeds. The average year-to-year fluctuations in the prices of fifty commodities studied by the United Nations Secretariat over the period from 1900 to 1950 was 14 per cent per annum.[2] As the value of exports fluctuates widely, a specialized country lacks control over national income, money supply, and hence over its rate of development.[3] It may be desirable, in these terms, to accept a somewhat lower degree of specialization and lower level of real income at the outset of a development program in order more surely to be in control of it. When Brazil, for example, was specializing successively in sugar, rubber, and coffee, it failed to get development effectively under way.

The instability argument rests partly on the proposition that demand is inelastic. It is possible to make a static case on this point. It is sometimes maintained that comparative advantage is well and good as far as a country has gone, but that additional investment in the export industry will depress prices. If demand is inelastic, calculation of marginal revenue for a given incremental unit must take into account not only the return on that unit but the impact on profits on inframarginal sales. It may then happen that a country will do well to leave resources currently engaged in exports where they are, but to invest additional available resources elsewhere. The average revenue in this case could be higher in exports than in an import-competing good, but marginal revenue lower. Average comparative advantage would dictate expanding exports, but marginal comparative advantage would lie with the import-competing good.

Or the difficulty may lie not so much in the price elasticity of demand abroad as in the income-inelasticity or uncertainty about the income-elasticity of alternative investments in the home market, as claimed by Nurkse. It was argued in Chapter 9 that balance in demand could be achieved by displacing existing producers; among the producers whom it is easiest to supersede are the foreigners. If foreign producers have built a market for shoes in a country, the country knows that it can invest safely in shoe production, provided it excludes the foreign product.

Another argument runs to the effect that specialization is an undesirable policy in the long run, since it condemns underdeveloped countries specializing in raw materials to ever-declining terms of trade, as contrasted with developed countries which produce manufactures. It was originally thought that the terms of trade would favor primary production, which obeyed the law of diminishing returns, and respond

[2] *Instability in Export Markets of Underdeveloped Countries*, United Nations, New York, 1952.

[3] See H. C. Wallich, *Monetary Problems of an Export Economy*, Harvard University Press, Cambridge, Mass., 1950.

adversely to manufactures, which followed the law of diminishing cost. But observation has made clear that there is no real evidence to support the view that the different sectors followed different laws of production, and some to suggest that, in fact, the terms of trade have run the other way. The major evidence cited was decidedly weak: primarily the inverse of the British terms of trade from 1870 to 1938. More generally, the theorem rests on generalizations such as Engel's law, which requires a progressive shift of resources out of foodstuffs into secondary and tertiary industry as world income per capita grows; but failing which, foodstuffs will be overproduced and hence decline in price relative to manufactures; or the increased efficiency in the consumption of raw materials used in manufacturing, which enables a given amount of raw-material production to support a higher and higher value of manufactured output. This means, of course, that if the physical outputs of raw materials and manufactures grow at equal rates, the terms of trade will shift against raw materials. Or the argument runs in terms of comparative monopoly power: increased efficiency in developed countries takes the form of higher prices for factors of production and constant prices for goods, whereas in underdeveloped countries, factor returns hold steady in spite of increased productivity and the benefit goes abroad to lower prices.

As it happens, there is evidence from Europe's terms of trade to suggest that, while there is no necessary trend in the terms of trade between manufactures and raw materials, the terms of trade seem to favor developed and run against underdeveloped countries.[4] The statements become reconciled when it is realized that many countries, such as Britain (coal), Germany (coal), and the United States (wheat and cotton), export primary products, and a number of underdeveloped countries export manufactures (Japan and India, textiles). The basis for the tendency of the terms of trade to deteriorate for underdeveloped countries, however, is found in their immobility of supply. They may be lucky and find themselves producing a commodity in which profitability is high, and imitators are kept at bay by natural advantages. But typically, the underdeveloped country finds that competitors swarm in when it does well, which limits the improvement possible in terms of trade, while it is unable readily to reallocate resources when demand shifts away from its products, which leads prices to fall. Supply is elastic for price increases and inelastic for price declines.

This tendency for the terms of trade to turn against underdeveloped

---

[4] See C. P. Kindleberger, *The Terms of Trade*, The Technology Press of Massachusetts Institute of Technology and John Wiley & Sons, Inc., New York, 1956, esp. chaps. 10 and 11.

countries is not, however, an argument against specialization in foreign trade. It supports, rather, greater flexibility in the allocation of resources so as to take advantage of the benefits in working for the foreign market and to limit losses when demand shrinks or a competitor outdoes the country.

Opposition to foreign trade based on the disparity between private and social costs is represented particularly by Manoilescu's *Theory of Protection,*[5] to which previous reference has been made. This holds that the existence of underemployment or disguised unemployment in the agricultural sector brings it about that private cost, on which comparative advantage calls for exports of agricultural products and imports of manufactures, is unrepresentative of social costs. In the agricultural sector, private cost is too low, because wages are depressed; in industry, private cost is too high, because manufacturers pay unduly high wages which would be lowered if the disguised unemployed freely competed in the labor market. Accordingly, Manoilescu recommended tariffs on imports to assist in the transfer of labor from unemployment in agriculture to employment in industry. This argument rests essentially on differing sets of factor proportions in different sectors, a dual economy. It fails to take account, however, of the possibility that the exact opposite condition exists in the capital market, that its private cost is below social cost in manufacturing and above in the agricultural sector. To the extent that this is true, part of the qualification of the theory of comparative advantage is offset. But a more general solution is to merge factor markets and equalize factor prices, rather than to interfere with specialization based on incorrect factor prices which are allowed to continue.

A somewhat different argument, equally based on imperfections in factor markets, is that made by Hla Myint, to which reference was made in the previous chapter. In his view, foreign enterprise which gives rise to international trade produces an initial productive change in technology and specialization, but tends to freeze the domestic factors at their initial productivity and rate of return. This, however, argues less for reducing foreign trade than for changing its basis.

This argument may be linked back to the classic exception to comparative advantage based on increasing returns, relying on the presumption that external economies—largely in training—are much more substantial in import substitution than in export expansion.[6] That this

[5] P. S. King & Staples, Ltd., London, 1931.

[6] The best statement of this point is by H. W. Singer in "The Distribution of Gains between Investing and Borrowing Countries," *American Economic Review, Papers and Proceedings,* May, 1950, p. 473.

is so is not proven, of course; and a number of economists such as
Viner would vigorously deny it.[7] Moreover, where export industries
are primary goods produced with scientific technology and using substantial amounts of capital—as in Middle Western, Antipodean, and
Danish agriculture, the training effect in the export industry may be
large and cumulative. There is nonetheless considerable evidence to
suggest that in labor-intensive economies, which imitate rather than
initiate technological change, there may be a larger developmental
gain in training from import substitution than export expansion. Japan
is perhaps the classic example. The textile, electrical equipment, steel,
machinery, and shipbuilding industries all had their start in protection.
Where trade is based on differences in factor endowments, as mentioned presently, limiting imports and encouraging the acquisition of
new techniques may be the path of more rapid development.

A more fundamental attack on comparative advantage, however,
has been made by Romney Robinson, who suggests that the doctrine
is more useful in explaining where a country has been than in indicating where it might go.[8] Factor endowments are not fixed. They change
with technology, as we have noticed above. They can also be altered
by international factor movements—at least of labor and capital. And,
where trade opens up opportunities for capital formation or labor
training, and imports of intermediate goods (which are hard to distinguish from factors) bulk large in relation to gross national product,
trade explains factor endowments rather than factor endowments
trade.[9] This is the most telling blow to the theory of comparative advantage, but there are lesser ones. Since diffusion of technology takes
place slowly, trade may be explained at a given time not by differences
in factor proportions but by differences in technology. Just because
airplane manufacture is labor-intensive does not mean that India is

[7] *International Trade and Economic Development,* Free Press, Glencoe, Ill.,
1952, esp. pp. 60ff.
[8] R. Robinson, "Factor Endowments and Comparative Advantage," *Quarterly
Journal of Economics,* May, 1956, part I, pp. 169–192; *ibid.,* August, 1956, part
II, pp. 346–363.
[9] Japan has abundant labor and capital but lacks raw materials. Where these
can be imported cheaply, and where markets are located not too far away, Japan
finds itself with a comparative advantage in textiles, steel products, chemicals, etc.,
although it lacks their basic ingredients. One could perhaps net out the import
content of exports, and calculate comparative advantages on the basis of values
added, but the question of whether it is profitable to import raw materials for
manufacture into particular exports depends partly on costs of transport and the
location of the factory site (Japan's is appallingly bad) and partly on the prices
of complementary labor and capital, which may be sufficiently low to overcome
high transport costs in one case but not in another. These reflections are based on
discussions with Prof. R. Komiya.

able to export airplanes. More than this, if a production function permits a very considerable amount of substitution along it, of land for capital and capital for land, the theory of comparative advantage has nothing to communicate: the United States with cheap capital can export rubber to Indonesia, or possibly Indonesia with cheap rubber-producing land can export rubber to the United States.

When technology is subject to change, in ways which will sharply alter the proportions of factor inputs, specialization involves a risk. Technological change may undermine the basis for specialization as the history of synthetic nitrates, rayon, nylon, detergents, atabrine, and similar products proves. It is all very well to put all one's rocks into one sturdy basket, for they do not get hurt when they spill. With fragile eggs, it's different.

Finally, exception can be taken to the assumption of the classic model about tastes. Tastes are frequently assumed for convenience to be identical before trade, and to be unaffected by commodity exchanges. But where an early result of new transport and communication is the demonstration effect, the gain from trade is offset, in some degree, by the change in tastes which trade brings about. Few would argue that isolation is possible or that taste changes are reversible in the event of a reduction in trade. But the classic economist should qualify his identification of more trade with more welfare to take account of the fact that economic intercourse may bring with it a shift of demand away from the abundant native product in the underdeveloped country toward the scarce imported commodity.

These, then, are the major bones of contention which have been picked with the theory of comparative advantage. It is not denied that the theory is correct, given its assumptions. But if, instead of perfect competition, demand curves slope downward; if factors within countries can change in quantity and have limited mobility, and immobility of factors between countries is not universally respected; if the state of the arts is permitted to change, and not all at once but continuously; if imperfect factor markets permit unemployment and disparities between social and private cost, the theory of comparative advantage may not be relevant to development.

Nonetheless, foreign trade is capable of assisting a developing country out of the impasse created by the need for sectoral and vertical balance of investment; and a historical review suggests that there have been occasions when foreign trade has been in fact a stimulus to economic growth. The fact of the matter is that there are at least three foreign-trade models of a developing country which ought to be examined, not one: instances of development where export industry represents a leading (or primary) sector; a lagging sector; or a balancing sector. After discussion of each, it will be time to indicate how a country engaged in development decides which model is applicable.

FOREIGN TRADE AS A LEADING SECTOR

The classic example in which foreign trade has played a leading role is that of Britain. Up to 1913 its major exports were coal and textiles. The expansion in textiles proceeded at a rate which averaged 6.75 per cent per annum from 1819 to 1840.[10] Thereafter it slowed down to 4.3 per cent for the next twenty years, and to 1.5 per cent from 1870 to 1913. Coal exports increased from 12.7 million tons in 1872 to 44.1 million in 1900 and to 73.4 million in 1913. W. A. Lewis, who on the whole does not give much attention to the possibility of exports leading economic development, ascribes a considerable portion of the slowdown in development after 1870 to the fact that the rate of increase in exports fell off from 6 per cent per annum to 2 per cent.[11] But this causation would hold only if exports as a leading sector were the only possible foreign-trade model. An equally effective explanation would be that of Svennilson: running into competition in textiles, coal, steel and engineering products, Britain's rate of growth had to slow down unless it succeeded in transforming the economy so as to develop in other sectors on the basis of new or imitated technology.[12] Germany provides a case where economic development occurred at a rapid rate, based largely on the home market and with limited dependence on foreign trade. But E. A. G. Robinson exaggerates when he implies that one method is surer than the other, or that Britain would have been better off if it had tried to develop along lines which limited foreign trade.[13] The model which has foreign trade as a leading sector makes the economy more dependent upon the events of the outside world, but it also makes it less dependent on internal balance.

Other examples than Britain are by no means lacking. The Swedish development after 1880, the Danish from the same period, Switzerland,

[10] P. Rousseaux, *Les Mouvements de fond de l'économie anglaise, 1800–1913,* Institut des Recherches Économiques et Sociales, Louvain, 1938, pp. 173ff.

[11] W. A. Lewis, *The Theory of Economic Growth,* Richard D. Irwin, Inc., Homewood, Ill., 1955, pp. 279, 345ff. For a contrary view see W. G. Hoffmann, *British Industry, 1700–1950* (trans. by W. O. Henderson and W. H. Chaloner), Basil Blackwell & Mott, Ltd., Oxford, 1955, where the decline in the rate of growth after 1860 is ascribed, among other things, to the reallocation of resources caused by the adoption of free trade.

[12] I. Svennilson, *Growth and Stagnation in the European Economy,* United Nations, Geneva, 1954, pp. 22ff.

[13] E. A. G. Robinson, "The Changing Structure of the British Economy," *Economic Journal,* September, 1954, esp. pp. 454–455.

the Low Countries, Canada from 1900 to 1913 and again after World War II come to mind. More significant for many underdeveloped countries today is the experience of Asia after 1950, when the Korean War touched off a scramble for raw materials. Export values more than doubled between the first half of 1950 and the first half of 1951. This expansion coincided with an increase of public investment undertaken under development programs initiated prior to the outbreak of war. The expansion in real income from exports provided the financial resources both internal and external to launch the development program. Even the decline in exports after the first half of 1951 did not completely reverse the development impetus.

It remains true that a country with a large proportion of national income generated by exports is dependent on the rate of growth and the state of economic fluctuations in the world market. Much depends on the income-elasticity, the technological prospects, and the short-run instability of the commodities concerned. Oil, rubber, watches, chemicals, aluminum, and high-grade steels are better bets than cotton textiles, grain, or coffee. But dependence on foreign markets is not complete. Improved techniques and research in demand for export products are frequently the most productive investment in an underdeveloped country, since they better the competitive position vis-à-vis other underdeveloped countries and broaden the market. To the extent that steps can be taken along these lines, the underdeveloped country is not completely dependent.

FOREIGN TRADE AS A LAGGING SECTOR

The Economic Commission for Latin America is persuaded that the foregoing models do not apply to modern development, at least in Latin America. In its view, foreign trade is doomed to lag behind domestic growth, partly because of the failure of developed countries to buy raw materials as their development proceeds, and partly because of the necessity of underdeveloped countries to buy capital goods from developed countries.

The factors limiting the demand of the developed countries have already been mentioned—Engel's law and the continuous increase in efficiency in the consumption of raw materials. Prebisch, the former Executive Director of the Commission, has put the income-elasticity of the United States demand for primary goods at 0.66, while that for Latin America for industrial products is 1.58.[14] If the volume (Q_x) is

[14] See R. Prebisch, comment on G. Myrdal, "Towards a More Closely Integrated Free-World Economy," in R. Lekachman (ed.), *National Policy for Economic*

fixed, and the developing country has no control over the prices of exports (P_x) or of imports (P_m), the country's total capacity to import is fixed. This, of course, leaves out the possibility of foreign loans discussed in the next chapter.

It is not altogether clear that it is appropriate to quote the income-elasticity of the United States for primary-products imports in connection with Latin American exports. A significant number of United States imports of primary products come from Southeast Asia. In addition, the foreign trade of a number of Latin American countries is closely tied with Europe and has grown substantially. In the period 1895 to 1899, for example, imports from Latin America accounted for 5 per cent, by value, of total British imports, whereas during the five years before World War I, they provided 10 per cent of a much enlarged import bill. During the fifteen years before World War I, moreover, production in Europe as a whole rose by 45 per cent, whereas imports from Latin America doubled.[15]

In stating that the capacity of underdeveloped countries to import is fixed, the Prebisch model omits the competitive effect. Total consumption of foodstuffs and raw materials may grow more slowly than consumption of services, for example; but it is by no means clear that total consumption determines the capacity of any country, or even of presently underdeveloped countries as a whole to produce. An underdeveloped country can expand its sales if it can outproduce its fellow underdeveloped countries or, except where tariff policy intervenes too strenuously, if it can outproduce the primary-goods sector of developed countries. Depletion is a factor assisting in this process, and as the example of oil shows, even where coal in the United States is abundant, the competition of oil against coal opens ever wider markets

---

Welfare at Home and Abroad, Doubleday & Company, Inc., New York, 1955, p. 278. In this passage Dr. Prebisch refers to the estimate of 0.66 per cent, representing the percentage change in imports of primary products associated with a given percentage change in income, as based on data of the Paley Commission. In the *Analyses and Projections of Economic Development, part I, Introduction to the Technique of Programming,* United Nations Economic Commission for Latin America, New York, 1955, p. 14, it is observed that according to a report of the Council of Economic Advisers, an increase of 1 per cent in domestic industrial production in the United States resulted in an increase in imports of 0.66 per cent. While the figure is identical, the concepts are different.

It should also be noted that, with equal percentage increases in income in the United States and Latin America, and lower income-elasticity in the former than the latter, it is still possible for the Latin American balance of payments to improve if, as is the case, national income is larger in the United States than in Latin America.

[15] *A Study of Trade between Latin America and Europe,* United Nations, Geneva, 1953, p. 1.

for primary production. Europe used to produce its own wheat, wool, flax, meat, dairy products, etc. For some of these income-elasticity is substantial. But for others, Engel's law and the increasing efficiency of raw-materials consumption in manufacturing notwithstanding, competition has enabled overseas areas to expand their sales at a much more rapid rate than total consumption.

The other element in the Prebisch model is that imports necessarily rise with economic development. In some instances, this is a consequence of the entry of workers into the market economy with an increasing part of their consumption imported,[16] in response to demonstration effect or competitive forces.[17] In addition, however, the necessity to import arises from the import content of the investment program, or the need for particular raw materials, especially fuel, for which no convenient substitutes are available. A development program will produce a shift in the import schedule. Even where the development program is financed in a noninflationary way, by increased savings, there is likely to be a considerable shift of the import schedule, since the import content of investment, which rises, is likely to be greater than that of consumption, which declines.

It is probably inevitable that the demand for capital goods from abroad rises in economic development.[18] This was not so significant for countries which developed in the nineteenth century, where technological innovations played an important role in the process, and new capital goods were developed at home. As noted in Chapter 10, development today is imitative to a much greater extent and hence relies on imported capital goods. If the demonstration effect among producers were less intense, however, it might be possible to economize on foreign exchange, as well as to fit domestic factor proportions more effectively, by buying obsolete and secondhand equipment.

The Economic Commission for Latin America illustrates these propositions with some figures for Latin America, showing the change in the proportions of imports by classes, and the relation of each class of imports to disposable income in the late 1920s as compared with the period 1946 to 1953. These data are given in Table 14.1. But these data appear to be strongly influenced by the experience of Argentina, at least as far as the declining share of consumer goods is concerned. The

---

[16] See *Processes and Problems of Industrialization in Underdeveloped Countries,* United Nations, New York, 1955, p. 59, which cites the budgets of Indonesian workers.

[17] Such as the displacement of the Indian handicraft textile industry by the English machine product in the nineteenth century.

[18] See the growth in the proportion of imports taken by capital goods, in Tables 14.1 and 14.2 below.

Table 14.1. Value of Imports by Classes and Related to
Income for Latin America

Class of imports as a percentage of total imports by value

Years	Consumer goods	Capital goods	Raw materials	Fuel
1925–1929	47.5	33.1	13.1	6.3
1946–1953	32.1	39.4	19.4	9.1

Imports as a percentage of expenditure

Years	Imports of consumption goods to consumption	Imports of investment goods to investment	Imports of raw materials to consumption	Imports of fuel to consumption
1925–1929	12.5	57.0	3.4	1.6
1946–1953	5.7	37.6	3.4	1.6

SOURCE: *Analyses and Projections of Economic Development*, United Nations
Economic Commission for Latin America, part I, p. 14.

United Nations Secretariat study shows remarkably differing patterns
for Argentina, Brazil, and Mexico in consumers' goods and raw materials, albeit for somewhat different years than those in Table 14.1.
This is shown in Table 14.2 on page 250.

From the slow growth in capacity to import (volume of exports
times the terms of trade) and the necessity to import capital goods
and possibly raw materials and fuel, the Economic Commission for
Latin America concludes that there is virtually certain to be a need
for borrowing abroad. This, they say, can be limited by import substitution in consumer goods. The desirability and importance of limiting consumption goods imports during the process of development
arise from the attempt to keep borrowing from abroad as low as possible, or, to put it the other way, maintain investment as high as possible, given the limited availability of foreign loans.

The Prebisch model, in which exports lag, is based upon planned
investment under a program of contrived growth. But the growth need
not be planned. It can partake of the nature of the market variety of
the species with, however, the leading sector a purely internal one.
Germany after 1870 is perhaps the outstanding example. If the focus
of investment is domestic, there is likely to be a necessity to limit imports, to prevent the spillage of income abroad from making the

Table 14.2. Value of Imports by Classes for Specified Countries †
Class of imports as a percentage of total imports by value

Years	Consumer goods	Capital goods	Raw materials	Fuel
Argentina				
1937–1939	40	32	20	8
1947–1949	21	44	25	11
1950–1952	12	38	31	19
Brazil				
1937–1939	42	32	17	10
1947–1949	35	41	12	12
1950–1952	35	40	13	13
Mexico				
1937–1939	32	38	28	2
1947–1949	29	51	16	4
1950–1952	30	50	17	3

† Percentages are given over a longer period for Australia and the Union of South Africa but with an incomparable breakdown. It is of interest, however, to observe that there are different trends within classes. In Australia, imports of foodstuffs declined from 15 per cent in 1914/15–1916/17, to 5.3 per cent in 1948/49–1950/51, whereas fully manufactured goods for consumers, where it was possible to determine a category, barely fell at all from 25 per cent to 23 per cent over the same period, after having been only as low as 18.5 per cent in the 1930s.

SOURCE: *Processes and Problems of Industrialization in Underdeveloped Countries*, United Nations, New York, 1955, p. 114.

balance-of-payments position intolerable. The German example does not apply, however, except insofar as food is concerned. In the investment sector and in armaments, the marginal propensity to import was low because of German capacity in capital goods. The difference between British and German development lies here. In Britain exports led, import-competing industry (in this case, agriculture) could be liquidated, and the balance of payments produced substantial surpluses for investment overseas. In Germany, on the other hand, internal investment took the lead, production of foodstuffs and textiles was sufficient, with moderate protection, to provide for consumption at relatively low rates of pay. There was less specialization and less overseas investment.

E. A. G. Robinson has argued that the British high degree of specialization, compared with Germany's, made its economy very fragile.[19] It is true that more specialization means more risk, and requires a greater transformation when other countries produce their own textiles, and coal is displaced as a world fuel by oil. There was a decline in the rate of expansion in export markets.[20] But this view seems to assume that capacity to transform is low and that a country should fix its degree of specialization for long periods of time. When the market for textiles becomes saturated, investment should shift to new products of high income-elasticity, at home or abroad. If capacity to produce these goods had been readily developed, the decline in the rate of increase in exports need not have been important for Britain in view of her low income-elasticity of demand for food. But where the rate of increase in exports sags after a country's capacity to transform has declined, it is not certain whether the slowdown in growth should be blamed on export markets or on resource inflexibility.

The growth model in which exports are the lagging sector may not apply to every country in Latin America today, as the Economic Commission for Latin America seems to imply; nor is it relevant to much of Africa, with highly skewed resources, nor to each Asian economy. It does appear, however, to represent the experience of Australia and the Union of South Africa, which have been growing rapidly in recent years but with the major emphasis on investment for the domestic market rather than for export. In Australia the deleterious effects on the balance of payments were offset for a time by improvement in the demand for wool, and later by an increase in efficiency of wool production. Over the longer period, however, import restrictions appear to be called for by buoyant domestic investment, the lag of capacity to import behind demand for imports, and the unavailability of capital imports on a large scale.

BALANCE THROUGH FOREIGN TRADE

It has been indicated in Chapter 9 that the foreign market relieves a developing country from the necessity to seek balance, whether as an outlet in demand balance or as a source of production in balance for supply. W. A. Lewis puts it that a country must either improve its productivity in agriculture or export manufactures (thereby enabling it to import food).[21] This seems to leave little room for the country

[19] *Op. cit.*, pp. 450ff.
[20] See also J. R. Meyer, "An Input-Output Approach to Evaluating the Influence of Exports on British Industrial Production in the Late Nineteenth Century," *Explorations in Entrepreneurial History*, October, 1955, pp. 12–34.
[21] *Op. cit.*, pp. 345ff.

which wants to specialize in exporting foodstuffs, such as Australia, New Zealand, and Burma, or to export raw materials and import food, such as Pakistan, Indonesia, etc. Nor is it necessary for food, raw materials, or manufactures to predominate in either exports or imports more than the other. The United States exports and imports food, raw materials, and manufactures and so do many countries for one or more of these categories.

Japan is cited by Lewis as the classic example of a country which undertook exports of manufactures in order to balance its output. It is also mentioned as a country which balanced its output by expanding productivity in agriculture. Further, there is evidence that Japan falls in the category of Britain, with foreign trade as a leading sector, at least in the early period when silk was the major export.[22]

In economic terms, the question of whether to achieve balance internally or through exporting manufactures turns, of course, on the long-run slopes of the demand and supply curves of manufactures and foodstuffs. If the demand for manufactures in the foreign market is elastic, and the domestic supply of food is inelastic with respect to price increases, a prima facie case for exports of manufactures and imports of food is made, unless the supply schedule for food abroad is even more steeply vertical than that at home. On the other hand, if foreign markets for manufactures are inelastic, and the supply of food at home is elastic, the presumption runs the other way.

Foreign trade always balances domestic demand and supply, and it may therefore be inappropriate to distinguish a special model of foreign trade which emphasizes this function.[23] And yet a separate model is useful to suggest a policy of foreign-trade expansion which differs from that in which expansion is demand-led (the leading model) or the policy of trade contraction (import substitution in the lagging model). Food may be imported to hold down agricultural prices and balance the demand for consumption, with supply-led expansion of exports in other lines. Or imports of capital goods or technicians' services may be undertaken to balance the supply of goods and services needed for development, and paid for with supply-led expansion of exports. In the leading model, the autonomous variable is foreign demand (coupled with technological change in the develop-

[22] Lakdawala puts it strongly in *International Aspects of Indian Economic Development*, Oxford University Press, London, 1951, p. 11: "It is believed that Japan's decision to industrialize . . . mainly succeeded because at the time there was a very keen American demand for silk, owing to the outbreak of the silkworm disease in Europe."

[23] This point was put to me by H. Kitamura. It may also be noted, as pointed out above, that the requirements of balance of the Nurkse kind—in demand— may call for displacing imports to gain an assured market.

ing country); in the lagging model, the impetus comes from domestic investment, which raises imports faster than exports grow. In the balancing model, the emphasis is on autonomous increases in exports brought about by supply pushes.

WHICH MODEL?

It seems evident that economic development is attainable by any of the three suggested routes—where foreign trade leads, where it lags, and where it balances. Indeed, development is possible in a closed economy, as the Soviet Union example shows. Which is the appropriate model to follow, therefore, depends on circumstances. The question is, which circumstances.

The answer clearly must be the skewness of resources, both human and natural. Where these resources are highly specialized, the potential gain from trade is large and justifies instability and risk. Where, on the other hand, natural resources are abundant and varied, and human mobility and skills permit labor to be productive over a range of tasks, the significance of the contribution of foreign trade is reduced. In the long run, the natural resources are the more significant, since workers can be trained to new tasks. In the short run, the quality of the labor force is a significant consideration.

A country such as Australia, with a variety of resources and an adaptable working force, can contemplate a long-run development with less and less attention to trade. Australia possesses rich coal and iron resources, which give it capacity for cheap steel-making once capital has been built up; oil has been discovered within the continental limits; density of population is such that food can be exported along with raw materials and ultimately manufactured products.

Whether India is similarly favored is difficult to judge. The first Five-Year Plan put its emphasis on food production, partly perhaps with the implicit view of a balanced program of investment in which increased food output was needed to stabilize the price of the wage good before one could expand industrial output. This is a closed-economy model. In part, however, India appears to have operated on the assumption that the long-run terms of trade would favor food over industrial products—a Colin Clark rather than a Prebisch position. There was, however, also a strong element of mercantilism involved. India did not want to depend on outsiders for its essential food. It was not clear whether considerations of foreign exchange or defense dominated. To the extent that foreign exchange played a part, it was simple import substitution, regardless of price. Growing food is something we can do at home. We will therefore do it, irrespective of the relative prices of food and other things. In this period, with high income-elasticity for food and investment attention given to the agricultural sector, the marginal propensity to import operated negatively. Income rose because food production increased (with investment and a good monsoon); and, as income rose, the demand for imports shifted downward, since home production was a substitute for imports.

In the second Five-Year Plan, investment emphasis is given to heavy industry. Here the import content of investment is high, but much of the output—steel, chemicals, heavy engineering products—will ultimately substitute for imports. India believes that its steel will be cheap,[24] that its resources are balanced, that it needs to pay little attention to specialization in foreign trade beyond continuing to sell abroad jute, tea, and textiles. But this model must take into account other resources than coal and iron deposits. A significant open question is whether Indian entrepreneurship and labor will be efficient in import-competing industries, along with natural resources.[25] If so, it may be that Indian lack of skewness in resources favors the lagging foreign-trade model.

One interesting case may be mentioned—Israel, where quantitative restrictions in exports and imports and domestic subsidies have so disrupted the internal price system that the national experts have difficulty in estimating how wide the limits may be within which it is possible to gain from trade.[26]

[24] It is not completely clear that India will ultimately have a comparative advantage in steel-making. Some casual discussions of the question have suggested that in recent years India has been unable to import steel at any price. If the price of imports is infinity, and the demand sufficiently inelastic, any country has a comparative advantage in producing for itself. But the nonavailability of supplies requires a different test. Can India produce steel more cheaply at home than it can contract for steel abroad on terms which would enable a producer to construct new capacity? The writer has been unable to find evidence to eliminate the possibility that India wants a steel industry "because every important country has one."

[25] It may be that skewness of resources brings with it skewness of personal capacities, and that this feeling underlies the Canadian Royal Commission inquiry into the question of whether Canada should continue to operate with exports of primary products as its leading sector. There can be little doubt that resource-based exports have produced impressive gains in income for Canada. But the "development of resources . . . is losing a little of its glamor as it becomes apparent that this is not itself a great provider of employment or of a humane life." "Inquiry into Canadian Prosperity," *Economist*, May 28, 1955, p. 746.

[26] Cf. "The price mechanism is seriously inadequate as a basis for judging the most economic allocation of the country's resources. This inadequacy stems from the manipulation of prices by a complicated web of subsidies, different exchange rates, the import licensing system, tariffs, and other indirect taxes." The Falk Project for Economic Research in Israel, *First Annual Report, 1954,* Jerusalem, 1955, p. 36.

It may be thought that a country which has decided on a program of economic development has no choice about what happens to its foreign trade. If demand for its products increases, well and good. But it cannot choose to follow the leading model. Otherwise, it is obliged to follow the lagging model, unless it wants to neglect agriculture and push some form of manufactured exports to balance its accounts. But this is hardly the case. Technology is not fixed, nor are the technological limits likely to be fully exploited by investment in the export sector. If increased investment can make exports cheaper, whether through widening the application of existing processes or devising and installing new, there is room to push exports for balance and even to the point where exports lead the development process. In uncontrived development the stimulus sometimes came from demand (cotton in the United States), sometimes from supply (cotton textiles in England, watches in Switzerland), and sometimes both (Swedish pulp and paper, Danish and New Zealand butter, bacon, eggs).

It is said that a distinguished economist, when he visits an underdeveloped country, first asks for a list of imports and considers which of the leading items can be manufactured domestically. An equally important question, which should not be neglected, is what exports can be produced more efficiently. In Malaya, for example, the replanting of rubber trees with higher-yielding, disease-resisting strains may be the most effective investment for development. Such increased investment should not be pursued in an export area where marginal comparative advantage is lacking, i.e., where marginal revenue is lower than in import substitution. But where a country sells its exports in competition with other countries, including the import-competing sector of the importing countries, marginal revenue is unlikely to be much below average revenue, and the possibilities of cost reduction in the export sector are worth careful examination.

COMMERCIAL POLICY

Space does not permit a detailed discussion of the problems of commercial policy in countries embarked on economic development. An enormous amount of attention has been devoted to this problem. Perhaps it will suffice here to say a few words by way of summary. This discussion is organized not around the devices of commercial policy— tariffs, quotas, exchange rate change, including multiple-exchange rates—but about the objectives. The most important of these may be said to be revenue, protection (or resource reallocation), defense of the balance of payments, stability, and maximization of income. It is assumed that the foreign-trade model is one where demand for exports lags in development, and that the primary sector in development is internal, say, social overhead capital.

We have already indicated that the revenue aspects of commercial policy for underdeveloped countries are important and that the need for revenue modifies the normal case for free trade.[27] While import tariffs on luxuries may not give rise to resource shifts because of inelasticity of supply, it may be well to ensure that such tariffs afford no protection by imposing a parallel domestic excise. Unfortunately, this cannot be paralleled in export taxes. Here, if the incidence is on the domestic producer, the allocation effect is inescapable, since foreign producers lie outside the reach of the local tax collector.

The protective effect is frequently invoked in tariffs to stimulate an infant industry. The economist always prefers a subsidy, but is obliged to recognize that he differs in this respect from domestic producers who somehow believe that a subsidy is degrading, while a tariff is businesslike. Multiple-exchange rates and exchange depreciation have their protective effects, along with ordinary tariffs and quota restrictions. When protection is given to an industry, there must be resources to move into it, available or readily released from other occupations. These resources include capital and land as well as labor, and labor of the appropriate skills and training. If this is not the case, the extra demand for resources in the absence of supply is inflationary.

The primary object of commercial policy in underdeveloped countries is likely to be defense of the balance of payments. This arises from the desires to limit borrowing and to avoid the necessity to cut domestic investment. Domestic investment may be excessive in relation to total resources, so that demand spills over into imports all along the line; or an equilibrium position is adversely affected by a shift from consumption to investment which maintains national income at the old level but increases the propensity to import as the import content of added investment exceeds the savings in imports from the subtracted consumption. Investment may be excessive not in periods of boom but only on the average over the cycle, which originates abroad.

Multiple-exchange rates, exchange depreciation, quota restrictions, and, to a lesser extent, tariffs, are mainly directed to the balance of payments. Depreciation is not likely to be effective in expanding the foreign-exchange value of exports, where there is either inelasticity of demand abroad or full employment at home. Nor is it likely to be of assistance in reducing imports, where the level of living and real wages are not readily compressible. The result is likely to be the most

[27] See above, pp. 200–206.

temporary relief. Accordingly, many countries have turned to multiple-exchange rates, or the disequilibrium system. This, as we have noted earlier, requires for its effective functioning the spur of incentives which will outweigh the opportunity to make a profit by operating illegally. If such incentive is absent, the disequilibrium system is likely to work with low efficiency, with antisocial incidence, despite the efforts of the authorities to favor necessities and penalize luxuries through the gradual distortion of investment and consumption.

In short, not commercial policy but monetary and fiscal restraint, or borrowing abroad, is the most effective means of coping with the balance-of-payments problem of developing countries in the long run. There are exceptions. Where resources are balanced, and not fully employed so that elasticities are high, import protection is likely to have considerable balance-of-payments effects, especially if the objects of protection—food and textiles in German development—have low income-elasticity, and the products with high income-elasticity—capital goods, housing services—are domestically produced. But this situation is rare in the underdeveloped parts of the world today.

Underdeveloped countries have talked much about the desirability of achieving stability through stabilization of the prices of primary products. A United Nations resolution called for the establishment of "fair and equitable" prices or terms of trade.[28] A majority opinion of an international group of five experts concluded that "fair and equitable" meant "long-run equilibrium"[29] but that it was desirable to reduce the amplitude of fluctuations about this level, if it could be determined. These experts, unfortunately, were unable to agree on any means for achieving this result; while opposing export restriction, they were disposed to favor neither international agreements with maximum and minimum prices and minimum quantities of exports and imports, on the one hand, nor buffer-stock arrangements on the other. A particularly difficult problem faced in the last-named device is that of deciding whether the buffer stock is to be financed by producers or consumers, or some combination of the two. The balance-of-payments position of underdeveloped countries is much more stable in the cycle, assuming prices and production unchanged, if buffer-stock purchases are financed abroad rather than at home.

Underdeveloped countries are most anxious to pursue commodity price stabilization policies on a world basis, and involving all commodities at once. The United States has been opposed to this, largely

[28] Resolution 86 of the General Assembly of the United Nations, adopted Dec. 21, 1952.

[29] *Commodity Trade and Economic Development*, United Nations, New York, 1952, chap. 1.

on doctrinal grounds, which become less effective in dealing with particular commodities in which United States interests are heavily involved: wheat, sugar, and to a lesser degree, tin. The doctrinal grounds are simple and sound: there is no basis for forecasting the long-run price. Producer interests usually outweigh those of consumers; the stabilized price is fixed too high, supply expands, and the agreement ultimately collapses. Bauer and Paish have proposed a long-run moving average as the basis for making payments to producers, in contrast with the West African Cocoa Marketing Board, which has stabilized the price to producers at a low level and permitted the world price to fluctuate (as the Board claims).[30] The method used by the Cocoa Marketing Board, or a similar device of sliding-scale export taxes on commodities, where the tax is borne by the producer and passed neither forward to foreigners nor backward on labor, will stabilize the incomes of producers in the export sector, not necessarily at the appropriate level, but will render the balance of payments and governmental revenue unstable.

Open economies are bound to be unstable in some particular—in balance of payments or income. If governments want to achieve internal stability of income and growth, they can choose among a variety of alternatives—stabilization of the price of exports, counter-cyclical export taxes, built-in stabilizers in tax and expenditure—but they must make sure that operations balance around the long-run level. The temptation is to set the export price too high on the average, or to spend the revenue and foreign exchange in prosperity which should be going into reserves for depression. The attempt to produce internal stability then results in inflation: exchange reserves and domestic sinking funds are unavailable when needed, and the balance of payments must be defended by quantitative or exchange restrictions.

Income stability in underdeveloped countries is attainable, but only with an impressive degree of discipline and self-control. In a few countries such as India, where income and imports are negatively correlated, at least for a period, stability is more readily obtained.

Finally, commercial and fiscal policy are used to maximize the resources available for economic development, to improve the terms of trade in merchandise, to redivide the gain from trade deriving from investments by foreigners, to convert marginal resources into foreign exchange without reducing the monopoly prices paid by prime exports. The capacity of underdeveloped countries to affect the prices of their

[30] See P. T. Bauer and F. W. Paish, "The Reduction of Fluctuations in the Incomes of Primary Producers," *Economic Journal,* December, 1952, pp. 750–780; and P. T. Bauer, *A Survey of West African Trade,* Cambridge University Press, London, 1955.

imports is certainly limited. Here they are price takers, not price makers. But in exports the position may be otherwise. A high degree of specialization means that demand is inelastic, at least in the short run; and where foreign investors have a large commitment, their capacity to escape the incidence of taxes—or the revenue effects on them of multiple-exchange systems—is low.

It is vital, however, to distinguish between the short-run and the long-run elasticity. Export taxes may be passed forward in a sellers' market, but sellers' markets do not last. Export restriction will raise prices briefly, but hold up an umbrella under which foreign competitors can gain a foothold. Expansion of output among rival producers and rival products lies one or two years off to limit the extent to which prices can be raised.

Commercial policy can hardly make much of a positive contribution to economic development. The next chapter will discuss the taxation of foreign investors, which is perhaps somewhat more useful and has produced substantial revenues for development over the last twenty or so years. Tariffs have their purposes, for revenue and for protection. But commercial policy still falls short of refinement to the point where short-run instability of prices of primary products exported by underdeveloped countries can be overcome or where its effects on development in underdeveloped countries can be smoothly offset.[31]

The United Nations has observed the paradox that economic development needs favorable terms of trade to follow the road to balanced economic development so that it will not have to depend on its terms of trade any longer. But the more competing countries balance their resources and withdraw resources from exports, the higher the gains from trade for those countries that continue to specialize.

---

[31] A rather more optimistic note is struck by G. Myrdal in his *An International Economy*, Harper & Brothers, New York, 1956, chap. XIII.

CHAPTER 15 *Borrowing Abroad*

THE NEED FOR FOREIGN CAPITAL

It is sometimes urged that foreign borrowing is necessary in economic development because the need for investment goods from abroad grows at a faster rate than the "capacity to import."[1] The latter variable, it will be recalled, is derived from the volume of exports and the terms of trade, both of which, it is claimed, lie outside the control of the developing country. If capacity to import grows at the rate of 2 per cent a year, while the need for investment goods requires an increase in the volume of imports at 3 per cent, capital imports at 1 per cent of the value of exports would be needed, on this showing, to preserve balance-of-payments equilibrium.

This emphasis on the behavior of specific variables like investment goods is appropriate only under certain limiting circumstances, and in the short run. The general case for borrowing abroad is to add to resources over-all, not to acquire particular resources. Foreign borrowing would be needed to obtain certain types of foreign equipment only if the economy had no capacity to redirect its efforts from one sector to another, or no time to effect such transformation. Since economic development absolutely requires such redirection, and is a time-consuming process, the view that it is necessary to borrow to get command of foreign investment equipment for developmental purposes can be said to be wrong.

One alternative to borrowing to finance capital-goods imports is increased domestic savings. Reduced consumption operates, in some part, directly on imports, which frees foreign exchange. In part, it

---

[1] See *Analyses and Projections of Economic Development, Part I, Introduction to the Technique of Planning*, United Nations, Economic Commission for Latin America, New York, 1955, p. 5; also H. J. Bruton, "Growth Models and Underdeveloped Countries," *Journal of Political Economy*, August, 1955, pp. 330ff.

liberates domestic resources which must then be reallocated to export or import-competing production to permit expansion in exports or a further reduction in imports.

Or foreign borrowing may be used to finance domestic capital formation without the necessity to purchase foreign capital equipment. As is well known, loans can be transferred in consumption goods. If capital formation requires mainly domestic resources, such as construction, the foreign loan may be used to import food which permits the transfer of workers from agriculture to construction without reducing current consumption.

Despite this error in reasoning, the need for foreign borrowing is frequently identified with the need for foreign capital goods, as if the existing balance of payments were in equilibrium and would be unaffected by shifts in resources needed to produce the domestic contribution to the new capital. Or there may be no error, but merely an assumption that transformation is impossible within the relevant time span, or to the necessary degree, or that foreign lending for development is a short-run rather than a long-run measure. Whether based on error or on restrictive assumptions, in its early loans and in many current negotiations, the International Bank for Reconstruction and Development lends usually only the foreign-exchange content of a project. Thus the loan of $27 million to Lebanon for the power and irrigation project on the Litani River covered "the services of foreign consultants and contractors and imports of power generation equipment, transmission lines and substations, construction equipment and some construction materials and supplies."[2] Local currency requirements of $13 million were provided by the Lebanese government. Similarly, and more important, in planning the High Dam at Aswan, it was contemplated that the United States and British governments and the International Bank would cover the $400 million of foreign-exchange expenditure required over the fifteen-year building period, whereas the remaining estimated $900 million of domestic expenditure would be furnished by Egypt. It was the difficulty of Egypt's fulfilling this part of its bargain which was used by the United States and Britain as the basis or pretext for withdrawing their offer of aid.

Domestic capital expenditure can, of course, be provided locally in a noninflationary manner if it is matched by new savings, and if the appropriate shifts in the economy occur. Income remains as before, but consumption declines and capital expenditure takes its place. Double resource shifts may be required, if, for example, resources most readily transferred into capital construction come out of produc-

[2] IBRD press release no. 420, Aug. 26, 1955.

tion for the export market. In this circumstance, the other resources released by saving must shift into new exports or into import-competing production.

The notion that foreign loans are needed for foreign capital goods is based on partial-equilibrium analysis, with all other things equal, *ceteris paribus*. This is an inappropriate line of reasoning, since the problem is of the general-equilibrium, or *mutatis mutandis* variety.

There is one important qualification to the foregoing, however. Internal investment can lead a development program without foreign loans and despite the need for foreign capital goods, if it is kept within the limits of total resources, but timing may produce a transitional balance-of-payments deficit to be covered by borrowing. After the initial shift of spending toward foreign goods, resources will have to be diverted into export or import-competing lines by depreciation or deflation to pay for incremental imports. If the process is export-led, the same rate of investment can be achieved without a transitional deficit. Whether development is export- or internal-investment led does not determine the need for foreign borrowing in general, which is a function of total expenditure in relation to total domestic production. Where expenditure is limited to the amount of resources, however, the way the process is initiated makes a difference for transitional borrowing.

The need for foreign capital is then determined by the rate of investment in relation to domestic savings. The equilibrium condition for national income is that domestic investment plus exports must equal imports plus domestic savings. If the balance of payments is to be in equilibrium, with no borrowing, exports are equal to imports, and domestic investment is limited to domestic savings. An increase in investment unaccompanied by an equal shift in the savings schedule must be financed in part by borrowing from abroad, since part of the increased income will spill over into imports (assuming a positive marginal propensity to import). Investment can increase without harm to the balance of payments only if exports expand simultaneously in the correct proportion, or if the savings schedule shifts upward or the import schedule downward.

CAPACITY TO ABSORB CAPITAL

The International Bank for Reconstruction and Development has said that the problem in development is not, or perhaps has not been, the supply of loans so much as the limited capacity to absorb capital.[3]

[3] See various submissions of the International Bank to United Nations publications, such as that mentioned in footnote 9 below, and see the early IBRD, *An-*

Millikan and Rostow have proposed that the developed countries of the world should make available to underdeveloped countries as much capital as they can absorb, by which they mean as much as can, with reasonable assurance, be productively used.[4]

The general-equilibrium view of the need for foreign capital leads to the conclusion that capacity to absorb capital is unlimited. And so it is. Limits can readily be set by establishing a criterion for productivity, such as 10 per cent per annum, but where "productive" means a return which is positive, and time is allowed for transformation, capacity to absorb for productive purposes is virtually unlimited. And of course if capital consumption is permitted, there is no question but that the sky is the limit. But if capacity to absorb capital is taken in the short run, and transformation is time-consuming, the notion of a limit has reality.

The International Bank's criterion for determining capacity is the existence of well-engineered designs for a given project, which must make economic sense in the context of a development program. The concept is restricted to projects because of the Bank's view that lending (as a general rule) should be restricted to the foreign-exchange content of investment projects. Where the rule has been departed from, the Bank has loaned for general exchange needs of an incremental nature arising out of a development program. While their primary emphasis is on programs, Millikan and Rostow also write in terms of projects, on the assumption that lending is likely to be limited to bankable projects.

The more general view, however, is that capital can be absorbed at a pace determined by the rate at which complementary factors and facilities can be made available.[5] This is evident enough with regard to the construction of a particular project. Construction needs manpower, roads, materials, etc. Where these are not available, it is not possible to proceed. But more is generally intended. The project must not only be built; to be "absorbed," it must be productive. This means that there must be complementary resources to be combined

---

nual Reports, especially the *Fourth Annual Report* for 1948–1949, pp. 8–9: "Perhaps the most striking single lesson which the Bank has learned in the course of its operations is how limited is the capacity of the underdeveloped countries to absorb capital quickly for really productive purposes. . . . In point of fact . . . the principal limitation upon Bank financing in the development field has not been lack of money but lack of well-prepared and well-planned projects ready for immediate execution."

[4] See M. F. Millikan and W. W. Rostow, *A Proposal: Key to an Effective Foreign Policy,* Harper & Brothers, New York, 1957, pp. 56ff.

[5] See S. H. Frankel, *Capital Investment in Africa,* Oxford University Press, London, 1938, p. 424.

with it in the production of further output and markets on which the product is sold. And when one leaves the project basis and moves on into broad investment undertakings, absorptive capacity is determined by complementary factors and facilities, including those for construction and those needed to make economic use of the capital. It is possible to build capital structures, such as the irrigation dam in the Helmand Valley,[6] without absorbing them. In contrast, Canadian borrowing in the period 1900–1913 was readily absorbed, despite the absence of any projects as such, because the investment undertakings of Dominion and provincial governments and of private enterprise could draw sufficient resources of the right sorts from home and abroad to construct the capital, and because the output of the newly formed capital was readily marketed.

It seems somewhat strained, however, to use the conception of absorptive capacity to cover both the act of capital formation and the subsequent economic justification of the capital where formed, without making a distinction between stages. Perhaps, then, capacity to absorb can be broken down between the first stage, where the question is one of capacity to form new capital, and a second, concerned with its efficient use. Both concepts should be included in absorptive capacity. The International Bank may emphasize more the first; and Millikan and Rostow, more the second. In either case, the capacity of a country to absorb foreign capital, in the short run, is simply a different way of referring to the balance in its development path. Its capacity to form capital with foreign loans refers to the consistency of its development plans in terms of physical requirements, whether for projects or for investment as a whole. Its capacity efficiently to use foreign capital, on the other hand, relates to vertical balance in supply and horizontal balance in demand which ensures that the newly constructed capital contributes to current production for which the demand is sufficiently income-elastic.

Few estimates of the world need for capital or ability to absorb it are worth a great deal. The United Nations experts who wrote *Measures for the Economic Development of Underdeveloped Countries*[7] calculated the foreign borrowing requirements of underdeveloped countries, excluding Europe and Japan, for a 2 per cent increase in income per capita by assuming an average capital/labor ratio of $2,500 per worker. This produced a total capital requirement of $19 billion. Domestic savings were estimated at $5.2 billion, leaving a gap of $13.8 billion. The authors assume that some of this gap would be

[6] See above, p. 145.
[7] New York, 1951.

filled by incremental savings, but the deficit to be made up by foreign lending came to more than $10 billion.

In commenting on this estimate, Higgins observes that a capital/labor ratio of $2,500 implies an incremental capital/output ratio, as of 1949, of 7.5, which is certainly high.[8] Moreover, China's requirements, which it appears to be determined to fill without foreign borrowing, account for about $4.7 billion of the deficit. Assuming a 2 per cent increase in income per capita, a capital/output ratio of 4 or 5, excluding China, the net excess of investment over current savings would be in the range of $4.7 to $7.1 billion.

Another, earlier estimate of the Food and Agriculture Organization proceeded by adding up the plans of underdeveloped countries for capital formation, subtracting reasonable estimates of domestic savings, and arrived at an annual need for foreign borrowing of about $8 billion.[9]

These methods evidently represent the over-all, long-run approach and neglect the question of capacity to absorb. Millikan and Rostow arrive at estimates of capacity to absorb capital of $2.5 to $3.5 billion a year by assuming that countries at the very early stages of development will be able on the average to absorb no more than 30 to 50 per cent more capital than they are currently forming, while countries with development well under way can increase the rate of capital formation more than the first group, but will be able to finance more of it themselves through a high marginal propensity to save.[10] This appears to assume that their development is of the Mexican type with skewed income distribution and a high rate of reinvestment of profits.

CAPACITY TO REPAY

The same distinction between short and long run applies to capacity to repay. In the short run, capacity to repay is dictated by the foreign-exchange impact of the investment undertaken, whether it be export-increasing or import-decreasing. Over time, the only determinant of the capacity to repay is the loan's contribution to productivity of the economy as a whole, and the capacities of the system to skim off the necessary portion of that productivity in taxes or pricing, and to re-

[8] See B. Higgins and W. Malenbaum, "Financing Economic Development," *International Conciliation*, March, 1955, pp. 291ff.

[9] See Food and Agriculture Organization, "Report on International Investment and Financing Facilities," in *Methods of Financing Economic Development in Underdeveloped Countries*, United Nations, Lake Success, New York, 1949, pp. 43–88.

[10] *Op. cit.*, pp. 98ff.

allocate resources so as to transfer debt service abroad. An increase in productivity brought about by foreign loans in purely domestic overhead, such as public utilities in an internal city, carries its own capacity to repay if the loan is productive. The requirement for repayment is that the fiscal system raise the necessary funds, and that transformation occur to shift resources into export-increasing or import-decreasing lines.

This is not to suggest that repayment is easy. It may seem so when the initial investment is made in an export industry, and so it is in the short run. In the long run, however, developing countries have a tendency for investment to exceed domestic savings, i.e., to borrow abroad. Any requirement for repayment is a requirement that savings exceed investment, and calls for an "uphill" movement of capital. It is appropriate for an individual loan, perhaps, to require amortization, and for an individual project to pay amortization out of its gross earnings. But a country as a whole typically borrows net in its developing stages. Amortization places a burden upon it since in the event that loans were suddenly unavailable, it would have to transfer capital outward instead of inward. The banking requirement of amortization gives underdeveloped economies the opposite problem from that of the International Bank and the Export-Import Bank which are receiving so much capital repayment in recent years that they have to lend very considerable amounts annually to prevent the capital movement from changing direction.

Similar considerations apply to capacity to pay interest on foreign loans. In the short run, the closer the project is to increasing exports or reducing imports, the more readily the interest on the debt can be paid. In the long run, the test is productivity in general, plus fiscal and transforming capacities. The notion that foreign resources made available to government for social overhead capital must be made on the basis of grants, rather than loans, is therefore based on short-run considerations.

A series of well-known articles on the repayment problem tends to ignore various of these considerations. W. S. Salant[11] and E. D. Domar[12] discuss mainly the effect on the lending country, and focus on the question of when the lender's balance of trade turns adverse. This occurs, they assert, when the rate of interest on outstanding loans, plus the rate of amortization, exceeds the rate of growth of lending, plus the rate of amortization. Conversely, underdeveloped countries must borrow at a rate higher than the rate of interest on outstanding

[11] "The Domestic Effects of Capital Export under the Point Four Program," *American Economic Review, Papers and Proceedings,* May, 1950, pp. 504ff.
[12] "The Effect of Foreign Investment on the Balance of Payments," *American Economic Review,* December, 1950, pp. 805–826.

issues (leaving amortization out of it) if they want to prevent the balance of trade from turning positive. But surely it is the current account and not the balance of trade which ought to be the criterion. If the current account is negative, and balanced by capital inflow, it is not appropriate to say that the country is borrowing abroad to pay interest on old debts. The positive capital formation pays interest on old debts, and new capital is being formed with the new capital inflow.[13]

The Salant-Domar analysis is thus applicable to income transfers rather than to capital movements. It fails to give attention to the increase in consumption in the lending country, which spills over in part into imports, and assists the balance of payments, or to the growth of capacity in the borrowing country, which, either directly or indirectly with the aid of transformation, makes possible the necessary expansion in exports. Income transfers, where the transfer is consumed in the receiving country and (possibly) comes out of new savings but produces no income in the remitting, require an entirely different analysis than capital movements.

The fact is that geometric growth can be made to do almost anything. If it is assumed that transformation will take place, and that growth will occur with a very high marginal propensity to save and a low capital/output ratio, a country can cease borrowing in short order despite payment of a relatively high rate of interest. Using "arbitrary" assumptions, Millikan and Rostow state:[14]

. . . if the initial rate of domestic investment is 5 per cent of national income, if foreign capital is supplied at a constant rate equal to one-third the initial level of domestic investment, if 25 per cent of all additions to income are saved and reinvested, if the capital output ratio is 3, and if interest and dividend service on foreign loans and private investments are paid at the rate of 6 per cent a year, the country will be able to discontinue net foreign borrowing after fourteen years and sustain a 3 per cent growth of income out of its own resources.

A general measure of capacity of a country to accept and service foreign borrowing has been devised in the investment/service ratio.[15]

[13] J. J. Polak in "Balance of Payments of Countries Reconstructing with the Help of Foreign Loans," *Quarterly Journal of Economics*, February, 1943, pp. 208–240 (reproduced in *Readings in the Theory of International Trade*, American Economic Association, Blakiston–Richard D. Irwin, Inc., Philadelphia, 1949, pp. 459–493) emphasizes the difference made by investment in the export sector on the one hand or the domestic sector on the other, but neglects, in his interest in an income model, all possibility of transformation.

[14] *Op. cit.*, pp. 157–158.

[15] See D. Finch, "Investment Service of Underdeveloped Countries," *Staff Papers*, September, 1951, pp. 60–85.

This is the relation of outgoing interest and amortization (which are debits in the balance of payments) to total exports of goods and services (a credit). Investment/service ratios as high as 30 per cent (Indonesia in the 1930s) are not unknown and result from the inclusion of large remitted profits in the content of export goods. These may not be difficult to transfer, since the requisite act of saving occurs simultaneously with the earning of profits.

The investment/service ratio should perhaps include pensions paid by colonies or newly independent states to civil servants retired in the mother country, since these virtually amount to a capital obligation. Some of these payments were in fact capitalized by India during the war[16] and payments under pension obligations to the Netherlands constituted a sizable item in the Indonesian balance of payments from the 1949 agreement with the Netherlands until its denunciation in 1956.

Investment/service ratios today are much lower than during the 1930s, but the rate of foreign lending has not increased on that account. The reasons for the reduction in the ratios include repayments on debt during the war, the rise of commodity prices relative to fixed interest payments on bonds, and the reduction of the profitability of direct investments, except in oil, due to increases in wages and in taxes on profits. That this reduction has not increased the volume of foreign lending is due to the profitability of direct investments in developed countries, to fears of exchange control or confiscation on the part of private investors, and to the failure to devise institutions capable of replacing the foreign bond in international investment.

FORMS OF FOREIGN BORROWING—DIRECT INVESTMENT

Direct investment has traditionally been viewed as a desirable form of international capital movement. The traditions on which this view is based, however, are largely those of the developed countries. The reasons given have been that this investment is accompanied by technical assistance and training possibilities for the country where the investment is made; the investor may, in the case of very large companies dealing in very underdeveloped areas, provide its own social and economic overhead capital, and the transfer of profits imposes a supportable burden on the economy, since these investments have been typically in the export sector, and the increased profits have been associated with increased exports which automatically transfer them. The training impact has been mentioned in an earlier chapter, and is

[16] See *Economic Development with Stability*, International Monetary Fund, Washington, 1953, p. 76.

intensively discussed in a number of studies of *United States Business Performance Abroad* undertaken by the National Planning Association (along with other aspects of that performance).[17] In several instances such as Venezuela, the countries in which large and profitable investments have taken place express themselves as thoroughly satisfied and levy taxes on the profits of foreign enterprises which are used to finance development investment.

There is, nonetheless, some dissent, largely over the questions of the training capacity of foreign enterprises, and the division of profits. The arguments of Myint and Hanson have been mentioned in Chapter 13. These regard foreign investment, at least in Burma and Latin America, respectively, as fossilizing techniques and the earning capacity of the native population, and collaborating with a small industrial class to preserve the large gap in levels of living between the mass of the workers and the small industrialist and landowning group. A still further argument of a different sort was adduced in Chapter 10, where it was suggested that in some instances foreign investment adopted too modern techniques with the result of creating a technological gap too wide to be bridged by the rest of the economy and "dual economy." Singer is the primary expositor of the corollary which follows from this, that the foreign-investment sector of an underdeveloped economy is really an enclave which belongs to the developed economy but happens to be located geographically somewhere else. The appropriate concept might then be national income, which is corrected for the contribution of foreign factors, rather than net national or net geographical product.

More recently a question has been raised about so-called import-decreasing foreign investments. E. T. Penrose, citing the case of the General Motors–Holden plant in Australia, has observed that the reinvestment of profits of an investment can give rise to a higher and higher equity on which profits, ultimately transferred abroad, impose a large burden on the balance of payments[18] and arouse, or did in the case of Australia, some resentment in the local populace.

The size of the profits is not the issue here—Creole Petroleum Corporation had a profit in 1954 which was 100 per cent of the stockholders' equity in 1945, and almost 33 per cent of current equity.[19] Nor is the fact that reinvestment in a going concern occurs more

[17] See the National Planning Association studies of Creole in Venezuela, Casa Grace in Peru, Sears Roebuck de Mexico, and the Philippine American Life Insurance Company. Others will be published in the series.

[18] See E. T. Penrose, "Foreign Investment and the Growth of the Firm," *Economic Journal*, June, 1956, pp. 220–235.

[19] W. C. Taylor and J. Lindeman, *The Creole Petroleum Corporation in Venezuela*, National Planning Association, Washington, 1955, appendix 2, pp. 85–86.

readily than new investment the crux. What raises difficulty for the economy is the fact that foreign investment of this sort indulges the demonstration effect unduly, encourages excessive spending, and hence gives rise to imbalance in national income and balance-of-payments accounts. G. M.–Holden tried to keep its profits down by lowering the price of its car below the equilibrium level, and built up a backlog of 12 months' orders; it limited dividend remittances by expanding its capacity from 40,000 automobiles annually to 100,000. But Australian demand for the product, not foreign investment, was basically responsible. If Australia were in any case to import the number of automobiles produced by G. M.–Holden, and the direct investment were import-reducing, the total effect would have been to assist the balance of payments: the payment of dividends to the parent company abroad would have been much less an expenditure of foreign exchange than the reduction in the value of imports, and the balance of payments would have improved, as well as productivity. If demand is highly price and income-elastic, however, the saving which comes from having the car cheaper is more than offset by the fact that the country raises its standard of living. It is comparable to the experience of most families which invest in a deepfreeze or buy wine by the case rather than the bottle: it would be possible to save money by sticking to the old level of living. In fact, however, one is likely to spend all the savings, and more, in an improved standard.

For this wide variety of reasons, a number of countries have much more timidity about foreign investment than used to be the case. Underdeveloped countries have become markedly ambivalent. Capital is wanted to add to total resources, yet countries are worried that they may be somehow unduly exploited by foreign capital. In the last few years a number of countries have twice passed legislation regulating foreign investment, first imposing severe restrictions on the entry of foreign capital—as if investors in developed countries were clamoring to enter—and later revising their regulations and going some distance to meet the objections to the first set of laws, made by such groups as the International Chamber of Commerce, in order to stimulate entry.

This ambivalence is perhaps best illustrated in India where a socialist state has been proclaimed, but private foreign investment is said to be given national treatment. In fact, the treatment of foreign investment in India is highly selective, as evidenced by the fact that one large United States motor company withdrew its investment in the country at a time when two oil companies were reaching agreements to construct refineries. Officially, the Indian government welcomes foreign investments which:

1. Have a genuine program for manufacturing, not trade or distribution

2. Are located in a field where domestic investment is inadequate or domestic technology below the level abroad

3. Help the foreign-exchange position by being export-increasing or import-decreasing

4. Increase productivity

5. Make provision for training Indian personnel for higher technical administrative posts

6. Admit Indian capital at all stages of the venture

The provisions relating to the foreign balance and to training and productivity have already been discussed. The requirement that the investment be in manufacturing is, of course, a classic example of the widespread fallacy of identifying secondary production with development and ignoring the contribution of distribution. Part of its roots are no doubt traceable to fear of foreign monopolists. The Indian stipulation that domestic capital be admitted at all stages is one which is increasingly adopted in underdeveloped countries but is often meaningless in the absence of sufficient savings or readiness to invest in industrial equities. The Hanson point about strengthening domestic monopolists is also relevant. In the present form, it furnishes a contrast to other views on the same subject. Frequent objection is made to the foreign entrepreneur who puts in the smallest possible amount of equity capital and borrows debt capital locally to increase his leverage. At one time it was explicitly stated by the Australian Prime Minister that his country was not prepared to encourage companies which put in only a small equity in dollars and borrowed the rest locally, since they would be earning dollars on sterling investments.[20]

The position in foreign direct investment today is something of a standoff such as frequently occurs in bilateral monopoly. Both parties would benefit from getting together and working out mutually advantageous arrangements. But the investor wants a high return to compensate him for the risks of confiscation, and the country where the investment takes place is inclined to confiscate because of the high return earned by the investor. The result is stalemate. Exceptions abound, such as Venezuela, which is content to share in the substantial profits made in its oil industry on the fifty-fifty basis which it devised. Until July, 1956, oil companies in the Middle East have gone forward with substantial investments in producing and refining facilities and pipelines, despite the risks of war, civil commotion, unilateral con-

[20] See "Australia Welcomes Dollar Investments," *New York Times*, Sept. 10, 1949.

tract revision, and confiscation, and have found these investments profitable despite high rates of depreciation. Some considerable revival of investment has occurred since 1952, as laws governing foreign investment have been modified to encourage foreign investment. But the contribution could be more substantial.

FORMS OF FOREIGN BORROWING—GOVERNMENT BONDS

The traditional form of borrowing up to 1914 was government bonds. Government was the borrower, but the lender was the private investor. After World War I, the market revived and shifted from Europe, and especially from London, to New York. During the depression it collapsed, in part because of its overinflation during the late 1920s. It has never revived.

Investors today want no part of foreign government bonds. They fear, based on the dismal experience of the 1930s, that governments either will not or cannot service these obligations—either willfully defaulting, or inflating to the point where the balance of payments deteriorates and then blocking interest and amortization. The facts that most of the predepression bonds were continuously serviced, and that arrears of old indebtedness have been gradually cleared up, albeit at pennies on the dollar, have not helped.

Equity financing of international development is important, but debt financing is needed, too. Where productive investment opportunities exist, a country, like a private company, is warranted in borrowing at fixed rates of interest. Where productive assets are of considerable durability, long-term debt borrowing is entirely appropriate. Governments, as it happens, sell neither equities nor mortgages. Since much of the investment is for government account, especially in social and economic overhead capital, the lack of a foreign bond market is a handicap to development.

FORMS OF FOREIGN BORROWING—LENDING BY INTERNATIONAL AGENCIES

In the vacuum created by the need for borrowing on government account and the absence of a private bond market, the Bretton Woods conference established the International Bank for Reconstruction and Development to serve as a link between borrowing governments, on the one hand, and lending governments and private capital, on the other. The complex arrangements of the Bank, which have been described too frequently elsewhere, amount to a sort of domestic government guarantee of some private lending in the country where the Bank's obligations are sold. The Bank then furnishes some government capital to underdeveloped countries and provides a channel whereby timid private capital can move with governmental help.

The initial flow of loans by the Bank was fairly small. Currently it has reached more than $400 million gross annually, and outstanding loans amount to almost $2.5 billion.[21] In addition to its lending, the Bank has conducted economic surveys of various countries' prospects for development, furnished experts to study development problems, helped to negotiate agreements, recruited technical personnel, and operated an Economic Development Institute.

As mentioned on a number of occasions earlier, the Bank's loans, with the outstanding exception of the three transactions amounting to $145 million for the development of southern Italy, are made on a project basis. The southern Italian loans were made to cover the import spillover of the investment program rather than the foreign-exchange content of specific projects. The Bank's charges, which under its articles of agreement are based on what it pays for money, plus a 1 per cent charge for administration and a fractional charge for reserves, amount to close to 5 per cent.

A variety of proposals has been made to expand the work of the International Bank, generally on a modified basis. Expansion is sought to make more funds available. Modification, for the incremental activity at least, is desired to change the degree of supervision, to alter the project basis, to reduce the rate of interest, or to put the assistance on a grant, rather than a loan, basis.

A familiar form of these proposals which long antedates the International Bank is the demand for an Inter-American Bank to raise subscriptions from and make loans to North and South America. The word "respectively" does not appear at the end of the sentence, but is understood. The main purpose of this project, the regional aspects of which will be discussed in the following chapter, is to make more capital available for Latin America.

The most recent international proposal, enthusiastically supported by the underdeveloped countries in the United Nations, is that for a Special United Nations Fund for Economic Development, or SUNFED, which would raise money from countries on the basis of their ability to contribute, and distribute it on a grant basis, presumably according to need.[22] The United States, which would be the largest contributor,

[21] See address by IBRD president E. R. Black before the Economic and Social Council of the United Nations, Apr. 18, 1956.

[22] See United Nations' experts' report, *Special United Nations Fund for Economic Development*, New York, 1954.

has consistently voted against the project in the Economic and Social Council, citing as its reason the remarks of President Eisenhower in his speech of April 13, 1953. On this occasion, the President stated that the United States would be pleased to contribute to economic development abroad and would do so as soon as a reduction in the necessity to spend money for armaments made it possible.

Whether foreign assistance should take the form of loans or grants does not, of course, turn on whether it is to be used for social and economic overhead capital or for primary or secondary production. This follows from the section above on capacity to repay. If the economy lacks capacity to transform because of zero supply elasticity in exports and in import-competing industries, or if demand abroad has price elasticity of unity or less, which prevents expansion in exports, and exporting industry abroad has zero supply elasticity, which prevents any reduction in imports with free trade through lowering the cost of import-competing goods, a grant may be necessary for overhead projects or a disequilibrium system on the international front cannot be avoided. On the whole, however, it is appropriate to say that capacity to repay foreign assistance is primarily a function of the productivity of the investment, and grants are needed for projects of low or uncertain dubious productivity. It is not clear that these should be undertaken on any basis, given the existence of certainly productive investments.

It is true that grants raise income more than loans, typically by $4\frac{3}{4}$ or 5 per cent annually, if the contrast is between SUNFED grants and IBRD loans. If this can be reinvested, or used in "productive consumption," there is reason to favor grants over loans, insofar as the borrower or grantee is concerned. But that the grantee would prefer not to pay in order to get more benefit from the capital transfer is different from saying that it cannot pay.

FORMS OF FOREIGN BORROWING—GOVERNMENTAL LOANS AND GRANTS

Where governmental assistance to economic development abroad is part of general foreign policy, and the country does not, because of the terms of its participation in an international lending agency, exercise some measure of control over the latter's actions, there is a strong argument for unilateral rather than international action. Particularly where each country has one vote, and a few countries contribute while numerous countries benefit, it becomes difficult to use international assistance as a tool of foreign policy except in a very long-run sense.

The international organization may assist unfriendly countries unduly or fail to be sufficiently heedful of the needs of friends.

A variety of unilateral forms of assistance has come into being. The Export-Import Bank in the United States was begun as a depression measure to assist United States exporters in selling abroad, and is still frequently used to bail these exporters out of situations in which credits extended to foreign importers have been blocked. This in fact is a frequently sought type of development loan—now wanted by Argentina, Brazil, Chile, or Turkey to clear up the arrears of past excessive consumption in order to enable the country to make a new start on capital formation.

Other direct assistance to developing countries is furnished by the International Cooperation Administration in the Department of State. Most of this is defense support, i.e., to meet consumption needs in areas such as Korea, Taiwan, and Vietnam, where the burden of defense is very large in relation to available resources. Some is technical assistance, without complementary capital. But a considerable element —$1,604 million out of a total economic aid of $4,648 million in the fiscal year ended June 30, 1956—consisted of capital assistance to underdeveloped countries. All of this took the form of grants.[23]

Considerable amounts of similar assistance are made available by the United Kingdom to her colonies, and by France in North Africa. The release of blocked sterling balances owned by countries or colonies which furnished supplies to England during World War II in advance of agreed schedules is a paradoxical form of "aid," and does increase unrequited exports in the short run. Soviet assistance to underdeveloped countries appears to take the form primarily of agreements in which the Soviet Union delivers capital goods and is later repaid in primary products. These carry a nominal 2 per cent rate of interest— well below that of the International Bank for Reconstruction and Development—for the credit advanced.

FORMS OF FOREIGN BORROWING—AGRICULTURAL SURPLUSES

The Agricultural Trade Development and Assistance Act of 1954 in the United States provides for the use of agricultural surpluses for economic development. The idea is attractive to those concerned with getting rid of surpluses. In addition, as we have seen, it is not necessary for foreign borrowing to take the form of imports of capital goods.

[23] See *Survey of Current Business*, Department of Commerce, Washington, October, 1956, p. 19.

Agricultural commodities can do as well if resources previously engaged in producing, say, food, are shifted out of agriculture into the export sector—to the extent that imported capital goods are needed, and into capital formation—to the extent that the demand is for domestic capital such as construction.

It would be possible, indeed, for agricultural surpluses to be used for capital formation without transformation if they replaced existing purchased imports and released foreign exchange for capital purchases or purchases of other consumption goods. The difficulty, however, is that the act of 1954 requires that exports be incremental to cash sales. It also stipulates that they must not impair the competitive position of friendly countries.

But the foremost assistance which agricultural surpluses can provide in economic development is to prevent capital formation from being choked off, or the balance of payments turned adverse, through a lack of consumer goods arising from inability of agriculture to respond to the stimulus of increased demand. As stated previously, the rate of capital formation turns on the capacity of the economy to provide consumer goods for the resources engaged in producing capital. It would be economic to borrow and spend exchange for this purpose, even though most economic planners are insufficiently sophisticated to appreciate the fact that capital imports can take the form of imported foodstuffs. Where imported foodstuffs are surplus in the exporting country, and hence unwanted there, total resources are increased by imported food and increased capital formation made possible. Where the rate of capital formation has already been raised to overly ambitious levels, the agricultural surpluses may justify them.

The mechanism works in ways already described in Chapter 9 in the discussion of balance, and again in Chapter 14 on the foreign trade as a balancing sector. As manpower is transferred out of agriculture into social overhead or industrial capital formation, the demand for food rises, both on the part of the workers left on the farm and those in nonagricultural areas. If domestic supply is inelastic, and if agriculture is protected by prohibitive tariffs or quotas, the terms of trade shift against industrial products and in favor of farmers. Or the demand may spill over into imports and turn the balance of trade adversely. The difficulty may originate in a short crop which encourages speculators to hoard grain, raise the price of foodstuffs, and threaten the program of capital formation by raising the price of the wage good. In either circumstance, agricultural surpluses, on hand or available from abroad, can steady the terms of trade between foodstuffs and

industrial products and sustain or enlarge the rate of capital formation. The 1951 wheat loan to India and the similar grant to Pakistan
saved the programs of those countries from setback when they were
threatened by a bad monsoon. The Pakistan episode illustrates the
need for food stockpiles. The mere arrival of the shipment was sufficient to induce wheat sales by speculators, with the consequence of a
sharp drop in price and the inability of the government to sell at appropriate prices all the wheat made available.

In 1956, on the other hand, the $360 million and $110 million wheat
loans to India and Brazil, respectively, provided development resources
for these countries permitting future real investment.

FOREIGN RESOURCES AND PLANNING

Much has been made of the fact that several countries have embarked on investment programs for development without all the resources in hand and relying on foreign aid. In particular, the second
Indian Five-Year Plan, on its initiation, provided for foreign assistance
of $2,310 million over the five years, compared with $883 million for
the first Five-Year Plan and was able to count on only $420 million of
drawings on external sterling balances, $442 million of various credits
from the United States, the United Kingdom, the Soviet Union, Germany, the Colombo Plan, the International Bank, etc., and an estimated $210 million of new inflow of private foreign capital, or a total
of $1,072 million. The balance of $1,238 million was not covered but
was to be sought from international agencies and in government-to-
government assistance. Other investment programs, notably the Pakistani, but also those of Ceylon, Argentina, Brazil, etc., presuppose the
availability of foreign credits.

Where foreign credits are needed to fund past-due obligations arising from inflationary consumption and to restore the country's credit,
the program depends directly on the granting of credit. But where a
country starts with reserves and embarks on a schedule of investment
projects, it is important to determine the margin of error in the original
calculations of import needs. In India this is large. With a good monsoon, imports decline and foreign exchange will be available for capital
goods imports. In Pakistan, the difference between good and bad
harvests is again critical, but operates through exports: good harvests
provide, rather than save, foreign exchange. In both cases the investment plans presuppose average harvests but reality can bring good,
bad, or indifferent. There is a chance, then, that foreign sources of

loans are not needed to the extent that the Plan calls for external financing or, if the planners are overly optimistic, a greater chance that more borrowing will be needed than indicated.

In short, calculation of the foreign-exchange content of an investment plan on a project basis, presupposing that exports and imports go on as before except as directly reduced and increased, respectively, is a risky business. *Ceteris* have a way of not being *paribus*. If planning were flexible, with investment projects capable of being advanced, postponed, speeded up in the time taken to accomplish them, or dragged out, it might be possible and desirable to take account of harvest-to-harvest changes in the need for and availability of foreign resources and to adjust investment undertakings as the program went along. This would involve fitting the requirements to resources, rather than the other way round. Since underdeveloped countries lack control over the monsoon and over the availability of foreign loans, there is some logic to looking at it this way. But to encourage loans, it may be best to put the other face on it to the world. This is what we must do; this is what we need from abroad, suppressing the qualification *plus or minus,* and this is what we need from developed countries in loans, or preferably grants.

SUMMARY

Borrowing abroad is needed to add to total resources available for economic development, not to make development possible by providing a limited range of resources which the country does not possess. Without loans, but with capacity to transform, a country could develop, though the rate would be slowed down by over-all lack of resources. With virtually unlimited loans, but without capacity to transform, economic development would be impossible. Foreign loans could be used to add to consumption, and possibly to increase productivity in existing lines to some slight degree. But development as a process would be impossible.

Borrowing, then, is a question of degree, not kind; and it comes after other questions of kind have been settled. Even foreign loans together with foreign technicians cannot produce development. They may be able to reproduce the physical setting of a developed economy, but without adaptability it will fail to produce.

How much should be borrowed abroad? As much as can be fruitfully used. This is determined by the capacity to transform, on the one hand, and the abundance of capital, on the other. When transforming ability is high, so too are savings. The country which makes a rapid start in development in its capacity to reallocate resources in response to economic stimuli can absorb capital in large amounts, and should so long as the marginal productivity of capital is higher there than in lending countries, and by more than the subjective risk premium. If transformation capacity grows and stays high, it is likely quickly to move the mature debtor and young creditor stages because of rapidly increasing savings.

CHAPTER 16   *Regional Cooperation*

WHAT IS A REGION?

In some economic contexts, the region is a unit smaller than a nation. In the present discussion, it is larger. The type of regional cooperation, collaboration, or integration frequently invoked for purposes of development is on an international scale.

In the draft charter of the International Trade Organization—an inoperative document but one of some significance in the history of ideas—a region was defined in terms of geographical propinquity. Neighboring countries together make a geographical unit which for some economic (and political) purposes may be said to form an entity. The British delegation argued long and hard against this restriction. To it the essence of a region was that it was a unit with political cohesion. Geography was secondary. The British Commonwealth was thus claimed to be a "region" for the purpose of collaboration for economic development, and entitled to any exemptions from general rules granted for this purpose.

Something must be granted to the British point, if not everything. Proximity between countries is not a sufficient condition of a basis for regional cooperation, as India and Pakistan, Egypt and Israel illustrate. There must be a basis of common interest, such as usually arises between neighbors, and a common if frequently limited purpose. On the other hand, geography cannot be abandoned altogether. Israel and Burma do not constitute a region, despite the friendship which has sprung up between the two countries;[1] nor can the British claim be admitted that political bonds are sufficient. But it is the contention of this chapter that the basic obstacle to regional cooperation for economic development is political, not economic. This applies in the

[1] See "Burmese Will Grow Wheat for Israelis," *New York Times*, May 8, 1956.

various types of economic cooperation to be discussed: trade preferences, commodity stabilization, river valley development, banking and
payments arrangements, and regional development planning. Only in
regional technical cooperation is the economic benefit so substantial
and the competitive element so small that regional cooperative arrangements find little obstacle in political indifference, although en-
mity may constitute a block.

TRADE PREFERENCES

The draft charter of the International Trade Organization had two
provisions under which new exceptions to the general rule of nondis-
crimination could be put into effect: one was customs unions, the
other, the granting of 100 per cent preferences in specific articles by
countries engaged in economic development. The customs union provision has been attacked as illogical: a 99 per cent preference is ruled
out, but one of 100 per cent is permitted. The distinction, however, is
that a customs union or free-trade area involves the agreement to
abandon use of tariffs in trade between two countries. Thus far among
developing countries there are no such unions or areas in being, although Syria and Jordan have signed a preliminary agreement for
"total economic union," including a customs union;[2] the Arab League,
consisting of Egypt, Iraq, Jordan, Lebanon, Libya, Saudi Arabia,
Yemen, and the Sudan, has embarked on a study of plans for economic
union;[3] and the Central American Committee on Economic Cooperation, formed by the Ministers of Economy of Guatemala, El Salvador,
Honduras, Nicaragua, and Costa Rica, has agreed on a multilateral
free-trade treaty, which in the summer of 1956 was awaiting ratification.[4]

The initial provisions of the ITO draft charter on preferences for
economic development were included at the insistence of the Arab
League. It is significant that five years went by without steps being
taken to translate them into concrete proposals. Indeed, these years
were marked by retrogression; every country in the Arab League, with
minor exceptions, arranged with one or more oil companies with investment in its area to establish an oil refinery to supply the local
market with products, rather than import products from efficient-sized
refineries located within neighboring boundaries. It is significant that

---

[2] "Arabs Say Soviet Plans Navy Visits," *New York Times*, Aug. 7, 1956.
[3] *Ibid.*
[4] "Central America to Knit Industry," *New York Times*, July 12, 1956; "Central
Americas Set Industry Plan," *ibid.*, July 22, 1956.

the stimulus to renewed efforts toward customs and economic union came after the Arab League's enhanced political cohesion resulting from the Egyptian seizure of the Suez Canal.[5]

In Central America, the free-trade treaty relates to certain limited articles, as provided by the defunct ITO charter. Certain industries are to be declared "regional industries" with immunity from local taxation and import taxes in the other members of the agreement: an existing paint company in Costa Rica, a cardboard container company ready to start operations in 1956 in Guatemala, and a tire company, also in Guatemala, in the early stages of investment. Other likely regional industries were expected to be designated in petroleum byproducts, ceramics, and rayon fiber. The five countries also established a Central American Development Fund, with a quota of $1 million for each country, to assist in starting regional industries. The combined market of the five countries is estimated at nine million of population compared with the three million in Guatemala, which is the largest of the five.

Despite these advances, the prospect for widespread regional cooperation through trade preferences and customs unions is not bright. Even where a high degree of political cohesion exists, as between the Netherlands and the Belgian-Luxembourg Economic Union, the road to customs union is long and weary.[6] Similarly, the European Common Market, initiated on March 25, 1957, provides for its full accomplishment only seventeen years after ratification; and this schedule may be lengthened as the period unfolds. It may be true that to establish a customs union in advance of industrialization encounters less opposition from vested interests. But, where political bonds are weak, as is true for the most part among developing countries, every country is prepared in principle to agree to preferences, but in practice is unable to see why the industry in question cannot be located within its borders. Each country is prepared to make concessions in abstract without being willing to cede a given industry in practice. The Central American Committee on Economic Cooperation, established in 1952 under the authorization of the Economic Commission for Latin America, represents the first and heartening evidence which would contravene this view.

Even Britain, which has long subscribed to Empire preference,

[5] Some of the resurgence of interest, however, antedates the Suez incident and goes back to a meeting of the League's Political Committee in Damascus on May 19, 1956. It is noteworthy that the Political Committee proposed the union.

[6] See J. E. Meade, *Negotiations for Benelux: An Annotated Chronicle 1943–56,* Princeton Studies in International Finance, Princeton, N.J., 1957.

where political considerations are equally or more significant than economic, is beginning to have misgivings when it contemplates the free entry of Indian textiles into Britain.

The principle of these trade preferences is unexceptional. To achieve technologically appropriate scale, the market is widened, but the infant industry is protected against the outside world. If the infant industry proves capable of competing in the long run, the customs union results in trade creation rather than trade diversion.[7] But the practice is hard to achieve, and there is a question whether the scarce resource of economic administrative talent should be used to pursue it.

The same considerations apply to political union. Here the most interesting project is that of the British Caribbean Federation which would unite fifty or more islands stretching over 1,300 miles and possibly British Honduras and British Guiana (which would add another 500 miles). The political basis for union is easier to see than the economic, since the islands, aided by Empire preference, are for the most part competitors in provisioning the British market with tropical products. In addition, the nature of their geographic links, in which each is virtually as accessible to the outside world as it is to the rest of the Federation, provides an artificial rather than a real basis of economic union.

STABILIZATION SCHEMES

Commodity stabilization schemes have already been touched upon in Chapter 14. Here we need only refer to the difficulties of negotiating and administering such arrangements exclusively among underdeveloped countries, and where they have to provide the finance to buy up surpluses. No such agreement exists today. The stabilization measures in effect in wheat, sugar, and tin all involve developed countries. Although the tin buffer-stock scheme is financed by the exporters, it is British and Dutch producer interests in Southeast Asia which provide the necessary leadership. A recent attempt by Brazil to organize a coffee stabilization scheme failed over the question of the distribution of costs. Brazil, Costa Rica, Colombia, and Guatemala were unable to work out a sharing arrangement which would take proper account of levels of income, importance of coffee to the national economy, quality of product grown, etc.

There is no economic reason why underdeveloped countries cannot

[7] This is a different case from that treated in J. Viner, *The Customs Union Issue,* Carnegie Endowment, New York, 1950, widely discussed, since the tariff level is initially unambiguously raised, with trade-diverting effects.

work out commodity arrangements to stabilize prices—although there is the general danger that the price will be set too high. The difficulty is finding the appropriate sharing basis among countries which are all poor and lack ties other than the common product.

TECHNICAL COOPERATION

The most substantial success achieved by regional cooperation has been in the field of technical cooperation. It remains true that the major source of technical assistance is the developed countries. But Colombo Plan experience in Asia, and a limited amount of United Nations experience elsewhere, has shown that there are real benefits to be gained from narrowing the technological gap between countries and having an underdeveloped country assisted by another which is not far in advance of it. This question has already been referred to in Chapter 10. The outstanding illustration is furnished by the technical assistance arrangements of the Colombo Plan, which undertakes training of individuals for development tasks in neighboring countries and uses experts from Asian as well as non-Asian membership of the Consultative Committee.

Of special interest is the possibility that Japan may be in a better position to furnish technical assistance for other parts of Asia than the United States and Western Europe, because of the narrower cultural as well as technical gap. In Asia, too, Indian experience with community development projects has been made available to visitors from other Asian countries and particularly through visits of Indian experts to Indonesia, where the program has been adopted.

Substantial technical assistance is furnished through regional meetings of experts. The United Nations regional commissions in Europe, Latin America, and Asia and the Far East serve less as planners of development projects or programs, discussed below, than as clearing houses for ideas. The same is true of the Colombo "Plan." Conferences are held on planning techniques, the process of development, and the analysis of developmental blocks. Experience is exchanged. It is evident that intellectual and technical cooperation is much the easiest to organize and carry out. Advice is cheap and can always be ignored. One can learn from strangers or even enemies—the latter is not only possible but advisable—and, where the process is mutual, among countries at not too different stages of growth, the highly structured relationship of teacher and pupil, with its inevitable appearance of patronization, is avoided. Not only does intellectual collaboration not require a solid political basis; it can help to build one. The process of intellectual communication and exchange may serve as the basis for ultimate collaboration of a more substantial and expensive sort.

REGIONAL PAYMENTS ARRANGEMENTS

The European Payments Union has been a distinct success. With a capital of $350 million, it has provided for multilateral clearing among the countries of Western Europe since 1950 and made possible a liberalization of mutual trade and a reduction of exchange barriers. But the idea involved is not necessarily useful in other contexts.

The Japanese delegation to the Bandung Conference in 1955 suggested the creation of an Asian Payments Union. At the Simla meeting of Asian countries in May, 1955, an attempt was made to reach an agreement under which $200 million of aid made available by the United States could be employed on a regional basis in Asia, presumably for payments arrangements. From time to time it is suggested that the Latin American countries adopt a regional payments pattern, or that the Arab League's customs union ultimately be broadened into a monetary union. The Asian Payments Union idea has been abandoned. The Simla Conference failed to get any agreement on how to use $200 million regionally. Latin American and Arabian monetary cooperation are remote possibilities. The experience of Europe is almost irrelevant to that of underdeveloped countries, because the underlying conditions are so different.

European countries participating in the European Payments Union have on the average about 60 per cent of their trade with other members of the union. If the United Kingdom were to be excluded, the percentage would rise to 65. Much of this trade, moreover, is highly competitive, which means that elasticities of demand and supply are relatively high. In underdeveloped regions, on the other hand, most trade is conducted by the countries in the region with the outside world, and very little inside the area. In Latin America, the average proportion of regional trade is close to 15 per cent. The percentage is higher in Asia, reflecting particularly the considerable proportion of Japanese trade within the region; but it is still relatively small—about 35 per cent. Moreover, the elasticities of demand and supply on regional trade are low. Argentina and Brazil are almost inevitably supplied by Venezuelan oil. Burmese and Thailand rice have few outlets other than Japan, Indonesia, and India.

There is room for particular deals, largely financed outside the area. The International Cooperation Administration in the Department of State has developed a number of these—for example, the provision of technical assistance to Burma in return for which that country would ship rice to Pakistan;[8] or sales of wheat to Japan against yen which would then be spent for capital goods made available to third countries.[9] It was reported from Simla that India and Japan were both interested in using the $200 million offered by the United States in this fashion, largely to finance Indian purchases of capital equipment in Japan. But this was a long way from the original proposal of a revolving fund, presumably one which would revolve more than once.

It is argued that one reason the $200 million offer of the United States at Simla was not accepted was that the sum was too small to make it worthwhile for the countries participating either to overcome their mutual suspicions or to use their imaginations to productive effect. If so, this was the remote cause. The proximate causes of failure were inability of the countries present to agree on a basis for sharing, and lack of any proposals which would enable the funds to be used more than twice, i.e., to pay A to provide goods to B.

Capacity to share requires a very high degree of social and political cohesion, as the European Recovery Program made clear. In Asia, a number of small countries have said that they wanted to deal bilaterally with outside benefactors and not to be told that their own plans had to be cut back in the interest of greater Asia. Such planning in the "common interest" was too reminiscent of the Greater East Asia Co-Prosperity Sphere. But even if the countries had been able to divide the amount, the United States proposal appeared to call for more than splitting a melon.

RIVER VALLEY DEVELOPMENT

Much is hoped for from international river valley development by underdeveloped countries. A number of rivers lend themselves to, or rather require, international treatment—the Nile, rising in Ethiopia, Kenya, and Tanganyika, flowing through the Sudan before reaching Egypt; the Jordan, with its source in Lebanon, serving as a border between Syria and Israel before flowing into Jordan; the Indus (Pakistan, Kashmir, and India); the Mekong (Tibet, Burma, Laos, Thailand, Cambodia, Vietnam); the Helmand, Salween, Zambezi, Congo, Amazon, Orinoco, etc., to name but a few. Some of these present few problems because of abundance of water, remoteness of the source, limited extent of the flow, or other reasons. But the international character of these leading rivers presents a great problem. The basic difficulty is

[8] "3-Way Rice Trade Proposed by U.S.," *New York Times,* Mar. 13, 1956.
[9] "U.S. Offers Japan 3-Way Trade Deals," *ibid.,* Mar. 9, 1956.

in the division of the water—either its diversion to irrigation, as in the Jordan and the Indus, or the amount of evaporation as a result of dams, which is the difficulty in the Nile and the Helmand. Whether power should be generated and floods controlled by one large dam downstream or many small ones upstream is a hotly debated issue in the United States. Where upstream and downstream lie in different countries, and small dams upstream may so regulate the flow and increase evaporation as to make it impossible to generate power and irrigate on the desired scale downstream, there is evidently room for disagreement. While the international regulation of navigation and power on the Rhine is well established and runs smoothly, the Danube has presented difficulties since the split of Europe, and even Canada and the United States have had disagreements on whether and how to develop rivers which run between or in both countries. When the countries are ancient rivals, competitors, or enemies, as in the Pakistan-India dispute and that between Israel and Lebanon-Syria-Jordan, the prospects for cooperation are dim.

These difficulties may not be unmixed curses. River valley development involves high costs and an uncertain and long-delayed return. Transport as a major object of investment may have a substantial payout, but irrigation and power suffer from high capital/output ratios and are dubious items of expenditure early in the development process. The multipurpose project too readily embarked on, following the TVA analogy, frequently results in monumental waste.

Where it is clear that the payout is high and near in time and the cost modest, river valley development has much to recommend it. All that is then needed is the political cohesion sufficient to agree on the division of the water, the division of expenses of joint projects, and the sharing of the joint benefits. This is a tall order among friends; impossible between enemies.

REGIONAL PROJECTS

Aside from rivers, it is difficult to find regional development projects. This is not for want of trying. The Inter-American political system, under its various forms, worked for many years before it hit upon the Inter-American Highway, the value of which is largely national and mainly symbolic on the international front, although it may ultimately lead some United States tourists beyond Mexico. In Europe, the European Coal and Steel Community offers an interesting and unique experiment in cooperation among six countries under supranational authority, which may be extended into other fields. Here the political basis is vastly more solid than in underdeveloped areas. But after long study, the Economic Commission for Europe, searching hard for an international project involving southern Europe, has been able to offer only another highway for the purpose of attracting tourists—this time from Trieste to Belgrade, Istanbul, Athens, Patras, (ferry to) Brindisi, Rome, and back to Trieste.[10]

REGIONAL PLANNING

Numerous writers have urged the creation of organs of regional planning or regional integration of national plans.[11] The Colombo Plan is sometimes cited as an example of what is intended, or reference is made to the European Recovery Program, which was thought to be a "coordinated" or "integrated" plan.

There is merit in expert and ministerial meetings to compare national development plans. This is the nature of the Colombo Plan, which is neither a plan nor an organization but a three-week annual meeting, which disappears for forty-nine weeks of the year, and at which the main task is an editorial one. There is no sharing of external contributions, since developmental aid, except for technical assistance, is furnished on a bilateral basis.[12]

The European Recovery Program went further. There were the recommendations for the amount and sharing of aid. In the single field of oil refining, there was integrated planning, assisted by the fact that the industry involved large units and a small number of companies which were able to lend their personnel to the respective governments for the purpose. A few absurd national projects were frowned upon by the group and abandoned. The Organization for European Economic Cooperation and the European Payments Union provided a means whereby pressure could be brought to bear by the group against the inflationary or other unwise internal policies of a given country, and

---

[10] "Southern European Bank," *The Times*, Mar. 31, 1956.

[11] See, e.g., W. Y. Elliott (ed.), *Foreign Economic Policy for the United States*, Henry Holt & Company, Inc., New York, 1955, esp. chap. 7.

[12] Cf. F. Benham, *The Colombo Plan and Other Essays*, Royal Institute of International Affairs, London, 1956, p. 2: "There is no general Colombo Plan Fund, from which loans or grants are allocated to the various Asian members. Each country has its own development programme, which, of course, it draws up and revises from time to time exactly as it pleases. Every offer of assistance, whether financial or technical, is the subject of bilateral negotiation between the two countries concerned, who settle all the details entirely between themselves. Nor does the Consultative Committee, or any other body, exercise any control over either the general planning of a country or its administration of its various projects."

in favor of trade liberalization, on a discriminatory and ultimately on a nondiscriminatory basis. But primarily integration was accomplished on a limited basis through the removal of trade barriers and the broad and rough harmonization of monetary and fiscal policies. During the period of acute shortages, the OEEC and the ECE allocated short supplies. Statistics of foreign trade and national income were made comparable and aggregated for the group. But planning in the sense that national programs were laid aside and a single international investment plan was agreed upon was not even remotely approached in the earlier period. Later six countries formed the European Coal and Steel Community, which is regarded widely as a venture in planning but is considered by its sponsors as a means of permitting international competition to allocate supply. A further step in this direction is contemplated in the proposed EURATOM in the field of atomic research and energy.

The nearest approach to investment planning thus far is that envisaged by the Central American Committee on Economic Cooperation. Beyond this, the regional meetings of technical experts and ministers in seminars or formal meetings may result in elimination of duplication in some projects. More positive results seem unlikely.

The fact is that there has been considerable disintegration and duplication in the recent course of developmental investment. The finely articulated jute and burlap industry of British India was divided by partition with jute production in East Pakistan and jute manufacture in the vicinity of Calcutta. Since partition, jute production had been started in India and jute manufacture in Pakistan. The oil refinery at Haifa in Israel has been isolated by blockade and duplicated by new installations at Sidon. The Anglo-Iranian Oil Company has built a large new refinery at Aden to replace the confiscated Abadan installation. The growth of textile industries in virtually every underdeveloped country has brought about world excess and overproduction.

The major contribution of regional development boards would be in arresting this trend toward duplication and autarchy within the region. In addition, there might be some tasks to be performed in dividing aid. Here, however, there is a considerable difficulty, not met in a world organization such as the International Bank, with its regional loans departments for Europe and Africa; Latin America; and Asia and the Middle East. If regional administrative boards were established, the division of economic aid on a world basis would have to be made once and for all between the various regions; and any attempt to modify the original division would be strongly resisted by the regions which were cut. In a global organization, on the other

hand, there is always the possibility of correcting and amending tenta-
tive regional breakdowns, by subtracting resources from, say, the
Europe-Africa area and making them available to Latin America. The
International Bank operates on the working level on a regional basis,
as any politico-economic organization must do. Objective criteria
governing assistance must be modified to make sure that every country
in good standing gets something, and that prizes are passed out for
economically good behavior. But there is no known continental division. If each region were given a quota, it would be much clearer that
a loan for A means less for its neighbor, B, which would be divisive
rather than unifying. And where the countries are themselves asked
to divide the aid, instead of enlisting the services of presumably objective and disinterested expert groups such as the International Bank,
the opportunities for friction are magnified.

THE POLITICAL BASIS OF REGIONAL COOPERATION

It is easy to exaggerate the political solidarity running among underdeveloped countries. United against "colonialism" and capitalistic exploitation and joined as a bloc in the United Nations to vote more
projects which aid economic development in general, their interests
are often opposed when it comes to development in particular. Some
countries have ties which bind them particularly to one developed
country or another—the Philippines to the United States, or Morocco
and Tunisia to France. In Latin America there is a basic cleavage between the countries belonging to the dollar bloc and those producing
commodities which compete with United States exports and maintaining close trade ties to Europe. The jealousy of Latin America over
United States concern for European recovery has not been concealed.
It would be easy to open up similar divergences of interest between
the Middle East and the Far East, or Asia and Latin America. The
growth of Ethiopian and Liberian production in coffee threatens
Brazilian long-run interests. The Egyptian assumption of leadership in
the Arab world arouses antithetical feelings of pride in Nasser's de-
fiance of the West and fear of his ascendancy over the other members
of the Moslem world.

Where the political basis for federation or union exists, as in the
British West Indies, or between Northern and Southern Rhodesia and
Nyasaland which are forming the Central African Federation, a clear
basis of economic integration exists. The resolve to share at whatever
cost has preceded the actual necessity to do so. The political compact
does not so much eliminate regional differences as it arranges for their

settlement in organized fashion, along with the agreement to face the outside world as a unit.

Where political cohesion falls short of this pitch, however, as is largely the position in the underdeveloped world, limited interests will coincide from time to time, and present opportunities for occasional cooperation. To attempt to force more substantial tasks of cooperation on these countries, regionally or otherwise, however, is to jeopardize whatever cohesion they may have achieved.

It has already been noted that the way to political cohesion may lie through efforts at economic cooperation. This is true. But before one can go far in economic joint effort, the political underpinning must be built into place.

The relations between economic and political action are full of paradox. The economic theorem that trade and factor movements can equalize factor prices has it exactly backwards. If free trade and large-scale factor movements be not imposed by the power of the sovereign, they are tolerated in a democratic society so long as some measure of political cohesion exists, and this cohesion requires an original rough degree of factor-price equalization. Factor-price equalization (or its original underlying social unity) produces free trade and free immigration rather than the reverse.[13]

The underdeveloped countries have this bond in common: they are poor. But there is a great difference in the solidarity of the poor when all know that they are likely to remain so, and the stresses and strains which arise among the poor as they compete to climb out of poverty. It may be true that all can make economic progress more effectively together than apart. But there is always the chance that one can move faster and farther alone. This possibility serves as a great inhibitor of regional economic cooperation.

[13] See G. Myrdal, *An International Economy*, Harper & Brothers, New York, 1956, chaps. I, II, and III.

CHAPTER 17   *Relations with Developed Countries*

THE ECONOMIC INTEREST

Among the numerous and varied interests of developed nations in countries engaged on programs of economic growth, the material ones include direct markets for exports, competition of new industries in third markets and in the home market, sources of supply for imports, and outlets for profitable investment. Growth brings changes in these relationships.

The impact of development on markets for exports of developed countries is a dual one. On the one hand is the market-destroying effort of the establishment of new industries, generally of an import-competing character, frequently designed specifically to substitute for imports. On the other, development raises income in general, which spills over into imports in general, and increases the demand, in particular, for imported capital equipment.

Which of these effects will predominate in any particular instance will depend upon the foreign-trade structure of the developed country and its capacity to transform. If a country is highly specialized in consumer goods exports, such as textiles, and fairly inflexible, as was Britain in the 1920s, development abroad may be adverse to its exporting interests. By and large, however, there is almost no doubt that the market-creating effects overwhelm the market-destroying. For United States goods, imports of developed countries run $5.80 per capita (in 1948), compared with $1.25 for a group of countries only moderately developed, and $0.70 for underdeveloped countries.[1] The correlation between the stage of growth and imports from the United States is not very high, however, as Figure 17.1 shows. Proximity plays a large role for countries in the Western Hemisphere, and special cases

[1] *Point 4,* Department of State, Washington, 1949, p. 10.

like Israel and Japan produce a level of imports higher than the norm. Statistical investigation indicates that more of world trade consists in machinery and vehicles, and less in food, drink, tobacco, raw materials, and textiles, while metals, chemicals, and miscellaneous products hold their own.[2]

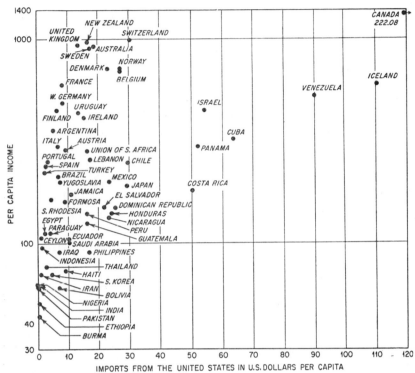

Figure 17.1. Imports from the United States compared with income per capita, 1953. SOURCES: Imports in U.S. dollars per capita, *Direction of International Trade, 1954*, United Nations, New York, 1954; *Demographic Yearbook, 1954*, United Nations, New York, 1954; income per capita, Table 1.1, Income per Capita in U.S. Dollars.

Within these broad groups have been changes involving loss of old markets and the creation of new. If developed countries have capacity to develop new products and new ways of producing old commodities, and to shift resources from old lines of production into new,

[2] See *Industrialization and Foreign Trade*, League of Nations, Geneva, 1945; E. Staley, *World Economic Development*, International Labour Office, Montreal, 1945; H. Tyszynski, "World Trade in Manufactured Commodities, 1899–1950," *Manchester School*, September, 1951, pp. 272–304; A. K. Cairncross and J. Faaland, "Long Term Trends in Europe's Trade," *Economic Journal*, March, 1952, pp. 25–34.

growth in poor countries is on balance stimulating. The old view that the export of machinery is economic suicide[3] is virtually dead, although traces of it are occasionally found.

Growth of competition in third markets and even in the home market is a wider extension of the market-destroying effect. The classic case used to be the expansion of Japanese textile trade which pressed Britain everywhere in her colonial empire until Empire preference was invoked to help. Today's classic case is India, inside the imperial preference system, long since a serious competitor for her own market and now shipping cotton gray goods to Britain. Market destruction in third markets and in developed countries must therefore be added to market destruction in the developing country itself. It is important in particular cases,[4] but still insignificant compared to market creation.

The view that the United States should foster the development of underdeveloped areas in order to expand supplies of imported raw materials was expressed in the Paley Report,[5] and has subsequently been voiced in official studies of the foreign economic policy of the United States.[6] This justification of aid to underdeveloped countries seems contrived. Neither the general necessity for expanded supplies of imported materials nor the likelihood that economic development abroad is needed to achieve them is clear. Where additional imports of iron or petroleum would be useful in keeping down raw-material costs, direct investment, frequently in such developed countries as Canada, may be capable of providing them without general plans of economic development. And such general plans, as a rule, leave little room for domestic investments in raw-materials production. Indeed, Colin Clark's prediction that the terms of trade will favor raw materials over manufactures by 1960[7] is based on the assumption that economic development will reallocate incremental or even infra-marginal resources to manufactures as opposed to raw materials in a measure which exceeds the requirements of the demand for manufactures. It can therefore be argued either way without much con-

[3] See A. O. Hirschman, "Effects of Industrialization on the Markets of Industrial Countries," in B. Hoselitz (ed.), *The Progress of Underdeveloped Areas*, Chicago, 1952, p. 276, quoting the title of a German tract of 1907.

[4] The Economic Commission for Europe has recently urged that Europe should further transform itself away from consumer industries and toward capital goods. See *Economic Survey of Europe in 1955*, United Nations, Economic Commission for Europe, Geneva, 1956, pp. 31–32.

[5] *Resources for Freedom*, President's Materials Policy Commission, Washington, 1952, vol. I, chap. 11 *et seq.*

[6] *Report to the President on Foreign Economic Policies* (Gray Report), Washington, 1950, pp. 59–60; Commission on Foreign Economic Policy (Randall Commission), *Report to the President and the Congress*, Washington, 1954, pp. 39ff.

[7] C. Clark, *The Economics of 1960*, Macmillan & Co., Ltd., London, 1942.

fidence in either outcome: development will enlarge or shrink the supply of imports available to developed countries. A policy of assisting development on any impressive scale, however, could hardly be based upon the view chosen.

Finally, it seems likely that economic development will hurt the investment interests of developed countries before it improves them. It is true that developed countries undertake investments in one another, particularly in import-competing, differentiated, and frequently patent-protected products. Canada and the United States both have investments across their mutual border. The United States invests in Europe and Europe in the United States. Before this stage is reached, however, a more painful and difficult period will probably have to be undergone. In this period, political independence and increasing self-confidence on the part of the underdeveloped country and its component sectors are likely to lead to higher wage costs, higher taxes, and increased regulation, if not nationalization or confiscation. The sovereignty of the underdeveloped country is likely to increase along parallel political and economic paths with reduced direction, increased complication, and a reduced share of profit for the owners in the developed country. That conditions will get better after they have gotten worse is some consolation—unless, to be sure, they have gone completely bad during the intermediate stage, and cannot recover. But it can hardly be maintained that economic development should be sought by developed countries so as to increase the profitability of their investments in countries now underdeveloped.

On this showing, it is hard to make a case that the development of presently undeveloped areas carries economic benefits for the developed countries which justify their assistance. The export-creating effect, coupled with the long-run favorable impact on direct investment, probably justifies the conclusion that growth is on balance favorable. But in any particular instance, the effect is uncertain, and may run the other way. Moreover, the receipt of benefits from development abroad depends on transformation, including innovation and reallocation of resources, and a country which is capable of these adjustments may be said to produce its own prosperity. It makes little sense as a precept for the conduct of business to subsidize one's customers, or even to teach one's competitors to run their businesses more successfully. There will be occasions, however, when it pays off handsomely.

We conclude, therefore, that economic interests are not sufficient to induce developed countries in assisting underdeveloped. Development abroad may redound favorably, and need not hurt. But the argument that no country can be prosperous in a world where there are countries which are not prosperous is rhetorical nonsense. Parts of a country can wax rich, despite poverty elsewhere in the nation and elsewhere in the world. A country needs only enough customers, at home or abroad, and not that every potential customer be as rich as it is. A country can become rich in a world of poverty even without exploiting the poor, as the example of the United States proves—though Marxists will not agree with this statement. To attempt to sustain prosperity through improving the economic condition of all underdeveloped countries runs the risk of neglecting capacity to transform, which is the critical condition of prosperity.

NONECONOMIC INTERESTS

The major noneconomic interests used to justify assistance to economic development today are defense and humanitarianism, to counter the designs of the Soviet Union, and to prevent unrest or revolution, which might spread so as to involve other countries and lead to war.

The defense argument is often put in a short-run context, sometimes in more long-run terms. In the former, development is needed to strengthen existing allies, to increase their allocation of resources to defense needs currently and their capacity to produce defense goods over time. In the latter, the underdeveloped country is regarded as committed to a program of development. To give assistance is to win its friendship so that it will become a defensive ally, or "neutral for" the West rather than neutral or active against.

To assist a country's economic development program for the sake of winning friends is not very different from assistance given to counter or match economic assistance given by the Soviet Union. The theory is identical. It assumes that if the West does not give aid, aid given by the Soviet Union will win allies, friendship, or benevolent neutrality for it, to the detriment of others. This, then, is a simple variant of the long-run defense interest.

Humanitarian or ethical considerations have been used on the part of mature nations to justify interest in the development of underdeveloped countries, in the Atlantic Charter, the United Nations Charter, the Articles of Agreement of the International Bank for Reconstruction and Development, and in many similar international documents. It is difficult, however, to distinguish selflessness from long-run enlightened self-interest. Even where the motives are clearly separable, the conduct may not be: witness the medical missionary such as Albert Schweitzer, and the oil company, each of which establishes clinics and ministers to the health of native peoples. The missionary is unaware, the oil company conscious of the feedback. Assistance to development on a humanitarian basis can be undertaken because of the existence of the need; or the same action may be forthcoming under enlightened self-interest in the realization that the need, left unfilled, may give rise to trouble. This may not be a specific kind of trouble —the spread of communism, an alliance with the Soviet Union, a fascist movement, or a similar disturbance. It is not necessary to foresee the nature of the untoward result; the more profound insights into social behavior, indeed, suggest that it is impossible to forecast clearly the nature of the outcome of what the sociologists call anomie.

It is obvious from the discussion of evolutionary and revolutionary aspects of economic development in Chapter 13 that it is equally impossible to forecast the social and political consequences of economic development. If development gets under way, and the growth of appetite outruns the capacity for satisfying it, or if development brings with it a marked increase in skewness of the distribution of economic wealth and political power, development itself may lead to anomie. All that can be said as justification of programs of assistance to economic development is that the chances of avoiding political and social disintegration, such as results from a sharp dichotomy between social needs and their fulfillment, is likely to be greater when economic development is assisted from abroad than when it is not. Such is the increase in communication and transport, and such the narrowing of intellectual distance, that economic aspirations of most countries have increased. In some cases, this increase has not yet penetrated deeply into the peasant, the *fellah*, the Latin American Indian, or the untouchable. But it is under way. National leaders, the middle class, the urban proletarian, all are conscious of the gap in levels of living and economic power between developed and underdeveloped nations, and are determined to close it by one means or another. A program of assistance to underdeveloped countries by developed ones will assuredly raise aspirations, along with capacity. It is likely, however, to raise capacity more than short-run aspiration, and hence to assist in closing the gap. So long as economic progress is being made with help from abroad, the chances of social breakdown with the creation of power vacuum into which new power is violently sucked are reduced.

This is not a solid argument or rationale for assistance from abroad to underdeveloped countries; it is nonetheless the primary argument. And it has an important corollary. The underdeveloped countries are bound and determined to make progress in economic development. If they receive assistance from the developed countries, they may or may not succeed in achieving that development while maintaining political freedom and benevolent neutrality internationally. If, on the other hand, they do not receive aid, their chances of failing to develop and therefore undergoing internal convulsions, or of adopting totalitarian methods to make progress toward development, and succeeding or failing, are increased. The gamble involved in assisting development may not be very appealing, but it may be more attractive than the gamble of standing idly by.

SHOULD DEVELOPED COUNTRIES ASSIST THE UNDERDEVELOPED?

It would seem, then, that, while there is no very clear and direct economic interest to be served, nor any certain noneconomic interest, the developed countries should come to the assistance of underdeveloped countries in getting on with the task at a faster rate than they could undertake by themselves. Part of the reason goes beyond the interests of the developed countries and touches upon morality, and the expectations concerning development which have been aroused. Responsibility derives from expectations created from outside. It was a great point in the Hungarian uprising of the fall of 1956 to determine whether Radio Free Europe had created expectations that active assistance would be given to an open revolt; for, if such expectations have been fostered, a moral obligation would have been incurred. Similarly, in international relations, when a country undertakes to come to the defense of another country if attacked, it commits itself to a course of conduct even though the commitment was entered into unwisely. Where no such commitment exists, a country may regret an attack on another but be able to consider itself not bound to assist.

The underdeveloped countries now have expectations of assistance in their development, arising from a variety of sources; but above all from the statements of United States officials, politicians, personalities, and intellectuals. If such assistance were available in the form of foreign loans, it would be possible to point to this means of securing capital without necessity to go further. But where the expectation has been fully aroused, and only partly satisfied through the International Bank, the Point Four, and similar programs, it is likely to prove impossible to escape action. If the United States were suddenly to change its political complexion and elect to power a long-term opponent of foreign assistance, such as the late Senator Taft, the expectations previously awakened would be rapidly revised. But the main stream of political thought cannot be quickly channeled into other directions.

The expectation having been aroused, the United States, at least, among the developed countries, is committed to some form of economic assistance to the development programs of the so-called free world. No such expectations have been awakened in the Soviet Union (after 1946) or in Red China.

LOANS OR GRANTS

The writer sees little merit in grants. Whether or not charity begins at home, it has nothing to do with development. The sharing of treasure is appropriate to defense, war, and reconstruction from war, and to alleviate human suffering from disaster. Defense, reconstruction, and relief grants are therefore appropriate. Grants may also assist in raising consumption, for which charity is appropriate. But development is a business matter. Since loans are not available privately on a business basis, governments which have awakened or heightened expectations as to rates of development can appropriately make loans for economic development. The significant questions are how much, and on what basis.

THE AMOUNT OF LOANS

Reference has been made in Chapter 14 to scientific attempts to establish the appropriate amount of international loans. Most of these are rather unscientific. The balance-of-payments criterion applied in the European Recovery Program (for the first year) is backwards—it is not the program which determines the balance-of-payments deficit so much as the balance-of-payments deficit that can be financed which determines the program.[8] Moreover, its incentives are perverse. The worse a country performs in terms of limiting consumption and raising the marginal propensity to save, the worse its balance of payments and the greater its need.

The concept of capacity to absorb capital, developed by Millikan and Rostow and discussed above,[9] is not entirely free from these am-

[8] See F. Machlup, "Three Concepts of the Balance of Payments and the So-called Dollar Shortage," *Economic Journal*, March, 1950, pp. 46–68. This dictum applies less completely to the European Recovery Program where the program was partly determined by the requirements of reconstruction, having in mind some historical and politically required levels of living, than it does to economic development. There may, however, be a touch of a politically necessary level of living in development, because of aroused expectations, which makes some of the causation run from the program to the deficit.

[9] See pp. 262–265.

biguities. Capacity to absorb capital is partly a balance-of-payments notion, with the proviso that consumption is held down and all the complementary resources for capital formation are available. But suppose that there are two countries which differ in no respect except the marginal propensity to save. Is their capacity to absorb capital equal or different? If they attempt to form the same amount of capital, and the one with the lower marginal propensity to save runs a higher balance-of-payments deficit, should it get greater foreign loans or not? What if the government made every effort to raise the marginal propensity to save, but failed because the country had previously always lived within its means and therefore lacked the heavy burden of agricultural debt which soaks up savings so rapidly when income rises?

Millikan and Rostow, moreover, tend to toss aside their criterion of loans on the basis of capacity to absorb. In estimating how much capital their program would absorb, they divide the underdeveloped countries into two classes: those whose development is already under way, and those not.[10] The latter are estimated to absorb something like 30 per cent to 50 per cent of the existing level of capital formation, and so are the former, even though their capacity to absorb capital is certainly higher.

One objective criterion would be strictly economic bidding, with a fixed amount of loans allocated among underdeveloped countries according to the rate of interest offered. But this sets an inappropriate standard. It is assumed that loans would be contracted at rates of interest approaching the marginal productivity of capital in the United States, or the rate at which asset holders are willing to part with their liquidity to hold United States bonds and the equivalent. This should be well below the marginal productivity of capital in underdeveloped areas after complementary resources have been found or provided for. The demand for capital should thus exceed the likely supply at the going price. Some basis for rationing should therefore be found.

There is no scientific basis for rationing. The process is clearly a political one. So is the international division of the costs of a war, or the agreement on contributions to the costs of the United Nations, or the quotas in the International Monetary Fund. Economic criteria can help approach the stage where the bargaining gets intense. In the League of Nations formula there was an amalgam of percentages of world income, world trade, etc., which gave the basis for final negotiation. In the final analysis there must be a consensus that the division of aid is somehow right. The more that appeals to economic formulae are

---

[10] See M. F. Millikan and W. W. Rostow, *A Proposal: Key to an Effective Foreign Policy,* Harper & Brothers, New York, 1957, pp. 98ff.

convincing, the more they assist in the political process. But it remains political.

The nature of the sharing process raises the question whether future allocations out of a possible second provision of loan assistance should be geared closely to performance on the first. The difficulty is that need and incentives may be perversely related: the better a country has used its initial aid, the less it needs and the more it deserves, and the converse. The point should be familiar to economists in public finance who worry about the effects of taxes on incentives. They conclude that all taxes on sales or on income have adverse effects on incentives, and welfare considerations require a most impractical system of lump-sum progressive taxes, i.e., taxes levied on capital, which leave people with the incentive to earn all they can, and progressive in that they take more revenue from the people with higher incomes (or capital).[11] The same holds true for subsidies or partial subsidies, which is what loans at less than the marginal productivity of capital come to: these should be lump-sum progressive subsidies so as not to distort incentives. This means that the loans should be decided on without reference to performance so that no country would have any incentive to waste its resources. But only those countries which have some capacity to form capital with foreign assistance should receive loans.

If foreign loans are not to be granted to the point where they equate the marginal efficiency of capital in the United States (and Western Europe) on the one hand, and the underdeveloped countries on the other, the amount of such loans on an annual basis is also a political question. How much should the United States spend on schools each year? There is no scientific answer because there is no necessary amount of training that a young man or woman should have, nor any necessary ratio of expenditure to students.[12] We should spend on schools what we feel is needed to bring them up (or down) to the

---

[11] See J. E. Meade, *Trade and Welfare*, Oxford University Press, London, 1955, p. 49.

[12] The scientific answer is, of course, that we should equalize the marginal utility of the tax dollar spent on schooling with that of every other dollar spent for given purposes. In the absence of capacity to measure this marginal value, it is possible to say only that we should spend a little more on this, and less on that, with a fixed government revenue or, if all objects of government expenditure have a higher marginal utility than objects of private expenditure, that we ought to increase taxes to meet new governmental needs. Senator Taft's frequently repeated warning that foreign aid would make the United States bankrupt meant primarily that he did not value foreign aid as much as he did objects of private expenditure, and so was unwilling to tax for the purpose. In part, however, it might have meant that the United States was prepared to spend on foreign aid without raising the necessary revenues in taxes for the purpose, which leads to inflation.

standard we have in mind, given the various other objectives of common expenditure, and the rate at which we are prepared to tax our-selves. The same is true of loans for foreign assistance.

The question of the amount to be spent for schools is somewhat easier than foreign aid because we have a long history of educating our children, and we are dealing not with a new objective of expenditure but with changes in an existing one. The same might be said of foreign loans except that most people are conscious of the fact that we are not doing nearly enough to meet the expectations that have been aroused, so that the change in the rate of expenditure should be substantial rather than of the normal order of magnitude of such changes.

My own view is that the Millikan and Rostow figure of a scale of lending of $2.5 to $3.5 billion a year is about right as a target. But the rationale is much simpler.

CONDITIONS OF AID

There is a considerable and persistent temptation on the part of various groups, represented in the Congress, to use the fact of international aid, as in the European Recovery Program, to gain short-run ends for the United States. Various special interests urge the restriction of aid to goods shipped in American bottoms, or goods covered by American insurance policies. Aid is sometimes tied to general United States interests, such as the provision of raw materials for the defense stockpile. Certain branches of government, including the legislative, are interested in acquiring local currencies for expenditure by the United States government, generally for purposes which would not have merited as much attention if it had been necessary to appropriate the monies directly for them, e.g., congressional travel and the construction of handsome embassy offices and residences.

Apart from these mundane interests, there is a temptation to use the bargaining power inherent in capacity to give or withhold aid to secure other United States interests, both political and ideological. In the political realm, aid may be offered as a reward for taking part in defense pacts, or to gain bases. Ideologically, there is the urge to advance United States positions on other fronts, particularly when this country is convinced that the United States position would benefit the other country as well. The abandonment of neutralism would be one such requirement, closely allied with defense pacts. Less politically touchy, the British loan was made to win British adherence to the doctrine of multilateral trade and convertible exchanges. Many voices were raised in the European Recovery Program to insist on agreements to an enlargement of the European economy through some sort of customs or economic union; others wanted to obtain renunciation of socialism as a *quid pro quo* of aid.

Opposed to these positions is one which would give assistance without any strings attached. In defense of this position it is asserted that to lay down conditions is to compromise the sovereignty of the country receiving aid, or to interfere in its internal politics. This is too simple and idealistic by half. Sovereignty is not inviolable, nor are internal politics sacrosanct where they stand in the way of development. Development by itself changes the balance of political forces, as Chapter 13 emphasized. And if the borrowing or assisted country chooses to reject aid which imposes conditions which will ensure its effective use, it protects its "sovereignty" at the expense of its long-run sovereign interest. Another, and the one advocated in these pages, is to require as a condition of aid that every possible effort be made to proceed expeditiously toward economic development, wasting neither domestic nor foreign resources, insofar as possible. This requires careful analysis of the development program of the country to ensure that its premises are realistic and its objectives within reach. It also generally entails some machinery for analysis of future plans and evaluation of current progress.

If the sole condition of foreign aid is that it be used effectively, the abridgment of sovereignty which comes from consultation with foreign missions, with the International Bank, or a United Nations agency is supportable. If such outside forces are to be effective, moreover, they must take positions on issues which are subjects of internal struggles, and thereby find themselves interfering in internal politics. Where very weak governments exist, it may even be helpful to establish a system of counterpart funds, under which the local-currency proceeds of goods procured with foreign aid and sold in the domestic economy are sequestered and spent only with the agreement of the granting agency or country. The deflationary effect of the foreign aid is more readily maintained when these proceeds cannot be spent without regard to their monetary impact. The forces in the government standing for monetary sobriety are strengthened. But counterpart funds are not the means to impose budgetary restraint on a country which lacks any semblance of it: central-bank loans to the government can inflate as rapidly as or more rapidly than any increase in counterpart funds can bring about contraction.

The administration of conditions of foreign aid is full of pitfalls. If a country is committed to manifestly uneconomic projects of development, it may be impossible to persuade it to modify its development program and undesirable for political reasons to withhold assistance altogether. United States–Egyptian experience over the High Dam at Aswan does not provide the appropriate illustration. This project was first supported and then rejected on political grounds, although the excuse given for rejection—that the project was too large and involved too long a commitment of too much Egyptian savings before any increment in output would be realized—should have been the basis for an initial refusal to give support. But when the Egyptian government or any other acquires an *idée fixe* in developmental programming, it is difficult to say yes or no.

Interference in domestic affairs is inevitable, as has been suggested, since all developmental change involves a shift in the strength of opposing political forces. Where the primary condition of assistance is its productive use, this may require foreigners to approve action which will harm the class in the society which is most friendly to them politically. This is hard. But where long-run and short-run interests are thus opposed, the former should prevail. Since underdeveloped countries are too poor and frequently too politically ineffective adequately to safeguard their long-run interests at the expense of the short-run, it is necessary to administer development loans in such a way as to promote the future when it is under attack from the present.

ADMINISTRATION

The major issue in the administration of loan assistance is whether it should be done by a political body or by experts, and whether in the former case the lending should be on an international or a bilateral basis. The issue is political rather than economic. But it is sufficiently important to warrant some attention.

The case against bilateral arrangements is that they provide opportunity for exploitation and political interference. The major argument in their favor is that international bodies have their own particular form of political behavior not free from logrolling, deals, or bloc voting. The suggestion that multilateral administration is somehow more likely to operate on the basis of principle instead of *ad hoc* expediency or power politics is frequently put forward but has little basis in fact. Where principles are well established to the point of being cut and dried, international administration is desirable but gains very little. Where objective criteria are elusive and principles of administration must be developed by accretion, it is safer to have programs prepared by experts, adopted by international bodies, but subject to the veto of the contributing nations—or roughly the formula of the Marshall Plan.

In a democratic country it is possible to have the many, through their representatives, tax the few for objects of common expenditure, since there is a fundamental political compact, whether written or understood, under which expenditures and taxes are voted. In international matters, such understanding is still lacking. The underdeveloped countries lack the power to tax the developed. They must therefore win their consent for the amount of subsidy contained in loans below the marginal product of capital in underdeveloped countries. It makes sense that this consent should be explicit in the continuous administration of intergovernmental developmental loans rather than implicit in the discontinuous replenishment of funds when the pool runs out. To give a contributor of 72 per cent of the funds only one vote in seventeen, where no objective principles of distribution have been devised, as was true of UNRRA, is to run the risk that the recipients and minor contributors will use the aid for purposes for which it was not created. And in these circumstances the project is likely to be wound up by the major donor when the fund runs out.

OTHER EFFECTS

Loans and grants are by no means the only way in which developed countries affect the rate of growth in underdeveloped countries. Direct aid is also provided through technical assistance, discussed in Chapter 10. But the indirect effects are also of great importance. In some of these the developed country may not even be conscious of the impact it has.

The most obvious, the most frequently cited, and the most important indirect means of assistance to underdeveloped countries is the stabilization of the economies of the developed countries at high levels of employment. This contributes to the steadiness of the prices and volume of exports of primary products in developing countries and to the stability of the availability of private capital, much of which is dependent for its investment in underdeveloped areas on the expansion of markets in developed.

With high, stable, or expanding levels of output in developed countries, it would still be possible to have considerable fluctuations in the demand for the exports of primary-producing countries if there are inventory cycles, generated by speculators or by business consumers. There is perhaps little that governments can do to counteract this source of instability for developing countries, except not to add to it. It was inexcusable at the time of Korea for the United States government, through its defense stockpile, first to join the private market in bidding up the prices of tin, rubber, wool, etc., and then at the top of the market actively to undertake to drive these prices down. Governments are expected to get less panicky than private dealers and to lean into the wind.

Whether it is possible for the developed countries to go further than abstaining from destabilizing speculation is a troubled question. Underdeveloped countries are naturally eager for schemes of commodity stabilization, financed by international contributions, which would come largely from developed countries. Until there is agreement on methods of such stabilization, there is little to be done. The United Nations experts gathered to study the problem finally contented themselves with the recommendation of establishing a board to keep a running watch on commodity problems;[13] but this was rejected by the developed countries as constituting a continuous pressure group for price supports.

Here again is an area, however, in which it is at least possible to establish a negative standard. The United States has a number of agricultural surpluses which it is engaged in disposing of abroad. If it is too much to ask the United States to hold up the price of, say, cotton, it should at least be possible to require that it not knock it down. It is not sufficient for the United States to assert that it is only selling at the world price. When a major supplier increases its sales substantially, the world price is driven down. Not all "incremental" sales enlarge the market by their full amount. It makes little sense for the United States and other developed countries to aid the underdeveloped in their mutual long-run interest while at the same time pursuing short-run ends which run contrary to the short- and long-run interests of underdeveloped areas.

But the major and most difficult negative requirement, perhaps, is to make aid to development through technical assistance and loans at less than the demand price for capital available to underdeveloped areas without insisting on short-run concessions in the area of defense and political commitments. There will be countries which will need defense aid, and will ask for it. Here it can be granted, along with but separately from developmental assistance. As other countries make developmental headway, moreover, their neutralism may be threatened from other directions which in turn may lead them into closer understanding of the defense problem. But an unwilling ally is of little help in crisis, and bought friendships are no bargain, however cheap.

[13] United Nations' experts' report, *Commodity Trade and Economic Development*, New York, 1953.

We conclude that North America, Western Europe, and the white dominions have a long-run political interest in assisting the rest of the world to catch up with their economic development, or at least to make a rapid start in raising their national income. There are many negative aspects to this interest: it is not economic, nor defense, nor diplomatic in the short run. It involves, moreover, a gamble; for there is a chance that economic development as a slogan creates larger appetites than it can satisfy and is politically disruptive. Nonetheless, it seems clear that the continuous shrinkage in the size of the world, and the heightened mutual awareness among continents and peoples which that shrinkage brings, call for greater political and social cohesion to preserve stability and the very survival of the earth. Toward the goal of this cohesion some equalization of incomes among nations is needed. Developed-country support for developing nations with no strings other than its efficient use is enlightened self-interest.

CHAPTER 18 *A Few Conclusions*

VICIOUS CIRCLES

One can conclude from the foregoing that economic development is a difficult and complicated business. There is the difficulty of charting a course and steering the developmental process after a start has been made. There is also the difficulty of getting development under way.

Poverty abounds in what the cliché expert calls vicious circles. The Malthusian circle keeps countries poor by expanding their numbers when increases in output occur. "The rich get richer and the poor get children." The capital circle is also familiar. At low incomes it is impossible to save enough to form new capital.[1] "It takes money to make money." But there are other circles and paradoxes.

It has been noted, for example, that industrialization needed to relieve population pressure tends at an early stage to introduce improved health. This increases the rural population, causes excessive fragmentation of land holdings, and becomes one of the chief sources of rural migration to the cities to increase population pressure there.[2] Or how does a developing country escape the paradox of income distribution: to accumulate savings on a nationwide basis requires austerity, which in turn demands equality of sacrifice and more equal income distribution which reduces savings; but to promote high profits as a source of savings for capital formation may lead to unrest, on the one hand, and may fail to produce socially desirable investment, on the other, since

[1] See "Extension Is Voted for Colombo Plan," *New York Times*, Oct. 2, 1955: "A vicious circle has developed . . . [in a number of countries in the area]. Development is checked for lack of financial resources; resources remain low for lack of development."
[2] *Processes and Problems of Industrialization in Underdeveloped Countries*, United Nations, New York, 1955, p. 121.

the profitmaking classes are not necessarily interested in the common good.[3]

Poor countries, which need strong government more than rich, have less chance of having it.[4]

Underdeveloped countries have difficulty with their terms of trade: when they are adverse, they lack the resources needed for economic development; when they are favorable, they lack the incentive.[5]

And yet, despite the barriers presented to economic development by this amount of negative feedback, economic development *has* occurred, generally as part of an unconscious process, and in not very densely populated areas. It has also occurred as a consciously willed objective, as in Japan and the Soviet Union, the former fairly densely populated. How does a country break out of the stable equilibrium or vicious circle of poverty into an area where the process of development becomes interacting and cumulative?

DEVELOPMENTAL STARTS

The answer to the foregoing question is that we don't know. Theories abound; opportunities for rigorous testing are limited.

In unplanned development, as in Western Europe, the most important dynamic force seems to have been the evolving character of the people, and particularly of the "new men," the merchants and bankers, who gradually worked themselves free from the confining embrace of feudalism. Where, in Southern and Eastern Europe, the middle class was weak and ineffective, dependent upon the landed classes and subservient to them, it was because it had failed to reach the size and strength to enable it to challenge the old order. Up to a certain critical level of the middle class, the vicious circle perpetuates itself; beyond it, change becomes the established order—self-perpetuating and interacting change in capital formation and technology.

The process has been historically slow. In Britain the Reformation of the sixteenth century led to political revolution of the seventeenth and the Industrial Revolution of the eighteenth century, before the rapid period of development in the nineteenth century. In France, Germany, northern Italy, western Austria, Bohemia, and Scandinavia,

---

[3] D. R. Gadgil, *Economic Policy and Development*, Gokhale Institute, Poona, 1955, p. 181.

[4] W. A. Lewis, *The Theory of Economic Growth*, Richard D. Irwin, Inc., Homewood, Ill., 1955, p. 382.

[5] *Repercussions of Changes in the Terms of Trade on the Economies of Countries in the Process of Development*, United Nations, E/2456, June 11, 1953 (mimeographed).

the pace was faster after a slow start. And in many areas—southern France, Spain, parts of Italy—commercial revolution failed to be followed by industrial revolution for reasons which are not clear.

Professor Rostow divides the growth process into the accomplishment of certain "preconditions"—the achievement of the appropriate combination of the propensities to seek material gain, to have families, to pursue pure science, to apply science to the material world, and so forth, and the process of development itself, which follows when the preconditions have been met.[6] But, as we have seen,[7] income can reach a substantial level during the commercial revolution, so that growth is not absent during the period when the preconditions are being met. Nor are the propensities unaffected by the subsequent process of cumulative capital formation and income growth. Even if it were possible to separate the preconditions from growth itself, if the preconditions were necessary but not sufficient, it is difficult to divide the responsibility for development between them and the subsequent capital-growth period. Between *causa remota* and *causa proxima* it is impossible to choose a *causa causans* if both are necessary and neither is sufficient.

One cannot quickly dismiss the role of climate in giving rise to the initial breakthrough from the vicious circles of underdevelopment. In the period of unconscious development, international communication was limited, cultures were isolated and independent, and culture change occurred primarily as a consequence of internal stimuli.[8] Where economic energy was required to produce an adequate level of living in temperate climates, it was relatively easy to develop more energy and for it to push on in other directions and break out of the restraints of tradition. Where the climate was benign, on the other hand, the output of economic energy was initially low, and lacked the internal stimulus to reach the cumulative, self-reinforcing stage. When the external stimulus was provided, however, as in Japan in the nineteenth century and in Asia and Africa in the twentieth, climate is seen not to be a barrier. Some such line of reasoning is needed to explain, with Huntington, why high levels of economic development have not been reached in the tropics in modern times, and still to leave room for the possibility of tropical development in future. As A. J. Brown, M. Bates,

[6] W. W. Rostow, *The Process of Economic Growth*, W. W. Norton & Co., Inc., New York, 1952, chap. 2.

[7] See pp. 100–101.

[8] This is subject to wide qualification, as for example the forcible impact of some cultures on others—Moorish and Christian, Spanish and Aztec and Incan, French and British and North American Indian, etc. In addition there was economic stimulus, such as that received by the Crusaders from the Moslem world.

and T. S. Simey have emphasized, the inhabitants of the tropics today are undernourished, not lazy, while the enervation experienced by the white man under tropical conditions is cultural, not physiological. When the external stimulus has been provided, there is sufficient energy to meet the requirements of growth.

With planned development, it is not clear how the vicious circle is broken. There may be no unique way. Japanese experience differs substantially from that of the Soviet Union. In the former instance the economy was kept open, imitation of Western technology took place on a wide front, an entrepreneurial class was grafted onto the old class society with the adoption of the institution of private enterprise and the use of the price system to allocate resources and distribute income. In the Soviet Union, on the other hand, the emphasis was on industrial capital formation, first and foremost, with the application of enough compulsion to achieve the necessary resource allocation and restricttion of consumption. The Soviet capital-cumulation pattern may or may not be capable of transformation into one where a desired degree of consumer choice and pattern of income distribution are achieved. The Malenkov experience of 1952 suggests that there are difficulties inherent in the process.

CUMULATIVE GROWTH

Once growth has started, the questions become what does it consist in, what keeps it going, what slows it down and brings it to a halt. Our discussion was divided into four ingredients and two aspects of change —resources, capital formation, social structure, and technology in the first category, and scale and transformation in the second. But these convenient labels for organizing the discussion, it will be recalled, are not necessarily conceptually distinct. Resources must be defined in terms of technology; technological change springs from the social structure, as does the capacity to transform or the desire to resist transformation. Once growth has started, the question is mainly whether it is further changes in people which speed the process, or primarily the accumulation of capital which feeds on itself.

It may be well to recur to the human analogy used in Chapter 1 to describe growth in relation to income per capita. What is the nature of the growth process in people? As a person grows, is the basic change physiological, or does it lie in the metamorphosis of his social, emotional, or technical capacity? Is a grown person more effective at producing income than a child because of his larger size, his wider technical education, his possession of more tools and implements, or his greater interest in economic well-being? The questions answer themselves. There is no unique way to describe the growth process, and it is foolish to insist on one. Growth involves a dynamic interacting system of linked changes. The *causa causans* lies deep in some control mechanism—possibly the endocrine glands insofar as physiology is concerned; but it has a variety of social and cultural dimensions which are linked to the physiological in ways unique for separate cultures. The economic equivalent of the endocrine glands remains perhaps to be discovered, but even when it is isolated it is not clear how much matters will have been advanced.

We have suggested in Chapter 2 that above a certain minimum volume of resources, resources are not critical, since changes in technology and increases in capital can be substituted for them. This is acceptable as a very general statement. Yet it is troublesome that Japan, which we regard as having been through the developmental process, has such a low income per capita. Is Japan developed or not? With $200 per capita of income in 1953, it ranked with Mexico, Yugoslavia, and Costa Rica as an underdeveloped country; and yet it has achieved scale, undergone transformation, and formed capital in cumulative fashion, which is the essence of the developmental process. Perhaps 1953 is not an appropriate year to measure the level of income in Japan; not until 1955 could it be said to have recovered from the war and the structural readaptation of its trade pattern to the changes in China. In 1955 and 1956 income per capita grew at rates approaching 10 per cent a year. But it would appear that resources have been so limited, and the rate of population increase so great, that growth has not brought with it much in the way of a lift in the income of the masses. Part of the explanation may be that technological capacity was insufficient to make up for the lack of resources. Japanese capacity for imitation has been high. But in few lines has its technological progress been autonomous.

STRATEGIC FACTORS IN GROWTH

The interrelations among resources, capital formation, social structure, technology, scale, and transformation are, as has been said, many and complex. The random elements in the growth process are innumerable and important. The contingencies, as the historians say, overwhelm the invariable relationships. And yet it appears that the social factor is in many ways the strategic element. This is true in a positive sense in unconscious or private-enterprise development; and negatively true where development is imposed from the top. Where private forces bear the brunt of the responsibility, capital formation and technical change are both functions of the social position. The open society, with social mobility, opportunities for workers with energy to rise to the middle class, and for the upper classes to achieve distinction in ways which are socially productive, provides incentives for saving and for innovation. In those societies where government assumes the leadership in efforts at economic betterment, development can be blocked by unwillingness or inability of the masses to respond to work incentives, to assume burdens of austerity, and to turn their backs on traditional ways without becoming rootless and restive.

Emphasis on the social element leads to priorities in investment in transport and communication, on the one hand, and in education, on the other. The distinction between producers' and consumers' goods is important here. Transport and communication are designed to link goods markets and personal contacts but not necessarily to provide for pilgrimages to religious places or for family visits. Education equally should be biased in practical ways and limited in its attention to the higher reaches of cultivation, beyond those important to social cohesion.

Transport links markets as well as people. As such it increases elasticities, improves the efficiency of the price system, and permits the achievement of economies of scale in production and distribution. Education also sends out its effects in many directions. The spread of calculation is basic to income maximization. Capacity to communicate is needed for organized markets with formal prices. A minimum of rationality and understanding of cause and effect are prerequisites for changes in techniques. And universal education through grade school (preferably high school) must underlie the effective recruitment of the foremen, supervisors, straw bosses, and shop stewards on whom effective organization of production and distribution at basis rests.

Transport (and communications) and education are therefore general investment priorities. Some observers add electric power. Decisions must be made in separate cases on the basis of the facts. But to admit electric power into the select circle of priority investments in principle is difficult. Electric power has a large element of demonstration effect in it; it requires the use of capital in factor proportions frequently inappropriate to the factor endowments existing and in short-run prospect in underdeveloped countries. Many of the multipurpose hydroelectric projects, as contrasted with thermal, imply a very low rate of interest. It is true that the International Bank has made many loans on power projects, and there may be an irreversibility about technology, which means that it is impossible to produce today with methods which were in vogue at the turn of the century when there was little electric power centrally distributed. Moreover, there is something to be said for the stimulus to technological assistance from developed countries, and from the young men and women of underdeveloped countries who have been educated abroad and "corrupted" by Western levels of living, which would come from the provision of electric power in houses—making possible air conditioning, food refrigeration, efficient lighting, etc. Charles Issawi at the Harris Foundation lectures in Chicago in 1951 mentioned the "four L's" of development, of which I recall only "literacy" and " 'lectricity." But it is possible to have reservations.

Are there strategic factors beyond investment priorities for transport and education? What about balance, the secret of all development problems, as Lewis says? Or cheap foodstuffs, which make capital formation possible? To emphasize transport and education is simply to assert the view that there are external economies to be had in investment in these areas. There may be other external economies. In particular situations, indeed, the economies in transport and education have been fully exploited. But balance as a secret of development means that the price system does not function at all, in contrast to external economies which claim that it does not function in all particulars. And if the price system is made or encouraged to work, increased investment in agriculture will be indicated when the price of foodstuffs has risen relative to other goods. One of the secrets of development, recommended here instead of balance, is the use of the price system to the fullest extent possible, taking into account economies of scale and without too many short cuts in anticipation of changes in demand supply or factors.

There is a temptation in developing countries to interfere in the price system in a variety of ways—overvaluing the exchange rate, buying up farm produce below the urban market price less transport, establishing controls over price, allocation, or distribution. Where governments interfere in the price system and then make investment decisions because the price system does not work effectively, there may be an opportunity to economize by eliminating two offsetting sets of actions.

Admittedly, the price system does not work perfectly, as the discussion of economies of scale makes clear. The question is whether to ignore it or work with it, whether to plan investment and to a considerable extent output, because elasticities of demand and supply are low —demand does not turn away from items in short supply, nor resources rush in to produce them—or whether to encourage more responsiveness to price, and to change prices where external economies, or internal economies blocked by monopoly behavior, make price ineffective. Again circumstances will alter cases, but the general predilection of the writer is to salvage the most that can be saved of the price system. It is more economical of administrative talent to rely on private incentives. There is less chance of the enormous errors which free-wheeling outside the price system can bring in monumental and wrong investments. An effective price system encourages those social responses which are the strategic basis of development—rationality in perception, specificity in interpersonal relations, and universalism in choice of roles. The market is a school as well as an engine of distribution.

RELATIVE VERSUS ABSOLUTE GROWTH

This book has focused on the problem of getting development started in underdeveloped countries, and of keeping it going. Very little attention has been paid to the *rate* of development, so long as it is positive, or to the question whether development can be revived after it slows down. Many of these problems belong to the economies of middle and old age rather than early youth. It makes little sense to worry whether a baby will end up five or six feet tall when the question is whether the growth process can be stimulated at all and brought safely through the problems of infancy, childhood, and adolescence.

For some purposes, however, growth is seen as a closing of the gap in the level of living between developed and underdeveloped countries. So long as the rate of growth in the United States is as high as anywhere in the world, growth is not taking place abroad on this showing, because the gap is widening rather than narrowing. This attention to relative rates of growth makes sense for some problems, particularly in fields of defense or long-run politics. But for the most part what counts is whether the underdeveloped country is growing at all. Differences between positive rates of change are less significant than the difference between a positive rate of change and static equilibrium. The slower rate of growth once under way can pick up speed—and of course can slow down too. And the higher rate of growth has the prospect of slowing down. The Gompertz or S curve of growth applies more or less roughly to growth problems. On only a small portion of it can geometric rates of growth be extrapolated, and then not for long. New technological change, or spurts of investment, or even deep-seated social resolves can stimulate new growth processes at the flattening part of the curve as rates of change die down. Institutionalized research and competitive innovational investment may even carry the secret of eternal economic youth. If so, they may be open for all countries when a higher level of income has been achieved. But I doubt it.

There is no reason, then, for a developing country to lose courage because of the gap between its level of living and that of developed countries, a gap which is growing wider in absolute and possibly even in relative terms. It is sufficient at the early stages to get the growth process started. Too little is known about it, much less about how these rates can be sustained and how rejuvenated when they slow down. It is a sufficient achievement, and very difficult, to get economic development under way.

Name Index

Subject Index